GENERAL EDITOR

THE RIGHT HONOURABLE LORD JUSTICE BROOKE
Vice-President of the Court of Appeal (Civil Division)

EDITOR OF CIVIL PROCEDURE NEWS

PROFESSOR I. R. SCOTT
University of Birmingham; Barrister; Honorary Bencher of Gray's Inn

SENIOR EDITORIAL BOARD

DISTRICT JUDGE R. N. HILL
Scarborough County Court and District Registry; Visiting Professor of Law, Leeds Metropolitan University

SENIOR COSTS JUDGE P. T. HURST
Supreme Court Costs Office

HIS HONOUR JUDGE NIC MADGE
Harrow Crown Court

PROFESSOR I. R. SCOTT
University of Birmingham; Barrister; Honorary Bencher of Gray's Inn

MASTER R. L. TURNER
Senior Master of the Supreme Court and Queen's Remembrancer

EDITORS

MR REGISTRAR BAISTER
A Bankruptcy Registrar of the High Court

DISTRICT JUDGE A. R. S. BASSETT CROSS
Principal Registry, Family Division

V. C. BELL
Barrister, Supreme Court Chancery Chambers

MASTER BRAGGE
Supreme Court, Chancery Division

M. BREALEY
Barrister

S. BURN
Solicitor; Deputy District Judge

HIS HONOUR JUDGE CHAMBERS Q.C.
Mercantile Judge for Wales and Chester

REGISTRAR DERRETT
A Bankruptcy Registrar of the High Court

P. DOBSON
Barrister; Visiting Professor of Law, Anglia Polytechnic University

A. R. DONNELLY
Of the Public Guardianship Office

M. GIBBON
Barrister

S. GROSZ
Solicitor

K. HOUGHTON
The Admiralty Marshal and Chief Clerk of the Admiralty and Commercial Registry

THE HONOURABLE MR JUSTICE JACKSON
Judge of the Queen's Bench Division of the High Court

R. JAY
Solicitor

E. JEARY
Of the Court Funds Office

B. KEITH
Principal Clerk, House of Lords

DISTRICT JUDGE M. LANGLEY
Central London County Court

C. LEWIS
Barrister

A. J. MACKERSIE
Judicial Clerk, House of Lords

MASTER MILLER
Admiralty Registrar and a Master of the Supreme Court, Queen's Bench Division

MASTER J. O'HARE
A Master of the Supreme Court Costs Office

R. J. B. PARKES Q.C.
One of Her Majesty's Counsel

DISTRICT JUDGE P. PEARL
Watford County Court

MASTER ROSE
A Master of the Supreme Court, Queen's Bench Division

C. SANDERS
Of the Official Solicitor and Public Trustee

MASTER VENNE
Head of the Civil Appeals Office

H. WARD
Barrister

HIS HONOUR JUDGE DAVID WILCOX
Technology and Construction Court, Queen's Bench Division

DR VICTORIA WILLIAMS
Barrister

CHIEF MASTER WINEGARTEN
Chief Master of the Supreme Court, Chancery Division

B. YOUNG
The Clerk to the Interim Applications Judge

MASTER YOXALL
A Master of The Supreme Court, Queen's Bench Division

ADVISORY EDITORS

P. ALLEN
Managing Partner, Hodge Jones & Allen Solicitors

HIS HONOUR JUDGE CHAMBERS Q.C.
Mercantile Judge of Wales and Chester

THE HONOURABLE MR JUSTICE LAWRENCE COLLINS
Judge of the Chancery Division of the High Court

HIS HONOUR JUDGE GRENFELL
Designated Civil Judge, Leeds

THE HONOURABLE MR JUSTICE JACKSON
Judge of the Queen's Bench Division of the High Court

THE RIGHT HONOURABLE LORD JUSTICE JACOB
Lord Justice of Appeal

THE HONOURABLE MR JUSTICE MOORE-BICK
Judge of the Queen's Bench Division of the High Court

CIVIL PROCEDURE 2004

Second Cumulative Supplement To the 2004 Edition

Up–to–date generally to August 31, 2004

TO ACCESS THE WHITE BOOK CIVIL PROCEDURE RULES WEBSITE AND TO REGISTER FOR THE FORMS ALERTER SERVICE YOU NEED TO ENTER THE FOLLOWING PASSWORD:
WB2004

LONDON
SWEET & MAXWELL
2004

Published in 2004 by Sweet & Maxwell Limited of
100 Avenue Road, London NW3 3PF.
European, International, Practice Directions and Rules reference tables typeset by Hobbs the Printers Ltd, Totton, Hampshire. All other typesetting by Sweet & Maxwell electronic publishing system
Printed in England by Bath Press, UK

No natural forests were destroyed to make this product; only farmed timber was used and replanted.

British Library Cataloguing in Publication Data
A catalogue record for this book is available from the British Library

ISBN 0 421 886803
All rights reserved. Crown Copyright material is reproduced with permission of the Controller of HMSO and the Queen's Printer for Scotland.

No part of this publication may be reproduced or transmitted in any form or by any means, or stored in any retrieval system of any nature without prior written permission, except for permitted fair dealing under the Copyright, Designs and Patents Act 1988, or in accordance with the terms of a licence issued by the Copyright Licensing Agency in respect of photocopying and/or reprographic reproduction. Application for permission for other use of copyright material including permission to reproduce extracts in other published works shall be made to the publishers. Full acknowledgment of author, publisher and source must be given.

Such permission is hereby granted to members of the legal profession (which expression does not include individuals or organisations engaged in the supply of services to the legal profession) to reproduce, transmit and store the text of the Forms set out in Volume 1 for the purpose of enabling them to conduct proceedings on behalf of, or to provide legal advice to, their clients.

©
Sweet & Maxwell Limited
2004

SERVICE INFORMATION

Generally up to-date-to August 31, 2004

Civil Procedure 2004 published in April 2004. The Second Cumulative Supplement brings the Rules and Practice Directions up to date to August 31, 2004 and incorporates changes introduced under:

- Civil Procedure Amendment Rules 2004
- Department of Constitutional Affairs Updates upto, and including, 36.

We have included all material published by the DCA up to August 31, 2004.

For further updates, see http://www.sweetandmaxwell.co.uk/whitebook. *You will need to enter your subscriber password: WB2004*

Civil Procedure Forms CD

Your 2004 subscription includes a CD–Rom containing all the forms provided in the Civil Procedure Forms Volume. Many of these forms are editable and downloadable. The Civil Procedure Forms Volume and the Civil Procedure Forms CD will be updated three times a year.

**Subscribers to the Civil Procedure CD and Print Service already receive the forms on their CD and will not receive an additional Forms CD.

Forms Alerter Service

As a White Book subscriber you are entitled to register for our Forms Alerter service. A registration form can be found at http://www.sweetandmaxwell.co.uk/whitebook.

You will need to enter your subscriber password which can be found on the inside cover of this Supplement.

Once you have registered your email address with us, an email alerter service will notify you of new forms and amendments to forms before they are published in the White Book Forms Volume. New and amended forms will be available for downloading from the White Book website.

Civil Procedure Forms Volume

If you were a subscriber to the White Book in 2003, please remember to retain your White Book Forms Volume. This will continue to be updated during the 2004 and subsequent subscription years. The ninth Forms Release is included with this Supplement.

Internet-based primary law updating - http://www.sweetandmaxwell.co.uk/whitebook

For full text of the CPR and Practice Directions annotated to show any amendments since the publication of Civil Procedure 2004, see - http://www.sweetandmaxwell.co.uk/whitebook

You will need to enter your subscriber password which can be found on the inside cover of this Supplement.

How to use Civil Procedure 2004

As ever, we have endeavoured to ensure that the content of the Civil Procedure follows a logical layout.

Civil Procedure Rules are now reproduced in bold to ensure they are easily distinguishable from editorial comment and Practice Directions. History notes have been added to provide a full record of changes to the Civil Procedure Rules.

A Table of Contents has been included in Volume 2.

Volume One

The Civil Procedure Rules and Practice Directions (including Schedules 1 and 2 containing those RSC and CCR still in force) are contained in Volume 1 with the following exceptions:

– *CPR on Specialist lists* – CPR Parts 58 – 63 (dealing with the Commercial Court, the Mercantile Courts, the Technology and Construction Court, Admiralty Claims and Arbitrations, and Patents and Other Intellectual Property Claims) are set out in Volume 2, Section 2A–F.

– *CPR Part 49 – Specialist proceedings* – the proceedings dealt with under the Practice Direction to Part 49 (Proceedings under the Companies Acts) are set out in Volume 2, Section 2G.

Miscellaneous Practice Directions, Pre–Action Protocols, procedural guides and a guide to time limits are reproduced in Volume One.

Volume Two

The main elements of Volume Two are the specialist areas of practice and procedure: the specialists lists dealt with by CPR Parts 58 – 63 and the specialist proceedings under CPR Part 49, other specialist proceedings (*e.g.* Housing and Consumer) and procedural legislation.

A quick guide to finding key materials is set out below.

How to find ...

... CPR Rules and Supplementary Practice Directions (Vol. 1, Section A)

The Civil Procedure Rules and Practice Directions are contained in Section A, which adopts the following paragraph system.

Part 3, r.1	Para. **3.1**
Commentary to Part 3, r.1	Para. 3.1.**1**, (3.1.**2** etc.)
Practice Direction supplementing Part 3	Para. 3**PD**.1
Second Practice Direction supplementing Part 3	Para. 3**B**PD.1

The paragraph numbers appear at the top outside corner of each page.

... Rules of the Supreme Court, County Court Rules and Supplementary Practice Directions

Section A also contains the re–enacted Rules of the Supreme Court and County Court Rules, with all supplementary Practice Directions. The following paragraph system is used:

RSC Order 52, r.1	Para. **sc**52.1
Commentary to RSC Order 52.1	Para. sc52.1.**1** (**sc52.1.2** etc.)
Practice Direction supplementing Order 52	Para. scpd52.1
CCR Order 1, r.6	Para. **cc**1.6
Commentary to CCR Order 1, r.6	Para. cc1.6.1

... Miscellaneous Practice Direction (Vol. 1, Section B)
Practice Directions which are not supplementary to a rule (*e.g.* the Practice Direction on Insolvency Proceedings) are contained in Section B, which adopts the following paragraph system.

Practice Direction Insolvency Proceedings, etc.	Para. B1–001

... Pre–Action Protocols (Vol. 1, Section C)
The Pre–Action Protocols are contained in Section C, which adopts the following paragraph system:

Practice Direction—Protocols	Para. C–001
Pre–Action Protocol for Personal Injury Claims	Para. C–001

... Chancery Guide
The Chancery Guide Appears in Section 1 of Volume 2 and is numbered para. 1-1 onwards.

... Specialist Practice Directions under CPR Parts 58–63 and Specialist Court Guides, Applications under the Companies Act
Specialist Proceedings under CPR Parts 58–63 and Specialist Court Guides, Applications under the Companies Act appear in Section 2 of Volume 2 as follows:

CPR 58	Commercial Court
CPR 59	Mercantile Courts
CPR 60	Technology and Construction Courts
CPR 61	Admiralty Claims
CPR 62	Arbitration Claims
CPR 63	Patents and other Intellectual Property Claims
Practice Direction to CPR 49	Applications Under the Companies Act

... Forms
The forms are located in the Civil Procedure Forms Volume and on the Forms CD.

Service Elements

The White Book Service allows you to choose a customised product to suit your requirements.
Civil Procedure Volumes 1 & 2
Annual subscription includes:
Civil Procedure 2004 Volume 1
Civil Procedure 2004 Volume 2
Civil Procedure Forms Volume
Civil Procedure Forms CD
Two supplements
Civil Procedure News
Internet–based primary law updating
Forms E–mail Alerter Service
Subscription price: £295

Civil Procedure 2004 Volume 1
Annual subscription includes:

Civil Procedure 2004 Volume 1
Civil Procedure Forms Volume
Civil Procedure Forms CD
Two supplements
Civil Procedure News
Internet–based primary law updating
Forms E–mail Alerter Service
Subscription price: £195

Civil Procedure CD and Print Service
Annual subscription includes:
All materials in Volumes 1 and 2 and the Forms Volume on one CD (plus 2 replacement CDs throughout the year)
Civil Procedure 2004 Volume 1
Civil Procedure 2004 Volume 2
Civil Procedure Forms Volume
Two paper supplements
Civil Procedure News
Internet–based primary law updating
Forms E–mail Alerter Service
Subscription price: £345 + £8.75 VAT

Premium Online Service

Please contact our WestlawUK helpdesk for further information on 0800 028 2200.

Customer Services

If you have a query relating to your subscription or you wish to purchase extra copies of Civil Procedure 2004, please call our Customer Services team in Swiss Cottage on:

UK direct customers: (0207) 449 1111
UK trade customers: (0207) 449 1104
International customers: +44 1264 343032

Or you can write to:

Customer Services
Sweet & Maxwell Limited
100 Avenue Road
London
England NW3 3PF
DX: 38861 Swiss Cottage
Website: http://www.sweetandmaxwell.co.uk

Comments and feedback

We are always pleased to receive comments and suggestions from customers. Address correspondence to: Publishing Editor, The White Book Service, Sweet & Maxwell, 100 Avenue Road, London, NW3 3PF or e–mail to *whitebook@sweetandmaxwell.co.uk*

November 2004

CONTENTS

Table of Statutes

[**References in bold** type are to the paragraph at which that section, or part of that section, is set out in full.]

Table of Statutory Instruments

[**References in bold** type are to the paragraph at which that section, or part of that section, is set out in full.]

TABLE OF CIVIL PROCEDURE RULES

References to paragraph numbers in square brackets are to Volume 2. **Figures in bold type** indicate where a rule is set out in full

TABLE OF RULES OF THE SUPREME COURT

References to paragraph numbers in square brackets are to Volume 2.

TABLE OF RULES OF THE COUNTY COURT

References to paragraph numbers in square brackets are to Volume 2.

TABLE OF PRACTICE DIRECTIONS

References to paragraph numbers in square brackets are to Volume 2.

TABLE OF INTERNATIONAL AND EUROPEAN LEGISLATION

References to paragraph numbers in square brackets are to Volume 2.

Secondary Legislation

TABLE OF CASES

Table of Cases

White v White [2001] UKHL 9; [2001] 1 W.L.R. 481; [2001] 2 All E.R. 43; [2001] 1 All E.R. (Comm) 1105; [2001] 1 Lloyd's Rep. 679; [2001] R.T.R. 25; [2001] 2 C.M.L.R. 1; [2001] Lloyd's Rep. I.R. 493; [2001] P.I.Q.R. P20; (2001) 98(15) L.S.G. 33; (2001) 151 N.L.J. 350; (2001) 145 S.J.L.B. 67; *The Times*, March 6, 2001; *Independent*, April 30, 2001 (C.S.) [illegible]

White Bank Ellis Chemicals [illegible] C.H.R. [illegible]

Wigan MBC v G (A Child). See Manchester City Council v G

Wilkinson v Lord Chancellor's Department; sub nom. Wilkinson v Official Solicitor; Wilkinson v S [2003] EWCA Civ 95; [2003] 1 W.L.R. 1254; [2003] 2 All E.R. 184; [2003] C.P. Rep. 37; [2003] 1 F.C.R. 741; (2003) 100(12) L.S.G. 29; (2003) 147 S.J.L.B. 178; *The Times*, February 8, 2003; *Independent*, February 12, 2003 [illegible]

[illegible] Official Solicitor; Wilkinson v S. See Wilkinson v Lord Chancellor's Department

Wilson v First County Trust Ltd (No.2); sub nom. Wilson v Secretary of State for Trade and Industry [2003] UKHL 40; [2004] 1 A.C. 816; [2003] 3 W.L.R. 568; [2003] 4 All E.R. 97; [2003] 2 All E.R. (Comm) 491; [2003] H.R.L.R. 33; [2003] U.K.H.R.R. 1085; (2003) 100(35) L.S.G. 39; (2003) 147 S.J.L.B. 872; *The Times*, July 11, 2003; *Independent*, November 3, 2003 (C.S.), HL; reversing [2001] EWCA Civ 633; [2002] Q.B. 74; [2001] 3 W.L.R. 42; [2001] 3 All E.R. 229; [2001] 2 All E.R. (Comm) 134; [2001] E.C.C. 37; [2001] H.R.L.R. 44; [2001] U.K.H.R.R. 1175; (2001) 98(24) L.S.G. 44; (2001) 145 S.J.L.B. 125; *The Times*, May 16, 2001; *Independent*, May 8, 2001; *Daily Telegraph*, May 8, 2001 [illegible]

— v Secretary of State for Trade and Industry. See Wilson v First County Trust Ltd (No.2)

Winans v Winans [1948] [illegible]

Woolley v Woolley, sub nom. S (A Minor) (Injunction to Restrain), Re [1993] Fam. 1; [1993] 3 W.L.R. 118; [1993] 3 All E.R. 385; [1993] 2 F.L.R. 119; [1993] Fam. Law 9; *The Times*, April 2, 1993; *Daily Telegraph*, April 22, 1993 [illegible]

Wright v Mortimer (1996) 28 H.L.R. 719; [1996] E.G.C.S. 51; (1996) 72 P. & C.R. D36 [illegible]

X v Brown [2003] EWCA Civ 181 [illegible]

[illegible] Tracy [1902] 1 K.B. 527, CA; reversing [1901] 1 Q.B. 112 [illegible]

[illegible] v Varnon [2003] EWCA Civ 7; [2003] 1 F.C.R. [illegible]; *The Times*, February 5, 2003; *Independent*, February 11, 2003 [illegible]

Zubaida v White [2003] E.M.L.R. 246 [illegible]

VOLUME 1

CIVIL PROCEDURE RULES

SECTION A

CIVIL PROCEDURE RULES 1998

PART 1

OVERRIDING OBJECTIVE

Editorial Introduction

After "Civil Procedure (Amendment) Rules 2003 (S.I. 2003 No. 364)" delete the full stop and add:

1.0.2 , Civil Procedure (Amendment No. 2) Rules 2003 (S.I. 2003 No. 1242), Civil Procedure (Amendment No. 3) Rules 2003 (S.I. 2003 No. 1329), Civil Procedure (Amendment No. 4) Rules 2003 (S.I. 2003 No. 2113), Civil Procedure (Amendment No. 5) Rules 2003 (S.I. 2003 No. 3361), Civil Procedure (Amendment) Rules 2004 (S.I. 2004 No. 1306), Civil Procedure (Amendment No. 2) Rules 2004 (S.I. 2004 No. 2072).

The overriding objective

Before the twelfth paragraph which begins "In Holmes v. S.G.B. Services" add:

1.3.2 In *Colley v. Council for Licensed Conveyancers* [2001] EWCA Civ 1137; [2002] 1 W.L.R. 160, CA, the Court of Appeal said (para. 45) there is a tension between the principle stated by Lord Bingham in *R. (Daly) v. Secretary of State for the Home Department* [2001] UKHL 26; [2001] 2 A.C. 532, H.L., that the right of access to a court may only be curtailed by clear and precise terms, and the provisions of CPR r.1.2.

Add at end of the penultimate paragraph:

In a case where a defendant is in danger of losing his home, the overriding objective does not require that his pleaded admission to the effect that the claimant had served the required statutory notice (though the fact was otherwise) should be disregarded (*Loveridge v. Healey* [2004] EWCA Civ 173, CA).

Cost and delay

Add after first paragraph:

1.3.4 Well before the CPR came into effect, the courts expressed their determination to clamp down on unnecessary delay. For example, when issuing *Practice Direction (Civil Litigation: Case Management)* [1995] 1 W.L.R. 508, the Lord Chief Justice and the Vice-Chancellor said the courts "have over the years been too ready to allow those who are litigating to dictate the pace at which cases proceed". Since the CPR came into effect it has been explained that "in contrast to the old regime the court will determine the length of the trial and what is to happen at the trial" (*Loveridge v. Healey* [2004] EWCA Civ 173, CA, at para. 30 *per* Buxton L.J.).

In the new fourth paragraph, add after "Swain v. Hillman [2001] All E.R. 91, CA":

; *Puma AG Rudolf Dassler Sport v. Sports Soccer Ltd* [2003] EWHC 2705 (Ch) (Etherton J.)

In the last paragraph before the sentence which begins "In Mitchell v. United Kingdom" add:

In *Eastaway v. United Kingdom (Application No.74976–01), The Times* August 9, 2004, ECtHR, following the collapse in 1990 of group of companies, proceedings brought by Secretary of State against a former company director under the 1986 Act were commenced on July 1, 1992, and completed on June 4, 2001. The ECtHR held that, in all the circumstances, the proceedings were not pursued with the diligence required by Art. 6, and there had been a violation of Art. 6 in that director's civil rights and obligations were not determined within a reasonable time.

Court's resources

Delete the last line of the second paragraph and substitute:

1.3.7 *Bhamjee v. Forsdick* [2003] EWCA Civ 1113; [2004] 1 W.L.R. 88, CA. A practice direction made under r. 3.11 contains provisions about the power of the court to make a civil restraint order against a litigant in the exercise of the jurisdiction explained by the Court of Appeal in this case.

CPR "a new procedural code"

In the first paragraph, for "The Civil Procedure Act 1997, s.2(7)" substitute:

1.3.9 The Civil Procedure Act 1997, s.1(3) (as amended)

Human Rights Act 1998 and the CPR

At the end of the fourth paragraph add:

1.3.10 As to the circumstances where Art. 6 may be said to have been violated by delays in completing proceedings,see para. 1.3.4 above.

Encouraging use of alternative dispute resolution (ADR) procedure

Add after the sixth paragraph:

1.4.11 In *Halsey v. Milton Keynes General NHS Trust* [2004] EWCA Civ 576, the Court of Appeal expressly adopted the propositions stated in the first two sentences of the paragraph immediately above. In this case the Court heard argument on the question whether the court has power to order parties to submit their disputes to mediation against their will. The Court said it was likely that compulsion of ADR would be regarded as an unacceptable constraint on the right to access to the court and, therefore, a violation of Art. 6 of the European Convention on Human Rights (see further below), and even if (contrary to the Court's view) the court does have jurisdiction to order unwilling parties to refer their disputes to mediation "we find it difficult to conceive of circumstances in which it would be appropriate to exercise it". (For earlier first instance authorities suggesting that a party might be ordered to submit his dispute to mediation against his will, see *Kinstreet Ltd. v. Balmargo Corporation Ltd*, August 3, 1999, unrep. (Arden J.); *Muman v. Nagasena* [2000] 1 W.L.R. 299, CA; *Shirayama Shokusan Company Ltd v. Donovo Ltd* [2003] EWHC 3006 (Ch) (Blackburne J.); see further para. C1A–007 below.)

In the new tenth paragraph, add after "Leicester Circuits Ltd v. Coates Brothers Plc [2003] EWCA Civ 333; March 5, 2003, CA, unrep.":

In *Reed Executive Plc v. Reed Business Information Ltd* [2004] EWCA Civ 159, the Court invited submissions on the relevance to the question of costs of the defendants' refusal of a number of offers to go to mediation. After noting that the defendants had engaged in serious settlement negotiations, Jacob L.J. said (para. 167) that such negotiations were not the same as mediation as "a good and tough mediator can bring about a sense of commercial reality to both sides which their own lawyers, however good, may not be able to convey".

Add to beginning of the new eleventh paragraph, beginning "In a given case it is quite conceivable...":

The question: when should the court impose a costs sanction against a successful litigant on the grounds that he has refused to take part in an alternative dispute resolution (ADR)? was considered by the Court of Appeal in *Halsey v. Milton Keynes General NHS Trust* [2004] EWCA Civ 576. The Court said the fundamental principle is that departure from the general rule (that the unsuccessful party should be ordered to pay the costs of the successful party) is not justified unless it is shown (the burden being on the unsuccessful party) that the successful party acted unreasonably in refusing to agree to ADR. The Court gave guidance (see especially para. 16) as to the factors that should be considered by the court in deciding whether a refusal to agree to ADR is unreasonable.

Add after the new thirteenth paragraph:

Practice Direction (Pilot Scheme for Mediation in Central London County Court) provides for a pilot scheme (operating from April 1, 2004, to March 31, 2005) enabling the Central London county court by a "notice of referral to mediation" to require parties to certain types of claims either to attend a mediation appointment or to give reasons for objecting to doing so (see para. 26BPD.1 below). As mediation is meant to be a consensual form of dispute resolution, it is provided that a party may object to referral to mediation; in which event the matter is referred to a district judge (para. 4.1). Apparently on the assumption that the court has jurisdiction to direct mediation, even though a party does not consent to this, it is further provided that the district judge may, despite any objection, direct "that a mediation appointment should proceed" (para. 4.1(2)).

In the new seventeenth paragraph, for "Shirayama Shokusan Company Ltd v. Danovo Ltd, December 5, 2003, unrep." substitute:

Shirayama Shokusan Company Ltd v. Danovo Ltd [2003] EWHC 3006 (Ch)

Delete the paragraph beginning "In Muman v. Nagasena..." and substitute:

Although the court has jurisdiction to order that parties should be adequately represented at a mediation, it has no jurisdiction to order that a particular person should attend, especially where that person was not a party to the proceedings (*Shirayama Shokusan Co. Ltd v. Danovo Ltd* (2004) 101(13) L.S.G. 34; *The Times*, March 22, 2004 (Blackburne J.) (D applying for order staying proceedings until conclusion of mediation attended by a third party (X) as a representative of C, where D contending that X's presence was essential to meaningful mediation)).

PART 2

APPLICATION AND INTERPRETATION OF THE RULES

After the definition of "child" add:

Interpretation

2.3

"civil restraint order" means an order restraining a party—

(a) from making any further applications in current proceedings (a limited civil restraint order);

(b) from issuing any further applications or making certain applications in specified courts (an extended civil restraint order); or

(c) from issuing any claim or making any application in specified courts (a general civil restraint order).

General note on interpretation of rules (rr.2.2 and 2.3)

In the fifth paragraph, for "The Civil Procedure Act 1997, s.2(7)" substitute:

2.3.1

The Civil Procedure Act 1997, s.1(3) (as amended)

In the same paragraph delete the full stop and add at the end:

; *Flynn v. Scougall*, [2004] EWCA Civ 873; [2004] 3 All E.R. 609, C.A. (payments into court). Cases have arisen where the failure of counsel to recognise that pre–CPR authorities continue to be of considerable persuasive force (if not strictly binding) have caused avoidable confusion and lead to unnecessary appeals (*e.g. Garratt v. Saxby* [2004] EWCA Civ 341; [2004] 1 W.L.R. 2152, CA (inadvertent disclosure of defendant's payment into court)).

Practice Directions as aids to interpretation

In the second paragraph, for "Leigh v. Michelin Tyre Plc [2003] EWCA Civ 1766; December 8, 2003, CA, unrep." substitute:

2.3.4

Leigh v. Michelin Tyre Plc [2003] EWCA Civ 1766; [2004] 1 W.L.R. 846, CA).

"civil restraint order"

Add new paragraph 2.3.10.1

2.3.10.1

This definition was inserted in r.2.3(1) when r.3.11 (Power of court to make civil restraint orders) and r.23.12 (Dismissal of totally without merit application) were added to the CPR, and rr.3.3, 3.4 and 52.10 were amended, by the Civil Procedure (Amendment No. 2) Rules 2004 (S.I. 2004 No. 2072), with effect from October 1, 2004. These amendments put into rule form the procedure outlined by the Court of Appeal in *Bhamjee v. Forsdick (Practice Note)* [2003] EWCA Civ 1113; [2004] 1 W.L.R. 88, CA, and amplified in *Mahajan v. Department of Constitutional Affairs* [2004] EWCA Civ 96, June 30, 2004, C.A., unrep. See further the commentary to Pt. 3.

"district judge of that Court"

Add at end:

2.4.2 References in any enactment, instrument or other document to a district judge or deputy district judge do not include (a) a district judge (magistrates' courts) or (b) a deputy district judge (magistrates' courts) (Courts Act 2003, s.65(3)).

Chancery Proceedings

For existing rule 5.1(j) substitute:

2BPD.5 **5.1**(j) making final orders under the Landlord and Tenant Acts 1927 and 1954, except (i) by consent, and (ii) orders for interim rents under sections 24A to 24D of the 1954 Act;

Existing heading of section 8 is amended:

COUNTY COURTS

Injunctions, Anti–social Behaviour Orders and Committal

2BPD.8 *Add new rule 8.1(d):*

8.1(d) where the injunction is to be made under any of the following provisions—

(i) section 153A, 153B or 153D of the Housing Act 1996; or

(ii) section 3 of the Protection from Harassment Act 1997.

Add new rule 8.1A:

8.1A A District Judge has jurisdiction to make an order under section 1B or 1D of the Crime and Disorder Act 1998 (anti–social behaviour).

In rule 8.3, delete "section 3 of the Protection from Harassment Act 1997,"

Trials and Assessments of Damages

2BPD.11 *Delete sub–paragraph (a) (ii) and substitute:*

11.1(a)(ii) for a new tenancy under section 24 or for the termination of a tenancy under section 29(2) of the Landlord and Tenant Act 1954;

In rule 11.1(b), after "land" delete the semi colon and add:

11.1(b) proceedings under section 82A(2) of the Housing Act 1985 or section 6A(2) of the Housing Act 1988 (demotion claims) or proceedings in a county court under Chapter 1A of the Housing Act 1996 (demoted tenancies)

Delete rule 11.1(d) and substitute:

(d) with the permission of the Designated Civil Judge in respect of that case, any other proceedings.

PART 3

THE COURT'S CASE MANAGEMENT POWERS

Prospective costs cap orders

Add at end:

3.1.8 In *King v. Telegraph Group Ltd* [2004] EWCA Civ 613, it was held that in a defamation case initiated under a conditional fee agreement without "after–the–event" insurance cover (as to which see r.43.2(k)) the court should consider making a costs capping order if there was a danger that, unless a cap was imposed, the freedom of the press would be jeopardised.

Civil restraint orders

Add at end:

Reference should also be made to r.3.11A, set out below, and to Practice Direction 3C—Civil Restraint Orders, set out in para. 3CPD.1, below. **3.1.12**

Court's power to make order of its own initiative

In rule 3.3 add new sub-paragraph (7):

3.3—(7) If the court of its own initiative strikes out a statement of case or dismisses an application, and it considers that the claim or application is totally without merit— **3.3**

(a) the court's order must record that fact; and

(b) the court must at the same time consider whether it is appropriate to make a civil restraint order.

Power to strike out a statement of case

In rule 3.4 add new sub-paragraph (6):

3.4—(6) If the court strikes out a claimant's statement of case and it considers that the claim is totally without merit— **3.4**

(a) the court's order must record that fact; and

(b) the court must at the same time consider whether it is appropriate to make a civil restraint order.

Where failure to comply was caused by the legal representative only

Add at end:

Where a claimant seeks relief in respect of a fault for which his legal representative is responsible, the court may take into account the detriment the claimant may suffer if the current proceedings are brought to an end and he is left to sue his legal representative instead (*Hansom v. E Rex Makin & Co.* [2003] EWCA Civ 1801 and *Flaxman–Binns v. Lincolnshire CC* [2004] EWCA Civ 424). **3.9.2**

Power of the court to make civil restraint orders

Add new rule 3.11:

3.11 A practice direction may set out— **3.11**

(a) the circumstances in which the court has the power to make a civil restraint order against a party to proceedings;

(b) the procedure where a party applies for a civil restraint order against another party; and

(c) the consequences of the court making a civil restraint order.

7. Vexatious Litigants

In paragraph 7.6 delete existing sub–paragraphs (3) and (4) and substitute:

7.6(3) make an order dismissing the application without a hearing; or **3PD.7**

(4) give directions for the hearing of the application.

PRACTICE DIRECTION—CIVIL RESTRAINT ORDERS

3CPD.1

This Practice Direction supplements CPR Rule 3.4

Introduction

Add new Practice Direction 3C:

1. This practice direction applies where the court is considering whether to make—

(a) a limited civil restraint order;
(b) an extended civil restraint order; or
(c) a general civil restraint order,

against a party who has issued claims or made applications which are totally without merit.

Rules 3.3(7), 3.4(6) and 23.12 provide that where a statement of case or application is struck out or dismissed and is totally without merit, the court order must specify that fact and the court must consider whether to make a civil restraint order. Rule 52.10(6) makes similar provision where the appeal court refuses an application for permission to appeal, strikes out an appellant's notice or dismisses an appeal.

2. Limited Civil Restraint Orders

3CPD.2

2.1 A limited civil restraint order may be made by a judge of any court where a party has made 2 or more applications which are totally without merit.

2.2 Where the court makes a limited civil restraint order, the party against whom the order is made—

(1) will be restrained from making any further applications in the proceedings in which the order is made without first obtaining the permission of a judge identified in the order;
(2) may apply for amendment or discharge of the order provided he has first obtained the permission of a judge identified in the order; and
(3) may apply for permission to appeal the order and if permission is granted, may appeal the order.

2.3 Where a party who is subject to a limited civil restraint order—

(1) makes a further application in the proceedings in which the order is made without first obtaining the permission of a judge identified in the order, such application will automatically be dismissed—
  (a) without the judge having to make any further order; and
  (b) without the need for the other party to respond to it;
(2) repeatedly makes applications for permission pursuant to that order which are totally without merit, the court may direct that if the party makes any further application for permission which is totally without merit, the decision to dismiss the application will be final and there will be no right of appeal, unless the judge who refused permission grants permission to appeal.

2.4 A party who is subject to a limited civil restraint order may not make an application for permission under paragraphs 2.2(1) or 2.2(2) without first serving notice of the application on the other party in accordance with paragraph 2.5.

2.5 A notice under paragraph 2.4 must—

(1) set out the nature and grounds of the application; and
(2) provide the other party with at least 7 days within which to respond.

2.6 An application for permission under paragraphs 2.2(1) or 2.2(2)—
(1) must be made in writing;
(2) must include the other party's written response, if any, to the notice served under paragraph 2.4; and
(3) will be determined without a hearing.

2.7 An order under paragraph 2.3(2) may only be made by—
(1) a Court of Appeal judge;
(2) a High Court judge or master; or
(3) a designated civil judge or his appointed deputy.

2.8 Where a party makes an application for permission under paragraphs 2.2(1) or 2.2(2) and permission is refused, any application for permission to appeal—
(1) must be made in writing; and
(2) will be determined without a hearing.

2.9 A limited civil restraint order—
(1) is limited to the particular proceedings in which it is made;
(2) will remain in effect for the duration of the proceedings in which it is made, unless the court otherwise orders; and
(3) must identify the judge or judges to whom an application for permission under paragraphs 2.2(1), 2.2(2) or 2.8 should be made.

3. Extended Civil Restraint Orders

3CPD.3

3.1 An extended civil restraint order may be made by—
(1) a judge of the Court of Appeal;
(2) a judge of the High Court; or
(3) a designated civil judge or his appointed deputy in the county court,

where a party has persistently issued claims or made applications which are totally without merit.

3.2 Unless the court otherwise orders, where the court makes an extended civil restraint order, the party against whom the order is made—
(1) will be restrained from issuing claims or making applications in—
   (a) any court if the order has been made by a judge of the Court of Appeal;
   (b) the High Court or any county court if the order has been made by a judge of the High Court; or
   (c) any county court identified in the order if the order has been made by a designated civil judge or his appointed deputy,

   concerning any matter involving or relating to or touching upon or leading to the proceedings in which the order is made without first obtaining the permission of a judge identified in the order;
(2) may apply for amendment or discharge of the order provided he has first obtained the permission of a judge identified in the order; and
(3) may apply for permission to appeal the order and if permission is granted, may appeal the order.

3.3 Where a party who is subject to an extended civil restraint order—

(1) issues a claim or makes an application in a court identified in the order concerning any matter involving or relating to or touching upon or leading to the proceedings in which the order is made without first obtaining the permission of a judge identified in the order, the claim or application will automatically be struck out or dismissed—
   (a) without the judge having to make any further order; and
   (b) without the need for the other party to respond to it;

(2) repeatedly makes applications for permission pursuant to that order which are totally without merit, the court may direct that if the party makes any further application for permission which is totally without merit, the decision to dismiss the application will be final and there will be no right of appeal, unless the judge who refused permission grants permission to appeal.

3.4 A party who is subject to an extended civil restraint order may not make an application for permission under paragraphs 3.2(1) or 3.2(2) without first serving notice of the application on the other party in accordance with paragraph 3.5.

3.5 A notice under paragraph 3.4 must—

(1) set out the nature and grounds of the application; and
(2) provide the other party with at least 7 days within which to respond.

3.6 An application for permission under paragraphs 3.2(1) or 3.2(2)—

(1) must be made in writing;
(2) must include the other party's written response, if any, to the notice served under paragraph 3.4; and
(3) will be determined without a hearing.

3.7 An order under paragraph 3.3(2) may only be made by—

(1) a Court of Appeal judge;
(2) a High Court judge; or
(3) a designated civil judge or his appointed deputy.

3.8 Where a party makes an application for permission under paragraphs 3.2(1) or 3.2(2) and permission is refused, any application for permission to appeal—

(1) must be made in writing; and
(2) will be determined without a hearing.

3.9 An extended civil restraint order—

(1) will be made for a specified period not exceeding 2 years;
(2) must identify the courts in which the party against whom the order is made is restrained from issuing claims or making applications; and
(3) must identify the judge or judges to whom an application for permission under paragraphs 3.2(1), 3.2(2) or 3.8 should be made.

3.10 The court may extend the duration of an extended civil restraint order, if it considers it appropriate to do so, but it must not be extended for a period greater than 2 years on any given occasion.

3.11 If he considers that it would be appropriate to make an extended civil restraint order—

(1) a master or a district judge in a district registry of the High Court must transfer the proceedings to a High Court judge; and

(2) a circuit judge or a district judge in a county court must transfer the proceedings to the designated civil judge.

4. General Civil Restraint Orders

3CPD.4

4.1 A general civil restraint order may be made by—

(1) a judge of the Court of Appeal;

(2) a judge of the High Court; or

(3) a designated civil judge or his appointed deputy in a county court,

where, despite the existence of an extended civil restraint order, the party against whom the order is made persists in issuing claims or making applications which are totally without merit.

4.2 Unless the court otherwise orders, where the court makes a general civil restraint order, the party against whom the order is made—

(1) will be restrained from issuing any claim or making any application in—

(a) any court if the order has been made by a judge of the Court of Appeal;

(b) the High Court or any county court if the order has been made by a judge of the High Court; or

(c) any county court identified in the order if the order has been made by a designated civil judge or his appointed deputy,

without first obtaining the permission of a judge identified in the order;

(2) may apply for amendment or discharge of the order provided he has first obtained the permission of a judge identified in the order; and

(3) may apply for permission to appeal the order and if permission is granted, may appeal the order.

4.3 Where a party who is subject to a general civil restraint order—

(1) issues a claim or makes an application in a court identified in the order without first obtaining the permission of a judge identified in the order, the claim or application will automatically be struck out or dismissed—

(a) without the judge having to make any further order; and

(b) without the need for the other party to respond to it;

(2) repeatedly makes applications for permission pursuant to that order which are totally without merit, the court may direct that if the party makes any further application for permission which is totally without merit, the decision to dismiss that application will be final and there will be no right of appeal, unless the judge who refused permission grants permission to appeal.

4.4 A party who is subject to a general civil restraint order may not make an application for permission under paragraphs 4.2(1) or 4.2(2) without first serving notice of the application on the other party in accordance with paragraph 4.5.

4.5 A notice under paragraph 4.4 must—

(1) set out the nature and grounds of the application; and
(2) provide the other party with at least 7 days within which to respond.

4.6 An application for permission under paragraphs 4.2(1) or 4.2(2)—
(1) must be made in writing;
(2) must include the other party's written response, if any, to the notice served under paragraph 4.4; and
(3) will be determined without a hearing.

4.7 An order under paragraph 4.3(2) may only be made by—
(1) a Court of Appeal judge;
(2) a High Court judge; or
(3) a designated civil judge or his appointed deputy.

4.8 Where a party makes an application for permission under paragraphs 4.2(1) or 4.2(2) and permission is refused, any application for permission to appeal—
(1) must be made in writing; and
(2) will be determined without a hearing.

4.9 A general civil restraint order—
(1) will be made for a specified period not exceeding 2 years;
(2) must identify the courts in which the party against whom the order is made is restrained from issuing claims or making applications; and
(3) must identify the judge or judges to whom an application for permission under paragraphs 4.2(1), 4.2(2) or 4.8 should be made.

4.10 The court may extend the duration of a general civil restraint order, if it considers it appropriate to do so, but it must not be extended for a period greater than 2 years on any given occasion.

4.11 If he considers that it would be appropriate to make a general civil restraint order—
(1) a master or a district judge in a district registry of the High Court must transfer the proceedings to a High Court judge; and
(2) a circuit judge or a district judge in a county court must transfer the proceedings to the designated civil judge.

5. General

3CPD.5 **5.1** The other party or parties to the proceedings may apply for any civil restraint order.

5.2 An application under paragraph 5.1 must be made using the Part 23 procedure unless the court otherwise directs and the application must specify which type of civil restraint order is sought.

5.3 Examples of a limited civil restraint order, an extended civil restraint order and a general civil restraint order are annexed to this practice direction. These examples may be modified as appropriate in any particular case.

6. Form N19

3CPD.6

Limited civil restraint order

Name of court	
Claim No.	
Name of Claimant	
Name of Defendant	
Date of issue	

Enter name and address of person against whom the order is made

SEAL

You must obey the directions contained in this order. If you do not you will be guilty of contempt of court and you may be sent to prison.

SECTION 1

Date of order

Name of Judge

Name of person against whom order is made

The judge has considered an application by the ☐ Claimant ☐ Defendant

OR

The court has considered, of its own initiative ☐

AND

Upon hearing

Upon reading

And has found that the above named person has made two or more applications in these proceedings which are totally without merit.

SECTION 2

The Order

It is ordered that you be restrained from making any further application in these proceedings without first obtaining the permission of

Name of Judge

OR

If unavailable

It is further ordered

☐ **This order will remain in effect for the duration of these proceedings**

OR

☐ until

N19 Limited civil restraint order

1. If you wish to apply for permission-

   (a) to make **an application** in these proceedings; **OR**

   (b) to make an application to **amend or discharge** this order,

   you must first serve notice of your application on the other party. The notice must set out the nature and grounds of the application and provide the other party with at least 7 days within which to respond. You must then apply for permission of the judge identified in the order. The application for permission must be made in writing and must include the other party's written response, if any, to the notice served. The application will be determined without a hearing.

2. If you repeatedly make applications for permission under 1 above which are totally without merit, the court may direct that if you make any further application for permission which is totally without merit, the decision to dismiss the application will be final and there will be no right of appeal, unless the judge who refused permission grants permission to appeal.

3. Any application for permission to appeal a refusal of an application under 1 above must be made in writing and will be determined without a hearing.

SECTION 3

Costs

☐ There is no order for costs

☐ It is ordered that you pay costs. The sum you must pay is ________

You must pay on or before ________

and send payment to the ☐ Claimant ☐ Defendant

Note

If you attempt to make a further application in these proceedings without first obtaining permission of the judge named in the order above, your application will automatically be dismissed without the judge having to make any further order and without the need for the other party to respond to it.

If this order was made in your absence, you may make an application to set aside, vary or stay the order. An application must be made within the period specified in the order or, where no period is specified, not more than 7 days after service of this order on you. You do not require permission of the court to make such an application.

If you do not understand anything in this order you should go to a Solicitor, Legal Advice Centre or a Citizens' Advice Bureau.

7. Form N19A

3CPD.7

Extended civil restraint order

Name of court	
Claim No.	
Name of Claimant	
Name of Defendant	
Date of issue	

Enter name and address of person against whom the order is made

SEAL

You must obey the directions contained in this order. If you do not you will be guilty of contempt of court and you may be sent to prison.

SECTION 1

Date of order

Name of Judge

Name of person against whom order is made

The judge has considered an application by the ☐ Claimant ☐ Defendant

OR

The court has considered, of its own initiative ☐

AND

Upon hearing

Upon reading

And has found that the above named person has persistently issued claims or made applications which are totally without merit.

SECTION 2

The Order

It is ordered that you be restrained from issuing claims or making applications in any court specified below concerning any matter involving or relating to or touching upon or leading to the proceedings in which this order is made without first obtaining the permission of

Name of Judge

OR

If unavailable

☐ Court of Appeal

☐ The High Court

☐ County Court(s)

☐ Any county court

☐ Any court

N19A Extended civil restraint order

It is further ordered

This order will remain in effect until

1. If you wish to apply for permission-

   (a) to make **an application** in these proceedings; **OR**

   (b) to make an application to **amend or discharge** this order,

   you must first serve notice of your application on the other party. The notice must set out the nature and grounds of the application and provide the other party with at least 7 days within which to respond. You must then apply for permission of the judge identified in the order. The application for permission must be made in writing and must include the other party's written response, if any, to the notice served. The application will be determined without a hearing.

2. If you repeatedly make applications for permission under 1 above which are totally without merit, the court may direct that if you make any further application for permission which is totally without merit, the decision to dismiss the application will be final and there will be no right of appeal, unless the judge who refused permission grants permission to appeal.

3. Any application for permission to appeal a refusal of an application under 1 above must be made in writing and will be determined without a hearing.

SECTION 3

Costs

☐ There is no order for costs

☐ It is ordered that you pay costs. The sum you must pay is

You must pay on or before

and send payment to the ☐ Claimant ☐ Defendant

Note

If you attempt to make a further application in these proceedings without first obtaining permission of the judge named in the order above, your application will automatically be dismissed without the judge having to make any further order and without the need for the other party to respond to it.

If this order was made in your absence, you may make an application to set aside, vary or stay the order. An application must be made within the period specified in the order or, where no period is specified, not more than 7 days after service of this order on you. You do not require permission of the court to make such an application.

If you do not understand anything in this order you should go to a Solicitor, Legal Advice Centre or a Citizens' Advice Bureau.

8. Form N19B

3CPD.8

General civil restraint order

Name of court	
Claim No.	
Name of Claimant	
Name of Defendant	
Date of issue	

Enter name and address of person against whom the order is made

SEAL

You must obey the directions contained in this order. If you do not you will be guilty of contempt of court and you may be sent to prison.

SECTION 1

Date of order

Name of Judge

Name of person against whom order is made

The judge has considered an application by the ☐ Claimant ☐ Defendant

OR

The court has considered, of its own initiative ☐

AND

Upon hearing

Upon reading

And has found that, despite the existence of an extended civil restraint order, the above named person persists in issuing claims or making applications which are totally without merit.

SECTION 2

The Order

It is ordered that you be restrained from issuing any claim or making any application in any court specified below without first obtaining the permission of

Name of Judge

OR

If unavailable

☐ Court of Appeal

☐ The High Court

☐ County Court(s)

☐ Any county court

☐ Any court

N19B General civil restraint order

It is further ordered

This order will remain in effect until

1. If you wish to apply for permission-

   (a) to make **an application** in these proceedings; **OR**

   (b) to make an application to **amend or discharge** this order,

   you must first serve notice of your application on the other party. The notice must set out the nature and grounds of the application and provide the other party with at least 7 days within which to respond. You must then apply for permission of the judge identified in the order. The application for permission must be made in writing and must include the other party's written response, if any, to the notice served. The application will be determined without a hearing.

2. If you repeatedly make applications for permission under 1 above which are totally without merit, the court may direct that if you make any further application for permission which is totally without merit, the decision to dismiss the application will be final and there will be no right of appeal, unless the judge who refused permission grants permission to appeal.

3. Any application for permission to appeal a refusal of an application under 1 above must be made in writing and will be determined without a hearing.

SECTION 3

Costs

☐ There is no order for costs

☐ It is ordered that you pay costs. The sum you must pay is

You must pay on or before

and send payment to the ☐ Claimant ☐ Defendant

Note

If you attempt to make a further application in these proceedings without first obtaining permission of the judge named in the order above, your application will automatically be dismissed without the judge having to make any further order and without the need for the other party to respond to it.

If this order was made in your absence, you may make an application to set aside, vary or stay the order. An application must be made within the period specified in the order or, where no period is specified, not more than 7 days after service of this order on you. You do not require permission of the court to make such an application.

If you do not understand anything in this order you should go to a Solicitor, Legal Advice Centre or a Citizens' Advice Bureau.

PART 4

FORMS

In 'Table 1', the following forms are added or amended:

Table 1

"N" FORMS

Contents:

4PD.3

No.	Title
N6	Claim form for demotion of tenancy
N7	Notes for defendant (mortgaged residential property)
N7A	Notes for defendant (rented residential property)
N7B	Notes for defendant—forfeiture of the lease
N7D	Notes for defendant—demotion claim
N11D	Defence form (demotion of tenancy)
N16A	Application for Injunction (general form)
N19	Limited civil restraint order
N19A	Extended civil restraint order
N19B	General civil restraint order
N119A	Notes of guidance on completing particulars of claim (rented residential premises)
N122	Particulars of claim for demtion of tenancy
N206D	Notice of issue (demotion claim)
N215	Certificate of service
N293A	Combined Certificate of Judgment and Request for Writ of Fieri Facias

PART 5

COURT DOCUMENTS

Supply of documents from court records—general

Delete existing rule 5.4 and substitute:

5.4 (1) A court or court office may keep a publicly accessible register of claims which have been issued out of that court or court office.

(2) Any person who pays the prescribed fee may, during office hours, search any available register of claims.

(The practice direction contains details of available registers.)

(3) A party to proceedings may, unless the court orders otherwise, obtain from the records of the court a copy of —

(a) a statement of case;

(b) a judgment or order given or made in public (whether made at a hearing or without a hearing);

(c) an application notice, other than in relation to—

(i) an application by a solicitor for an order declaring that he has ceased to be the solicitor acting for a party; or

(ii) an application for an order that the identity of a party or witness should not be disclosed;

(d) any written evidence filed in relation to an application, other than a type of application mentioned in sub–paragraph (c)(i) or (ii);

(e) a notice of payment into court;

(f) an appellant's notice or respondent's notice.

(4) A party to proceedings may, if the court gives permission, obtain from the records of the court a copy of any other document filed by a party or communication between the court and a party or another person.

(5) Any other person may—

(a) unless the court orders otherwise, obtain from the records of the court a copy of —

(i) a claim form, subject to paragraph (6) and to any order of the court under paragraph (7);

(ii) a judgment or order given or made in public (whether made at a hearing or without a hearing), subject to paragraph (6); and

(b) if the court gives permission, obtain from the records of the court a copy of any other document filed by a party, or communication between the court and a party or another person.

(6) A person may obtain a copy of a claim form or a judgment or order under paragraph (5)(a) only if—

(a) where there is one defendant, the defendant has filed an acknowledgment of service or a defence;

(b) where there is more than one defendant, either—

(i) all the defendants have filed an acknowledgment of service or a defence;

(ii) at least one defendant has filed an acknowledgment of service or a defence, and the court gives permission;

(c) the claim has been listed for a hearing; or

(d) judgment has been entered in the claim.

(7) The court may, on the application of a party or of any person identified in the claim form—

(a) restrict the persons or classes of persons who may obtain a copy of the claim form;

(b) order that persons or classes of persons may only obtain a copy of the claim form if it is edited in accordance with the directions of the court; or

(c) make such other order as it thinks fit.

(8) A person wishing to obtain a copy of a document under paragraph (3), (4) or (5) must pay any prescribed fee and—

(a) if the court's permission is required, file an application notice in accordance with Part 23; or

(b) **if permission is not required, file a written request for the document.**

(9) **An application for permission to obtain a copy of a document, or for an order under paragraph (7), may be made without notice, but the court may direct notice to be given to any person who would be affected by its decision.**

(10) **Paragraphs (3) to (9) of this rule do not apply in relation to any proceedings in respect of which a rule or practice direction makes different provision.**

Supply of documents to Attorney–General from court records

Add new rule 5.4A:

5.4A **5.4A (1) The Attorney–General may search for, inspect and take a copy of any documents within a court file for the purpose of preparing an application or considering whether to make an application under section 42 of the Supreme Court Act 1981 or section 33 of the Employment Tribunals Act 1996 (restriction of vexatious proceedings).**

(2) **The Attorney–General must, when exercising the right under paragraph (1)—**

(a) **pay any prescribed fee; and**

(b) **file a written request, which must—**

(i) **confirm that the request is for the purpose of preparing an application or considering whether to make an application mentioned in paragraph (1); and**

(ii) **name the person who would be the subject of the application.**

Effect of rule

At the beginning add:

5.4.1 This rule was substituted by the Civil Procedure (Amendment No. 2) Rules 2004 with effect from October 1, 2004, and changed the former provision in some significant respects. The rule is supplemented by Practice Direction (Court Documents) para. 4, specifying the courts or court offices maintaining the registers referred to in r.5.4(1).

Supply of documents from court records

Delete existing paragraph 4 and substitute:

5PD.4 **4.1** Registers of claims which have been issued are available for inspection at the following offices of the High Court at the Royal Courts of Justice:

(1) the Central Office of the Queen's Bench Division;

(2) Chancery Chambers.

4.2 No registers of claims are at present available for inspection in county courts or in District Registries or other offices of the High Court.

4.3 An application under rule 5.4(4), 5.4(5)(b) or 5.4(6)(b)(ii) for permission to obtain a copy of a document, even if made without notice, must be made under CPR Part 23 and the application notice must identify the document or class of document in respect of which permission is sought and the grounds relied upon.

4.4 An application under rule 5.4(7) by a party or a person identified in a claim form must be made—

(1) under CPR Part 23; and

(2) to a Master or district judge, unless the court directs otherwise.

PART 6

SERVICE OF DOCUMENTS

Address for service

For the third and fourth paragraphs substitute:

6.5.3 Where the defendant has nominated solicitors as the address for service, service of the claim form on the defendant rather than the solicitors was not valid service: *Nanglegan v. Royal Free Hampstead NHS Trust* [2001] EWCA Civ 127; [2002] 1 W.L.R. 1043. The Defendant's argument that r.6.5(3) implies that claim forms (as opposed to other documents) can validly be served on the defendant, notwithstanding his instruction of solicitors, was not accepted by the Court of Appeal. In this case the defendant's solicitors had confirmed they had instructions to accept service, so the court made no finding on whether this was a prerequisite. In *Smith v. Probyn* (2000) 97(12) L.S.G. 44; (2000) 144 S.J.L.B. 1342 service on solicitors who had been corresponding with one of the parties to a dispute, but who had not been nominated to accept service by the eventual defendant, was not valid service.

When the claimant did not receive the defendant's loss adjuster's letter nominating a solicitor to accept service and the solicitor had not confirmed willingness to accept, service on the defendant was valid service (*James v. First Bristol Buses Ltd* [2003] C.L.Y. 454). *Firstdale Ltd v. Quinton* [2004] EWHC 1926, (Comm.) decided that an indication by a defendant's solicitor that he was authorised to accept service of proceedings by a particular claimant, could not ordinarily be taken to have indicated his authority to accept service of a claim form arising from the same dispute but from a different claimant, an assignee. Service on the defendant directly was, therefore, valid service.

In the fifth paragraph delete the second and third sentences and substitute:

But in a number of cases the courts have said that if the claimant opts to effect service (rather than the court doing so) the answer depends upon whether the claimant has taken reasonable steps to locate the defendant. In *Mersey Docks Property Holdings v. Kilgour* [2004] EWHC 1638 the High Court decided that where the claimant knows the defendant has moved he cannot simply serve at the old address without making reasonable enquiries. The defendant was an architect. The claimant knew he no longer practised at his 1998 business address. Internet searches of directory enquiries and of the Royal Institute of British Architects directory of architect's practices did not reveal a new address (because Mr Kilgour had changed his firm name to MKA.) The court decided that the claimant did not take reasonable steps as they left the checking of the address until the end of the limitation period, and did not search in the individual architects directory or Yellow Pages or contact the RIBA. The claim form was not validly served.

Scope of provision

At the end of the second paragraph add:

6.8.1 *Shiblaq v. Sadikoglu (Application to Set Aside) (No.2)* 2004 EWHC 1890 (Comm.) was decided similarly in a case in which the claimant served proceedings on the defendant in Turkey via a notary public, which was not permitted under Turkish law (only for domestic proceedings). Neither CPR 6.8 nor 6.9 should be used to avoid a defect in service that was inconsistent with a service convention between the jurisdiction and the country of service.

At the beginning of the last paragraph delete "In Knauf UK GMBH v. British Gypsum Ltd & Others October 24, 2001, unreported, CA" and substitute:

Knauf UK GmbH v. British Gypsum Ltd [2001] EWCA Civ 1570; [2002] 1 W.L.R. 907

Add at end:

However the discretion under CPR 6.8(1) is much broader that impracticality and where service would involve very extensive delay in a case which was already stale and there were good grounds for supposing that delay was the sole aim of the defendant, permission would be given for alternative service within the jurisdiction onsolicitors who were actively involved in the proceedings on behalf of the defendant (*Marconi Communications International Ltd v. PT Pan Indonesia Bank TBK* [2004] EWHC 129; [2004] 1 Lloyd's Rep 594 (Comm)).

Certificate of service

Delete the first paragraph and subsections (a) and (b) and substitute:

6.10 Where a rule, practice direction or court order requires a certificate of service, the certificate must state the details set out in the following table **6.10**

Scope of provision

Delete the first paragraph

At the end of the second paragraph add: **6.10.1**

From June 30, 2004 rule 6.10 was amended so that a certificate of service is no longer required to state that the document served has not been returned undelivered. But a statement of truth is required instead (see Form N215).

Scope of provision

Add at end:

Society of Lloyds v. Tropp [2004] EWHC 33 (Comm): this case confirmed that service of the claim form in accordance with contractual arrangements is valid service including when the individual defendant to be served had not personally authorised the contract and was domiciled outside the jurisdiction. (Tropp was a citizen of the USA and objected to service on a UK based agent for Lloyds' names.) **6.15.2**

Burden and Standard of Proof

Add at end:

See also *Bank of Tokyo–Mitsubishi Ltd v. Baskan Gida Sanayi Ve Pazarlama AS* [2004] EWHC 945 (Ch); [2004] I.L.Pr. 26. **6.19.8**

Matters Relating to Tort, Delict or Quasi Delict

At the end of the fourth paragraph add:

See *Bank of Tokyo–Mitsubishi Ltd v. Baskan Gida Sanayi Ve Pazarlama AS* [2004] EWHC 945 (Ch); [2004] I.L.Pr. 26 for the place of loss where banks within the jurisdiction are victims of a conspiracy in which a letter of credit is drawn outside the jurisdiction. **6.19.12**

Priority of Jurisdiction

At the end of the second paragraph, delete the full stop and add:

; see also *Tavoulareas v. Tsavliris (The Atlas Pride)* [2004] EWCA Civ 48; [2004] 1 Lloyd's Rep. 445. **6.19.16**

Degree to which Proceedings must be "Related"

After the quote from Lord Saville regarding Sarrio SA v. Kuwait Investment Authority add:

For a further consideration of the relevant criteria see *Bank of Tokyo–Mitsubishi Ltd v. Baskan Gida Sanayi Ve Pazarlama AS* [2004] EWHC 945; [2004] I.L.Pr. 26. **6.19.20**

Counterclaims

Add new paragraph 6.19.20.1:

Article 6(3) of the Judgment Regulations (Article 6(3) of the Brussels Convention) provides that a person domiciled in a Contracting State may also be sued on a counterclaim arising from the same contract or facts on which the original claim was based, in the court in which the original claim is pending. This situation does not cover a Part 20 claim against a claimant by a party, nor a defendant in the proceedings, in respect of discrete groups of facts that enjoy a common background: *Dollfus Mieg et Compagnie v. CDW International Ltd* [2004] I.L.Pr. 12. **6.19.20.1**

Jurisdiction Agreements

Delete the fourth paragraph "It is difficult to see how a jurisdiction..."

6.19.22 *Add at end:*

Where a court is seised of jurisdiction under Article 21 of the Brussels Convention, it is that court which must decide whether it lacks jurisdiction by reason of a jurisdiction agreement: *Erich Gasser GmbH v. Misat Srl (C116/02)* [2004] 1 Lloyd's Rep. 222; [2004] I.L.Pr. 7.

The standard of proof required when a defendant seeks to rely on a foreign jurisdiction agreement in a case where, apart from the alleged agreement, the English court would have jurisdiction under the Judgments Regulation is that of a good arguable case; *Bank of Tokyo–Mitsubishi Ltd v. Baskan Gida Sanayi Ve Pazarlama AS* [2004] EWHC 945; [2004] I.L.Pr. 26.

Service out of the jurisdiction where the permission of the court is required

After "will be served" add:

6.20 **6.20—(3) (otherwise than in reliance on this paragraph)**

The written evidence

At the end of sub–paragraph (d) add:

6.21.6 (d) See *MRG (Japan) Ltd v. Engelhard Metals Japan Ltd* [2003] EWHC 3418; [2004] 1 Lloyd's Rep. 731 for a rather more robust approach.

Add after the second paragraph:

In *MRG (Japan) Ltd v. Engelhard Metals Japan Ltd* [2003] EWHC 3418; [2004] 1 Lloyd's Rep. 731 Toulson J. held that the duty to make full disclosure is confined to disclosure of all that is relevant to considering the criteria relevant to permission to serve out of the jurisdiction and does not include an obligation to set out matters that would go no further than showing that the defendant had or might have arguable grounds for disputing the validity of contracts relied upon to found jurisdictions. Practitioners would do well to err on the side of caution.

Principles upon which permission to serve outside the jurisdiction is granted

After "De Molestina v. Ponton [2002] 1 Lloyd's Rep. 271" add:

6.21.15 (2) ; *Swiss Reinsurance v. United India* [2002] EWHC 741 (Comm); [2004] I.L.Pr. 4

The test is the same as a "reasonable prospect of success" (*BAS Capital Funding Corp v. Medfinco Ltd* [2003] EWHC 1798; [2004] 1 Lloyd's Rep. 652.)

Jurisdiction clauses

After the sentence which ends "Mercury Communications Ltd v. Telesystems International [1999] 2 All E.R. 33; Jogia, Re [1988] 2 All E.R. 328" add:

6.21.19 Very strong grounds are required to override a choice of English jurisdiction (*BAS Capital Funding Corp v. Medfinco Ltd* [2003] EWHC 1798; [2004] 1 Lloyd's Rep. 652).

At the end of the fifth paragraph add:

In some cases the fact that the clause was non–exclusive might make it easier to displace the strong presumption in favour of giving effect to them, particularly where more than one jurisdiction was chosen and one feature that may be highly relevant is where there are already proceedings in a foreign country which involve overlapping issues, especially if they have been commenced by a party which subsequently seeks to sue in England (see *BAS Capital Funding Corp* above).

Restraint of foreign proceedings

At end of the seventh paragraph delete the sentence "The presence of a non–exclusive jurisdiction clause might have the effect of lightening the burden in the applicant of establishing vexatious or oppressive conduct" and substitute:

6.21.23 1. Where foreign proceedings are properly commenced abroad by a party that is subsequently a defendant in proceedings within the jurisdiction brought by the defendant on the foreign proceedings and those proceedings have no unconscionable vexatious or oppressive aspect, they will not be restrained by an anti–suit injunction. This is particularly so where the foreign proceedings have been fully contested over an appreciable period. The presence of a non–exclusive jurisdiction clause might lighten the burden of an applicant in establishing vexatious or oppressive conduct but will not be construed as giving primacy to the English courts in any conflict arising from the prospect of virtually simultaneous trials in parallel proceedings:

For the eighth paragraph substitute:

The Brussels Convention is to be interpreted as precluding the grant of an injunction whereby a court of a Contracting State prohibits a party to proceedings pending before it from commencing or continuing legal proceedings before a court of another Contracting State, even where that party is acting in bad faith with a view to frustrating the existing proceedings: *Turner v. Grovit* (C159/02), [2004] I.L.Pr. 25.

Add at end:

The longer the delay in making applications for an anti-suit injunction, the more likely it is that there will be good reason to refuse it, but there is not culpable delay where it is caused by a party taking approriate steps to challenge the jurisdiction in a foreign forum (*Advent Capital Plc v. GN Ellinas Importers–Exporters Ltd* [2003] EWHC 3330; [2004] I.L.Pr. 23).

Governed by English law (r.6.20(5)(c))

Add at end:

6.21.35 Article 3.3 of the Rome Convention provides an exception to the freedom of parties to choose the applicable law where that choice is designed to circumvent the mandatory rules of the country which is alone concerned with the transaction. In applying the article, the relevant elements are not those laid down by the mandatory rules of the law of the country in question: *Caterpillar Financial Services Corp v. SNC Passion* [2004] EWHC 569 (Comm); [2004] 2 Lloyd's Rep. 99.

Rule 6.20(8) claims in tort

At the end of the first paragraph delete the last sentence and substitute:

6.21.39 See *Morin v. Bonhams & Brooks Ltd* [2003] EWCA Civ 1802; [2004] 1 Lloyd's Rep. 702 for the proper approach to rule 6.20(8) and the irrelevance of other provisions and authorities.

General

Add new paragraph 6.26.3

6.26.3 Where it is common ground that the defendant has not received actual notice of the proceedings, the onus is on the claimant to show that the method of service adopted was adequate and in compliance with the local rules: *Arros Invest Ltd v. Rafik Nishanov* [2004] EWHC 576 (Ch); [2004] I.L.Pr. 22.

Service out of the jurisdiction where permission of the Court is not required

Delete existing statement and substitute:

6BPD.2 **1.2** "I state that the High Court of England and Wales has power under the Civil Jurisdiction and Judgments Act 1982, the claim having as its object rights *in rem* in immovable property or tenancies in immovable property (or otherwise in accordance with the provisions of Article 16 of Schedule 1 or 3C to that Act, or paragraph 11 of Schedule 4 to that Act) to which any of those provisions applies, to hear the claim and that no proceedings are pending between the parties in Scotland, Northern Ireland or another Convention territory of any contracting state as defined by Section 1(3) of the Act".

Delete existing statement and substitute:

1.3 "I state that the High Court of England and Wales has power under the Civil Jurisdiction and Judgments Act 1982, the defendant being a party to an agreement conferring jurisdiction to which Article 17 of Schedule 1 or 3C to that Act or paragraph 12 of Schedule 4 to that Act applies, to hear the claim and that no proceedings are pending between the parties in Scotland, Northern Ireland or another Convention territory of any contracting state as defined by Section 1(3) of the Act."

Add new paragraph 1.3D:

1.3D In proceedings to which Rule 6.19(2) applies, the statement should be:

"I state that the High Court of England and Wales has power to hear this claim under [state the provisions of the relevant enactment] which satisfies the requirements of rule 6.19(2), and that no proceedings are pending between the parties in Scotland or Northern Ireland, or in another Contracting State or Regulation State as defined by section 1(3) of the Civil Jurisdiction and Judgments Act 1982."

In paragraph 1.4, for "or 1.3C" substitute:

1.4 , 1.3C or 1.3D

Service with the permission of the Court under certain Acts

Delete sub–paragraph 5.2(8) and substitute:

6BPD.6 **5.2**(8) The Inheritance (Provision for Family and Dependants) Act 1975,

PART 7

HOW TO START PROCEEDINGS—THE CLAIM FORM

Effect of rule

Add at end:

7.2.1 Note that Moneyclaimsonline has been made more permanent.

Salford City Council v. Garner 2004 AER (D) 465 Feb CA decided that the power of the court to decide a claim was brought when the claim form was received in the court office, rather than when it was issued (see the Practice Direction paragraph 5.1) only applies when a limitation date under the Limitation Acts is imminent, and not in other situations (here a one year time limit from the date of an introductory tenancy to issue possession proceedings.)

Effect of rule

After the penultimate paragraph add:

7.6.1 *Chare v. Fairclough* [2003] EWHC 180 decided that lodging the claim form with the Queen's Bench Masters for onward transmission to consular services to arrange service out of the jurisdiction did not fall within CPR, r.7.6(3)(a) as the court was not serving the claim form, only acting as a conduit. The claimant's solicitor therefore, should check within the 6 month period from issue of the claim form whether service has been effected, and if not apply prospectively for an extension of time. A retrospective application would be considered under CPR, r.7.6(3)(b) and the application would have had to be made promptly—it was not in this case.

Mersey Docks Property Holdings v. Kilgour [2004] EWHC 1638 decided that reasonable steps must be taken to locate a defendant before serving at his last known address (see notes to r.6.5 Address for Service).

Supported by evidence

Add at end:

7.6.2

The rules do not prescribe the evidence that is required. The Court of Appeal has decided that for an extension to be granted the claimant must put forward a valid reason. In *Hashtroodi v. Hancock* 2004 EWCA Civ 652 the claimant applied ex parte for an extension of time of three weeks to serve the claim form one day before the expiry of the claim form. The extension was granted. The claim form was apparently put in the DX within the three weeks but never arrived. The Master decided to allow the claim to continue. The Court of Appeal said that the power to extend time prospectively must be exercised in accordance with the overriding objective which means a valid reason must be advanced in the application; no reason was advanced in this case—the delay was due to the solicitor's incompetence and the extension should not have been granted.

Extension of time for serving particulars of claim

Delete "Austen v. Newcastle Chronicle..." and substitute:

Austin v. Newcastle Chronicle & Journal Ltd [2001] EWCA Civ 834

7.6.4

The provisions of the Act

Delete "section 139(a)" and substitute:

3.1(5) section 139(1)(a)

7BPD.3

PRACTICE DIRECTION—PRODUCTION CENTRE

General

In sub-paragraph 1.4(4) for "Paragraph 8.3" substitute:

7CDP.1

Paragraph 7.3

PART 8

ALTERNATIVE PROCEDURE FOR CLAIMS

Editorial Introduction

In the first paragraph, delete the last sentence.

In the last paragraph, after "the use of alternative procedure" add:

8.0.2

, *e.g.* claims under the Inheritance (Provision for Family and Dependants) Act 1975 (CPR, r.57.16(1)).

Move the last two paragraphs of 8.0.3 to the end of 8.0.2.

Add at end:

Modifications to Part 8 procedure apply in the Commercial Court and reference should be made to the Admiralty and Commercial Courts Guide, Part B4.

Appeals

In the first paragraph, after "any appeal from a final judgment" add:

in a Pt 8 claim other than given by a High Court judge

8.0.3

Further Part 8 Practice Direction

Delete the last paragraph.

Related Sources

8.0.4

After "Part 8 acknowledgment of service (N210)" add:

- *Costs—Only Part 8 Claim* (**N210A**)

8.0.6

Add at end:

- Admiralty and Commercial Courts Guide (Part B4)

Contents of the Claim Form

In the second paragraph after "set out in summary form only" add:

8.2.1 the facts and

Rule 8.3

Delete paragraph 8.3.1 and substitute:

8.3.1 Rule 8.3 does not apply by reason of para. B12 to PD B to applications listed in section B, Table 2 to the Part 8 Practice Direction. An acknowledgment of service should be verified by a statement of truth; see r.22.1(1)(e) and para. 1.1(4) of PD to Part 22. Particular attention should be paid to section E of Form N210.

Defendant's evidence

In the first paragraph, add at end:

8.5.2 Attention is drawn to section E in Form N210.

Timings

After "acknowledgment of service by the defendant" add:

8.5.3 Attention is drawn to the provisions of paras 5.5 and 5.6 of the Pt 8 Practice Direction concerning the Limits on agreements to extend time.

Add at end:

in the acknowledgment of service.

Evidence

Add at end:

8.6.1 including allocation to a track.

Procedure where defendant objects to use Part 8 procedure

In the first paragraph after "taken by a defendant" add:

8.8.1 in section D of Form 210 (Acknowledgment of Service)

In the second paragraph, for the sentence beginning "A person who uses the Pt 8 procedure..." substitute:

A person who uses the Pt 8 procedure inappropriately, *e.g.* knowing that there are significant issues of fact, and incurs a defendant in costs will be likely to be the subject to an order for summary assessment of costs.

Practice Direction—Alternative Procedure for Claims

Managing the claim 4.3

8PD.4 *In paragraph 4.3 delete ", such as a consent application under section 38 of the Landlord and Tenant Act 1954,"*

SECTION B

Application

Delete sub–paragraph B.1(2).

8BPD.6 *In Table 2 the following entries are deleted:*

TABLE 2

Schedule Rule
RSC O.98, r.2(1)
CCR O.49, r.5(1)
CCR O.49, r.6B(1)
CCR O.49, r.10(3)

PART 11

DISPUTING THE COURT'S JURISDICTION

Effect of Part 11

At the end of the fourth paragraph add:

Compliance with CPR r.6.19(1)(A) in relation to one cause of action among several should not have the effect that service of the proceedings is necessarily set aside. Such an omission can be cured by use of CPR r.3.10: *Bank of Tokyo–Mitsubishi Ltd v.Baskan Gida Sanayi Ve Pazarlama AS* [2004] EWHC 945; [2004] I.L.Pr. 26. **11.1.1**

PART 12

DEFAULT JUDGMENT

Scope of provision

Add at end:

Part 55.7(4) provides that Part 12 does not apply to possession claims. **12.2.1**

Allocation

In the first paragraph after "disposal hearing without allocation" add:

However allocation to track is now considered to be better practice. **12.7.6**

Evidence

Delete sub–paragraph 4.3(c) and substitute:

4.3(c) the claim has been properly served in accordance with Article 20 of Schedule 1 or 3C to the Act, paragraph 15 of Schedule 4 to the Act, or Article 26 of the Judgments Regulation. **12PD.4**

PART 13

SETTING ASIDE OR VARYING DEFAULT JUDGMENT

Effect of rule

In the second paragraph delete the sentence that begins "The phrase "real prospect of success" reflects..." **13.3.1**

Effect of rule

In the third paragraph for "an affidavit" substitute:

a witness statement **13.4.1**

Claimant's duty to apply to set aside judgment

Rule 13.5 was revoked by Civil Procedure Rules 2004 (S.I. 2004 No. 1306)

13.5 [Revoked] **13.5**

Delete paragraph 13.5.1

PART 14

ADMISSIONS

Effect of rule **13.5.2**

Delete the first sentence.

Disposal hearing

For "Paragraph 12.8 of the Practice Direction which supplements Part 26 (26PD.6)" substitute:

14.6.6 Paragraph 12.2 of the Practice Direction which supplements Part 26 (26PD.12)

PART 15

DEFENCE AND REPLY

Effect of rule

For sub–paragraph (3) substitute:

15.4.2 (3) where, before the defence is filed, the claimant applies for summary judgment on the whole of the claim or on a particular issue (as to the time for filing a defence in such a case see r.24.4(2); an application for summary judgment made by a defendant does not extend the period for filing the defence but does prevent the claimant obtaining judgment in default until the application has been disposed of (see r.12.3(3));

PART 18

FURTHER INFORMATION

Editorial Introduction

At the end of the first sentence delete "than heretofore"

18.0.2 *In the second paragraph delete the sentence which begins "Some of the former rules..."*

Delete the fifth paragraph

Practice Direction—Further Information

PRACTICE DIRECTION—FURTHER INFORMATION

Preliminary Request for Further Information or Clarification

Add new paragraph 1.7:

18PD.1 **1.7** Subject to the provisions of paragraphs 3.1 to 3.3 of the Practice Direction to Part 6, a request should be served by e–mail if reasonably practicable.

PART 19

PARTIES AND GROUP LITIGATION

Giving notice to the Crown

Add at end:

19.4A.2 Click on the links for "Crown Proceedings Act".

III. GROUP LITIGATION

Editorial Introduction

Delete the second paragraph and substitute:

19.10.0 The Final Access to Justice Report (July 1996) in Chapter 17 recommended that experience had shown (1) that there were definite limits to the weight representative actions (O.15, r.4) (now CPR, r.19.6) could bear, (2) that consolidation (O.15, r.4) (now CPR, r.19.2) deals with situations where actions have already been commenced, and it is better that multi–party litigation be dealt with on a collective basis before then, and (3) that joinder is not satisfactory where the interests of claimants differ. It addition it was said that the existing procedures were difficult to use and had proved disproportionately costly.

Delete the sixth paragraph.

Delete the first sentence in the seventh paragraph and substitute:

Rules 19.10 to 19.15 of this section of Part 19 are designed to achieve the objectives stated in the Final Report.

Comment

Delete the second paragraph and substitute:

19.11.1

PF19 should be used with appropriate adaptions. Parties are invited to submit to the Senior Master, Room E115 or the Chief Chancery Master in advance of the hearing their own draft order, to enable a check to be made on whether the necessary ingredients have been included. In the Chancery Division parties are advised to contact the Chancery Lawyer, Ms Vicky Bell (Room TM 5.06, Thomas More Building, Royal Courts of Justice, Strand, London, WC2A 2LL, tel. 020 7947 6080) at the earliest opportunity if they are contemplating making an application to the Chief Master for a GLO.

In the third paragraph after the first sentence add:

In the Chancery Division the register may alternatively be maintained by the lead solicitors but kept by the court or it may be kept and maintained by the court (the distinction is relevant to the rules for inspecting the register under 19BPD 6.6).

Delete the fourth paragraph and substitute:

An amendment to the Practice Direction (PDB para.6.1A) now makes it clear that individual claimants must issue their own claim form (and pay the issue fee) before their claim can be entered on a group register.

At the end of the sixth paragraph delete the last sentence.

Delete the seventh paragraph and substitute:

In the Queen's Bench Division the Senior Master arranges for details of GLO's to be published on the court service website (www.courtservice.gov.uk/cms/guidesnotices.htm) and in various reports as appropriate, and in the Chancery Division the Chief Chancery Master makes similar arrangements.

ANNEX

Delete paragraphs 19PD.7 to 19PD.10 inclusive and substitute:

19PD.7

CABINET OFFICE

CROWN PROCEEDINGS ACT 1947

List of Authorised Government Departments and the names and addresses for service of the person who is, or is acting for the purposes of the Act as, Solicitor for such Departments, published by the Minister for the Civil Service in pursuance of Section 17 of the Crown Proceedings Act 1947.

This list supersedes the list published on 5 April 2003

AUTHORISED GOVERNMENT DEPARTMENTS	SOLICITOR AND ADDRESSES FOR SERVICE

Advisory, Conciliation and Arbitration Service)	
Assets Recovery Agency)	
Board of Trade)	
Cabinet Office)	
Central Office of Information)	
Crown Prosecution Service)	
Department for Constitutional Affairs)	
Department for Culture, Media and Sport)	
Department for Education and Skills)	
Department for International Development)	
Department for Transport)	
Department of Trade and Industry)	
Director General of Telecommunications)	
Export Credits Guarantee Department)	
Foreign and Commonwealth Office)	
Government Actuary's Department)	The Treasury Solicitor
Health and Safety Executive)	Queen Anne's Chambers
Her Majesty's Chief Inspector of)	28 Broadway
Schools in England)	Westminster
Her Majesty's Chief Inspector of)	London SW1H 9JS
Schools in Wales)	
Her Majesty's Treasury)	
Home Office)	(see Notes (1) and (2))
The International Rail Regulator)	
Lord Chancellor's Department)	
Ministry of Defence)	
National Savings and Investments)	
Northern Ireland Office)	
Office for National Statistics)	
Office of Fair Trading)	
Office of the Deputy Prime Minister)	
Ordnance Survey)	
Privy Council Office)	
Public Record Office)	
Public Works Loan Board)	
The Rail Regulator)	
Royal Mint)	
Serious Fraud Office)	
Wales Office (Office of the Secretary of)	
State for Wales) (see Note (3)))	

Commissioners of Customs and Excise	The Solicitor for the Customs and Excise New King's Beam House 22 Upper Ground London SE1 9PJ
Commissioners of Inland Revenue	The Solicitor of Inland Revenue Somerset House The Strand London WC2R 1LB
Crown Estate Commissioners	The Solicitor to the Crown Estate Commissioners Crown Estate Office 16 Carlton House Terrace London SW1Y 5AH
Department for Environment, Food and Rural Affairs (see Note (3)) Forestry Commissioners	The Solicitor to the Department for Environment, Food and Rural Affairs Nobel House 17 Smith Square London SW1P 3JR
Department of Health Department for Work and Pensions Food Standards Agency	The Solicitor to the Department for Work and Pensions and the Department of Health New Court 48 Carey Street London WC2A 2LS
Director General of Water Services	Head of Legal Services The Office of Water Services Centre City Tower 7 Hill Street Birmingham B5 4UA
Gas and Electricity Markets Authority	General Counsel Office of Gas and Electricity Markets 9 Millbank London SW1P 3GE
National Assembly for Wales	The Counsel General to the National Assembly for Wales Cathays Park Cardiff CF10 3NQ

Postal Services Commission	The Chief Legal Adviser Postal Services Commission Hercules House 6 Hercules Road London SE1 7DB

NOTES

(1) Section 17(3) and section 18 of the Crown Proceedings Act 1947 provide as follows:

17(3) Civil proceedings against the Crown shall be instituted against the appropriate authorised Government department, or, if none of the authorised Government departments is appropriate or the person instituting the proceedings has any reasonable doubt whether any and if so which of those departments is appropriate, against the Attorney General.

18 All documents required to be served on the Crown for the purpose of or in connection with any civil proceedings by or against the Crown shall, if those proceedings are by or against an authorised Government department, be served on the solicitor, if any, for that department, or the person, if any, acting for the purposes of this Act as solicitor for that department, or if there is no such solicitor and no person so acting, or if the proceedings are brought by or against the Attorney General, on the Solicitor for the affairs of His Majesty's Treasury.

(2) The above-mentioned provisions do not apply to Scotland, where in accordance with the Crown Suits (Scotland) Act 1857, as amended by the Scotland Act 1998, civil proceedings against the Crown (other than the Scottish Administration) or any Government Department (other than the Scottish Executive) may be directed against the Advocate General for Scotland. The Advocate General's address for service is the Office of the Solicitor to the Advocate General for Scotland, Victoria Quay, Edinburgh EH6 6QQ. Civil proceedings against the Scottish Administration may be directed against the Scottish Ministers at St.Andrew's House, Edinburgh EH1 3DG, or against the Lord Advocate for and on behalf of the Scottish Executive. The Lord Advocate's address for service is 25 Chambers Street, Edinburgh, EH1 1LA.

(3) The Solicitor and address for service for the purposes of or in connection with civil proceedings brought by or against the Crown which relate to those matters for which the Secretary of State is responsible in Wales and for which the Secretary of State for Environment, Food and Rural Affairs is responsible is the Solicitor to the Department for Environment, Food and Rural Affairs, Nobel House, 17 Smith Square, London, SW1P 3JR. The Treasury Solicitor is the Solicitor acting for the Wales Office (Office of the Secretary of State for Wales) in all other civil proceedings affecting that Office.

CABINET OFFICE
WHITEHALL
LONDON SW1

Andrew Turnbull

(Signed) SIR ANDREW TURNBULL

6 January 2004

PART 22

STATEMENTS OF TRUTH

Editorial Introduction

At the beginning of the fourth paragraph delete the first two sentences.

22.0.2

False statements

22.1.18

For "paras. 27.1 to 27.4 (see para. 32PD.27 below)" substitute:

paras. 28.1 to 28.4 (see para. 32PD.28 below)

PRACTICE DIRECTION—STATEMENTS OF TRUTH

Documents to be verified by a statement of truth

Add new sub–paragraph 1.1(6):

22PD.1 **1.1**(6) a certificate of service.

Penalty

Delete "paragraph 27" and substitute:

22PD.5 **5.** paragraph 28

PART 23

GENERAL RULES ABOUT APPLICATIONS FOR COURT ORDERS

When does Part 23 apply?

At the beginning of the sixth paragraph delete the first sentence and substitute:

23.0.3 Where former RSC and CCR have been replaced by new Parts and supplemented by practice directions, usually the role of the Pt 23 provisions has been clarified.

Successive applications for same relief

In the first paragraph delete the sentence which begins "This was recognised in the Access to Justice Final Report..."

23.0.14 *In the sentence that follows for "was" substitute:*
is

Dismissal of totally without merit applications

Add new rule 23.12:

23.12 **23.12 If the court dismisses an application and it considers that the application is totally without merit—**

(a) **the court's order must record that fact; and**

(b) **the court must at the same time consider whether it is appropriate to make a civil restraint order.**

Effect of rule

Add new paragraph 23.12.1:

23.12.1 This rule was added by Civil Procedure (Amendment No. 2) Rules 2004 (S.I. 2004 No. 2072) with effect from October 1, 2004. The circumstances in which the court has power to make a civil restraint order against a party to proceedings, the procedure where a party applies for a civil restraint order against another party, and the consequences of the court making such an order, are set out in the practice direction supplementing r.3.11, and "civil restraint order" is defined in r.2.3(1).

Application "totally without merit"

Add new paragraph 23.12.2:

23.12.2 In r.3.4 (Power to strike out a statement of case) it is provided that, if the court strikes out a claimant's statement of case, and it considers that the claim is totally without merit, the court's order must record that fact, and the court must at the same time consider whether it is appropriate to make a civil restraint order (r.3.4(6)). The court has the same responsibilities where, of its own initiative, in these circumstances it strikes out a statement of case or dismisses an application (r.3.3(7)). (It may be noted that, whereas r.3.3(7) refers to the striking out of "a statement of case", r.3.4(6) refers to the striking out of "a claimant's statement of case".) An appeal court also has these responsibilities where it refuses an application for permission to appeal, strikes out an appellant's notice, or dismisses an appeal, and it considers the application, the notice of the appeal to be totally without merit (r.52.10(5) & (6)).

Rule 23.12 applies to applications generally and is not confined to applications under r.3.4 or those referred to in r.52.10. Practice Direction (Civil Restraint Orders), which supplements r.3.11, applies where the court is considering whether to make a civil restraint order, and should be read together with r.23.12 (and with r.3.4 and r.52.10).

It is important that there should be an effective way of ensuring that orders made by courts, either to the effect that an application or action has been dismissed as being totally devoid of merit, or that a civil restraint order has been made, are made widely known to other judges and courts who may be concerned with the same litigant (*Mahajan v. Department of Constitutional Affairs* [2004] EWCA Civ 96, June 30, 2004, C.A., unrep., at para. 46, per Brooke L.J.).

Amongst other things, r.23.12 and the similar provisions referred to above are designed to prevent court resources from being wasted. Thus, they may be seen as an example of the carrying into effect of the policy referred to in the overriding objective (r.1.1) of allotting to each case an appropriate share of the court's resources, while taking into account the need to allot resources to other cases (see para.1.3.7). They also help further the policy of avoiding a multiplicity of proceedings (see para. 1.4.15).

PART 25

INTERIM REMEDIES AND SECURITY FOR COSTS

Inherent jurisdiction

For "Bhamjee v. Forsdick [2003] EWCA Civ 1113..." substitute:

Bhamjee v. Forsdick (Practice Note) [2003] EWCA Civ 1113; [2004] 1 W.L.R. 88, CA **25.1.5**

Add at end:

See also, *Mahajan v. Department of Constitutional Affairs* [2004] EWCA Civ 946, June 30, 2004, CA, unrep. Towards the end of 2004, this aspect of the Court's inherent jurisdiction was put into rule form by the addition to the CPR of r.3.11 (Power of the court to make civil restraint order).

Interim injunction (r.25.1(1)(a))

After the seventh paragraph add:

25.1.9 Where the Attorney General applies to the High Court under the Supreme Court Act 1981 s.42 (Restriction of vexatious legal proceedings), the Court has jurisdiction to grant an interim injunction against the respondent, limiting his access to the courts pending the hearing of the application (*Attorney General v. Bhamjee* [2003] EWHC 2687 (Admin), July 31, 2003, D.C., unrep.).

Anti-suit injunction

At the end of the first paragraph add:

See paras. 6.19.19 and 6.21.23 above. **25.1.12**

Injunctions restraining publication of confidential information

In the last paragraph, for "Cream Holdings Ltd v. Banerjee [2003] EWCA Civ 103; The Times, February 28, 2003, CA" substitute:

Cream Holdings Ltd v. Banerjee [2003] EWCA Civ 103; [2003] 3 W.L.R. 999, CA **25.1.13**

In the last paragraph after "publication should not be allowed" add:

See also *Emerson Developments v. Avery* [2004] EWHC 194 (QB); January 26, 2004, unrep. (Field J.).

Who can apply for security for costs

Add at end:

25.12.3 An order for security for costs can be made in favour of a claimant in respect of a counterclaim brought against him if the counterclaim raises issues which go beyond the defence of his claim (*Thistle Hotels Ltd v. Gamma Four Ltd* [2004] EWHC 322; [2004] 2 B.C.L.C. 174).

Subsequent applications for security

Add at end:

25.12.11 Rules 12 and 13 are wide enough to permit applications against a claimant for security for the costs of proceedings at first instance to be provided pending an appeal brought by the defendant even though the defendant will not be entitled to such costs unless the appeal is successful (*Dar International FEF Co. v. Aon Ltd* [2004] 1 W.L.R 1395 CA; compare *Stabilad Ltd v. Stephens & Carter Ltd (No.1)* [1999] 1 W.L.R. 1201, noted in para. 25.12.13, below). In *DAR International FEF Co. v. Aon Ltd* the defendant obtained an order for security for costs pre–trial. Judgment was given against the defendant and the security (which took the form of a bank guarantee) expired a short time later. The trial judge refused to order reinstatement of the security pending the defendant's appeal. The Court of Appeal held that, although it had jurisdiction to make the order sought, in the circumstances, it was not appropriate to do so in this case.

No discrimination against claimants resident in other States

Add at end:

25.13.6 No formal evidence is required in order to prove the obstacles or difficulties of enforcement which may arise. Whilst there must be a proper basis for considering that such problems exist, the court will take note of obvious realities (*Thistle Hotels Ltd v. Gamma Four Ltd* [2004] EWHC 322).

In *Texuna International Ltd v. Cairn Energy Ltd* [2004] EWHC 1102 the court estimated the additional costs of enforcement in that case at £50,000 if enforcement took place in Hong Kong and also allowed a further £50,000 to cover the risk that enforcement would become more complex or that enforcement proceedings might have to be brought in another country; the claimant was ordered to provide security in the sum of £100,000.

Companies Act 1985, s.726(1)

In the penultimate paragraph, add at end:

25.13.13 In *Brimko Holdings Ltd v. Eastman Kodak Company* [2004] EWHC 1343, the claimant successfully demonstrated that an order for security in the amount sought by the defendant would stifle its claim. Instead, the court made an order for security in a sum slightly larger than the sum which the claimant had volunteered to provide.

PART 26

CASE MANAGEMENT—PRELIMINARY STAGE

Matters relevant to allocation

Add at end:

26.8.1 Note that additional matters which are relevant to allocation are contained in CPR Part 55.9 (possession claims) and Part 65.19 (demotion claims).

Effect of rule

In "Khiaban v. Beard", for "[2003] EWCA Civ 358; March 10, 2003" substitute:

26.8.4 *Khiaban v. Beard* [2003] EWCA Civ 358; [2003] 1 W.L.R. 1626

8. The Small Claims Track—Allocation and Case Management

8.1 Allocation

26PD.8 *In sub-paragraph 8.1(1)c, for "those for possession" substitute:*

opposed claims under Part 56, disputed claims for possession under Part 55 and demotion claims whether in the alternative to possession claims or under Part 65.

10. The Multi-Track

In paragraph 10.1 delete "The following paragraphs do not apply to" and substitute:

10.1 Paragraph 10.1 does not apply to— **26PD.10**

In sub-paragraph 10.1(1), for "where the defendant has filed a defence" substitute:

or a demotion claim whether in the alternative to a possession claim or under Part 65;

PART 29

THE MULTI-TRACK

Controlling costs

Add at end:

In *King v. Telegraph Group Ltd* [2004] EWCA Civ 613, it was held that in a defamation case initiated under a conditional fee agreement without "after-the-event" insurance cover (as to which see r.43.2(k)) the court should consider making a costs capping order if there was a danger that, unless a cap was imposed, the freedom of the press would be jeopardised. **29.2.3**

PART 30

TRANSFER

Existing title is amended. Delete existing rule 30.8 and substitute:

Transfer of competition law claims **30.8**

30.8—(1) This rule applies if, in any proceedings in the Queen's Bench Division, a district registry of the High Court or a county court, a party's statement of case raises an issue relating to the application of—

(a) **Article 81 or Article 82 of the Treaty establishing the European Community; or**

(b) **Chapter I or II of Part I of the Competition Act 1998**

(2) **Rules 30.2 and 30.3 do not apply.**

(3) **The court must transfer the proceedings to the Chancery Division of the High Court at the Royal Courts of Justice.**

PART 31

DISCLOSURE AND INSPECTION OF DOCUMENTS

Legal professional privilege

In the final paragraph, for "Disclosure of a privileged professional document for a limited purpose does not without legal professional move constitute a general waiver or lost of privilege," substitute:

Disclosure of this type of privileged document for a limited purpose does not without more constitute a general waiver or loss of privilege, **31.3.5**

(a) *Communications privileged although no litigation was contemplated or pending— "legal advice privilege"*

Solicitor and client

In the fourth paragraph after "in the context of obtaining legal advice" add:

31.3.6 *i.e.* advice concerning legal rights and obligations

In the fourth paragraph, for "Legal advice privilege does not extend to documents communicated to a client or to his solicitor for advice to be taken on them. Nor has the concept of "dominant purpose" any application or relevance to legal advice privilege, Three Rivers District Council v. Governor & Company of The Bank of England (No. 5) [2003] EWCA Civ 474; [2003] QB 1556; [2003] 1 W.W.R. 667 CA" substitute:

The purpose of the communication may be construed broadly and in terms of its dominant purpose but the mere fact that advice is given by a solicitor in the now fairly wide scope of the ordinary business of a solicitor does not of itself attract the privilege, *Three Rivers DC v. Bank of England (Disclosure) (No.5)* [2003] EWCA Civ 474, CA; [2003] QB 1556, and *Three Rivers DC v. Bank of England (Disclosure) (No.6)* [2004] EWCA Civ 218; [2004] Q.B. 916; [2004] 2 W.L.R. 1065; [2004] 3 All E.R. 168, CA

In the fourth paragraph after "submissions to the Bingham Inquiry" add:

and the subject matter of advice as to presentation

Other grounds of privilege

Without prejudice communications

In the eighth paragraph, for "see Berry Trade Ltd v. Moussavi, The Times, June 3, 2003, CA." substitute:

31.3.40 see *Berry Trade Ltd v. Moussavi* [2003] EWCA Civ 715; *The Times*, June 3, 2003, CA. In *Savings & Investments Bank Ltd v. Fincken* [2003] EWCA Civ 1630; [2004] 1 W.L.R. 667; [2004] 1 All E.R. 1125, CA, it was held that the unambiguous impropriety exception is confined to instances where it is established that the privelege is itself being abused.

Rule 31.16(3)(a), (b) and (d)

Add after first paragraph:

31.16.3 In *Rose v. Lynx Express Ltd* [2004] EWCA Civ 447, the court of appeal held "that courts should be hesitant, in the context of an application for pre–action disclosure, about embarking upon any determination of substantive issues in the case. In our view it will normally be sufficient to found an application under CPR 31.16(3) for the substantive claim pursued in the proceedings to be properly arguable and to have a real prospect of success, and it will normally be appropriate to approach the conditions in CPR 31.16(3) on that basis."

Claim for disclosure and production (The former action for discovery)

At the end of the first paragraph add:

31.18.3 See too *Carlton Film Distributors Ltd v. VCI Plc* [2003] EWHC 616; [2003] F.S.R. 47 p.876 extension of Norwich Pharmacal principle to an intended claim in contract situation resulting in an order for disclosure by a third party who had manufactured goods at the behest of the intended defendant to enable intended claimant to plead accurately its claim in contract.

Subsequent use of disclosed documents

In "BASF AG v. SmithKline Beecham Plc" delete "; Subs and" and add:

31.22.1 [2004] 1 W.L.R. 1479;

PART 32

EVIDENCE

Effect of rule

Delete full stop and add:

32.7.1 to this extent, directing that the defendant's cross–examination be limited accordingly.

PENALTY

Delete "paragraph 27.2(1) and substitute:

32PD.28 **28.3** paragraph 28.2(1)

PART 34

WITNESSES, DEPOSITIONS AND EVIDENCE FOR FOREIGN COURTS

"inferior court or tribunal"

Add at end:

34.4.1 The Chairman of the Parole Board Panel is entitled to give directions under Rule 9 of the Parole Board Rules 1997 including a direction requiring a party to the proceedings (*i.e.*, the prisoner or the Secretary of State) to apply for a witness summons from the county court or High Court under rule 34.4; see *The Queen (on the Application of Brooks) v. The Parole Board* [2004] EWCA Civ 80.

Arbitration porceedings

Add new paragraph 34.4.1A:

34.4.1A Section 43 of the Arbitration Act 1996 provides that a party to arbitral proceedings may use the same court procedures as are available in relation to legal proceedings to secure the attendance before the tribunal of a witness in order to give oral testimony or to produce documents or other material evidence. This may only be done with the permission of the tribunal or the agreement of the other parties and the court procedures may only be used if–the witness is in the United Kingdom, and the arbitral proceedings are being conducted in England and Wales or, as the case may be, Northern Ireland. Section 43(4) states that a person shall not be compelled by virtue of this section to produce any document or other material evidence which he could not be compelled to produce in legal proceedings. A party who wishes to rely on s.43 of the 1996 Act must apply for a witness summons in accordance with Part 34; see para. 7.1 of the Part 62 Arbitration Practice Direction. There is no power under s.43 of the 1996 Act for a court to order disclosure against a non–party as opposed to issuing a witness summons for the production of specific documents; see *BNP Paribas v. Deloitte and Touche LLP* [2003] EWHC 2874 (Comm); [2004] 1 Lloyd's Rep 233.

Purpose of rule

In the first paragraph after the first sentence add:

34.8.1 In *Barratt v. Shaw & Ashton and Another* [2001] EWCA Civ 137, the Court of Appeal said that the primary purpose of r.34.8 is the taking of evidence on deposition and introducing it in that form at the trial from a witness whom it would be impossible to bring to court for trial. However, that court was prepared to accept that it might be appropriate to order a deposition to be taken where justice required that the evidence to be given by the deponent be available prior to the hearing taking place. The example given was where a party wishes to pursue or resist an application for summary judgment under Part 24, and he could not adduce the necessary evidence for that purpose without having the evidence taken on deposition—perhaps because the witness was refusing to provide a statement.

Effect of rule

Add at end:

34.11.1 In *Barratt* v. Shaw & Ashton and Another [2001] EWCA Civ 137, r.34.11(4) was described as "a fallback procedure for when it seems preferable that the trial judge should hear some of the evidence orally."

Effect of rule

Add at end:

34.12.1 In *Dendron GmbH and Others v. The Regents of the University of California and Anor* [2004] EWHC 589 (Patents) Laddie J., the court rejected the submission that r.34.12 was the only limitation on the use of depositions or that CPR Part 34 was intended to be a definitive code in relation to the collateral use of evidence. Dealing with a deposition obtained through a court in the USA (see r.34.13) and a deposition obtained though a requested court in a Regulation State (see r.34.23), it was held that there exists an implied obligation not to use, without the permission of the (requesting) court or the consent of the witness, evidence obtained by compulsion under letters of request. A distinction was drawn with CPR Part 31 (which is said to be a complete code relating to disclosure) on the basis that CPR Part 31 was not concerned with the taking of evidence under compulsion. Although the *Dendron* case was concerned with evidence obtained under letters of request, it is strongly arguable that such an implied obligation also arises with depositions taken in England and Wales for use in England and Wales.

Delete list and substitute:

Hague Convention countries

34.13.7

Argentina	Israel	Singapore
Australia	Italy	Slovak Republic
Barbados	Kuwait	Slovenia
Belarus	Latvia	South Africa
Bulgaria	Lithuania	Spain
China	Luxembourg	Sri Lanka
Cyprus	Mexico	Sweden
Czech Republic	Monaco	Switzerland
Denmark	Norway	Turkey
Estonia	Netherlands	Ukraine
Finland	Poland	United Kingdom and possessions
France	Portugal	United States and possessions
Germany	Romania	Venezuela
Hungary	Russian Federation	

Add at end:

Hungary and Seychelles must be added to the list. According to the Hague Convention website, the United Kingdom has not yet declared acceptance of the accession of the following countries: China, Kuwait, Lithuania, Romania, Slovenia, Sri Lanka and Seychelles. The Special Administrative Regions of Hong Kong and Macao should no longer appear separately in the list. The Convention still applies to those regions but since Hong Kong and Macao have been restored to the Peoples' Republic of China by the United Kingdom and Portugal respectively, the information relating to these two regions (*i.e.*, reservations, declarations, contact details of the authorities and dates of entry into force) has been added to the information for the Peoples' Republic of China.

II. EVIDENCE FOR FOREIGN COURTS

Scope and interpretation

For "a Regulation State" substitute:

34.16 34.16—(1) **another Regulation State.**

Powers of the Court

Before the third paragraph add:

34.21.4 In *USA v. Philip Moris Inc and Others* [2004] EWCA Civ 330, the judge at first instance included in his order a direction that the applicant (the Claimant) supply to the non–party witness and one of the defendants a paginated bundle of documents on which it intended to rely at the examination, together with a written indication of the proposed lines of questioning with reference to documents together with sample questions. He also fixed a directions hearing at which he would hear objections by the witness and the defendant and give further directions as appropriate. The Court of Appeal approved this approach. The case was complex, involved numerous documents and it was likely that the witness would raise issues of legal professional privilege.

Where a person to be examined is in another Regulation State

After "who is" add:

34.23 34.23—(1) **in another Regulation State**

Note

Add new paragraph 34.23.1:

34.23.1 See *Dendron GmbH v. University of California (Parallel Proceedings: Use of Evidence)* [2004] EWHC 589 (Patents) Laddie J. (above).

PART 35

EXPERTS AND ASSESSORS

Editorial Introduction

Add at end of the eleventh paragraph:

35.0.2 In *X v. Brown* [2003] EWCA Civ 181, the trial judge preferred the evidence of the defendant's psychiatrist that the claimant would have developed a disabling psychogenic illness in any event regardless of the accident to that of the claimant's expert. The Court of Appeal said the reasoning the judge had applied to his analysis of the expert evidence did not support his conclusions and adjusted the damages award.

Effect of rule

Add at end:

35.1.1 In a dispute arising from a contract to supply an IT system the judge said it was unhelpful that no expert evidence was called *Peregrine Systems Ltd v. Stena Ltd* 2004 EWHC 275, (TCC) and in *IPC Media Ltd v. Highbury Leisure Publishing Ltd* 2004 EWHC 1967, (Ch) a copyright dispute, the parties were given permission only two months before trial to adduce expert evidence on the similarities between the design features of the two magazines.

Effect of rule

Add at end:

35.3.1 In *Hussein v. William Hill Group* [2004] EWHC 208, QB, a personal injury claim, two doctors who were friends of the claimant and who provided medical reports later in the proceedings which supported his claim were criticised by the judge and their reports were disregarded. The judge found that the claimant had greatly and deliberately exaggerated his injuries. The conduct of the doctors was referred to the General Medical Council.

C (A Child) (Immunisation: Parental Rights), Re & F (A Child) (Immunisation: Parental Rights), Re [2003] EWCA Civ 1148; [2003] 2 F.L.R. 1095 were disputes between parents concerning the immunisation of their children. The homeopath who gave evidence for the mothers (who were against the immunisation) was criticised by the judge for allowing her deeply held feelings about immunisation to overrule her duty to the court to give objective evidence.

Preaction protocols and disclosure of expert reports

Add at end:

35.4.3 The Preaction Protocol for Construction and Engineering has similar provisions. The Housing Disrepair Protocol provides for joint selection and instruction of a single joint expert in a similar way to the personal injury protocol.

Effect of rule

Move the sixteenth paragraph "The Queen's Bench Guide helpfully advises..." so it appears before the fourteenth paragraph "There have been a number of helpful decisions..."

35.7.1 *After the twentieth paragraph add:*

Piper v. Clifford Kent Ltd [2003] EWCA Civ 1692 a claim in smell nuisance from a chicken farm, the single joint expert, upon whose evidence the judge had relied, had failed to measure the wind direction on his visit: on appeal the case was remitted back to the county court for a retrial.

Privilege

Existing paragraph 35.10.5 is renumbered "35.10.4".

35.10.4 **Literature to be served with reports**

Add new paragraph 35.10.5:

35.10.5 *Wardlaw v. Farrar* [2003] EWCA Civ 1719 decided that in clinical negligence claims being conducted in the county courts or District Registries, the judges should adopt the standard direction of the Queens' Bench Masters that any material or literature upon which an expert wished to rely must be served either with his report or at the latest one month before trial. Permission would be needed from the trial judge before an expert witness could introduce additional material at trial. The point of principle is applicable to experts' reports in any discipline.

Assessor preparing report for court (r.35.15(3)(a))

Add at end:

35.15.4 In *Owners of the Bow Spring v. Owners of the Manzanillo II* [2004] EWCA Civ 1007 a dispute arising from a nautical collision, the Court of Appeal, obiter, said that the judge was correct to invite counsel to comment upon the questions he intended to put to the nautical assessors but he should have done likewise with the assessors' answers before deciding whether to accept the assessors' advice.

PART 36

OFFERS TO SETTLE AND PAYMENTS INTO COURT

Content limitations

For "Mitchell & others v. James & others [2002] EWCA Civ 997; [2003] 2 All E.R. 1064" substitute:

36.5.2 *Mitchell & others v. James & others* [2002] EWCA Civ 997; [2004] 1 W.L.R. 158; [2003] 2 All E.R. 1064

Note

Add at end:

36.8.1 A Part 36 offer is effected once received by the offeree without any need to comply with the provisions as to service contained in Part 6, see *Charles v. NTL Group Ltd* [2002] EWCA Civ 2004; [2003] C.P. Rep. 44, CA.

Interlocutory proceedings and a Part 36 payment (r.36.19(2))

For the last paragraph substitute:

36.19.1 The rule is directory not compulsive and upon breach the court has a discretion whether to continue or to recuse. It will usually continue where to do so will cause no injustice, see *Millensted*, above. These principles were reaffirmed in *Garratt v. Saxby* [2004] EWCA Civ 341; [2004] 1 W.L.R. 2152, CA, in which it was said that it was proper to take into account any additional time, cost and difficulty involved were the hearing to be aborted.

Under this rule, the payment in can only be used on arguments as to cost, see *Johnson v.Gore Wood & Co (No.2)* [2004] EWCA Civ 14 (attempt to use same in relation to causation of damages disallowed).

"...order interest ... at a rate not exceeding 10% above base rate ..."

Delete full stop and add:

36.21.2 , affirmed on this point [2004] EWCA Civ 277.

PART 37

MISCELLANEOUS PROVISIONS ABOUT PAYMENTS INTO COURT

Payment into court by life assurance company

Delete "an application notice" and substitute:

37PD.7 **7.1** a witness statement or an affidavit

Delete "application notice" and substitute:

(6) witness statement or an affidavit

After "witness statement" add:

7.2 or affidavit

Payment into court under Trustee Act 1925

Delete "an application notice" and substitute:

37PD.9

9.1 a witness statement or an affidavit

Delete "application notice" and substitute:

9.2 witness statement or an affidavit

Payment Into Court Under Vehicular Access Across Common And Other Land (England) Regulations 2002

Delete "an application notice" and substitute:

37PD.11

11.2 a witness statement or an affidavit

Delete "application notice" and substitute:

11.3 witness statement or an affidavit

Delete "application notice" and substitute:

11.4 witness statement or an affidavit

PART 39

MISCELLANEOUS PROVISIONS RELATING TO HEARINGS

"If the defendant does not attend" (r.39.3(1)(c))

Add at end:

39.3.5

As to whether or not a party was absent at trial, see *Rouse v. Freeman The Times* January 8, 2002 Gross J. (whether individual claimant present through solicitor) and *Watson v. Bluemoor Properties* [2002] EWCA Civ 1875; December 10, 2002 (whether defendant company present through director).

"the court may grant the application only if . . ." (r.39.3(5))

In the second paragraph, add after "(Garland v. Stedman, December 7, 2000, CA, unreported, but noted by Lawtel).":

39.3.7

It has been held on an application to set aside judgement, following the refusal of an application to adjourn a trial on medical grounds due to the lack of a medical certificate, that it was wrong to reject evidence of a medical condition in the absence of the defendant's cross–examination, where there was no reason to infer untrustworthiness and where there was no proper basis to reject such evidence (*St Ermin's Property Company Ltd v. Draper* [2004] EWHC 697 (ChD) January 27, 2004).

Start following text beginning "See too Regency Rolls Ltd v. Carnall" as a new paragraph.

See too *Regency Rolls Ltd v. Carnall*, October 16, 2000, CA, unreported, but noted in *Civil Procedure News*, April 23, 2001, where an application to set aside was dismissed because although the applicant had a good reason for not attending trial (he was "indisposed"), (1) his version of events was inherently incapable of belief and he could not be described as having reasonable prospects of success and (2) he had not acted promptly—the application under CPR r.39.3 was made over four weeks after the hearing. Arden L.J. pointed out that "The dictionary meaning of 'promptly' is 'with alacrity'". Simon Brown L.J. said, "I would accordingly construe 'promptly' here to require, not that an applicant has been guilty of no needless delay whatever, but rather that he has acted with all reasonable celerity in the circumstances." The Court of Appeal has held that a company acted promptly when, in a case involving "a considerable amount of documentation", an application to set aside was issued six weeks after judgment (*Watson v. Bluemoor Properties Ltd* [2002] EWCA Civ 1875; December 10, 2002).

After the penultimate paragraph add:

The reasonable prospect of success condition in 39.3(5) does not offend any fundamental principle of justice or any principle of ECHR jurisprudence (*Hackney LBC v. Driscoll* [2003] EWCA Civ 1037; [2003] 1 WLR 2602).

For "Hackney LBC v. Driscoll [2003] EWCA Civ 1037; [2003] 1 WLR 2602; The Times, August 29, 2003" substitute:

Hackney LBC v. Driscoll [2003] EWCA Civ 1037; [2003] 1 W.L.R. 2602; [2003] 4 All E.R. 1205; *The Times*, August 29, 2003

"Representation at trial of companies or other corporations" (r.39.6)

39.6.1

For "Avinue Ltd v. Sunrule Ltd The Times, December 5, 2003; November 26, 2003" substitute:

Avinue Ltd v. Sunrule Ltd [2003] EWCA Civ 1942; [2004] 1 W.L.R. 634.

Representation

39.6.2

For "(see para 5PD.1)" substitute:

(see para. 5.1)

Memorandum from the Lord Chief Justice and the Attorney General

Requests for the Appointment of an Advocate to the Court

39.8.2

1. The memorandum has been agreed between the Attorney General and the Lord Chief Justice. It gives guidance about making a request for the appointment of an Advocate to the Court (formerly called an "*amicus curiae*").
2. In most cases, an Advocate to the Court is appointed by the Attorney General, following a request by the court. In some cases, an Advocate to the Court will be appointed by the Official Solicitor or the Children & Family Court Advisory Service (CAFCASS) (see paragraphs 11 and 12 below).

The role of an Advocate to the Court

39.8.3

3. A court may properly seek the assistance of an Advocate to the Court when there is a danger of an important and difficult point of law being decided without the court hearing relevant argument. In those circumstances the Attorney General may decide to appoint an Advocate to the Court.
4. It is important to bear in mind that an Advocate to the Court represents no–one. His or her function is to give to the court such assistance as he or she is able on the relevant law and its application to the facts of the case. An Advocate to the Court will not normally be instructed to lead evidence, cross– examine witnesses, or investigate the facts. In particular, it is not appropriate for the court to seek assistance from an Advocate to the Court simply because a defendant in criminal proceedings refuses representation.
5. The following circumstances are to be distinguished from those where it will be appropriate for the court to seek the assistance of an Advocate to the Court:
   i. where a point of law which affects a government department is being argued in a case where the department is not represented and where the court believe that the department may wish to be represented;
   ii. where the Attorney believes it is necessary for him to intervene as a party in his capacity as guardian of the public interest;
   iii. where the court believes it is appropriate for a litigant in person to seek free (pro bono) assistance;
   iv. where, in a criminal trial, the defendant is unrepresented and the Advocate to the Court would be duplicating the prosecutor's duty as a minister of justice "to assist the court on all matters of law applicable to the case";
   v. where in a criminal case in relation to sentencing appeals there are issues of fact which are likely to arise and the prosecution ought to be represented, or it would be reasonable to ask the prosecutor to be present and address the court as to the relevant law.

6. In the first of these five cases, the court may invite the Attorney to make arrangements for the advocate to be instructed on behalf of the department. In the second, the court may grant the Attorney permission to intervene, in which case the advocate instructed represents the Attorney. In neither case is the advocate an Advocate to the Court.
7. In the third case the court may grant a litigant in person an adjournment to enable him or her to seek free (pro bono) assistance. In doing so, the court should bear in mind that it is likely to take longer to obtain free (pro bono) representation than funded representation. In contrast to an Advocate to the Court, a free (pro bono) legal representative will obtain his or her instructions from the litigant and will represent the interests of that party. His or her role before the court and duty to the court will be identical to that of any other representative of the parties. Accordingly it will not be appropriate for the court to take such a course where the type of assistance required is that provided by an Advocate to the Court.
8. In the fourth case the prosecutor's special duty is akin to an Advocate to the Court. In the fifth case, in relation to appeals against sentence where the defendant is represented, it may be preferable to request the attendance of the prosecutor who will be able to address the court on issues of fact and law. It would not be proper for an Advocate to the Court to take instructions from the prosecuting authority in relation to factual matters relating to the prosecution. An Advocate to the Court should only be asked to address the court as to the relevant law.

Making a request to the Attorney General

39.8.4

9. A request for an Advocate to the Court should be made by the Court as soon as convenient after it is made aware of the point of law which requires the assistance of an Advocate to the Court. The request should set out the circumstances which have occurred, identifying the point of law upon which assistance is sought and the nature of the assistance required. The court should consider whether it would be sufficient for such assistance to be in writing in the form of submissions as to the law, or whether the assistance should include oral submissions at the hearing. The request should ordinarily be made in writing and be accompanied by the papers necessary to enable the Attorney to reach a decision on the basis of a proper understanding of the case.
10. The Attorney will decide whether it is appropriate to provide such assistance and, if so, the form such assistance should take. Before reaching a decision he may seek further information or assistance from the court. The Attorney will also ask the court to keep under review the need for such assistance. Where the circumstances which gave rise to the original request have changed, such that the court may now anticipate hearing all relevant argument on the point of law without the presence of an Advocate to the Court, either the Court or the Attorney may ask the Advocate to the Court to withdraw.

Requests to the Official Solicitor or CAFCASS

39.8.5

11. A request for an Advocate to the Court may be made to the Official Solicitor or CAFCASS (Legal Services and Special Casework) where the issue is one in which their experience of representing children and adults under disability gives rise to special experience. The division of responsibility between them is outlined in Practice Notes reported at [2001] 2 FLR 151 and [2001] 2 FLR 155.
12. The procedure and circumstances for requesting an Advocate to the Court to be appointed by the Official Solicitor or CAFCASS are the same as those applying to requests to the Attorney General. In cases of extreme urgency, telephone requests may be made. In some cases, the Official Solicitor himself will be appointed as Advocate to the Court. He may be given directions by the Court authorising him to obtain documents, conduct investigations and enquiries and to advise the Court. He may appear by counsel or an in–house advocate.

The Attorney General
Lord Goldsmith QC

The Lord Chief Justice
The Right Hon. The Lord Woolf
19 December 2001

Requests for an Advocate to the Court should be addressed as follows:
The Legal Secretary,
The Legal Secretariat to the Law Officers,
Attorney General's Chambers,
9 Buckingham Gate,
London
SW1E 6JP
Telephone:020 7271 2417 (criminal)
020 7271 2413 (civil)
Fax: 020 7271 2434

Official Solicitor to the Supreme Court,
81 Chancery Lane,
London
WC2A 1DD
Telephone: 020 7911 7127
Fax: 020 7911 7105

CAFCASS (Legal Services and Special Casework) Newspaper House,
8–16 Great New Street,
London
EC4A 3BN
Telephone: 020 7904 0867
Fax: 020 7904 0868/9

For information about free (pro bono) services:
Bar Pro Bono Unit,
7 Gray's Inn Square,
London
WC1R 5AZ
Telephone: 020 7831 9711
Fax: 020 7831 9733
Email: enquiries[@00ba]rprobonounit.f9.co.uk

PART 40

JUDGMENTS, ORDERS, SALE OF LAND ETC.

Effect of judgment before entry

In the seventh paragraph, for "judges routinely make available to parties" substitute:

40.2.1 judges routinely make available to parties' legal advisers

In the seventh paragraph, for "written judgment to the parties in draft" substitute:
written judgment to the advisers in draft

Written Judgments

After "(see Vol. 2 para. 1–89)" add:

40.2.5 , Patents Court Guide para. 20 (see Vol. 2 para. 2F–130)

Add at end:

In accordance with these directions, a judge may make available to parties' legal advisers on a confidential basis his judgment before formally handing it down. See further para. 40.2.1, above. The normal practice is that the parties should not be shown a judgment until half an hour before it is handed down. However, in order to facilitate parties' understanding of a judgment, a judge may on terms permit the parties' legal advisers to release copies of it to them at an earlier stage (*Crown Dilmun v. Sutton* [2004] EWHC 821 (QB); April 1, 2004, unrep. (Peter Smith J.)).

Effect of rule

After "The application is made by" add:

Part 23 **40.16.1**

Sale by personal representatives of real estate

Delete "O.85, r.2(3)(d)" and add:

CPR 64.2 and PD to Part 64 para. 1(2)(G). **40.16.2**

Discharge of incumbrances on sale

Delete the three existing paragraphs and substitute:

Paragraph 1.2 of Part 1 or PD D to Part 40 provides that where land subject to any incumbrance is sold or exchanged any party may apply to the court for a direction under L.P.A. 1925, s.50. **40.16.3**

Directions

Delete existing paragraph and substitute:

The directions that in particular the court will make are set out in paragraph 2 of Part 1 or PD to Part 40. **40.16.5**

Leave to bid

Delete the last paragraph. **40.16.6**

Certifying result of sale

Delete existing paragraph and substitute:

Paragraphs 4.1 and 4.2 of Part 1 or PD to Part 40 applies. **40.16.7**

Non-compliance with a judgment or order

In paragraph 9.1, for "the penal notice" substitute: **40BPD.9**

a penal notice

PART 42

CHANGE OF SOLICITOR

Change of solicitor—duty to give notice

For existing rule 42.2(5)(a) substitute:

42.2—(5) (a) **notice is filed and served in accordance with paragraph (2); or** **42.2**

Revocation or discharge of legal aid certificate

For "the previously legally aided party" substitute:

the previously publicly funded party **42.2.4**

Appointment of new solicitors

Add at end:

As to the power to grant an injunction to restrain a particular advocate or legal advisor from acting, see *Skjevesland v. Geveran Trading Co. Ltd* [2002] EWCA Civ 1567; October 30, 2002. **42.4.3**

PART 43

SCOPE OF COST RULES AND DEFINITIONS

Costs Estimates

Add at end:

43.2.2 In *King v. Telegraph Group Ltd* [2004] EWCA Civ 613, the Court of Appeal said that the view expressed by Gage J. in *AB and Ors v. Leeds Teaching Hospitals NHS Trust* [2003] EWHC 1034 (QB), to the effect that the court possesses the power to make a costs capping order in an appropriate case, is correct. In the King case the Court said:

"The language of Section 51 of the Supreme Court Act 1981 is very wide and CPR 3.2(m) confers the requisite power. Needless to say, in deciding what order to make the court should take the principles set out in CPR 44.3 (which govern the retrospective assessment of costs) as an important point of reference".

In this case the Court also referred to the judgment of Dyson L.J. in *Leigh v. Michelin Tyre Plc* [2003] EWCA Civ 1766; [2004] 2 All E.R. 175, CA, where his lordship expressed the opinion that the prospective fixing of costs budgets was likely to achieve the objective of controlling the costs of litigation more effectively than estimates.

PART 44

GENERAL RULES ABOUT COSTS

Comment

After the sixth paragraph add:

44.3.1 An award of costs that simply looks at the number of issues won and lost does not fairly reflect the realities of the case. Where successful claimants had lost a good many issues it was not unreasonable, in particular in the light of the misleading conduct of three of the defendants, for the claimants to have raised the issues that they did. The claimants were awarded a percentage of their costs: *Douglas v. Hello Ltd* [2004] EWHC 63 (Ch) Lindsay J.

Costs in proceedings before trial

Discretion as to costs

Add at end:

44.3.5 The Court of Appeal has repeatedly stated that, when making an order for costs, the Judge should clearly state his reasons, particularly where the costs incurred are disproportionate to the amount in issue: see *English v. Emery Reimbold & Strick Ltd* [2002] EWCA Civ 605; *Verrechia v. Commissioner of Police for the Metropolis* [2002] EWCA Civ 605; [2002] 3 All ER 385 CA; *Lavelle v. Lavelle* [2004] EWCA Civ 223, CA.

Judicial Review

In sub–paragraph (d), add at end:

44.3.7 (d) And see *R. (on the application of Payne) v. Caerphilly CBC (Costs)* [2004] EWCA Civ 433.

Rule 44.3(2)

After the first paragraph add:

44.3.8 A Judge making an award of costs has essentially to determine whether to apply the general rule that costs follow the event, or award costs on an issue by issue basis. It is not appropriate to consider in that determination, a claimant's ability to recover damages in an action overall. In a case where the claimant had succeeded in two thirds of his pleaded causes of action and the trial had not been prolonged by the unsuccessful cause of action, it was appropriate that the costs should follow the event: *Flemming v. Chief Constable of Sussex* [2004] EWCA Civ 4.

Rule 44.3(4)

Delete full stop at the end of the second paragraph and add:

44.3.10 and *Kastor Navigation Co. Ltd v. Axa Global Risks (UK) Ltd (The Kastor Too)* [2004] EWCA Civ 277.

Add after the seventh paragraph:

Where the court found that there were reasonable grounds for suspecting that the testatrix had lacked knowledge and approval of the contents of her will, the defendants were entitled to test their case on that part of the claim. The court held that the beneficiary should not have to pay any part of her own costs of defending herself against allegations of undue influence which failed. The defendants were ordered to pay one half of the claimant beneficiary's costs: *Good (Deceased) (Costs), Re*; *Carapeto v. Good* [2002] W.T.L.R. 1305, Rimer J.

After the sixteenth paragraph add:

In a successful claim brought by the client against the solicitor who had acted for him in litigation, the solicitor joined counsel instructed by them in the original action as a third party. On appeal the solicitor was found to be liable as to 80 per cent and counsel as to 20 per cent of the damages awarded. The solicitor argued that costs should be apportioned in the same percentages. The court held that the costs order should reflect the fact that the matter should not have been defended by the solicitor and that both the solicitor and counsel had entered into an unnecessary and costly mud slinging contest. The solicitor was ordered to pay the full costs of the trial. Counsel was ordered to pay 20 per cent of the Part 20 proceedings. The solicitor was required to pay one third of its own costs of the appeal, the balance to be paid by counsel: *Moy v. Pettman Smith (A Firm) (Costs)* [2003] EWCA Civ 467; [2003] P.N.L.R. 31, CA.

Add at end:

Where the Judge making an order for costs is in a position to deal with the issue of conduct, by reason of his involvement in the case, it is the duty of the party wishing to raise the issue to raise it before that Judge. If the paying party does not raise the issue when it is open to him to do so, it is not open to him, when the costs come to be assessed, to raise the issue of conduct under r.44.5(3) as a ground for the reduction of costs which he would otherwise have to pay. If the paying party is uncertain as to whether a matter which he wishes to raise fall within that category, he should in any event raise it with the Judge, who can then consider whether he should deal with it or specifically direct that the Costs Judge deal with it on assessment. In the case of an order by consent, the paying party may seek to include in the consent order, a provision taking account of the matter which he wishes to raise by providing that he was not to pay the whole of the costs, or which specifically refers the matter in question to the Costs Judge for determination. A paying party who does not protect himself in those ways runs the risk that the Costs Judge will decide that the matter in question is one which should appropriately have been raised with the Judge making the costs order and which should not be raised before him. It is an abuse of the court's process to raise an issue before the Costs Judge which was not, but should have been, raised before the Judge making the order for payment of costs. The court could see no conflict with the mandatory provisions of rule 44.5(3)(a): *Aaron v. Shelton* [2004] EWHC 1162, (QB); [2004] 3 All E.R. 561 Jack J.

Rule 44.3(5)

After the third paragraph add:

44.3.11 In *Halsey v. Milton Keynes General NHS Trust* [2004] EWCA Civ 576 the Court of Appeal addressed the question of ADR in greater detail. The court indicated that the burden was on the unsuccessful party to show why there should be a departure from the general rule on costs, in the form of an order to deprive the successful party of some or all of his costs on the grounds that he refused to agree to ADR. A fundamental principal was that such a departure was not justified unless it had been shown that the successful party had acted unreasonably in refusing to agree to ADR. In deciding whether a party had acted unreasonably the court should bear in mind the advantages of ADR over the court process and have regard to all the circumstances of the particular case. The factors that could be relevant included:

(i) the nature of the dispute;
(ii) the merits of the case;
(iii) the extent to which other settlement methods had been attempted;
(iv) whether the costs of ADR were disproportionately high;
(v) whether any delay in setting up and attending the ADR would have been prejudicial;

(vi) whether the ADR had a reasonable prospect of success.

Where a successful party had refused to agree to ADR, despite the court's encouragement, that was a fact that the court would take into account when deciding whether his refusal was unreasonable. The court went on to decide that there was no basis for the court to discriminate against successful public bodies when deciding whether a refusal to agree to ADR should result in a cost penalty. The "ADR" pledge announced in March 2001 by the Lord Chancellor was no more than an undertaking that ADR would be considered and used whenever the other party accepts it in all suitable cases by all Government departments and agencies. It was difficult to see in what circumstances it would be right to give great weight to the pledge. The court's role was to encourage not compel ADR. It was likely that compulsion of ADR would be regarded by the European Court of Human Rights as an unacceptable constraint on the right of access to court and therefore a violation of Article 6 ECHR.

Add at end:

There is a long line of authority pre-CPR to the effect that a court is entitled to take into account pre-proceedings conduct by a party when exercising its discretion over costs. Rule 44.3(5)(a) specifically includes a reference to pre-proceedings conduct. Any suggestion that the conduct had to be conduct within the proceedings themselves (as stated in *Hall v. Rover Financial Services* [2002] EWCA Civ 1514) should be interpreted as no more than the description of the contemporary practice of Judges of the Commercial Court where the court is used to dealing with business people who "not infrequently do not follow the Queensbury Rules in their dealings with each other": *Groupama Insurance v. Overseas Partners & Aon Ltd* [2003] EWCA Civ 1846.

Rule 44.3(6)

Add at end:

44.3.12 "In any event in principle there seems no reason why the court should not [award interest] where a party has had to put up money paying its solicitor and been out of the use of that money in the meanwhile" *per* Waller L.J. in *Bim Kemi AB v. Blackburn Chemicals Ltd (Costs)* [2003] EWCA Civ 889. The court has expressed the view that the appropriate dates,when seeking to measure the extent to which a party has been out of pocket, would be the dates on which the invoices were actually paid. The appropriate time for interest to stop would be when interest on costs is replaced by judgment interest: *Douglas v. Hello Ltd* [2004] EWHC 63 (Ch) Lindsay J."

Costs on the Indemnity Basis

Add after third paragraph:

44.4.2 A respondent wishing to protect himself against costs of an appeal cannot rely on an offer to settle made before trial. The particular appeal turned on a pure point of construction to which there could be only one answer. In those circumstances the claimant could not be expected to have offered to give up a substantial part of its judgment. The claimant was awarded costs on the indemnity basis with interest from the mid point between the lapse of the offer and the date of the appeal hearing: *CEL Group Ltd v Nedlloyd Lines UK Ltd* [2003] EWCA Civ 1871.

Comment

Add after second paragraph:

44.5.1 Where four different commercial interests commenced separate proceedings against the same defendant, which were not consolidated, the court awarded the successful claimants their costs but directed that the Costs Judge was free to consider the four actions as if they had been consolidated at the date of the order for mutuality of evidence. Regard had to be had to the reasonableness of the claimants maintaining separate representation and separate expert witnesses during the period after that order: *Cipla Ltd v. Glaxo Group Ltd and other actions* [2004] EWHC 819, Pumfrey J.

Procedure

For "reduction is sought" substitute:

44.16.2 reduction sought is accepted

PART 45

FIXED COSTS

In the Table of Contents add:

Contents 45.0.1

IV. Fixed percentage increase in employers liability claims

II. ROAD TRAFFIC ACCIDENTS—FIXED RECOVERABLE COSTS IN COSTS-ONLY POCEEDINGS

Disbursements

In sub-paragraph (b) for "body of a prescribed description within the meaning of section 30(1) of the Access to Justice Act 1999" substitute:

45.10—(2) (b) **membership organisation** 45.10

At the end of sub-paragraph (b) add:

("membership organisation" is defined in rule 43.2(1)(n)).

III. FIXED PERCENTAGE INCREASE IN ROAD TRAFFIC ACCIDENT CLAIMS

Add new Section III:

Scope and interpretation 45.15

45.15—(1) This Section sets out the percentage increase which is to be allowed in the cases to which this Section applies.

(Rule 43.2(1)(l) defines "percentage increase" as the percentage by which the amount of a legal representative's fee can be increased in accordance with a conditional fee agreement which provides for a success fee).

(2) This Section applies where—

(a) **the dispute arises from a road traffic accident; and**

(b) **the claimant has entered into a funding arrangement of a type specified in rule 43.2(k)(i).**

(3) This Section does not apply if the proceedings are costs only proceedings to which Section II of this Part applies.

(4) This Section does not apply—

(a) **to a claim which has been allocated to the small claims track;**

(b) **to a claim not allocated to a track, but for which the small claims track is the normal track; or**

(c) **where the road traffic accident which gave rise to the dispute occurred before 6th October 2003.**

(5) The definitions in rule 45.7(4) apply to this Section as they apply to Section II.

(6) In this Section—

(a) **a reference to "fees" is a reference to fees for work done under a conditional fee agreement or collective conditional fee agreement;**

(b) **a reference to "trial" is a reference to the final contested**

hearing or to the contested hearing of any issue ordered to be tried separately;

(c) a reference to a claim concluding at trial is a reference to a claim concluding by settlement after the trial has commenced or by judgment; and

(d) "trial period" means a period of time fixed by the court within which the trial is to take place and where the court fixes more than one such period in relation to a claim, means the most recent period to be fixed.

Percentage increase of solicitors' fees

45.16 **45.16—(1) Subject to rule 45.18, the percentage increase which is to be allowed in relation to solicitors' fees is—**

(a) 100% where the claim concludes at trial; or

(b) 12.5% where—

(i) the claim concludes before a trial has commenced; or

(ii) the dispute is settled before a claim is issued.

Percentage increase of counsel's fees

45.17 **45.17—(1) Subject to rule 45.18, the percentage increase which is to be allowed in relation to counsel's fees is—**

(a) 100% where the claim concludes at trial;

(b) if the claim has been allocated to the fast track—

(i) 50% if the claim concludes 14 days or less before the date fixed for the commencement of the trial; or

(ii) 12.5% if the claim concludes more than 14 days before the date fixed for the commencement of the trial or before any such date has been fixed;

(c) if the claim has been allocated to the multi-track

(i) 75% if the claim concludes 21 days or less before the date fixed for the commencement of the trial; or

(ii) 12.5% if the claim concludes more than 21 days before the date fixed for the commencement of the trial or before any such date has been fixed;

(d) 12.5% where—

(i) the claim has been issued but concludes before it has been allocated to a track; or

(ii) in relation to costs-only proceedings, the dispute is settled before a claim is issued.

(2) Where a trial period has been fixed, if—

(a) the claim concludes before the first day of that period; and

(b) no trial date has been fixed within that period before the claim concludes,

the first day of that period is treated as the date fixed for the commencement of the trial for the purposes of paragraph (1).

(3) Where a trial period has been fixed, if—

(a) the claim concludes before the first day of that period; but

(b) before the claim concludes, a trial date had been fixed within that period,

the trial date is the date fixed for the commencement of the trial for the purposes of paragraph (1).

(4) Where a trial period has been fixed and the claim concludes—

(a) on or after the first day of that period; but

(b) before commencement of the trial,

the percentage increase in paragraph (1)(b)(i) or (1)(c)(i) shall apply as appropriate, whether or not a trial date has been fixed within that period.

(5) For the purposes of this rule, in calculating the periods of time, the day fixed for the commencement of the trial (or the first day of the trial period, where appropriate) is not included.

Application for an alternative percentage increase where the fixed increase is 12.5%

45.18—(1) This rule applies where the percentage increase to be allowed— **45.18**

(a) in relation to solicitors' fees under the provisions of rule 45.16; or

(b) in relation to counsel's fees under rule 45.17,

the percentage increase in paragraph (1)(b)(i) or (1)(c)(i) shall apply as appropriate, whether or not a trial date has been fixed within that period.

is 12.5%.

(2) A party may apply for a percentage increase greater or less than that amount if—

(a) the parties agree damages of an amount greater than £500,000 or the court awards damages of an amount greater than £500,000; or

(b) the court awards damages of £5£00,000 or less but would have awarded damages greater than £500,000 if it had not made a finding of contributory negligence; or

(c) the parties agree damages of £500,000 or less and it is reasonable to expect that, but for any finding of contributory negligence, the court would have awarded damages greater than £500,000.

(3) In paragraph (2), a reference to a lump sum of damages includes a reference to periodical payments of equivalent value.

(4) If the court is satisfied that the circumstances set out in paragraph (2) apply it must—

(a) assess the percentage increase; or

(b) make an order for the percentage increase to be assessed.

Assessment of alternative percentage increase

45.19—(1) This rule applies where the percentage increase of fees is assessed under rule 45.18(4). **45.19**

(2) If the percentage increase is assessed as greater than 20% or less than 7.5%, the percentage increase to be allowed shall be that assessed by the court.

(3) If the percentage increase is assessed as no greater than 20% and no less than 7.5%

(a) the percentage increase to be allowed shall be 12.5%; and

(b) the costs of the application and assessment shall be paid by the applicant.

IV. FIXED PERCENTAGE INCREASE IN EMPLOYERS LIABILITY CLAIMS

Add new Section IV:

45.20

Scope and interpretation

45.20—(1) Subject to paragraph (2), this Section applies where—

(a) **the dispute is between an employee and his employer arising from a bodily injury sustained by the employee in the course of his employment; and**

(b) **the claimant has entered into a funding arrangement of a type specified in rule 43.2(1)(k)(i).**

(2) **This Section does not apply—**

(a) **twhere the dispute—**

(i) **relates to a disease;**

(ii) **relates to an injury sustained before 1st October 2004; or**

(iii) **arises from a road traffic accident (as defined in rule 45.7(4)(a)); or**

(b) **tto a claim—**

(i) **which has been allocated to the small claims track; or**

(ii) **not allocated to a track, but for which the small claims track is the normal track.**

(3) **For the purposes of this Section—**

(a) **"employee" has the meaning given to it by section 2(1) of the Employers' Liability (Compulsory Insurance) Act 1969; and**

(b) **a reference to "fees" is a reference to fees for work done under a conditional fee agreement or collective conditional fee agreement.**

Percentage increase of solicitors' and counsel's fees

45.21

45.21 In the cases to which this Section applies, subject to rule 45.22 the percentage increase which is to be allowed in relation to solicitors' and counsel's fees is to be determined in accordance with rules 45.16 and 45.17, subject to the modifications that—

(a) **the percentage increase which is to be allowed in relation to solicitors' fees under rule 45.16(b) is—**

(i) **27.5% if a membership organisation has undertaken to meet the claimant's liabilities for legal costs in accordance with section 30 of the Access to Justice Act 1999; and**

(ii) **25% in any other case; and**

(b) **the percentage increase which is to be allowed in relation to counsel's fees under rule 45.17(1)(b)(ii), (1)(c)(ii) or (1)(d) is 25%.**

("membership organisation" is defined in rule 43.2(1)(n)).

Alternative percentage increase

45.22

45.22—(1) In the cases to which this Section applies, rule 45.18(2)–(4) applies where—

(a) **the percentage increase of solicitors' fees to be allowed in accordance with rule 45.21 is 25% or 27.5%; or**

(b) **the percentage increase of counsel's fees to be allowed is 25%.**

(2) Where the percentage increase of fees is assessed by the court under rule 45.18(4) as applied by paragraph (1) above—

(a) **if the percentage increase is assessed as greater than 40% or less than 15%, the percentage increase to be allowed shall be that assessed by the court; and**

(b) **if the percentage increase is assessed as no greater than 40% and no less than 15%—**

(i) **the percentage increase to be allowed shall be 25% or 27.5%(as the case may be); and**

(ii) **the costs of the application and assessment shall be paid by the applicant.**

PRACTICE DIRECTION RELATING TO PART 45

FIXED COSTS

Section 24 Fixed Costs in Small Claims

45PD.1

24.1 Under Rule 27.14 the costs which can be awarded to a claimant in a small claims track case include the fixed costs payable under Part 45 attributable to issuing the claim.

24.2 Those fixed costs shall be the sum of

(a) the fixed commencement costs calculated in accordance with Table 1 of Rule 45.2 and;

(b) the appropriate court fee or fees paid by the claimant.

Section 25 Fixed Costs on the Issue of a Default Costs Certificate

45PD.2

25.1 Unless paragraph 24.2 applies or unless the court orders otherwise, the fixed costs to be included in a default costs certificate are £80 plus a sum equal to any appropriate court fee payable on the issue of the certificate.

25.2 The fixed costs included in a certificate must not exceed the maximum sum specified for costs and court fee in the notice of commencement.

Section 25A — Road Traffic Accidents: Fixed Recoverable Costs in Costs-Only Proceedings

Scope

45PD.3

25A.1 Section II of Part 45 ('the Section') provides for certain fixed costs to be recoverable between parties in respect of costs incurred in disputes which are settled prior to proceedings being issued. The Section applies to road traffic accident disputes as defined in rule 45.7(4)(a), where the accident which gave rise to the dispute occurred on or after 6th October 2003.

25A.2 The Section does not apply to diputes where the total agreed value of the damages is within the small claims limit or exceeds £10,000. Rule 26.8(2) sets out how the financial value of a claim is assessed for the purposes of allocation to track.

25A.3 Fixed recoverable costs are to be calculated by reference to the amount of agreed damages which are payable to the receiving party. In calculating the amount of these damages—

(a) account must be taken of both general and special damages and interest;

(b) any interim payments made must be included;

(c) where the parties have agreed an element of contributory negligence, the amount of damages attributed to that negligence must be deducted;

(d) any amount required by statute to be paid by the compensating party directly to a third party (such as sums paid by way of compensation recovery payments and National Health Service expenses) must not be included.

25A.4 The Section applies to cases which fall within the scope of the Uninsured Drivers Agreement dated 13 August 1999. The section does not apply to cases which fall within the scope of the Untraced Drivers Agreement dated 14 February 2003.

Additional costs for work in specified areas

45PD.5 **25A.6** The area referred to in rule 45.9(2) consists of

PART 47

PROCEDURE FOR DETAILED ASSESSMENT OF COSTS AND DEFAULT PROVISIONS

Privilege and the power to order disclosure

Before the penultimate paragraph add:

47.14.3 The court cannot order disclosure of "without prejudice" negotiations against the wishes of one of the parties to those negotiations. This may mean that in some cases the court, when it comes to the question of costs, cannot decide whether one side or the other was unreasonable in refusing mediation. The court does not have power to order any disclosure of the detail of the "without prejudice" negotiations for the purposes of deciding the question of costs: *Reed Executive Plc v. Reed Business Information Ltd* [2004] EWCA Civ 887. The rule in *Walker v. Wilshire* [1889] 23 QBD 335 remains good law.

The hourly rate

After the sixth paragraph add:

47.14.17 In deciding whether or not it is disproportionate to instruct distant solicitors, the court should take into account other factors such as the fact that the solicitors were usually instructed by the clients on the particular type of case (*e.g.* infringement of trade mark), that the solicitors had knowledge of the client's products and the skill and resources available to operate speedily (to obtain a search order) and that when the solicitors had been instructed the defendant's location and the extent of its counterfeit operation might not have been known: *Mattel Inc v. RSW Plc* [2004] EWHC 1610, (Ch), H.H.J. Hegarty Q.C.

PRACTICE DIRECTION—PILOT SCHEME FOR DETAILED ASSESSMENT BY THE SUPREME COURT COSTS OFFICE OF COSTS OF CIVIL PROCEEDINGS IN LONDON COUNTY COURTS

47BPD.1 *This Practice Direction supplements* CPR Part 47

Delete existing Practice Direction 47B and substitute:

1. This practice direction applies, instead of paragraph 31.1 of the CPR Costs Practice Direction, to requests for a detailed assessment hearing which are filed between 6th July 2004 and 5th July 2005, pursuant to a judgment or order for the payment of costs by one party to another in civil proceedings in any of the following County Courts:

Barnet, Bow, Brentford, Central London, Clerkenwell, Croydon, Edmonton, Ilford, Lambeth, Mayors and City of London, Romford, Shoreditch, Wandsworth, West London, Willesden and Woolwich.

2. Where this practice direction applies, unless the court orders otherwise—

(1) the receiving party must file any request for a detailed assessment hearing in the Supreme Court Costs Office, Cliffords Inn, Fetter Lane, London EC4A 1DQ, DX 44454 Strand; and

(2) the Supreme Court Costs Office is the appropriate office for the purpose of CPR 47.4(1), and therefore all applications and requests in the detailed assessment proceedings must be made to that Office.

PART 48

COSTS—SPECIAL CASES

Comment

After the penultimate paragraph add:

48.2.1 The Court of Appeal held that a lawyer who had had a costs order made against him for personally intervening in an action against the first defendant could not be criticised for assisting the defendant financially in instructing solicitors of high standing and for assisting him in attempting to discharge his costs liabilities, particularly since a freezing order limited access to the defendant's own funds. There was no logical basis for finding that the lawyer's actions, which had the desired consequence of ensuring that the defendants' case did not go by default, so transformed the nature of the lawyer's involvement as to justify a costs order against him. There was no suggestion that the lawyer was personally interested in the outcome of the litigation: *Gulf Azov Shipping v. Idisi* [2004] EWCA Civ 292.

Improper, unreasonable or negligent

In the last paragraph delete the sentence "Where a solicitors firm missed a time limit..." and substitute:

48.7.4 Unless an applicant for a wasted costs order can establish that the legal representative acted in a way that was not only "improper, unreasonable or negligent" but was also in some way in breach of any duty to the court, the court cannot make a wasted costs order. Where a legal representative had been found to have acted negligently, the act had occurred at a time when there were no legal proceedings on foot and therefore there could be no question of that negligence representing any sort of breach of any duty to the court: *Charles v. Gillian Radford & Co* [2003] EWHC 3180, (Ch) Neuberger J.

GENERAL PRINCIPLES AND CASE LAW RELATING TO COSTS AND THEIR ASSESSMENT

1. Costs in Specific Courts and Other Tribunals

Employment appeal tribunal

Before the last paragraph add:

48.12.7 In deciding whether or not to make an order for costs against a party who has acted unreasonably in conducting the proceedings, the crucial question is whether in all the circumstances of the case a claimant (*e.g.* who withdrew a claim), had conducted the proceedings unreasonably, not whether the withdrawal of the claim was in itself unreasonable. It would be wrong for Employment Tribunals to take the line that it was unreasonable conduct for claimants to withdraw claims, and unfortunate if claimants were deterred from withdrawing by the prospect of an order for costs which might well not have been made against them had they failed in their claim after a full hearing. Equally, tribunals should not follow a practice on costs which might encourage speculative claims by allowing claimants to start cases in the hope of receiving an offer to settle failing which they could drop the case without any risk of a costs sanction: *McPherson v. BNP Paribas* [2004] EWCA Civ 569; [2004] 3 All ER 266, CA.

2. Costs relating to specific statutes

Coroner's Act 1988

Add at end:

48.13.2 The established practice of the court is to make no order for costs against an inferior court or tribunal which does not appear before it, except where there has been a flagrant incidence of improper behaviour or when the inferior court or tribunal unreasonably declined or neglected to sign a consent order disposing of the proceedings. The courts will treat an inferior court or tribunal which resists an application actively by way of argument, so as to make itself an active party to the litigation, as if it were such a party, so that in the normal course of events costs would follow the event. If, on the other hand, the inferior court or tribunal appeared in the proceedings in order to assist the court neutrally on questions of jurisdiction, procedure, specialist case law and the like the court would treat it as a neutral party and would not make an order for costs in its favour or against it whatever the outcome of the application. That approach might need to be modified so that a successful applicant who had to finance his own litigation might be fairly compensated out of a source of public funds and not be put to irrecoverable expense in asserting his rights, after a coroner (or other inferior tribunal) had gone wrong in law and where there was no other very obvious candidate available to pay his costs. An inferior tribunal which simply puts in a witness statement will not be at risk of an adverse costs order: *R (Davies) v. HM Deputy Coroner for Birmingham (No.2)* [2004] EWCA Civ 207 (Touche above not followed).

4. Costs relating to particular types of parties and miscellaneous

Bankruptcy

Add at end:

48.15.1 A costs certificate referring to the joint costs of three defendants represents a sufficiently detailed debt for the purpose of a statutory demand. The submission that three separate costs certificates should have been issued was rejected. The final costs certificate which had been issued referred to all three defendants jointly in respect of the total amount. Payment to one joint creditor would discharge the entire debt. A creditor was entitled to serve a statutory demand requiring payment of the whole sum of money to him: *Mahmood v. Penrose* [2004] EWHC 1500, (Ch), Mann J.

Liquidation

After the first paragraph add:

48.15.5 In the normal course of events any costs orders made against liquidators in relation to civil proceedings undertaken by them have priority over the general expenses of the liquidation (see *London Metallurgical Co, Re* [1895] 1 Ch 758): *Digital Equipment Ltd v. Bower* [2003] EWHC 2895 (Ch) Laddie J.

Patents

Add at end:

48.15.6 In patent proceedings concerning alleged infringement and invalidity which succeeded in part, the court make a percentage order. When such an order was made all costs were notionally allocated to the issues of infringement or invalidity, the successful party was assumed to recover all its reasonable costs of the action and the percentage deduction was made from that overall sum: *Apotex Europe Ltd v. SmithKline Beecham Plc* [2004] EWHC 964, (Ch) Pumfrey J.

PART 51

TRANSITIONAL ARRANGEMENTS AND PILOT SCHEMES

Stay of existing proceedings after one year

After the fifth paragraph add:

51.1.4 In *Flaxman–Binns v. Lincolnshire CC* [2004] EWCA Civ 424, CA, a circuit judge dismissed a student's (C) application under para. 19(2) for the automatic stay to be lifted on his negligence claim against a local education authority (D), first brought when C was a child. In allowing C's appeal the Court of Appeal said (1) no criticism should attach to C for taking no step to prevent the operation of the automatic stay as (a) at that stage he was a litigant in person and (b) until Autumn 2000 decisions of the House of Lords relevant to C's claim were pending, (2) on the evidence (including additional evidence), the judge was wrong to assume that during the period of further delay, for which C's solicitor accepted full responsibility, no efforts were made by or on behalf of C to chase the solicitor, (3) D had not sought to advance a positive case by appropriate evidence of significant prejudice to the conduct of the defence caused to them by the additional delay.

Commencement dates for statutory instruments amending CPR

Add at end:

51.1.5 Civil Procedure (Amendment) Rules 2004 (S.I. 2004 No. 1306) — June 1 and June 30, 2004

Civil Procedure (Amendment No. 2) Rules 2004 (S.I. 2004 No. 2072) — September 1 and October 1, 2004

Add at end:

51.1.7 The Civil Procedure (Amendment No. 5) Rules 2003 (S.I. 2003 No. 3361), which came into effect on February 1, March 1, April 1 and May 1, 2004, contain no transitional provisions.

The Civil Procedure (Amendment) Rules 2004 (S.I. 2004 No. 1306) made changes to CPR Pt. 56 (Landlord and Tenant Claims, Etc.) as a result of the coming into effect of amendments made to the Landlord and Tenant Act 1954 by the Regulatory Reform (Business Tenancies) (England and Wales) Order 2003. In particular, r.15 amended r.56.2 and r.16 substituted r. 56.3. These amendments came into effect on June 1, 2004. Rule 20(1) of these Rules contains transitional provisions and states:

> "In the circumstances where article 29(1) or (4) of the Regulatory Reform (Business Tenancies) (England and Wales) Order 2003 applies—
>
> (a) the amendments to Part 56 made by rules 15 and 16 of these Rules shall not apply; and
>
> (b) Part 56 shall continue to apply on and after 1st June, 2004, as if those amendments had not been made."

Further, the Civil Procedure (Amendment) Rules 2004 also amended the CPR by inserting Pt. 65 (Proceedings Relating to Anti–Social Behaviour and Harassment) and, as a consequence, revoking Sched. 2 CCR Ord. 49, r.6B. These amendments came into effect on June 30, 2004. Rule 20(2) of these Rules contains transitional provisions and states:

> "Where an application for an injunction under Chapter III or Part V of the Housing Act 1996 has been issued before 30th June 2004:
>
> (a) Section I of Part 65 shall not apply in relation to that application; and
>
> (b) CCR Order 49, rule 6B shall continue to apply on and after 30th June as if it had not been revoked."

Furthermore, it should be noted CPR Pt. 45 Section III (Fixed Percentage Increase in Road Traffic Claims), added by the Civil Procedure (Amendment) Rules 2004, with effect from June 1, 2004, does not apply where the accident occurred before October 6, 2003 (r.45.15(4)(c)).

The Civil Procedure (Amendment No. 2) Rules 2004 (S.I. 2004 No. 2072), which came into effect on September 1 and October 1, 2004, contain no transitional provisions. But it should be noted that CPR Pt. 45 Section IV (Fixed Percentage Increase in Employers Liability Claims), added to the CPR by these Rules with effect from October 1, 2004, does not apply where the dispute relates to an injury sustained before that date (r.45.20(2)(a)).

PART 52

APPEALS

Appeal court's powers

Add new sub-paragraphs (5) and (6):

52.10 **52.10—(5) If the appeal court—**

(a) **refuses an application for permission to appeal;**

(b) **strikes out an appellant's notice; or**

(c) **dismisses an appeal,**

and it considers that the application, the appellant's notice or the appeal is totally without merit, the provisions of paragraph (6) must be complied with.

(6) **Where paragraph (5) applies—**

(a) **the court's order must record the fact that it considers the application, the appellant's notice or the appeal to be totally without merit; and**

(b) **the court must at the same time consider whether it is appropriate to make a civil restraint order.**

52PD.1

PRACTICE DIRECTION—APPEALS

This Practice Direction supplements CPR Part 52

Contents of this Practice Direction

For existing Practice Direction 52 substitute:

1.1 This Practice Direction is divided into four sections:

- Section I – General provisions about appeals
- Section II – General provisions about statutory appeals and appeals by way of case stated
- Section III – Provisions about specific appeals
- Section IV – Provisions about reopening appeals

Section I

GENERAL PROVISIONS ABOUT APPEALS

52PD.2 **2.1** This practice direction applies to all appeals to which Part 52 applies except where specific provision is made for appeals to the Court of Appeal.

2.2 For the purpose only of appeals to the Court of Appeal from cases in family proceedings this Practice Direction will apply with such modifications as may be required.

ROUTES OF APPEAL

52PD.2A **2A.1** Subject to paragraph 2A.2, the following table sets out to which court or judge an appeal is to be made (subject to obtaining any necessary permission):

Decision of:	Appeal made to:
District judge of a county court	Circuit judge
Master or district judge of the High Court	High Court judge
Circuit judge	High Court judge
High Court judge	Court of Appeal

2A.2 Where the decision to be appealed is a final decision—

(1) in a Part 7 claim allocated to the multi–track; or

(2) made in specialist proceedings (under the Companies Acts 1985 or 1989 or to which Sections I, II or III of Part 57 or any of Parts 58 to 63 apply),

the appeal is to be made to the Court of Appeal (subject to obtaining any necessary permission).

2A.3 A "final decision" is a decision of a court that would finally determine (subject to any possible appeal or detailed assessment of costs) the entire proceedings whichever way the court decided the issues before it.

2A.4 A decision of a court is to be treated as a final decision for routes of appeal purposes where it:

(1) is made at the conclusion of part of a hearing or trial which has been split into parts; and

(2) would, if it had been made at the conclusion of that hearing or trial, have been a final decision.

2A.5 An order made:

(1) on a summary or detailed assessment of costs; or

(2) on an application to enforce a final decision,

(Section 16(1) of the Supreme Court Act 1981 (as amended); section 77(1) of the County Courts Act 1984 (as amended); and the Access to Justice Act 1999 (Destination of Appeals) Order 2000 set out the provisions governing routes of appeal)

2A.6(1) Where the decision to be appealed is a final decision in a Part 8 claim treated as allocated to the multi–track under rule 8.9(c), the court to which the permission application is made should, if permission is given, and unless the appeal would lie to the Court of Appeal in any event, consider whether to order the appeal to be transferred to the Court of Appeal under rule 52.14.

(2) An appeal against a final decision on a point of law in a case which did not involve any substantial dispute of fact would normally be a suitable appeal to be so transferred.

(See also paragraph 10.1)

GROUNDS FOR APPEAL

52PD.3

3.1 Rule 52.11(3)(a) and (b) sets out the circumstances in which the appeal court will allow an appeal.

3.2 The grounds of appeal should—

(1) set out clearly the reasons why rule 52.11(3)(a) or (b) is said to apply; and

(2) sspecify, in respect of each ground, whether the ground raises an appeal on a point of law or is an appeal against a finding of fact.

PERMISSION TO APPEAL

52PD.4 **4.1** Rule 52.3 sets out the circumstances when permission to appeal is required.

4.2 The permission of—

(1) the Court of Appeal; or

(2) where the lower court's rules allow, the lower court,

is required for all appeals to the Court of Appeal except as provided for by statute or rule 52.3.

(The requirement of permission to appeal may be imposed by a practice direction—see rule 52.3(b).)

4.3 Where the lower court is not required to give permission to appeal, it may give an indication of its opinion as to whether permission should be given.

Rule 52.1(3)(c) defines "lower court".)

Appeals from case management decisions

52PD.5 **4.4** Case management decisions include decisions made under rule 3.1(2) and decisions about:

(1) disclosure

(2) filing of witness statements or experts reports

(3) directions about the timetable of the claim

(4) adding a party to a claim

(5) security for costs.

4.5 Where the application is for permission to appeal from a case management decision, the court dealing with the application may take into account whether:

(1) the issue is of insufficient significance to justify the costs of an appeal;

(2) the procedural consequences of an appeal (*e.g.* loss of trial date) outweigh the significance of the case management decision;

(3) it would be more convenient to determine the issue at or after trial.

Court to which permission to appeal application should be made

52PD.6 **4.6** An application for permission should be made orally at the hearing at which the decision to be appealed against is made.

4.7 Where:

(a) no application for permission to appeal is made at the hearing; or

(b) the lower court refuses permission to appeal,

an application for permission to appeal may be made to the appeal court in accordance with rules 52.3(2) and (3).

4.8 There is no appeal from a decision of the appeal court to allow or refuse permission to appeal to that court (although where the appeal court, without a hearing, refuses permission to appeal, the person seeking permission may request that decision to be reconsidered at a hearing). See section 54(4) of the Access to Justice Act and rule 52.3(2), (3), (4) and (5).

Second appeals

4.9 An application for permission to appeal from a decision of the High Court or a county court which was itself made on appeal must be made to the Court of Appeal. **52PD.7**

4.10 If permission to appeal is granted the appeal will be heard by the Court of Appeal.

Consideration of permission without a hearing

4.11 Applications for permission to appeal may be considered by the appeal court without a hearing. **52PD.8**

4.12 If permission is granted without a hearing the parties will be notified of that decision and the procedure in paragraphs 6.1 to 6.6 will then apply.

4.13 If permission is refused without a hearing the parties will be notified of that decision with the reasons for it. The decision is subject to the appellant's right to have it reconsidered at an oral hearing. This may be before the same judge.

4.14 A request for the decision to be reconsidered at an oral hearing must be filed at the appeal court within 7 days after service of the notice that permission has been refused. A copy of the request must be served by the appellant on the respondent at the same time.

Permission hearing

4.14A(1) This paragraph applies where an appellant, who is represented, makes a request for a decision to be reconsidered at an oral hearing. **52PD.9**

(2) The appellant's advocate must, at least 4 days before the hearing, in a brief written statement—

(a) inform the court and the respondent of the points which he proposes to raise at the hearing;

(b) set out his reasons why permission should be granted notwithstanding the reasons given for the refusal of permission; and

(c) confirm, where applicable, that the requirements of paragraph 4.17 have been complied with (appellant in receipt of services funded by the Legal Services Commission).

4.15 Notice of a permission hearing will be given to the respondent but he is not required to attend unless the court requests him to do so.

4.16 If the court requests the respondent's attendance at the permission hearing, the appellant must supply the respondent with a copy of the appeal bundle (see paragraph 5.6A) within 7 days of being notified of the request, or such other period as the court may direct. The costs of providing that bundle shall be borne by the appellant initially, but will form part of the costs of the permission application.

Appellants in receipt of services funded by the Legal Services Commission applying for permission to appeal

4.17 Where the appellant is in receipt of services funded by the Legal **52PD.10**

Services Commission (or legally aided) and permission to appeal has been refused by the appeal court without a hearing, the appellant must send a copy of the reasons the appeal court gave for refusing permission to the relevant office of the Legal Services Commission as soon as it has been received from the court. The court will require confirmation that this has been done if a hearing is requested to re–consider the question of permission.

Limited permission

52PD.11 **4.18** Where a court under rule 52.3(7) gives permission to appeal on some issues only, it will—

(1) refuse permission on any remaining issues; or

(2) reserve the question of permission to appeal on any remaining issues to the court hearing the appeal.

4.19 If the court reserves the question of permission under paragraph 4.18(2), the appellant must, within 14 days after service of the court's order, inform the appeal court and the respondent in writing whether he intends to pursue the reserved issues. If the appellant does intend to pursue the reserved issues, the parties must include in any time estimate for the appeal hearing, their time estimate for the reserved issues.

4.20 If the appeal court refuses permission to appeal on the remaining issues without a hearing and the applicant wishes to have that decision reconsidered at an oral hearing, the time limit in rule 52.3(5) shall apply. Any application for an extension of this time limit should be made promptly. The court hearing the appeal on the issues for which permission has been granted will not normally grant, at the appeal hearing, an application to extend the time limit in rule 52.3(5) for the remaining issues.

4.21 If the appeal court refuses permission to appeal on remaining issues at or after an oral hearing, the application for permission to appeal on those issues cannot be renewed at the appeal hearing. See section 54(4) of the Access to Justice Act 1999.

Respondent's costs of permission applications

52PD.12 **4.22** In most cases, applications for permission to appeal will be determined without the court requesting—

(1) submissions from, or

(2) if there is an oral hearing, attendance by the respondent.

4.23 Where the court does not request submissions from or attendance by the respondent, costs will not normally be allowed to a respondent who volunteers submissions or attendance.

4.24 Where the court does request—

(1) submissions from; or

(2) attendance by the respondent,

the court will normally allow the respondent his costs if permission is refused.

APPELLANT'S NOTICE

52PD.13 **5.1** An appellant's notice must be filed and served in all cases. Where an application for permission to appeal is made to the appeal court it must be applied for in the appellant's notice.

Human Rights

52PD.14

5.1A(1) This paragraph applies where the appellant seeks—
(a) to rely on any issue under the Human Rights Act 1998; or
(b) a remedy available under that Act,
for the first time in an appeal.
(2) The appellant must include in his appeal notice the information required by paragraph 15.1 of the practice direction supplementing Part 16.
(3) Paragraph 15.2 of the practice direction supplementing Part 16 applies as if references to a statement of case were to the appeal notice.

5.1B CPR rule 19.4A and the practice direction supplementing it shall apply as if references to the case management conference were to the application for permission to appeal.

(The practice direction to Part 19 provides for notice to be given and parties joined in certain circumstances to which this paragraph applies)

Extension of time for filing appellant's notice

52PD.15

5.2 If an appellant requires an extension of time for filing his notice the application must be made in the appellant's notice. The notice should state the reason for the delay and the steps taken prior to the application being made.

5.3 Where the appellant's notice includes an application for an extension of time and permission to appeal has been given or is not required the respondent has the right to be heard on that application. He must be served with a copy of the appeal bundle (see paragraph 5.6A). However, a respondent who unreasonably opposes an extension of time runs the risk of being ordered to pay the appellant's costs of that application.

5.4 If an extension of time is given following such an application the procedure at paragraphs 6.1 to 6.6 applies.

Applications

52PD.16

5.5 Notice of an application to be made to the appeal court for a remedy incidental to the appeal (*e.g.* an interim remedy under rule 25.1 or an order for security for costs) may be included in the appeal notice or in a Part 23 application notice.

(Rule 25.15 deals with security for costs of an appeal)

(Paragraph 11 of this practice direction contains other provisions relating to applications)

Documents

52PD.17

5.6(1) This paragraph applies to every case except where the appeal—
(a) relates to a claim allocated to the small claims track; and
(b) is being heard in a county court or the High Court.
(Paragraph 5.8 applies where this paragraph does not apply)
(2) The appellant must file the following documents together with an appeal bundle (see paragraph 5.6A) with his appellant's notice—

(a) two additional copies of the appellant's notice for the appeal court; and
(b) one copy of the appellant's notice for each of the respondents;
(c) one copy of his skeleton argument for each copy of the appellant's notice that is filed (see paragraph 5.9);
(d) a sealed copy of the order being appealed;
(e) a copy of any order giving or refusing permission to appeal, together with a copy of the judge's reasons for allowing or refusing permission to appeal;
(f) any witness statements or affidavits in support of any application included in the appellant's notice.

5.6A(1) An appellant must include in his appeal bundle the following documents:
(a) a sealed copy of the appellant's notice;
(b) a sealed copy of the order being appealed;
(c) a copy of any order giving or refusing permission to appeal, together with a copy of the judge's reasons for allowing or refusing permission to appeal;
(d) any affidavit or witness statement filed in support of any application included in the appellant's notice;
(e) a copy of his skeleton argument;
(f) a transcript or note of judgment (see paragraph 5.12), and in cases where permission to appeal was given by the lower court or is not required those parts of any transcript of evidence which are directly relevant to any question at issue on the appeal;
(g) the claim form and statements of case (where relevant to the subject of the appeal);
(h) any application notice (or case management documentation) relevant to the subject of the appeal;
(i) in cases where the decision appealed was itself made on appeal (eg from district judge to circuit judge), the first order, the reasons given and the appellant's notice used to appeal from that order;
(j) in the case of judicial review or a statutory appeal, the original decision which was the subject of the application to the lower court;
(k) in cases where the appeal is from a Tribunal, a copy of the Tribunal's reasons for the decision, a copy of the decision reviewed by the Tribunal and the reasons for the original decision and any document filed with the Tribunal setting out the grounds of appeal from that decision;
(l) any other documents which the appellant reasonably considers necessary to enable the appeal court to reach its decision on the hearing of the application or appeal; and
(m) such other documents as the court may direct.

(2) All documents that are extraneous to the issues to be considered on the application or the appeal must be excluded. The appeal bundle may include affidavits, witness statements, summaries, experts' reports and exhibits but only where these are directly relevant to the subject matter of the appeal.

(3) Where the appellant is represented, the appeal bundle must contain a certificate signed by his solicitor, counsel or other representative to the effect that he has read and understood paragraph (2) above and that the composition of the appeal bundle complies with it.

5.7 Where it is not possible to file all the above documents, the appellant must indicate which documents have not yet been filed and the reasons why they are not currently available. The appellant must then provide a reasonable estimate of when the missing document or documents can be filed and file them as soon as reasonably practicable.

Small Claims

52PD.18

5.8(1) This paragraph applies where—
- (a) the appeal relates to a claim allocated to the small claims track; and
- (b) the appeal is being heard in a county court or the High Court.

(2) The appellant must file the following documents with his appellant's notice—
- (a) a sealed copy of the order being appealed; and
- (b) any order giving or refusing permission to appeal, together with a copy of the reasons for that decision.

(3) The appellant may, if relevant to the issues to be determined on the appeal, file any other document listed in paragraph 5.6 or 5.6A in addition to the documents referred to in sub–paragraph (2).

(4) The appellant need not file a record of the reasons for judgment of the lower court with his appellant's notice unless sub–paragraph (5) applies.

(5) The court may order a suitable record of the reasons for judgment of the lower court (see paragraph 5.12) to be filed—
- (a) to enable it to decide if permission should be granted; or
- (b) if permission is granted to enable it to decide the appeal.

Skeleton arguments

52PD.19

5.9(1) The appellant's notice must, subject to (2) and (3) below, be accompanied by a skeleton argument. Alternatively the skeleton argument may be included in the appellant's notice. Where the skeleton argument is so included it will not form part of the notice for the purposes of rule 52.8.

(2) Where it is impracticable for the appellant's skeleton argument to accompany the appellant's notice it must be lodged and served on all respondents within 14 days of filing the notice.

(3) An appellant who is not represented need not lodge a skeleton argument but is encouraged to do so since this will be helpful to the court.

Content of skeleton arguments

52PD.20

5.10(1) A skeleton argument must contain a numbered list of the points which the party wishes to make. These should both define and confine the areas of controversy. Each point should be stated as concisely as the nature of the case allows.

(2) A numbered point must be followed by a reference to any document on which the party wishes to rely.

(3) A skeleton argument must state, in respect of each authority cited—

(a) the proposition of law that the authority demonstrates; and

(b) the parts of the authority (identified by page or paragraph references) that support the proposition.

(4) If more than one authority is cited in support of a given proposition, the skeleton argument must briefly state the reason for taking that course.

(5) The statement referred to in sub–paragraph (4) should not materially add to the length of the skeleton argument but should be sufficient to demonstrate, in the context of the argument—

(a) the relevance of the authority or authorities to that argument; and

(b) that the citation is necessary for a proper presentation of that argument.

(6) The cost of preparing a skeleton argument which—

(a) does not comply with the requirements set out in this paragraph; or

(b) was not filed within the time limits provided by this Practice Direction (or any further time granted by the court),

will not be allowed on assessment except to the extent that the court otherwise directs.

5.11 The appellant should consider what other information the appeal court will need. This may include a list of persons who feature in the case or glossaries of technical terms. A chronology of relevant events will be necessary in most appeals.

Suitable record of the judgment

52PD.21 **5.12** Where the judgment to be appealed has been officially recorded by the court, an approved transcript of that record should accompany the appellant's notice. Photocopies will not be accepted for this purpose. However, where there is no officially recorded judgment, the following documents will be acceptable:

Note of judgment

52PD.23 (2) When judgment was not officially recorded or made in writing a note of the judgment (agreed between the appellant's and respondent's advocates) should be submitted for approval to the judge whose decision is being appealed. If the parties cannot agree on a single note of the judgment, both versions should be provided to that judge with an explanatory letter. For the purpose of an application for permission to appeal the note need not be approved by the respondent or the lower court judge.

Advocates' notes of judgments where the appellant is unrepresented

52PD.24 (3) When the appellant was unrepresented in the lower court it is the duty of any advocate for the respondent to make his/her note of judgment promptly available, free of charge to the appellant where there is no officially recorded judgment or if the court so directs. Where the appellant was represented in the lower court it is the duty of his/her own former advocate to make his/her note available in these circumstances. The appellant should submit the note of judgment to the appeal court.

Reasons for judgment in tribunal cases

(4) A sealed copy of the Tribunal's reasons for the decision. **52PD.25**

5.13 An appellant may not be able to obtain an official transcript or other suitable record of the lower court's decision within the time within which the appellant's notice must be filed. In such cases the appellant's notice must still be completed to the best of the appellant's ability on the basis of the documentation available. However it may be amended subsequently with the permission of the appeal court.

Advocates' notes of judgments

5.14 Advocates' brief (or, where appropriate, refresher) fee includes: **52PD.26**

(1) remuneration for taking a note of the judgment of the court;
(2) having the note transcribed accurately;
(3) attempting to agree the note with the other side if represented;
(4) submitting the note to the judge for approval where appropriate;
(5) revising it if so requested by the judge,
(6) providing any copies required for the appeal court, instructing solicitors and lay client; and
(7) providing a copy of his note to an unrepresented appellant.

Transcripts or notes of evidence

5.15 When the evidence is relevant to the appeal an official transcript of the relevant evidence must be obtained. Transcripts or notes are generally not needed for the purpose of determining an application for permission to appeal. **52PD.27**

Notes of evidence

5.16 If evidence relevant to the appeal was not officially recorded, a typed version of the judge's notes of evidence must be obtained. **52PD.28**

Transcripts at public expense

5.17 Where the lower court or the appeal court is satisfied that an unrepresented appellant is in such poor financial circumstances that the cost of a transcript would be an excessive burden the court may certify that the cost of obtaining one official transcript should be borne at public expense. **52PD.29**

5.18 In the case of a request for an official transcript of evidence or proceedings to be paid for at public expense, the court must also be satisfied that there are reasonable grounds for appeal. Whenever possible a request for a transcript at public expense should be made to the lower court when asking for permission to appeal.

Filing and service of appellant's notice

5.19 Rule 52.4 sets out the procedure and time limits for filing and serving an appellant's notice. The appellant must file the appellant's no- **52PD.30**

tice at the appeal court within such period as may be directed by the lower court which should not normally exceed 28 days or, where the lower court directs no such period, within 14 days of the date of the decision that the appellant wishes to appeal.

(Rule 52.15 sets out the time limit for filing an application for permission to appeal against the refusal of the High Court to grant permission to apply for judicial review)

5.20 Where the lower court judge announces his decision and reserves the reasons for his judgment or order until a later date, he should, in the exercise of powers under rule 52.4(2)(a), fix a period for filing the appellant's notice at the appeal court that takes this into account.

5.21(1) Except where the appeal court orders otherwise a sealed copy of the appellant's notice, including any skeleton arguments must be served on all respondents in accordance with the timetable prescribed by rule 52.4(3) except where this requirement is modified by paragraph 5.9(2) in which case the skeleton argument should be served as soon as it is filed.

(2) The appellant must, as soon as practicable, file a certificate of service of the documents referred to in paragraph (1).

5.22 Unless the court otherwise directs a respondent need not take any action when served with an appellant's notice until such time as notification is given to him that permission to appeal has been given.

5.23 The court may dispense with the requirement for service of the notice on a respondent. Any application notice seeking an order under rule 6.9 to dispense with service should set out the reasons relied on and be verified by a statement of truth.

5.24(1) Where the appellant is applying for permission to appeal in his appellant's notice, he must serve on the respondents his appellant's notice and skeleton argument (but not the appeal bundle), unless the appeal court directs otherwise.

(2) Where permission to appeal—

(a) has been given by the lower court; or

(b) is not required,

the appellant must serve the appeal bundle on the respondents with the appellant's notice.

Amendment of appeal notice

52PD.31 **5.25** An appeal notice may be amended with permission. Such an application to amend and any application in opposition will normally be dealt with at the hearing unless that course would cause unnecessary expense or delay in which case a request should be made for the application to amend to be heard in advance.

PROCEDURE AFTER PERMISSION IS OBTAINED

52PD.32 **6.1** This paragraph sets out the procedure where:

(1) permission to appeal is given by the appeal court; or

(2) the appellant's notice is filed in the appeal court and—

(a) permission was given by the lower court; or

(b) permission is not required.

6.2 If the appeal court gives permission to appeal, the appeal bundle must be served on each of the respondents within 7 days of receiving the order giving permission to appeal.

(Part 6 (service of documents) provides rules on service.)

6.3 The appeal court will send the parties—

(1) notification of—

(a) the date of the hearing or the period of time (the 'listing window') during which the appeal is likely to be heard; and

(b) in the Court of Appeal, the date by which the appeal will be heard (the 'hear by date');

(2) where permission is granted by the appeal court a copy of the order giving permission to appeal; and

(3) any other directions given by the court.

6.3A(1) Where the appeal court grants permission to appeal, the appellant must add the following documents to the appeal bundle—

(a) the respondent's notice and skeleton argument (if any);

(b) those parts of the transcripts of evidence which are directly relevant to any question at issue on the appeal;

(c) the order granting permission to appeal and, where permission to appeal was granted at an oral hearing, the transcript (or note) of any judgment which was given; and

(d) any document which the appellant and respondent have agreed to add to the appeal bundle in accordance with paragraph 7.11.

(2) Where permission to appeal has been refused on a particular issue, the appellant must remove from the appeal bundle all documents that are relevant only to that issue.

Appeal Questionnaire in the Court of Appeal

6.4 The Court of Appeal will send an Appeal Questionnaire to the appellant when it notifies him of the matters referred to in paragraph 6.3. **52PD.33**

6.5 The appellant must complete and file the Appeal Questionnaire within 14 days of the date of the letter of notification of the matters in paragraph 6.3. The Appeal Questionnaire must contain:

(1) if the appellant is legally represented, the advocate's time estimate for the hearing of the appeal;

(2) where a transcript of evidence is relevant to the appeal, confirmation as to what parts of a transcript of evidence have been ordered where this is not already in the bundle of documents;

(3) confirmation that copies of the appeal bundle are being prepared and will be held ready for the use of the Court of Appeal and an undertaking that they will be supplied to the court on request. For the purpose of these bundles photocopies of the transcripts will be accepted;

(4) confirmation that copies of the Appeal Questionnaire and the appeal bundle have been served on the respondents and the date of that service.

Time estimates

6.6 The time estimate included in an Appeal Questionnaire must be **52PD.34**

that of the advocate who will argue the appeal. It should exclude the time required by the court to give judgment. If the respondent disagrees with the time estimate, the respondent must inform the court within 7 days of receipt of the Appeal Questionnaire. In the absence of such notification the respondent will be deemed to have accepted the estimate proposed on behalf of the appellant.

RESPONDENT

52PD.35 **7.1** A respondent who wishes to ask the appeal court to vary the order of the lower court in any way must appeal and permission will be required on the same basis as for an appellant.

(Paragraph 3.2 applies to grounds of appeal by a respondent.)

7.2 A respondent who wishes only to request that the appeal court upholds the judgment or order of the lower court whether for the reasons given in the lower court or otherwise does not make an appeal and does not therefore require permission to appeal in accordance with rule 52.3(1).

(Paragraph 7.6 requires a respondent to file a skeleton argument where he wishes to address the appeal court)

7.3(1) A respondent who wishes to appeal or who wishes to ask the appeal court to uphold the order of the lower court for reasons different from or additional to those given by the lower court must file a respondent's notice.

(2) If the respondent does not file a respondent's notice, he will not be entitled, except with the permission of the court, to rely on any reason not relied on in the lower court.

7.3A Paragraphs 5.1A, 5.1B and 5.2 of this practice direction (Human Rights and extension for time for filing appellant's notice) also apply to a respondent and a respondent's notice.

Time limits

52PD.36 **7.4** The time limits for filing a respondent's notice are set out in rule 52.5(4) and (5).

7.5 Where an extension of time is required the extension must be requested in the respondent's notice and the reasons why the respondent failed to act within the specified time must be included.

7.6 Except where paragraph 7.7A applies, the respondent must file a skeleton argument for the court in all cases where he proposes to address arguments to the court. The respondent's skeleton argument may be included within a respondent's notice. Where a skeleton argument is included within a respondent's notice it will not form part of the notice for the purposes of rule 52.8.

7.7(1) A respondent who—

(a) files a respondent's notice; but

(b) does not include his skeleton argument within that notice,

must file and serve his skeleton argument within 14 days of filing the notice.

(2) A respondent who does not file a respondent's notice but who files a skeleton argument must file and serve that skeleton argument at least 7 days before the appeal hearing.

(Rule 52.5(4) sets out the period for filing and serving a respondent's notice)

7.7A(1) Where the appeal relates to a claim allocated to the small claims track and is being heard in a county court or the High Court, the respondent may file a skeleton argument but is not required to do so.

(2) A respondent who is not represented need not file a skeleton argument but is encouraged to do so in order to assist the court.

7.7B The respondent must—

(1) serve his skeleton argument on—

(a) the appellant; and

(b) any other respondent,

at the same time as he files it at the court; and

(2) file a certificate of service.

Content of skeleton arguments

52PD.37

7.8 A respondent's skeleton argument must conform to the directions at paragraphs 5.10 and 5.11 with any necessary modifications. It should, where appropriate, answer the arguments set out in the appellant's skeleton argument.

Applications within respondent's notices

52PD.38

7.9 A respondent may include an application within a respondent's notice in accordance with paragraph 5.5 above.

Filing respondent's notices and skeleton arguments

52PD.39

7.10(1) The respondent must file the following documents with his respondent's notice in every case:

(a) two additional copies of the respondent's notice for the appeal court; and

(b) one copy each for the appellant and any other respondents.

(2) The respondent may file a skeleton argument with his respondent's notice and—

(a) where he does so he must file two copies; and

(b) where he does not do so he must comply with paragraph 7.7.

7.11 If the respondent wishes to rely on any documents which he reasonably considers necessary to enable the appeal court to reach its decision on the appeal in addition to those filed by the appellant, he must make every effort to agree amendments to the appeal bundle with the appellant.

7.12(1) If the representatives for the parties are unable to reach agreement, the respondent may prepare a supplemental bundle.

(2) If the respondent prepares a supplemental bundle he must file it, together with the requisite number of copies for the appeal court, at the appeal court—

(a) with the respondent's notice; or

(b) if a respondent's notice is not filed, within 21 days after he is served with the appeal bundle.

7.13 The respondent must serve—

(1) the respondent's notice;

(2) his skeleton argument (if any); and
(3) the supplemental bundle (if any),

on—

(a) the appellant; and
(b) any other respondent,

at the same time as he files them at the court.

APPEALS TO THE HIGH COURT

Application

52PD.40 **8.1** This paragraph applies where an appeal lies to a High Court judge from the decision of a county court or a district judge of the High Court.

8.2 The following table sets out the following venues for each circuit—

(a) Appeal centres – court centres where appeals to which this paragraph applies may be filed, managed and heard. Paragraphs 8.6 to 8.8 provide for special arrangements in relation to the South Eastern Circuit.

(b) Hearing only centres – court centres where appeals to which this paragraph applies may be heard by order made at an appeal centre (see paragraph 8.10).

Circuit	Appeal Centres	Hearing Only Centres
Midland Circuit	Birmingham Nottingham	Lincoln Leicester Northampton Stafford
North Eastern Circuit	Leeds Newcastle Sheffield	Teesside
Northern Circuit	Manchester Liverpool Preston	Carlisle
Wales and Chester Circuit	Cardiff Swansea Chester	
Western Circuit	Bristol Exeter Winchester	Truro Plymouth
South Eastern Circuit	Royal Courts of Justice Lewes Luton Norwich Reading Chelmsford St Albans Maidstone Oxford	

8.3 Paragraphs 8.4 and 8.5 apply where the lower court is situated on a circuit other than the South Eastern Circuit.

8.4 The appellant's notice must be filed at an appeal centre on the circuit in which the lower court is situated. The appeal will be managed and heard at that appeal centre unless the appeal court orders otherwise.

8.5 A respondent's notice must be filed at the appeal centre where the appellant's notice was filed unless the appeal has been transferred to another appeal centre, in which case it must be filed at that appeal centre.

Venue for appeals and filing of notices on the South Eastern Circuit

52PD.41

8.6 Paragraphs 8.7 and 8.8 apply where the lower court is situated on the South Eastern Circuit.

8.7 The appellant's notice must be filed at an appeal centre on the South Eastern Circuit. The appeal will be managed and heard at the Royal Courts of Justice unless the appeal court orders otherwise. An order that an appeal is to be managed or heard at another appeal centre may not be made unless the consent of the Presiding Judge of the circuit in charge of civil matters has been obtained.

8.8 A respondent's notice must be filed at the Royal Courts of Justice unless the appeal has been transferred to another appeal centre, in which case it must be filed at that appeal centre.

General provisions

52PD.42

8.9 The appeal court may transfer an appeal to another appeal centre (whether or not on the same circuit). In deciding whether to do so the court will have regard to the criteria in rule 30.3 (criteria for a transfer order). The appeal court may do so either on application by a party or of its own initiative. Where an appeal is transferred under this paragraph, notice of transfer must be served on every person on whom the appellant's notice has been served. An appeal may not be transferred to an appeal centre on another circuit, either for management or hearing, unless the consent of the Presiding Judge of that circuit in charge of civil matters has been obtained.

8.10 Directions may be given for—

(a) an appeal to be heard at a hearing only centre; or

(b) an application in an appeal to be heard at any other venue,

instead of at the appeal centre managing the appeal.

8.11 Unless a direction has been made under 8.10, any application in the appeal must be made at the appeal centre where the appeal is being managed.

8.12 The appeal court may adopt all or any part of the procedure set out in paragraphs 6.4 to 6.6.

8.13 Where the lower court is a county court:

(1) appeals and applications for permission to appeal will be heard by a High Court Judge or by a person authorised under paragraphs (1), (2) or (4) of the Table in section 9(1) of the Supreme Court Act 1981 to act as a judge of the High Court; and

(2) other applications in the appeal may be heard and directions in the appeal may be given either by a High Court Judge or by any person authorised under section 9 of the Supreme Court Act 1981 to act as a judge of the High Court.

8.14 In the case of appeals from Masters or district judges of the High

Court, appeals, applications for permission and any other applications in the appeal may be heard and directions in the appeal may be given by a High Court Judge or by any person authorised under section 9 of the Supreme Court Act 1981 to act as a judge of the High Court.

Appeals to a judge of a county court from a district judge

52PD.43 **8A.1** The Designated Civil Judge in consultation with his Presiding Judges has responsibility for allocating appeals from decisions of district judges to circuit judges.

Re–hearings

52PD.44 **9.1** The hearing of an appeal will be a re–hearing (as opposed to a review of the decision of the lower court) if the appeal is from the decision of a minister, person or other body and the minister, person or other body—

(1) did not hold a hearing to come to that decision; or

(2) held a hearing to come to that decision, but the procedure adopted did not provide for the consideration of evidence.

Appeals transferred to the Court of Appeal

52PD.45 **10.1** Where an appeal is transferred to the Court of Appeal under rule 52.14 the Court of Appeal may give such additional directions as are considered appropriate.

Applications

52PD.46 **11.1** Where a party to an appeal makes an application whether in an appeal notice or by Part 23 application notice, the provisions of Part 23 will apply.

11.2 The applicant must file the following documents with the notice

(1) one additional copy of the application notice for the appeal court and one copy for each of the respondents;

(2) where applicable a sealed copy of the order which is the subject of the main appeal;

(3) a bundle of documents in support which should include:

(a) the Part 23 application notice; and

(b) any witness statements and affidavits filed in support of the application notice.

DISPOSING OF APPLICATIONS OR APPEALS BY CONSENT

Dismissal of applications or appeals by consent

52PD.47 **12.1** These paragraphs do not apply where any party to the proceedings is a child or patient.

12.2 Where an appellant does not wish to pursue an application or an appeal, he may request the appeal court for an order that his application or appeal be dismissed. Such a request must contain a statement that the appellant is not a child or patient. If such a request is granted it will usually be on the basis that the appellant pays the costs of the application or appeal.

12.3 If the appellant wishes to have the application or appeal dismissed without costs, his request must be accompanied by a consent signed by the respondent or his legal representative stating that the respondent is not a child or patient and consents to the dismissal of the application or appeal without costs.

12.4 Where a settlement has been reached disposing of the application or appeal, the parties may make a joint request to the court stating that none of them is a child or patient, and asking that the application or appeal be dismissed by consent. If the request is granted the application or appeal will be dismissed.

Allowing unopposed appeals or applications on paper

52PD.48 **13.1** The appeal court will not normally make an order allowing an appeal unless satisfied that the decision of the lower court was wrong, but the appeal court may set aside or vary the order of the lower court with consent and without determining the merits of the appeal, if it is satisfied that there are good and sufficient reasons for doing so. Where the appeal court is requested by all parties to allow an application or an appeal the court may consider the request on the papers. The request should state that none of the parties is a child or patient and set out the relevant history of the proceedings and the matters relied on as justifying the proposed order and be accompanied by a copy of the proposed order.

Procedure for structured settlements and consent orders involving a child or patient

52PD.49 **13.2** Settlements relating to appeals and applications where one of the parties is a child or a patient; and structured settlements which are agreed upon at the appeal stage require the court's approval.

Child

52PD.50 **13.3** In cases involving a child a copy of the proposed order signed by the parties' solicitors should be sent to the appeal court, together with an opinion from the advocate acting on behalf of the child.

Patient

52PD.51 **13.4** Where a party is a patient the same procedure will be adopted, but the documents filed should also include any relevant reports prepared for the Court of Protection and a document evidencing formal approval by that court where required.

Structured settlements

52PD.52 **13.5** Where a structured settlement has been negotiated in a case which is under appeal the documents filed should include those which would be required in the case of a structured settlement dealt with at first instance. Details can be found in the Practice Direction which supplements CPR Part 40.

SUMMARY ASSESSMENT OF COSTS

52PD.53 **14.1** Costs are likely to be assessed by way of summary assessment at the following hearings:

(1) contested directions hearings;

(2) applications for permission to appeal at which the respondent is present;

(3) dismissal list hearings in the Court of Appeal at which the respondent is present;

(4) appeals from case management decisions; and
(5) appeals listed for one day or less.

14.2 Parties attending any of the hearings referred to in paragraph 14.1 should be prepared to deal with the summary assessment.

OTHER SPECIAL PROVISIONS REGARDING THE COURT OF APPEAL

Filing of documents

52PD.54 **15.1**(1) The documents relevant to proceedings in the Court of Appeal, Civil Division must be filed in the Civil Appeals Office Registry, Room E307, Royal Courts of Justice, Strand, London, WC2A 2LL.

(2) The Civil Appeals Office will not serve documents and where service is required by the CPR or this practice direction it must be effected by the parties.

Core Bundles

52PD.55 **15.2** In cases where the appeal bundle comprises more than 500 pages, exclusive of transcripts, the appellant's solicitors must, after consultation with the respondent's solicitors, also prepare and file with the court, in addition to copies of the appeal bundle (as amended in accordance with paragraph 7.11) the requisite number of copies of a core bundle.

15.3(1) The core bundle must be filed within 28 days of receipt of the order giving permission to appeal or, where permission to appeal was granted by the lower court or is not required, within 28 days of the date of service of the appellant's notice on the respondent.

(2) The core bundle—

(a) must contain the documents which are central to the appeal; and

(b) must not exceed 150 pages.

Preparation of bundles

52PD.56 **15.4** The provisions of this paragraph apply to the preparation of appeal bundles, supplemental respondents' bundles where the parties are unable to agree amendments to the appeal bundle, and core bundles.

(1) **Rejection of bundles.** Where documents are copied unnecessarily or bundled incompletely, costs may be disallowed. Where the provisions of this Practice Direction as to the preparation or delivery of bundles are not followed the bundle may be rejected by the court or be made the subject of a special costs order.

(2) **Avoidance of duplication.** No more than one copy of any document should be included unless there is a good reason for doing otherwise (such as the use of a separate core bundle—see paragraph 15.2).

(3) **Pagination**

(a) Bundles must be paginated, each page being numbered individually and consecutively. The pagination used at trial must also be indicated. Letters and other documents should normally be included in chronological order. (An exception to consecutive page numbering arises in the case of core bundles where it may be preferable to retain the original numbering).

(b) Page numbers should be inserted in bold figures at the bottom of the page and in a form that can be clearly distinguished from any other pagination on the document.

(4) **Format and presentation**

(a) Where possible the documents should be in A4 format. Where a document has to be read across rather than down the page, it should be so placed in the bundle as to ensure that the text starts nearest the spine.

(b) Where any marking or writing in colour on a document is important, the document must be copied in colour or marked up correctly in colour.

(c) Documents which are not easily legible should be transcribed and the transcription marked and placed adjacent to the document transcribed.

(d) Documents in a foreign language should be translated and the translation marked and placed adjacent to the document translated. The translation should be agreed or, if it cannot be agreed, each party's proposed translation should be included.

(e) The size of any bundle should be tailored to its contents. A large lever arch file should not be used for just a few pages nor should files of whatever size be overloaded.

(f) Where it will assist the Court of Appeal, different sections of the file may be separated by cardboard or other tabbed dividers so long as these are clearly indexed. Where, for example, a document is awaited when the appeal bundle is filed, a single sheet of paper can be inserted after a divider, indicating the nature of the document awaited. For example, 'Transcript of evidence of Mr J Smith (to follow)'.

(5) **Binding**

(a) All documents, with the exception of transcripts, must be bound together. This may be in a lever arch file, ring binder or plastic folder. Plastic sleeves containing loose documents must not be used. Binders and files must be strong enough to withstand heavy use.

(b) Large documents such as plans should be placed in an easily accessible file. Large documents which will need to be opened up frequently should be inserted in a file larger than A4 size.

(6) **Indices and labels**

(a) An index must be included at the front of the bundle listing all the documents and providing the page references for each. In the case of documents such as letters, invoices or bank statements, they may be given a general description.

(b) Where the bundles consist of more than one file, an index to all the files should be included in the first file and an index included for each file. Indices should, if possible, be on a single sheet. The full name of the case should not be inserted on the index if this would waste space. Documents should be identified briefly but properly.

(7) **Identification**

(a) Every bundle must be clearly identified, on the spine and on the front cover, with the name of the case and the Court of

Appeal's reference. Where the bundle consists of more than one file, each file must be numbered on the spine, the front cover and the inside of the front cover.

(b) Outer labels should use large lettering eg ' Appeal Bundle A' or 'Core Bundle'. The full title of the appeal and solicitors' names and addresses should be omitted. A label should be used on the front as well as on the spine.

(8) **Staples etc.** All staples, heavy metal clips etc, must be removed.

(9) **Statements of case**

(a) Statements of case should be assembled in 'chapter' form – i.e claim followed by particulars of claim, followed by further information, irrespective of date.

(b) Redundant documents, eg particulars of claim overtaken by amendments, requests for further information recited in the answers given, should generally be excluded.

(10) **New Documents**

(a) Before a new document is introduced into bundles which have already been delivered to the court, steps should be taken to ensure that it carries an appropriate bundle/page number so that it can be added to the court documents. It should not be stapled and it should be prepared with punch holes for immediate inclusion in the binders in use.

(b) If it is expected that a large number of miscellaneous new documents will from time to time be introduced, there should be a special tabbed empty loose–leaf file for that purpose. An index should be produced for this file, updated as necessary.

(11) **Inter–solicitor correspondence.** Since inter–solicitor correspondence is unlikely to be required for the purposes of an appeal, only those letters which will need to be referred to should be copied.

(12) **Sanctions for non–compliance.** If the appellant fails to comply with the requirements as to the provision of bundles of documents, the application or appeal will be referred for consideration to be given as to why it should not be dismissed for failure to so comply.

Master in the Court of Appeal, Civil Division

52PD.57 **15.5** When the Head of the Civil Appeals Office acts in a judicial capacity pursuant to rule 52.16, he shall be known as Master. Other eligible officers may also be designated by the Master of the Rolls to exercise judicial authority under rule 52.16 and shall then be known as Deputy Masters.

Respondent to notify Civil Appeals Office whether he intends to file respondent's notice

52PD.58 **15.6** A respondent must, no later than 21 days after the date he is served with notification that—

(1) permission to appeal has been granted; or

(2) the application for permission to appeal and the appeal are to be heard together,

inform the Civil Appeals Office and the appellant in writing whether—

(a) he proposes to file a respondent's notice appealing the order or seeking to uphold the order for reasons different from, or additional to, those given by the lower court; or

(b) he proposes to rely on the reasons given by the lower court for its decision.

(Paragraph 15.11B requires all documents needed for an appeal hearing, including a respondent's skeleton argument, to be filed at least 7 days before the hearing)

Listing and hear-by dates

52PD.59

15.7 The management of the list will be dealt with by the listing officer under the direction of the Master.

15.8 The Civil Appeals List of the Court of Appeal is divided as follows:

- *The applications list*—applications for permission to appeal and other applications.
- *The appeals list*—appeals where permission to appeal has been given or where an appeal lies without permission being required where a hearing date is fixed in advance. (Appeals in this list which require special listing arrangements will be assigned to the special fixtures list)
- *The expedited list*—appeals or applications where the Court of Appeal has directed an expedited hearing. The current practice of the Court of Appeal is summarised in *Unilever plc v. Chefaro Proprietaries Ltd* (Practice Note) [1995]1 W.L.R. 243.
- *The stand-out list*—Appeals or applications which, for good reason, are not at present ready to proceed and have been stood out by judicial direction.
- *The second fixtures list*—[see paragraph 15.9A(1) below].
- *The second fixtures list*—if an appeal is designated as a 'second fixture' it means that a hearing date is arranged in advance on the express basis that the list is fully booked for the period in question and therefore the case will be heard only if a suitable gap occurs in the list.
- *The short-warned list*—appeals which the court considers may be prepared for the hearing by an advocate other than the one originally instructed with a half day's notice, or such other period as the court may direct.

Special provisions relating to the short-warned list

52PD.60

15.9(1) Where an appeal is assigned to the short-warned list, the Civil Appeals Office will notify the parties' solicitors in writing. The court may abridge the time for filing any outstanding bundles in an appeal assigned to this list.

(2) The solicitors for the parties must notify their advocate and their client as soon as the Civil Appeals Office notifies them that the appeal has been assigned to the short-warned list.

(3) The appellant may apply in writing for the appeal to be removed from the short-warned list within 14 days of notification of its assignment. The application will be decided by a Lord Justice, or the Master, and will only be granted for the most compelling reasons.

(4) The Civil Appeals Listing Officer may place an appeal from the short–warned list 'on call' from a given date and will inform the parties' advocates accordingly.

(5) An appeal which is 'on call' may be listed for hearing on half a day's notice or such longer period as the court may direct.

(6) Once an appeal is listed for hearing from the short warned list it becomes the immediate professional duty of the advocate instructed in the appeal, if he is unable to appear at the hearing, to take all practicable measures to ensure that his lay client is represented at the hearing by an advocate who is fully instructed and able to argue the appeal.

Special provisions relating to the special fixtures list

52PD.61 **15.9A**(1) The special fixtures list is a sub–division of the appeals list and is used to deal with appeals that may require special listing arrangements, such as the need to list a number of cases before the same constitution, in a particular order, during a particular period or at a given location.

(2) The Civil Appeals Office will notify the parties' representatives, or the parties if acting in person, of the particular arrangements that will apply. The notice—

(a) will give details of the specific period during which a case is scheduled to be heard; and

(b) may give directions in relation to the filing of any outstanding documents.

(3) The listing officer will notify the parties' representatives of the precise hearing date as soon as practicable. While every effort will be made to accommodate the availability of counsel, the requirements of the court will prevail.

Requests for directions

52PD.62 **15.10** To ensure that all requests for directions are centrally monitored and correctly allocated, all requests for directions or rulings (whether relating to listing or any other matters) should be made to the Civil Appeals Office. Those seeking directions or rulings must not approach the supervising Lord Justice either directly, or via his or her clerk.

Bundles of authorities

52PD.63 **15.11**(1) Once the parties have been notified of the date fixed for the hearing, the appellant's advocate must, after consultation with his opponent, file a bundle containing photocopies of the authorities upon which each side will rely at the hearing.

(2) The bundle of authorities should, in general—

(a) have the relevant passages of the authorities marked;

(b) not include authorities for propositions not in dispute; and

(c) not contain more than 10 authorities unless the scale of the appeal warrants more extensive citation.

(3) The bundle of authorities must be filed—

(a) at least 7 days before the hearing; or

(b) where the period of notice of the hearing is less than 7 days, immediately.

(4) If, through some oversight, a party intends, during the hearing, to refer to other authorities the parties may agree a second agreed bundle. The appellant's advocate must file this bundle at least 48 hours before the hearing commences.

(5) A bundle of authorities must bear a certification by the advocates responsible for arguing the case that the requirements of sub–paragraphs (3) to (5) of paragraph 5.10 have been complied with in respect of each authority included.

Supplementary skeleton arguments

15.11A(1) A supplementary skeleton argument on which the appellant wishes to rely must be filed at least 14 days before the hearing. **52PD.64**

(2) A supplementary skeleton argument on which the respondent wishes to rely must be filed at least 7 days before the hearing.

(3) All supplementary skeleton arguments must comply with the requirements set out in paragraph 5.10.

(4) At the hearing the court may refuse to hear argument from a party not contained in a skeleton argument filed within the relevant time limit set out in this paragraph.

Papers for the appeal hearing

15.11B(1) All the documents which are needed for the appeal hearing must be filed at least 7 days before the hearing. Where a document has not been filed 10 days before the hearing a reminder will be sent by the Civil Appeals Office. **52PD.65**

(2) Any party who fails to comply with the provisions of paragraph (1) may be required to attend before the Presiding Lord Justice to seek permission to proceed with, or to oppose, the appeal.

Disposal of bundles of documents

15.11C(1) Where the court has determined a case, the official transcriber will retain one set of papers. The Civil Appeals Office will destroy any remaining sets of papers not collected within 21 days of— **52PD.66**

(a) where one or more parties attend the hearing, the date of the court's decision;

(b) where there is no attendance, the date of the notification of court's decision.

(2) The parties should ensure that bundles of papers supplied to the court do not contain original documents (other than transcripts). The parties must ensure that they—

(a) bring any necessary original documents to the hearing; and

(b) retrieve any original documents handed up to the court before leaving the court.

(3) The court will retain application bundles where permission to appeal has been granted. Where permission is refused the arrangements in sub–paragraph (1) will apply.

(4) Where a single Lord Justice has refused permission to appeal on paper, application bundles will not be destroyed until after the time limit for seeking a hearing has expired.

Availability of Reserved judgments before hand down

52PD.67 **15.12** This section applies where the presiding Lord Justice is satisfied that the result of the appeal will attract no special degree of confidentiality or sensitivity.

15.13 A copy of the written judgment will be made available to the parties' legal advisers by 4 p.m. on the second working day before judgment is due to be pronounced or such other period as the court may direct. This can be shown, in confidence, to the parties but only for the purpose of obtaining instructions and on the strict understanding that the judgment, or its effect, is not to be disclosed to any other person. A working day is any day on which the Civil Appeals Office is open for business.

15.12 The appeal will be listed for judgment in the cause list and the judgment handed down at the appropriate time.

Attendance of advocates on the handing down of a reserved judgment

52PD.68 **15.15** Where any consequential orders are agreed, the parties' advocates need not attend on the handing down of a reserved judgment. Where an advocate does attend the court may, if it considers such attendance unnecessary, disallow the costs of the attendance. If the parties do not indicate that they intend to attend, the judgment may be handed down by a single member of the court.

Agreed orders following judgment

52PD.69 **15.16**(1) The parties must, in respect of any draft agreed orders—

(a) fax a copy to the clerk to the presiding Lord Justice; and

(b) file four copies in the Civil Appeals Office,

no later than 12 noon on the working day before the judgment is handed down.

15.17 A copy of a draft order must bear the Court of Appeal case reference, the date the judgment is to be handed down and the name of the presiding Lord Justice.

Corrections to the draft judgment

52PD.70 **15.18** Any proposed correction to the draft judgment should be sent to the clerk to the judge who prepared the draft with a copy to any other party.

Application for leave to appeal

52PD.71 **15.19** Where a party wishes to apply for leave to appeal to the House of Lords under section 1 of the Administration of Justice (Appeals) Act 1934 the court may deal with the application on the basis of written submissions.

15.20 A party must, in relation to his submission—

(a) fax a copy to the clerk to the presiding Lord Justice; and

(b) file four copies in the Civil Appeals Office,

no later than 12 noon on the working day before the judgment is handed down.

15.21 A copy of a submission must bear the Court of Appeal case reference, the date the judgment is to be handed down and the name of the presiding Lord Justice.

Section II

GENERAL PROVISIONS ABOUT STATUTORY APPEALS AND APPEALS BY WAY OF CASE STATED

16.1 This section of this practice direction contains general provisions about statutory appeals (paragraphs 17.1–17.6) and appeals by way of case stated (paragraphs 18.1–18.20). **52PD.72**

16.2 Where any of the provisions in this section provide for documents to be filed at the appeal court, these documents are in addition to any documents required under Part 52 or section 1 of this practice direction.

STATUTORY APPEALS

17.1 This part of this section— **52PD.73**

(1) applies where under any enactment an appeal (other than by way of case stated) lies to the court from a Minister of State, government department, tribunal or other person ("statutory appeals"); and

(2) is subject to any provision about a specific category of appeal in any enactment or Section III of this practice direction.

Part 52

17.2 Part 52 applies to statutory appeals with the following amendments: **52PD.74**

Filing of appellant's notice

17.3 The appellant must file the appellant's notice at the appeal court within 28 days after the date of the decision of the lower court he wishes to appeal. **52PD.75**

17.4 Where a statement of the reasons for a decision is given later than the notice of that decision, the period for filing the appellant's notice is calculated from the date on which the statement is received by the appellant.

Service of appellant's notice

17.5 In addition to the respondents to the appeal, the appellant must serve the appellant's notice in accordance with rule 52.4(3) on the chairman of the tribunal, Minister of State, government department or other person from whose decision the appeal is brought. **52PD.76**

Right of Minister etc. to be heard on the appeal

17.6 Where the appeal is from an order or decision of a Minister of State or government department, the Minister or department, as the case may be, is entitled to attend the hearing and to make representations to the court. **52PD.77**

APPEALS BY WAY OF CASE STATED

18.1 This part of this section— **52PD.78**

(1) applies where under any enactment—

(a) an appeal lies to the court by way of case stated; or

(b) a question of law may be referred to the court by way of case stated; and

(2) is subject to any provision about to a specific category of appeal in any enactment or Section III of this practice direction.

Part 52

52PD.79 **18.2** Part 52 applies to appeals by way of case stated subject to the following amendments.

Case stated by Crown Court or Magistrates' Court

Application to state a case

52PD.80 **18.3** The procedure for applying to the Crown Court or a Magistrates' Court to have a case stated for the opinion of the High Court is set out in the Crown Court Rules 1982 and the Magistrates' Courts Rules 1981 respectively.

Filing of appellant's notice

52PD.81 **18.4** The appellant must file the appellant's notice at the appeal court within 10 days after he receives the stated case.

Documents to be lodged

52PD.82 **18.5** The appellant must lodge the following documents with his appellant's notice:

(1) the stated case;

(2) a copy of the judgment, order or decision in respect of which the case has been stated; and

(3) where the judgment, order or decision in respect of which the case has been stated was itself given or made on appeal, a copy of the judgment, order or decision appealed from.

Service of appellant's notice

52PD.83 **18.6** The appellant must serve the appellant's notice and accompanying documents on all respondents within 4 days after they are filed or lodged at the appeal court.

Case stated by Minister, government department, tribunal or other person

Application to state a case

52PD.84 **18.7** The procedure for applying to a Minister, government department, tribunal or other person ("Minister or tribunal etc.") to have a case stated for the opinion of the court may be set out in—

(1) the enactment which provides for the right of appeal; or

(2) any rules of procedure relating to the Minister or tribunal etc.

Signing of stated case by Minister or tribunal etc.

52PD.85 **18.8** A case stated by a tribunal must be signed by the chairman or president of the tribunal. A case stated by any other person must be signed by that person or by a person authorised to do so.

Service of stated case by Minister or tribunal etc.

52PD.86 **18.9** The Minister or tribunal etc. must serve the stated case on—

(1) the party who requests the case to be stated; or
(2) the party as a result of whose application to the court, the case was stated.

18.10 Where an enactment provides that a Minister or tribunal etc. may state a case or refer a question of law to the court by way of case stated without a request being made, the Minister or tribunal etc. must—
(1) serve the stated case on those parties that the Minister or tribunal etc. considers appropriate; and
(2) give notice to every other party to the proceedings that the stated case has been served on the party named and on the date specified in the notice.

Filing and service of appellant's notice

18.11 The party on whom the stated case was served must file the appellant's notice and the stated case at the appeal court and serve copies of the notice and stated case on— **52PD.87**
(1) the Minister or tribunal etc. who stated the case; and
(2) every party to the proceedings to which the stated case relates,
within 14 days after the stated case was served on him.

18.12 Where paragraph 18.10 applies the Minister or tribunal etc. must—
(1) file an appellant's notice and the stated case at the appeal court; and
(2) serve copies of those documents on the persons served under paragraph 18.10
within 14 days after stating the case.

18.13 Where—
(1) a stated case has been served by the Minister or Tribunal etc. in accordance with paragraph 18.9; and
(2) the party on whom the stated case was served does not file an appellant's notice in accordance with paragraph 18.11,
any other party may file an appellant's notice with the stated case at the appeal court and serve a copy of the notice and the case on the persons listed in paragraph 18.11 within the period of time set out in paragraph 18.14.

18.14 The period of time referred to in paragraph 18.13 is 14 days from the last day on which the party on whom the stated case was served may file an appellant's notice in accordance with paragraph 18.11.

Amendment of stated case

18.15 The court may amend the stated case or order it to be returned to the Minister or tribunal etc. for amendment and may draw inferences of fact from the facts stated in the case. **52PD.88**

Right of Minister etc. to be heard on the appeal

18.16 Where the case is stated by a Minister or government department, that Minister or department, as the case may be, is entitled to appear on the appeal and to make representations to the court. **52PD.89**

Application for order to state a case

18.17 An application to the court for an order requiring a minister or **52PD.90**

tribunal etc. to state a case for the decision of the court, or to refer a question of law to the court by way of case stated must be made to the court which would be the appeal court if the case were stated.

18.18 An application to the court for an order directing a Minister or tribunal etc. to—

(1) state a case for determination by the court; or

(2) refer a question of law to the court by way of case stated,

must be made in accordance with CPR Part 23

18.19 The application notice must contain—

(1) the grounds of the application;

(2) the question of law on which it is sought to have the case stated; and

(3) any reasons given by the minister or tribunal etc. for his or its refusal to state a case.

18.20 The application notice must be filed at the appeal court and served on—

(1) the minister, department, secretary of the tribunal or other person as the case may be; and

(2) every party to the proceedings to which the application relates,

within 14 days after the appellant receives notice of the refusal of his request to state a case.

Section III

PROVISIONS ABOUT SPECIFIC APPEALS

52PD.91 **20.1** This section of this Practice Direction provides special provisions about the appeals to which the following table refers. This Section is not exhaustive and does not create, amend or remove any right of appeal.

20.2 Part 52 applies to all appeals to which this section applies subject to any special provisions set out in this section.

20.3 Where any of the provisions in this section provide for documents to be filed at the appeal court, these documents are in addition to any documents required under Part 52 or sections I or II of this practice direction.

52PD.92

Appeals to the Court of Appeal	Paragraph
Articles 81 and 82 of the EC Treaty and Chapters I and II of Part I of the Competition Act 1998	21.10A
Competition Appeal Tribunal	21.10
Contempt of Court	21.4
Decree nisi of divorce	21.1
Immigration Appeal Tribunal	21.7
Lands Tribunal	21.9
Nullity of marriage	21.1
Patents Court on appeal from Comptroller	21.3
Revocation of patent	21.2
Social Security Commissioners	21.5
Special Commissioner (where the appeal is direct to the Court of Appeal)	21.8

Value Added Tax and Duties Tribunals (where the appeal is direct to the Court of Appeal)	21.6

52PD.93

Appeals to the High Court	Paragraph
Agricultural Land Tribunal	22.7
Architects Act 1997, s.22	22.3
Charities Act 1993	23.8A
Chiropractors Act 1994, s.31	22.3
Clergy Pensions Measure 1961, s.38(3)	23.2
Commons Registration Act 1965	23.9
Consumer Credit Act 1974	22.4
Dentists Act 1984, s.20 or s.44	22.3
Extradition Act 2003	22.6A
Friendly Societies Act 1974	23.7
Friendly Societies Act 1992	23.7
Industrial and Provident Societies Act 1965	23.2, 23.7
Industrial Assurance Act 1923	23.2, 23.7
Industrial Assurance Act 1923, s.17	23.6
Inheritance Tax Act 1984, s.222	23.3
Inheritance Tax Act 1984, s.225	23.5
Inheritance Tax Act 1984 , ss.249(3) and 251	23.4
Land Registration Act 1925	23.2
Land Registration Act 2002	23.2, 23.8B
Law of Property Act 1922, para. 16 of Sched. 15	23.2
Medical Act 1983, s.40	22.3
Medicines Act 1968, ss.82(3) and 83(2)	22.3
Mental Health Review Tribunal	22.8
Merchant Shipping Act 1995	22.2
Nurses, Midwives and Health Visitors Act 1997, s.12	22.3
Opticians Act 1989, s.23	22.3
Osteopaths Act 1993, s.31	22.3
Pensions Act 1995, s.97	23.2
Pension Schemes Act 1993, ss.151 and 173	23.2
Pensions Appeal Tribunal Act 1943	22.5
Pharmacy Act 1954	22.3
Social Security Administration Act 1992	22.6
Stamp Duty Reserve Tax Regulations 1986, reg. 10	23.5
Taxes Management Act 1970, ss.53 and 100C(4)	23.4
Taxes Management Act 1970, s.56A	23.5
Value Added Tax and Duties Tribunal	23.8
Water Resources Act 1991, s.205(4)	23.2

52PD.94

Appeals to the County Court	Paragraph
Local Government (Miscellaneous Provisions) Act 1976	24.1
Housing Act 1996, ss.204 and 204A	24.2
Immigration and Asylum Act 1999, Pt II	24.3

APPEALS TO THE COURT OF APPEAL

Appeal against decree nisi of divorce or nullity of marriage

52PD.95

21.1(1) The appellant must file the appellant's notice at the Court of Appeal within 28 days after the date on which the decree was pronounced.

(2) The appellant must file the following documents with the appellant's notice—

(a) the decree; and

(b) a certificate of service of the appellant's notice.

(3) The appellant's notice must be served on the appropriate district judge (see sub-paragraph (6)) in addition to the persons to be served under rule 52.4(3) and in accordance with that rule.

(4) The lower court may not alter the time limits for filing of the appeal notices.

(5) Where an appellant intends to apply to the Court of Appeal for an extension of time for serving or filing the appellant's notice he must give notice of that intention to the appropriate district judge (see sub-paragraph 6) before the application is made.

(6) In this paragraph "the appropriate district judge" means, where the lower court is—

(a) a county court, the district judge of that court;

(b) a district registry, the district judge of that registry;

(c) the Principal Registry of the Family Division, the senior district judge of that division.

Appeal against order for revocation of patent

52PD.96

21.2(1) This paragraph applies where an appeal lies to the Court of Appeal from an order for the revocation of a patent.

(2) The appellant must serve the appellant's notice on the Comptroller-General of Patents, Designs and Trade Marks (the "Comptroller") in addition to the persons to be served under rule 52.4(3) and in accordance with that rule.

(3) Where, before the appeal hearing, the respondent decides not to oppose the appeal or not to attend the appeal hearing, he must immediately serve notice of that decision on—

(a) the Comptroller; and

(b) the appellant

(4) Where the respondent serves a notice in accordance with paragraph (3), he must also serve copies of the following documents on the Comptroller with that notice—

(a) the petition;

(b) any statements of claim;

(c) any written evidence filed in the claim.

(5) Within 14 days after receiving the notice in accordance with paragraph (3), the Comptroller must serve on the appellant a notice stating whether or not he intends to attend the appeal hearing.

(6) The Comptroller may attend the appeal hearing and oppose the appeal—
(a) in any case where he has given notice under paragraph (5) of his intention to attend; and
(b) in any other case (including, in particular, a case where the respondent withdraws his opposition to the appeal during the hearing) if the Court of Appeal so directs or permits.

Appeal from Patents Court on appeal from Comptroller

21.3 Where the appeal is from a decision of the Patents Court which was itself made on an appeal from a decision of the Comptroller–General of Patents, Designs and Trade Marks, the appellant must serve the appellant's notice on the Comptroller in addition to the persons to be served under rule 52.4(3) and in accordance with that rule. **52PD.97**

Appeals in cases of contempt of court

21.4 In an appeal under section 13 of the Administration of Justice Act 1960 (appeals in cases of contempt of court), the appellant must serve the appellant's notice on the court from whose order or decision the appeal is brought in addition to the persons to be served under rule 52.4(3) and in accordance with that rule. **52PD.98**

Appeals from Social Security or Child Support Commissioners

21.5(1) This paragraph applies to appeals under section 25 of the Child Support Act 1991, section 15 of the Social Security Act 1998 and paragraph 9 of Schedule 7 to the Child Support, Pensions and Social Security Act 2000 (appeals from the decision of a Commissioner on a question of law). **52PD.99**

(2) The appellant must file the appellant's notice within 6 weeks after the date of the Commissioner's decision on permission to appeal to the Court of Appeal was given in writing to the appellant.

(3) The appellant must serve the appellant's notice on—
(a) the Secretary of State; and
(b) any person appointed by him to proceed with a claim

in addition to the persons to be served under rule 52.4(3) and in accordance with that rule.

Appeals from Value Added Tax and Duties Tribunals

21.6(1) An application to the Court of Appeal for permission to appeal from a value added tax and duties tribunal direct to that court must be made within 28 days after the date on which the tribunal certifies that its decision involves a point of law relating wholly or mainly to the construction of— **52PD.100**
(a) an enactment or of a statutory instrument; or
(b) any of the Community Treaties or any Community Instrument,

which has been fully argued before and fully considered by it.

(2) The application must be made by the parties jointly filing at the Court of Appeal an appellant's notice that—
(a) contains a statement of the grounds for the application; and

(b) is accompanied by a copy of the decision to be appealed, endorsed with the certificate of the tribunal.

(3) The court will notify the appellant of its decision and—

(a) where permission to appeal to the Court of Appeal is given, the appellant must serve the appellant's notice on the chairman of the tribunal in addition to the persons to be served under rule 52.4(3) within 14 days after that notification.

(b) where permission to appeal to the Court of Appeal is refused, the period for appealing to the High Court is to be calculated from the date of the notification of that refusal.

Appeals from Immigration Appeals Tribunal

52PD.101 **21.7**(1) This paragraph applies to appeals under section 103(1) of the Nationality, Immigration and Asylum Act 2002 (appeal on a point of law from a determination of the Immigration Appeal Tribunal).

(2) The appellant's notice must be filed at the Court of Appeal within 14 days after the appellant is served in accordance with the Immigration and Asylum Appeals (Procedure) Rules 2003 with written notice of the Tribunal's decision to grant or refuse permission to appeal.

(3) The appellant must serve the appellant's notice in accordance with rule 52.4(3) on—

(a) the persons to be served under that rule; and

(b) the President of the Tribunal.

Appeal from Special Commissioners

52PD.102 **21.8**(1) An application to the Court of Appeal for permission to appeal from the Special Commissioners direct to that court under section 56A of the Taxes Management Act 1970 must be made within 28 days after the date on which the Special Commissioners certify that their decision involves a point of law relating wholly or mainly to the construction of an enactment which has been fully argued before and fully considered before them.

(2) The application must be made by the parties jointly filing at the Court of Appeal an appellant's notice that—

(a) contains a statement of the grounds for the application; and

(b) is accompanied by a copy of the decision to be appealed, endorsed with the certificate of the tribunal.

(3) The court will notify the parties of its decision and—

(a) where permission to appeal to the Court of Appeal is given, the appellant must serve the appellant's notice on the Clerk to the Special Commissioners in addition to the persons to be served under rule 52.4(3) within 14 days after that notification.

(b) where permission to appeal to the Court of Appeal is refused, the period for appealing to the High Court is to be calculated from the date of the notification of that refusal.

Appeal from Lands Tribunal

52PD.103 **21.9** The appellant must file the appellant's notice at the Court of Appeal within 28 days after the date of the decision of the tribunal.

Appeal from Competition Appeal Tribunal

21.10(1) Where the appellant applies for permission to appeal at the hearing at which the decision is delivered by the tribunal and— **52PD.104**

(a) permission is given; or

(b) permission is refused and the appellant wishes to make an application to the Court of Appeal for permission to appeal,

the appellant's notice must be filed at the Court of Appeal within 14 days after the date of that hearing.

(2) Where the appellant applies in writing to the Registrar of the tribunal for permission to appeal and—

(a) permission is given; or

(b) permission is refused and the appellant wishes to make an application to the Court of Appeal for permission to appeal,

the appellant's notice must be filed at the Court of Appeal within 14 days after the date of receipt of the tribunal's decision on permission.

(3) Where the appellant does not make an application to the tribunal for permission to appeal, but wishes to make an application to the Court of Appeal for permission, the appellant's notice must be filed at the Court of Appeal within 14 days after the end of the period within which he may make a written application to the Registrar of the tribunal.

Appeals relating to the application of Articles 81 and 82 of the EC Treaty and Chapters I and II of Part I of the Competition Act 1998

21.10A(1) This paragraph applies to any appeal to the Court of Appeal relating to the application of— **52PD.105**

(a) Article 81 or Article 82 of the Treaty establishing the European Community; or

(b) Chapter I or Chapter II of Part I of the Competition Act 1998.

(2) In this paragraph—

(a) 'the Act' means the Competition Act 1998;

(b) 'the Commission' means the European Commission;

(c) 'the Competition Regulation' means Council Regulation (EC) No. 1/2003 of 16 December 2002 on the implementation of the rules on competition laid down in Articles 81 and 82 of the Treaty;

(d) 'national competition authority' means—

(i) the Office of Fair Trading; and

(i) any other person or body designated pursuant to Article 35 of the Competition Regulation as a national competition authority of the United Kingdom;

(e) 'the Treaty' means the Treaty establishing the European Community.

(3) Any party whose appeal notice raises an issue relating to the application of Article 81 or 82 of the Treaty, or Chapter I or II of Part I of the Act, must—

(a) state that fact in his appeal notice; and

(b) serve a copy of the appeal notice on the Office of Fair Trading at the same time as it is served on the other party to the appeal (addressed to the Director of Competition Policy Co–

ordination, Office of Fair Trading, Fleetbank House, 2–6 Salisbury Square, London EC4Y 8JX).

(4) Attention is drawn to the provisions of article 15.3 of the Competition Regulation, which entitles competition authorities and the Commission to submit written observations to national courts on issues relating to the application of Article 81 or 82 and, with the permission of the court in question, to submit oral observations to the court.

(5) A national competition authority may also make written observations to the Court of Appeal, or apply for permission to make oral observations, on issues relating to the application of Chapter I or II.

(6) If a national competition authority or the Commission intends to make written observations to the Court of Appeal, it must give notice of its intention to do so by letter to the Civil Appeals Office at the earliest opportunity.

(7) An application by a national competition authority or the Commission for permission to make oral representations at the hearing of an appeal must be made by letter to the Civil Appeals Office at the earliest opportunity, identifying the appeal and indicating why the applicant wishes to make oral representations.

(8) If a national competition authority or the Commission files a notice under sub-paragraph (6) or an application under sub-paragraph (7), it must at the same time serve a copy of the notice or application on every party to the appeal.

(9) Any request by a national competition authority or the Commission for the court to send it any documents relating to an appeal should be made at the same time as filing a notice under sub-paragraph (6) or an application under sub-paragraph (7).

(10) When the Court of Appeal receives a notice under sub-paragraph (6) it may give case management directions to the national competition authority or the Commission, including directions about the date by which any written observations are to be filed.

(11) The Court of Appeal will serve on every party to the appeal a copy of any directions given or order made—

(a) on an application under sub-paragraph (7); or

(b) under sub-paragraph (10).

(12) Every party to an appeal which raises an issue relating to the application of Article 81 or 82, and any national competition authority which has been served with a copy of a party's appeal notice, is under a duty to notify the Court of Appeal at any stage of the appeal if they are aware that—

(a) the Commission has adopted, or is contemplating adopting, a decision in relation to proceedings which it has initiated; and

(b) the decision referred to in (a) above has or would have legal effects in relation to the particular agreement, decision or practice in issue before the court.

(13) Where the Court of Appeal is aware that the Commission is contemplating adopting a decision as mentioned in sub-

paragraph (12)(a), it shall consider whether to stay the appeal pending the Commission's decision.

(14) Where any judgment is given which decides on the application of Article 81 or 82, the court shall direct that a copy of the transcript of the judgment shall be sent to the Commission.

Judgments may be sent to the Commission electronically to comp–amicus@.eu.int or by post to the European Commission—DG Competition, B–1049, Brussels.

Appeal from Proscribed Organisations Appeal Commission

21.11(1) The appellant's notice must be filed at the Court of Appeal within 14 days after the date when the Proscribed Organisations Appeal Commission— **52PD.106**

(a) granted; or
(b) where section 6(2)(b) of the Terrorism Act 2000 applies, refused permission to appeal.

APPEALS TO THE HIGH COURT—QUEEN'S BENCH DIVISION

22.1 The following appeals are to be heard in the Queen's Bench Division. **52PD.107**

Statutory Appeals

Appeals under the Merchant Shipping Act 1995

22.2(1) This paragraph applies to appeals under the Merchant Shipping Act 1995 and for this purpose a re–hearing and an application under section 61 of the Merchant Shipping Act 1995 are treated as appeals. **52PD.108**

(2) The appellant must file any report to the Secretary of State containing the decision from which the appeal is brought with the appellant's notice.

(3) Where a re–hearing by the High Court is ordered under sections 64 or 269 of the Merchant Shipping Act 1995, the Secretary of State must give reasonable notice to the parties whom he considers to be affected by the re–hearing.

Appeals against decisions affecting the registration of architects and health care professionals

22.3(1) This paragraph applies to an appeal to the High Court under— **52PD.109**

(a) section 22 of the Architects Act 1997;
(b) section 82(3) and 83(2) of the Medicines Act 1968;
(c) section 12 of the Nurses, Midwives and Health Visitors Act 1997;
(cc) article 38 of the Nursing and Midwifery Order 2001;
(d) section 10 of the Pharmacy Act 1954;
(e) section 40 of the Medical Act 1983;
(f) section 29 or section 44 of the Dentists Act 1984;
(g) sections 23 of the Opticians Act 1989;
(h) section 31 of the Osteopaths Act 1993; and
(i) section 31 of the Chiropractors Act 1994.

(2) Every appeal to which this paragraph applies must be supported by written evidence and, if the court so orders, oral evidence and will be by way of re–hearing.

(3) The appellant must file the appellant's notice within 28 days after the decision that the appellant wishes to appeal.

(4) In the case of an appeal under an enactment specified in column 1 of the following table, the persons to be made respondents are the persons specified in relation to that enactment in column 2 of the table and the person to be served with the appellant's notice is the person so specified in column 3.

1 Enactment	2 Respondents	3 Person to be served
Architects Act 1997, s.22	The Architects' Registration Council of the United Kingdom	The registrar of the Council
Medicines Act 1968, s.82(3) and s.83(2)	The Pharmaceutical Society of Great Britain	The registrar of the Society
Nurses, Midwives and Health Visitors Act 1997, s.12; Nursing and Midwifery Order 2001, art.38	The Nursing and Midwifery Council	The Registrar of the Council
Pharmacy Act 1954, s.10	The Royal Pharmaceutical Society of Great Britain	The registrar of the Society
Medical Act 1983, s.40	The General Medical Council	The Registrar of the Council
Dentists Act 1984, s.29 or s.44	The General Dental Council	The Registrar of the Council
Opticians Act 1989, s.23	The General Optical Council	The Registrar of the Council
Osteopaths Act 1993, s.31	The General Osteopathic Council	The Registrar of the Council
Chiropractors Act 1994, s.31	The General Chiropractic Council	The Registrar of the Council

Consumer Credit Act 1974: appeal from Secretary of State

52PD.110 **22.4**(1) A person dissatisfied in point of law with a decision of the Secretary of State on an appeal under section 41 of the Consumer Credit Act 1974 from a determination of the Director General of Fair Trading who had a right to appeal to the Secretary of State, whether or not he exercised that right, may appeal to the High Court.

(2) The appellant must serve the appellant's notice on—

(a) the Secretary of State;

(b) the original applicant, if any, where the appeal is by a licensee under a group licence against compulsory variation, suspension or revocation of that licence; and

(c) any other person as directed by the court.

(3) The appeal court may remit the matter to the Secretary of State to the extent necessary to enable him to provide the court with such further information as the court may direct.

(4) If the appeal court allows the appeal, it shall not set aside or vary the decision but shall remit the matter to the Secretary of State with the opinion of the court for hearing and determination by him

The Pensions Appeal Tribunal Act 1943

52PD.111

22.5(1) In this paragraph "the judge" means the judge nominated by the Lord Chancellor under section 6(2) of the Pensions Appeal Tribunals Act 1943 ("the Act").

(2) An application to the judge for permission to appeal against a decision of a Pensions Appeal Tribunal—

(a) may not be made unless an application was made to the tribunal and was refused; and

(b) must be made within 28 days after the date of the tribunal's refusal.

(3) The appellant's notice seeking permission to appeal from the judge must contain—

(a) the point of law as respects which the appellant alleges that the tribunal's decision was wrong; and

(b) the date of the tribunal's decision refusing permission to appeal.

(4) The court officer shall request the chairman of the tribunal to give the judge a written statement of the reasons for the tribunal's decision to refuse permission to appeal, and within 7 days after receiving the request, the chairman must give the judge such a statement.

(5) Where permission to appeal was given by—

(a) the tribunal, the appellant must file and serve the appellant's notice;

(b) the judge, the appellant must serve the appellant's notice,

within 28 days after permission to appeal was given.

(6) Within 28 days after service of the notice of appeal on him, the chairman of the tribunal must—

(a) state a case setting out the facts on which the decision appealed against was based;

(b) file the case stated at the court; and

(c) serve a copy of the case stated on the appellant and the respondent.

(7) A copy of the judge's order on the appeal must be sent by the court officer to the appellant, the respondent and the chairman of the tribunal.

The Social Security Administration Act 1992

52PD.112

22.6(1) Any person who by virtue of section 18 or 58(8) of the Social Security Administration Act 1992 ("the Act") is entitled and wishes to appeal against a decision of the Secretary of State on a question of law must, within the prescribed period, or within such further time as the Secretary of State may allow, serve on the Secretary of State a notice requiring him to state a case setting out—

(a) his decision; and

(b) the facts on which his decision was based.

(2) Unless paragraph (3) applies the prescribed period is 28 days after receipt of the notice of the decision.

(3) Where, within 28 days after receipt of notice of the decision, a request is made to the Secretary of State in accordance with regulations made under the Act to furnish a statement of the grounds of the decision, the prescribed period is 28 days after receipt of that statement.

(4) Where under section 18 or section 58(8) of the Act, the Secretary of State refers a question of law to the court, he must state that question together with the relevant facts in a case.

(5) The appellant's notice and the case stated must be filed at the appeal court and a copy of the notice and the case stated served on—

(a) the Secretary of State; and

(b) every person as between whom and the Secretary of State the question has arisen,

within 28 days after the case stated was served on the party at whose request, or as a result of whose application to the court, the case was stated.

(6) Unless the appeal court otherwise orders, the appeal or reference shall not be heard sooner than 28 days after service of the appellant's notice.

(7) The appeal court may order the case stated by the Secretary of State to be returned to the Secretary of State for him to hear further evidence.

Appeals under the Extradition Act 2003

52PD.113 22.6A(1) In this paragraph, 'the Act' means the Extradition Act 2003.

(2) Appeals to the High Court under the Act must be brought in the Administrative Court of the Queen's Bench Division.

(3) Where an appeal is brought under section 26 or 28 of the Act—

(a) the appellant's notice must be filed and served before the expiry of 7 days, starting with the day on which the order is made;

(b) the appellant must endorse the appellant's notice with the date of the person's arrest;

(c) the High Court must begin to hear the substantive appeal within 40 days of the person's arrest; and

(d) the appellant must serve a copy of the appellant's notice on the Crown Prosecution Service, if they are not a party to the appeal, in addition to the persons to be served under rule 52.4(3) and in accordance with that rule.

(4) The High Court may extend the period of 40 days under paragraph (3)(c) if it believes it to be in the interests of justice to do so.

(5) Where an appeal is brought under section 103 of the Act, the appellant's notice must be filed and served before the expiry of 14 days, starting with the day on which the Secretary of State informs the person under section 100(1) or (4) of the Act of the order he has made in respect of the person.

(6) Where an appeal is brought under section 105 of the Act, the appellant's notice must be filed and served before the expiry of 14 days, starting with the day on which the order for discharge is made.

(7) Where an appeal is brought under section 108 of the Act the appellant's notice must be filed and served before the expiry of 14 days, starting with the day on which the Secretary of State informs the person that he has ordered his extradition.

(8) Where an appeal is brought under section 110 of the Act the appellant's notice must be filed and served before the expiry of 14 days, starting with the day on which the Secretary of State informs the person acting on behalf of a category 2 territory, as defined in section 69 of the Act, of the order for discharge.

(Section 69 of the Act provides that a category 2 territory is that designated for the purposes of Part 2 of the Act).

(9) Subject to paragraph (10), where an appeal is brought under section 103, 105, 108 or 110 of the Act, the High Court must begin to hear the substantive appeal within 76 days of the appellant's notice being filed.

(10) Where an appeal is brought under section 103 of the Act before the Secretary of State has decided whether the person is to be extradited—

(a) the period of 76 days does not start until the day on which the Secretary of State informs the person of his decision; and

(b) the Secretary of State must, as soon as practicable after he informs the person of his decision, inform the High Court—

(i) of his decision; and

(ii) of the date on which he informs the person of his decision.

(11) The High Court may extend the period of 76 days if it believes it to be in the interests of justice to do so.

(12) Where an appeal is brought under section 103, 105, 108 or 110 of the Act, the appellant must serve a copy of the appellant's notice on—

(a) the Crown Prosecution Service; and

(b) the Home Office,

if they are not a party to the appeal, in addition to the persons to be served under rule 52.4(3) and in accordance with that rule.

Appeals by way of case stated

Reference of question of law by Agriculture Land Tribunal

52PD.114

22.7(1) A question of law referred to the High Court by an Agricultural Land Tribunal under section 6 of the Agriculture (Miscellaneous Provisions) Act 1954 shall be referred by way of case stated by the Tribunal.

(2) Where the proceedings before the tribunal arose on an ap-

plication under section 11 of the Agricultural Holdings Act 1986, an—

(a) application notice for an order under section 6 that the tribunal refers a question of law to the court; and

(b) appellant's notice by which an appellant seeks the court's determination on a question of law,

must be served on the authority having power to enforce the statutory requirement specified in the notice in addition to every other party to those proceedings and on the secretary of the tribunal.

(3) Where, in accordance with paragraph (2), a notice is served on the authority mentioned in that paragraph, that authority may attend the appeal hearing and make representations to the court.

Case stated by Mental Health Review Tribunal

52PD.115 **22.8**(1) In this paragraph "the Act" means the Mental Health Act 1983 and "party to proceedings" means—

(a) the person who initiated the proceedings; and

(b) any person to whom, in accordance with rules made under section 78 of the Act, the tribunal sent notice of the application or reference or a request instead notice of reference.

(2) A party to proceedings shall not be entitled to apply to the High Court for an order under section 78(8) of the Act directing the tribunal to state a case for determination by court unless—

(a) within 21 days after the decision of the tribunal was communicated to him in accordance with rules made under section 78 of the Act he made a written request to the tribunal to state a case; and

(b) either the tribunal

(i) failed to comply with that request within 21 days after it was made; or

(ii) refused to comply with it.

(3) The period for filing the application notice for an order under section 78(8) of the Act is—

(a) where the tribunal failed to comply with the applicant's request to state a case within the period mentioned in paragraph (i)(3)(b)(i), 14 days after the expiration of that period;

(b) where the tribunal refused that request, 14 days after receipt by the applicant of notice of the refusal of his request.

(4) A Mental Health Review Tribunal by whom a case is stated shall be entitled to attend the proceedings for the determination of the case and make representations to the court.

(5) If the court allows the appeal, it may give any direction which the tribunal ought to have given under Part V of the Act.

APPEALS TO THE HIGH COURT—CHANCERY DIVISION

52PD.116 **23.1** The following appeals are to be heard in the Chancery Division.

Determination of appeal or case stated under various Acts

52PD.117 **23.2** Any appeal to the High Court, and any case stated or question referred for the opinion of that court under any of the following enactments shall be heard in the Chancery Division—

(1) paragraph 16 of Schedule 15 to the Law of Property Act 1922;
(2) the Industrial Assurance Act 1923;
(3) the Land Registration Act 1925;
(4) section 205(4) of the Water Resources Act 1991;
(5) section 38(3) of the Clergy Pensions Measure 1961;
(6) the Industrial and Provident Societies Act 1965;
(7) section 151 of the Pension Schemes Act 1993;
(8) section 173 of the Pensions Schemes Act 1993; and
(9) section 97 of the Pensions Act 1995.
(10) the Charities Act 1993
(11) section 13 and 13B of the Stamp Act 1891;
(12) section 705A of the Income and Corporation Taxes Act 1988;
(13) regulation 22 of the General Commissioners (Jurisdiction and Procedure) Regulations 1994;
(14) section 53, 56A or 100C(4) of the Taxes Management Act 1970;
(15) section 222(3), 225, 249(3) or 251 of the Inheritance Tax Act 1984;
(16) regulation 8(3) or 10 of the Stamp Duty Reserve Tax Regulations 1986;
(17) the Land Registration Act 2002.

(This list is not exhaustive.)

Statutory appeals

Appeal under section 222 of the Inheritance Tax Act 1984

52PD.118

23.3(1) This paragraph applies to appeals to the High Court under section 222(3) of the Inheritance Tax Act 1984 (the "1984 Act") and regulation 8(3) of the Stamp Duty Reserve Tax Regulations 1986 (the "1986 Regulations").

(2) The appellant's notice must—

(a) state the date on which the Commissioners of Inland Revenue (the "Board") gave notice to the appellant under section 221 of the 1984 Act or regulation 6 of the 1986 Regulations of the determination that is the subject of the appeal;

(b) state the date on which the appellant gave to the Board notice of appeal under section 222(1) of the 1984 Act or regulation 8(1) of the 1986 Regulations and, if notice was not given within the time permitted, whether the Board or the Special Commissioners have given their consent to the appeal being brought out of time, and, if they have, the date they gave their consent; and

(c) either state that the appellant and the Board have agreed that the appeal may be to the High Court or contain an application for permission to appeal to the High Court.

(3) The appellant must file the following documents with the appellant's notice—

(a) 2 copies of the notice referred to in paragraph 2(a);

(b) 2 copies of the notice of appeal (under section 222(1) of the

1984 Act or regulation 8(1) of the 1986 Regulations) referred to in paragraph 2(b); and

(c) where the appellant's notice contains an application for permission to appeal, written evidence setting out the grounds on which it is alleged that the matters to be decided on the appeal are likely to be substantially confined to questions of law.

(4) The appellant must—

(a) file the appellant's notice at the court; and

(b) serve the appellant's notice on the Board,

within 30 days of the date on which the appellant gave to the Board notice of appeal under section 222(1) of the 1984 Act or regulation 8(1) of the 1986 Regulations or, if the Board or the Special Commissioners have given consent to the appeal being brought out of time, within 30 days of the date on which such consent was given.

(5) The court will set a date for the hearing of not less than 40 days from the date that the appellant's notice was filed.

(6) Where the appellant's notice contains an application for permission to appeal—

(a) a copy of the written evidence filed in accordance with paragraph (3)(c) must be served on the Board with the appellant's notice; and

(b) the Board—

(i) may file written evidence; and

(ii) if it does so, must serve a copy of that evidence on the appellant, within 30 days after service of the written evidence under paragraph (6)(a).

(7) The appellant may not rely on any grounds of appeal not specified in the notice referred to in paragraph (2)(b) on the hearing of the appeal without the permission of the court.

Appeals under section 53 and 100C(4) of the Taxes Management Act 1970 and section 249(3) or 251 of the Inheritance Tax Act 1984

52PD.119 **23.4**(1) The appellant must serve the appellant's notice on—

(a) the General or Special Commissioners against whose decision, award or determination the appeal is brought; and

(b) (i) in the case of an appeal brought under section 100C(4) of the Taxes Management Act 1970 or section 249(3) of the Inheritance Tax Act 1984 by any party other than the defendant than the defendant in the proceedings before the Commissioners, that defendant; or

(ii) in any other case, the Commissioners of Inland Revenue.

(2) The appellant must file the appellant's notice at the court within 30 days after the date of the decision, award or determination against which the appeal is brought.

(3) Within 30 days of the service on them of the appellant's notice the General or Special Commissioners, as the case may be, must—

(a) file 2 copies of a note of their findings and of the reasons for their decision, award or determination at the court; and

(b) serve a copy of the note on every other party to the appeal.

(4) Any document to be served on the General or Special Commissioners may be served by delivering or sending it to their clerk.

Appeals under section 56A of the Taxes Management Act 1970, section 225 of the Inheritance Tax Act 1984 and regulation 10 of the Stamp Duty Reserve Tax Regulations 1986

23.5(1) The appellant must file the appellant's notice— **52PD.120**

(a) where the appeal is made following the refusal of the Special Commissioners to issue a certificate under section 56A(2)(b) of the Taxes Management Act 1970, within 28 days from the date of the release of the decision of the Special Commissioners containing the refusal;

(b) where the appeal is made following the refusal of permission to appeal to the Court of Appeal under section 56A(2)(c) of that Act, within 28 days from the date when permission is refused; or

(c) in all other cases within 56 days after the date of the decision or determination that the appellant wishes to appeal.

Appeal under section 17 of the Industrial Assurance Act 1923

23.6 The appellant must file the appellant's notice within 21 days after the date of the Commissioner's refusal or direction under section 17(3) of the Industrial Assurance Act 1923. **52PD.121**

Appeals affecting industrial and provident societies etc.

23.7(1) This paragraph applies to all appeals under— **52PD.122**

(a) the Friendly Societies Act 1974;
(b) the Friendly Societies Act 1992;
(c) the Industrial Assurance Act 1923; and
(d) the Industrial and Provident Societies Act 1965

(2) At any stage on an appeal, the court may—

(a) direct that the appellant's notice be served on any person;
(b) direct that notice be given by advertisement or otherwise of—
  (i) the bringing of the appeal;
  (ii) the nature of the appeal; and
  (iii) the time when the appeal will or is likely to be heard; or
(c) give such other directions as it thinks proper to enable any person interested in—
  (i) the society, trade union, alleged trade union or industrial assurance company; or
  (ii) the subject matter of the appeal, to appear and be heard at the appeal hearing.

Appeal from Value Added Tax and Duties Tribunal

23.8(1) A party to proceedings before a Value Added Tax and Duties Tribunal who is dissatisfied in point of law with a decision of the tribunal may appeal under section 11(1) of the Tribunals and Inquiries Act 1992 to the High Court. **52PD.123**

(2) The appellant must file the appellant's notice—

(a) where the appeal is made following the refusal of the Value Added Tax and Duties Tribunal to grant a certificate under article 2(b) of the Value Added Tax and Duties Tribunal Appeals Order 1986, within 28 days from the date of the release of the decision containing the refusal;

(b) in all other cases within 56 days after the date of the decision or determination that the appellant wishes to appeal.

Appeal against an order or decision of the Charity Commissioners

23.8A(1) In this paragraph—

'the Act' means the Charities Act 1993; and

'the Commissioners' means the Charity Commissioners for England and Wales.

(2) The Attorney–General, unless he is the appellant, must be made a respondent to the appeal.

(3) The appellant's notice must state the grounds of the appeal, and the appellant may not rely on any other grounds without the permission of the court.

(4) Sub–paragraphs (5) and (6) apply, in addition to the above provisions, where the appeal is made under section 16(12) of the Act.

(5) If the Commissioners have granted a certificate that it is a proper case for an appeal, a copy of the certificate must be filed with the appellant's notice.

(6) If the appellant applies in the appellant's notice for permission to appeal under section 16(13) of the Act—

(a) the appellant's notice must state—

(i) that the appellant has requested the Commissioners to grant a certificate that it is a proper case for an appeal, and they have refused to do so;

(ii) the date of such refusal;

(iii) the grounds on which the appellant alleges that it is a proper case for an appeal; and

(iv) if the application for permission to appeal is made with the consent of any other party to the proposed appeal, that fact;

(b) if the Commissioners have given reasons for refusing a certificate, a copy of the reasons must be attached to the appellant's notice;

(c) the court may, before determining the application, direct the Commissioners to file a written statement of their reasons for refusing a certificate;

(d) the court will serve on the appellant a copy of any statement filed under sub–paragraph (c).

Appeal against a decision of the adjudicator under section 111 of the Land Registration Act 2002

52PD.124 **23.8B**(1) A person who is aggrieved by a decision of the adjudicator and who wishes to appeal that decision must obtain permission to appeal.

(2) The appellant must serve on the adjudicator a copy of the appeal court's decision on a request for permission to appeal as soon as reasonably practicable and in any event within 14 days of receipt by the appellant of the decision on permission.

(3) The appellant must serve on the adjudicator and the Chief Land Registrar a copy of any order by the appeal court to stay a decision of the adjudicator pending the outcome of the appeal as soon as reasonably practicable and in any event within 14 days of receipt by the appellant of the appeal court's order to stay.

(4) The appellant must serve on the adjudicator and the Chief Land Registrar a copy of the appeal court's decision on the appeal as soon as reasonably practicable and in any event within 14 days of receipt by the appellant of the appeal court's decision.

Appeals by way of case stated

Proceedings under the Commons Registration Act 1965

52PD.125

23.9 A person aggrieved by the decision of a Commons Commissioner who requires the Commissioner to state a case for the opinion of the High Court under section 18 of the Commons Registration Act 1965 must file the appellant's notice within 42 days from the date on which notice of the decision was sent to the aggrieved person.

APPEALS TO A COUNTY COURT

Local Government (Miscellaneous Provisions) Act 1976

52PD.126

24.1 Where one of the grounds upon which an appeal against a notice under sections 21, 23 or 35 of the Local Government (Miscellaneous Provisions) Act 1976 is brought is that—

(a) it would have been fairer to serve the notice on another person; or

(b) that it would be reasonable for the whole or part of the expenses to which the appeal relates to be paid by some other person,

that person must be made a respondent to the appeal, unless the court, on application of the appellant made without notice, otherwise directs.

Appeals under sections 204 and 204A of the Housing Act 1996

24.2(1) An appellant should include appeals under section 204 and 204A of the Housing Act 1996 in one appellant's notice.

(2) If it is not possible to do so (for example because an urgent application under section 204A is required) the appeals may be included in seperate appellant's notices.

(3) An appeal under section 204A may include an application for an order under section 204A(4)(a) requiring the authority to secure that accommodation is available for the applicant's occupation.

(4) If, exceptionally, the court makes an order under section 204A(4)(a) without notice, the appellant's notice must be served on the authority together with the order. Such an order will normally require the authority to secure that accomodation is available until a hearing date when the authority can make representations as to whether the order under section 204A(4)(a) should be continued.

Appeal under Part II of the Immigration and Asylum Act 1999 (carriers' liability)

24.3(1) A person appealing to a county court under section 35A or section 40B of the Immigration and Asylum Act 1999 ("the Act") against a decision by the Secretary of State to impose a penalty under section 32 or a charge under section 40 of the Act must, subject to paragraph (2), file the appellant's notice within 28 days after receiving the penalty notice or charge notice.

(2) Where the appellant has given notice of objection to the Secretary of State under section 35(4) or section 40A(3) of the Act within the time prescribed for doing so, he must file the appellant's notice within 28 days after receiving notice of the Secretary of State's decision in response to the notice of objection.

(3) Sections 35A and 40B of the Act provide that any appeal under those sections shall be a re–hearing of the Secretary of State's decision to impose a penalty or charge, and therefore rule 52.11(1) does not apply.

Section IV

PROVISIONS ABOUT REOPENING APPEALS

Reopening of Final Appeals

52PD.127 **25.1** This paragraph applies to applications under rule 52.17 for permission to reopen a final determination of an appeal.

25.2 In this paragraph, "appeal" includes an application for permission to appeal.

25.3 Permission must be sought from the court whose decision the applicant wishes to reopen.

25.4 The application for permission must be made by application notice and supported by written evidence, verified by a statement of truth.

25.5 A copy of the application for permission must not be served on any other party to the original appeal unless the court so directs.

25.6 Where the court directs that the application for permission is to be served on another party, that party may within 14 days of the service on him of the copy of the application file and serve a written statement either supporting or opposing the application.

25.7 The application for permission, and any written statements supporting or opposing it, will be considered on paper by a single judge, and will be allowed to proceed only if the judge so directs.

PART 53

DEFAMATION CLAIMS

Editorial Introduction

53.0.2 *Delete ", although not new as matters of law,".*

PRACTICE DIRECTION–DEFAMATION CLAIMS

Offer of amends as a defence

After "(section 4(3))" add:

This imports a bad faith or malice test, which will rarely be satisfied: see *Milne v. Express Newspapers* [2002] EWHC 2564 (QB); [2003] 1 W.L.R. 927, Eady J., affirmed [2004] EWCA (Civ) 664. **53PD.11.1**

The section 4 procedure

Delete the last sentence of the second paragraph and substitute:

It is only intended to shut out those who have acted in bad faith, *i.e.* maliciously (see *Milne v. Express Newspapers* [2002] EWHC 2564 (QB); [2003] 1 WLR 927, Eady J., affirmed [2004] EWCA (Civ) 664. **53PD.12.3**

Ruling on meaning

Delete "Jameel v. Wall Street Journal [2003] EWCA Civ 1694" and substitute:

Jameel v. Wall Street Journal [2004] E.M.L.R. 6, CA **53PD.13.1**

Procedure

At the end of the penultimate sentence, after "application to the judge" add:

(see *Phillips v. Associated Newspapers Ltd* [2004] EWHC 190; [2004] 1 W.L.R. 2106). **53PD.15.2**

At the end of the final sentence, after "direct to the judge" add:

(see *Phillips*, ibid).

Where a statement is opposed

At the end of the final sentence, after "refused leave to make a statement)" add:

It would be quite exceptional for the court to refuse permission for the making of a reasonable and proportionate statement: see *Phillips v. Associated Newspapers Ltd* [2004] EWHC 190; [2004] 1 W.L.R. 2106. Note that in that case Eady J. held that where a claimant has accepted a Part 36 payment or offer, the costs of any application to make a unilateral statement, and of the making of the statement itself, will generally fall to be paid by the defendant as an integral part of the costs of the action. **53PD.15.3**

PART 54

JUDICIAL REVIEW AND STATUTORY REVIEW

I. JUDICIAL REVIEW

Scope and Interpretation

Delete subsections (b), (c) and (d). **54.1**

Against Whom Does Judicial Review Lie

At the end of the fourth paragraph for "(2nd ed)" substitute:

(3rd ed). **54.1.2**

Procedural Impropriety

For "R v. North and East Devon Health Authorities, ex p. Coughlan [2000] 2 W.L.R. 622" substitute:

R v. North and East Devon Health Authority, ex p. Coughlan [2001] Q.B. 213 **54.1.6**

Abuse of power generally

Delete full stop and add at end:

: see also *E v. Secretary of State for the Home Department* [2004] EWCA Civ 49; [2004] Q.B. 1044. **54.1.8**

Prerogative remedies renamed

For "Rule 54.1(1)" substitute:

54.1.12 Supreme Court Act 1981, s.29 as amended by the Civil Procedure (Modification of the Supreme Court Act 1981) Order 2004

When This Section May Be Used

Delete sub-paragraph (2) and substitute:

54.3 **54.3—(2) A claim for judicial review may include a claim for damages, restitution or the recovery of a sum due but may not seek such a remedy alone. (Section 31(4) of the Supreme Court Act 1981 sets out the circumstances in which the court may award damages, restitution or the recovery of a sum due on a claim for judicial review)**

Prospective amendment—r.54.3—in force May 1, 2004

54.3.1A *Delete paragraph 54.3.1A.*

Cases when the judicial review procedure may be used

54.3.1 *Delete the second sentence*

Interim Relief to give effect to European Union law

In the second paragraph after "Atlanta Fruchthandelsgesellschaft mbH v. Bundesamt fur Ernahrung und Forstwirschaft [1995] E.C.R. I–3761" delete the full stop and add:

54.3.7 and see *R. (on the application of ABNA Ltd) v. Secretary of State for Health* [2003] EWHC 2420; [2004] Eu. L.R. 88.

Procedure for determining applications for permission

In the second paragraph, delete from "However, under the former provisions of RSC Order 53..." to the end of the paragraph.

54.4.1 *Delete the third paragraph.*

Costs at the permission stage

In the frist paragraph delete the second sentence and substitute:

54.12.5 Where the claimant is granted permission, the costs will be costs in the case unless the judge granting permission makes a different order: *Practice Statement (QBD (Admin Ct): Judicial Review: Costs)* [2004] 1 W.L.R. 1760.

Response and written evidence

At the end of the second paragraph delete the full stop and add:

54.14.1 and *R. (on the application of Leung) v. Imperial College of Science, Technology and Medicine* [2002] EWHC 1358; [2002] E.L.R. 653.

Listing of judicial review claims

Existing title is amended

54.16.3 *In the first paragraph for "Applications" substitute:*
Claims

Hearing of substantive judicial review claims

54.16.5 *Existing title is amended*

Application for review

Delete sub-paragraph (3)(a) and substitute:

54.22 **54.22—(3) (a) the immigration or asylum decision to which the proceedings relate, and any document giving reasons for that decision;"; and**

Rule 54.22(5) was revoked by The Civil Procedure (Amendment No. 3) Rules 2003 (S.I. 2003 No. 1329).

(5) **[Revoked]**

Application for review

Add new paragraph 54.22.1:

54.22.1 Applications should normally be made under this procedure and not by a claim for judicial review: *R. (on the application of G) v. Immigration Appeal Tribunal* [2004] EWHC 588; [2004] 3 All E.R. 286.

PART 55

POSSESSION CLAIMS

Related Sources

After "Part 26 (Case Management – Preliminary Stage)" add:

55.0.3

- Part 65 and PD65 (Proceedings Relating to Anti-Social Behaviour and Harassment)
- Anti-Social Behaviour Act 2003

For "Housing Acts 1980 and 1988" substitute:

- Housing Acts 1980, 1985, 1988 and 1996

I. GENERAL RULES

Interpretation

Delete 55.1(c) and substitute:

55.1

55.1(c) **"mortgage" includes a legal or equitable mortgage and a legal or equitable charge and "mortgagee" is to be interpreted accordingly**

(d) **"the 1985 Act" means the Housing Act 1985.**

(e) **"the 1988 Act" means the Housing Act 1988.**

(f) **"a demotion claim" means a claim made by a landlord for an order under section 82A of the 1985 Act or section 6A of the 1988 Act ("a demotion order"); and.**

(g) **"a demoted tenancy" means a tenancy created by virtue of a demotion order..**

Add new paragraph 55.1.1:

55.1.1

Housing Act 1985 See para. 3A–322.

Housing Act 1988 See para. 3A–655.

demotion claims See Housing Act 1985, s.82A (para. 3A–356) and Housing Act 1988, s.6A (para. 3A–697 and 65.11.3).

Scope

After 55.2(1)(c) add:

55.2 **55.2 (Where a demotion claim is made in the same claim form in which a possession claim is started, this Section of this Part applies as modified by rule 65.12. Where the claim is a demotion claim only, Section III of Part 65 applies).**

Demotion claims

Add new paragraph 55.2.5:

55.2.5 See Housing Act 1985, s.82A (para. 3A–356) and Housing Act 1988, s.6A (para. 3A–697). See too the commentary at 65.11.3.

Proceedings against Trespassers

Add at end:

55.4.5 In a claim against trespassers (CPR, r.55.1(b)), a separate unoccupied area should be included in a possession order if, and only if, the land owner is entitled to an injunction quia timet against occupants in relation to the separate area (*Drury v. Secretary of State for the Environment, Food and Rural Affairs* [2004] EWCA Civ 200; *The Times*, March 15, 2004; *Ministry of Agriculture, Fisheries & Food v. Heyman* (1990) 59 P. & C.R. 48, QBD; and *University of Essex v. Djemal* [1980] 1 W.L.R. 1301; CA). The threshold requirement is for convincing evidence of a real danger of actual violation. The inclusion in a possession order of an unoccupied area should be exceptional. The necessary evidence should usually take the form of an intention to decamp to the other area, of a history of movement between the two areas from which a real danger of repetition can be inferred, or of such propinquity and similarity between the two areas as to command the inference of a real danger of decampment from one to the other.

Demotion claims

Add new paragraph 55.4.5.1:

55.4.5.1 PD65, para.5.1 provides that if a demotion order is sought as an alternative to possession, the particulars of claim must—

(1) state whether the demotion claim is a claim under Housing Act 1985, s.82A(2) or under Housing Act 1988, s.6A(2);

(2) state whether the claimant is a local housing authority, a housing action trust or a registered social landlord;

(3) provide details of any statement of express terms of the tenancy served on the tenant under Housing Act 1985, s.82A(7) or under Housing Act 1988, s.6A(10), as applicable; and

(4) state details of the conduct alleged.

Failure to comply with CPR, r.55.4

Add at end:

55.4.7 See, in another context, *Gwynedd CC v. Grunshaw* [2000] 1 W.L.R 494, CA.

Allocation

Delete 55.9(1)(c) and (d) and substitute:

55.9 **55.9**—(1) (c) **the importance to the defendant of retaining possession of the land;**

(d) **the importance of vacant possession to the claimant; and**

(e) **if applicable, the alleged conduct of the defendant.**

Allocation to track

55.9.5 *In the second paragraph, delete "PD55, para. 6.1 states that the financial value of the claim is not necessarily the most important factor. A possession claim may be allocated to the fast track even though the value of the property is in excess of £15,000."*

II. ACCELERATED POSSESSION CLAIMS OF PROPERTY LET ON AN ASSURED SHORTHOLD TENANCY

When this section may be used

For 55.11(1)(b) substitute:

55.11—(1) (b) **subject to rule 55.12(2), all the conditions listed in rule 55.12(1) are satisfied.** **55.11**

Add new subsection (3):

(3) **In this Section of this Part, a "demoted assured shorthold tenancy" means a demoted tenancy where the landlord is a registered social landlord.**

(By virtue of section 20B of the 1988 Act, a demoted assured shorthold tenancy is an assured shorthold tenancy)

Demoted assured shorthold tenancy

Add new paragraph 55.11.3.1:

See Housing Act 1988, s.20B (para. 3A–614) and the commentary at 65.11.3. **55.11.3.1**

Conditions

At the beginning of rule 55.12 insert subsection number (1).

55.12(1) The conditions referred to in rule 55.11(1)(b) are that— **55.12**

Add new subsection 55.12(2):

(2) **If the tenancy is a demoted assured shorthold tenancy, only the conditions in paragraph (1)(b) and (f) need be satisfied.**

Demoted assured shorthold tenancy

Add new paragraph 55.12.2:

See Housing Act 1988, s.20B (para. 3A–614) and the commentary at 65.11.3. **55.12.2**

The application

For 55.22(3)(b) substitute:

55.22—(3)(b) **written evidence.** **55.22**

PRACTICE DIRECTION — POSSESSION CLAIMS

SECTION I GENERAL RULES

Starting the claim

Add new paragraph 1.9:

1.9 Where the claim form includes a demotion claim, the claim must be started in the county court for the district in which the land is situated. **55PD.1**

Residential property let on a tenancy

For "2.3 and 2.4" substitute:

2.2 2.3. 2.4 and 2.4A **55PD.3**

Add new paragraph 2.4A:

2.4A If the claim for possession relates to the conduct of the tenant, the particulars of claim must state details of the conduct alleged.

Possession claim in relation to a demoted tenancy by a housing action trust or a local housing authority

Add new paragraph 2.7:

55PD.5A **2.7** If the claim is a possession claim under section 143D of the Housing Act 1996 (possession claim in relation to a demoted tenancy where the landlord is a housing action trust or a local housing authority), the particulars of claim must have attached to them a copy of the notice to the tenant served under section 143E of the 1996 Act.

Allocation

Paragraph 6.1 is revoked by Civil Procedure Rules 2004 (S.I. 2004 No. 1306)

55PD.9 **6.1** [Revoked]

PART 56

LANDLORD AND TENANT CLAIMS AND MISCELLANEOUS PROVISIONS ABOUT LAND

Editorial Introduction

Add at end:

56.0.2 Significant amendments were made to Part 56 and PD 56 by the Civil Procedure (Amendment) Rules 2004 S.I. 2004 No. 1306 (L. 8). The amendments implement changes in procedure required by the substantive law amendments to Landlord and Tenant Act 1954 Part II (security of tenure for business tenants) brought about by Regulatory Reform (Business Tenancies) (England and Wales) Order 2003 S.I. 2003 No. 3096. The amendments to the substantive law and to Part 56 and PD 56 only apply to cases where notices were served on or after June 1st 2004—see the Regulatory Reform (Business Tenancies) (England and Wales) Order 2003 S.I. 2003 No. 3096 para. 29(1) (at 3B–89) and the Civil Procedure (Amendment) Rules 2004 S.I. 2004 No. 1306 (L. 8)) which states:

Transitional provisions

20.—(1) In the circumstances where article 29(1) or (4) of the Regulatory Reform (Business Tenancies) (England and Wales) Order 2003 applies—

(a) **the amendments to Part 56 made by rules 15 and 16 of these Rules shall not apply; and**

(b) **Part 56 shall continue to apply on and after 1st June 2004 as if those amendments had not been made.**

(2) **Where an application for an injunction under Chapter III of Part V of the Housing Act 1996 has been issued before 30th June 2004—**

(a) **Section I of Part 65 shall not apply in relation to that application; and**

(b) **CCR Order 49, rule 6B shall continue to apply on and after 30th June 2004 as if it had not been revoked.**

Related Sources

Add at end:

56.0.3

- the Regulatory Reform (Business Tenancies) (England and Wales) Order 2003 S.I. 2003 No. 3096.

Starting the claim

For "paragraphs (2) or (4) apply" substitute:

56.2—(1) paragraph (2) applies **56.2**

Delete 56.2(4).

Landlord and Tenant Act 1954 s.38(4)

Add at end:

56.2.1 *Note* Part 56.2(4), which dealt with proceedings under Landlord and Tenant Act 1954 s.38(4) (former power to exclude security of tenure provisions of Landlord and Tenant Act 1954) was revoked by the Civil Procedure (Amendment) Rules 2004 in the light of the repeal of s.38(4) by the Regulatory Reform (Business Tenancies) (England and Wales) Order 2003 S.I. No. 3096—although these repeals do not apply to agreements to exclude Part II made before June 1st 2004—see the Regulatory Reform (Business Tenancies) (England and Wales) Order 2003 S.I. No. 3096 para. 29(2) at 3B–89.

Delete existing rule 56.3 and substitute:

56.3

Claims for a new tenancy under section 24 and for the termination of a tenancy under section 29(2) of the Landlord and Tenant Act 1954[1]

56.3—(1) This rule applies to a claim for a new tenancy under section 24 and to a claim for the termination of a tenancy under section 29(2) of the 1954 Act.

(2) In this rule—

(a) "the 1954 Act" means the Landlord and Tenant Act 1954;

(b) "an unopposed claim" means a claim for a new tenancy under section 24 of the 1954 Act in circumstances where the grant of a new tenancy is not opposed;

(c) "an opposed claim" means a claim for—

(i) a new tenancy under section 24 of the 1954 Act in circumstances where the grant of a new tenancy is opposed; or

(ii) the termination of a tenancy under section 29(2) of the 1954 Act.

(3) Where the claim is an unopposed claim—

(a) the claimant must use the Part 8 procedure, but the following rules do not apply—

(i) rule 8.5; and

(ii) rule 8.6;

(b) the claim form must be served within 2 months after the date of issue and rules 7.5 and 7.6 are modified accordingly; and

(c) the court will give directions about the future management of the claim following receipt of the acknowledgment of service.

(4) Where the claim is an opposed claim—

(a) the claimant must use the Part 7 procedure; but

(b) the claim form must be served within 2 months after the date of issue, and rules 7.5 and 7.6 are modified accordingly.

(The practice direction to this Part contains provisions about evidence, including expert evidence in opposed claims)

Add new paragraph 56.3.0:

56.3.0 See note at 56.0.2. Significant amendments to CPR 56.3 and PD 56 were made by the Civil Procedure (Amendment) Rules 2004 S.I. 2004 No. 1306 (L. 8).However these amend-

[1] 1954 c.56. Section 24 was amended by article 3 of S.I. 2003 No. 3096. Section 29(2) was substituted by article 5 of S.I. 2003 No. 3096.

ments only apply to cases where notices were served on or after June 1st 2004—see the Civil Procedure (Amendment) Rules 2004 S.I. 2004 No. 1306 (L. 8), para. 29 which is set out in full at 56.0.2. The former provisions continue to apply where notices were served before June 1st 2004.

Starting the claim

For "The claimant" substitute:

56PD.2 **2.1** Subject to paragraph 2.1A, the claimant

Add new paragraph 2.1A:

2.1A Where the landlord and tenant claim is a claim for—

(1) a new tenancy under section 24 of the 1954 Act in circumstances where the grant of a new tenancy is opposed; or

(2) the termination of a tenancy under section 29(2) of the 1954 Act,

the claimant must use the Part 7 procedure as modified by Part 56 and this practice direction.

In paragraph 2.2 delete "or rule 56.2(4) applies"

Claims for a New Tenancy under Section 24 and Termination of a enancy under Section 29(2) of the 1954 Act

Delete paragraphs 56PD.3 to 56PD.7 inclusive and substitute:

56PD.3 **3.1** This paragraph applies to a claim for a new tenancy under section 24 and termination of a tenancy under section 29(2) of the 1954 Act where rule 56.3 applies and in this paragraph.

(1) "an unopposed claim" means a claim for a new tenancy under section 24 of the 1954 Act in circumstances where the grant of a new tenancy is not opposed;

(2) "an opposed claim" means a claim for—

(a) a new tenancy under section 24 of the 1954 Act in circumstances where the grant of a new tenancy is opposed; or

(b) the termination of a tenancy under section 29(2) of the 1954 Act; and

(3) "grounds of opposition" means—

(a) the grounds specified in section 30(1) of the 1954 Act on which a landlord may oppose an application for a new tenancy under section 24(1) of the 1954 Act or make an application under section 29(2) of the 1954 Act; or

(b) any other basis on which the landlord asserts that a new tenancy ought not to be granted.

Precedence of claim forms where there is more than one application to the court under section 24(1) or section 29(2) of the 1954 Act

56PD.4 **3.2** Where more than one application to the court under section 24(1) or section 29(2) of the 1954 Act is made, the following provisions shall apply—

(1) once an application to the court under section 24(1) of the 1954 Act has been served on a defendant, no further application to the court in respect of the same tenancy whether under section 24(1) or section 29(2) of the 1954 Act may be served by that defendant without the permission of the court;

(2) if more than one application to the court under section 24(1) of the 1954 Act in respect of the same tenancy is served on the same day, any landlord's application shall stand stayed until further order of the court;

(3) if applications to the court under both section 24(1) and section 29(2) of the 1954 Act in respect of the same tenancy are served on the same day, any tenant's application shall stand stayed until further order of the court; and

(4) if a defendant is served with an application under section 29(2) of the 1954 Act ("the section 29(2) application") which was issued at a time when an application to the court had already been made by that defendant in respect of the same tenancy under section 24(1) of the 1954 Act ("the section 24(1) application"), thc service of the section 29(2) application shall be deemed to be a notice under rule 7.7 requiring service or discontinuance of the section 24(1) application within a period of 14 days after the service of the section 29(2) application.

Defendant where the claimant is the tenant making a claim for a new tenancy under section 24 of the 1954 Act

3.3 Where a claim for a new tenancy under section 24 of the 1954 Act is made by a tenant, the person who, in relation to the claimant's current tenancy, is the landlord as defined in section 44 of the 1954 Act must be a defendant. **56PD.4A**

Contents of the claim form in all cases

3.4 The claim form must contain details of— **56PD.5**

(1) the property to which the claim relates;

(2) the particulars of the current tenancy (including date, parties and duration), the current rent (if not the original rent) and the date and method of termination;

(3) every notice or request given or made under sections 25 or 26 of the 1954 Act; and

(4) the expiry date of—

(a) the statutory period under section 29A(2) of the 1954 Act; or

(b) any agreed extended period made under section 29B(1) or 29B(2) of the 1954 Act.

Claim form where the claimant is the tenant making a claim for a new tenancy under section 24 of the 1954 Act

3.5 Where the claimant is the tenant making a claim for a new tenancy under section 24 of the 1954 Act, in addition to the details specified in paragraph 3.4, the claim form must contain details of— **56PD.6**

(1) the nature of the business carried on at the property;

(2) whether the claimant relies on section 23(1A), 41 or 42 of the 1954 Act and, if so, the basis on which he does so;

(3) whether the claimant relies on section 31A of the 1954 Act and, if so, the basis on which he does so;

(4) whether any, and if so what part, of the property comprised in the tenancy is occupied neither by the claimant nor by a person employed by the claimant for the purpose of the claimant's business;

(5) the claimant's proposed terms of the new tenancy; and
(6) the name and address of—
 (a) anyone known to the claimant who has an interest in the reversion in the property (whether immediate or in not more than 15 years) on the termination of the claimant's current tenancy and who is likely to be affected by the grant of a new tenancy; or
 (b) if the claimant does not know of anyone specified by sub-paragraph (6)(a), anyone who has a freehold interest in the property.

3.6 The claim form must be served on the persons referred to in paragraph 3.5(6)(a) or (b) as appropriate.

Claim form where the claimant is the landlord making a claim for a new tenancy under section 24 of the 1954 Act

56PD.7 **3.7** Where the claimant is the landlord making a claim for a new tenancy under section 24 of the 1954 Act, in addition to the details specified in paragraph 3.4, the claim form must contain details of—
(1) the claimant's proposed terms of the new tenancy;
(2) whether the claimant is aware that the defendant's tenancy is one to which section 32(2) of the 1954 Act applies and, if so, whether the claimant requires that any new tenancy shall be a tenancy of the whole of the property comprised in the defendant's current tenancy or just of the holding as defined by section 23(3) of the 1954 Act; and
(3) the name and address of—
 (a) anyone known to the claimant who has an interest in the reversion in the property (whether immediate or in not more than 15 years) on the termination of the claimant's current tenancy and who is likely to be affected by the grant of a new tenancy; or
 (b) if the claimant does not know of anyone specified by sub-paragraph (3)(a), anyone who has a freehold interest in the property.

3.8 The claim form must be served on the persons referred to in paragraph 3.7(3)(a) or (b) as appropriate.

Claim form where the claimant is the landlord making an application for the termination of a tenancy under section 29(2) of the 1954 Act

56PD.7A **3.9** Where the claimant is the landlord making an application for the termination of a tenancy under section 29(2) of the 1954 Act, in addition to the details specified in paragraph 3.4, the claim form must contain—
(1) the claimant's grounds of opposition;
(2) full details of those grounds of opposition; and
(3) the terms of a new tenancy that the claimant proposes in the event that his claim fails.

Acknowledgment of service where the claim is an unopposed claim and where the claimant is the tenant

56PD.7B **3.10** Where the claim is an unopposed claim and the claimant is the tenant, the acknowledgment of service is to be in form N210 and must state with particulars—

(1) whether, if a new tenancy is granted, the defendant objects to any of the terms proposed by the claimant and if so—
  (a) the terms to which he objects; and
  (b) the terms that he proposes in so far as they differ from those proposed by the claimant;

(2) whether the defendant is a tenant under a lease having less than 15 years unexpired at the date of the termination of the claimant's current tenancy and, if so, the name and address of any person who, to the knowledge of the defendant, has an interest in the reversion in the property expectant (whether immediate or in not more than 15 years from that date) on the termination of the defendant's tenancy;

(3) the name and address of any person having an interest in the property who is likely to be affected by the grant of a new tenancy; and

(4) if the claimant's current tenancy is one to which section 32(2) of the 1954 Act applies, whether the defendant requires that any new tenancy shall be a tenancy of the whole of the property comprised in the claimant's current tenancy.

Acknowledgment of service where the claim is an unopposed claim and the claimant is the landlord

3.11 Where the claim is an unopposed claim and the claimant is the landlord, the acknowledgment of service is to be in form N210 and must state with particulars— **56PD.7C**

(1) the nature of the business carried on at the property;

(2) if the defendant relies on section 23(1A), 41 or 42 of the 1954 Act, the basis on which he does so;

(3) whether any, and if so what part, of the property comprised in the tenancy is occupied neither by the defendant nor by a person employed by the defendant for the purpose of the defendant's business;

(4) the name and address of—
  (a) anyone known to the defendant who has an interest in the reversion in the property (whether immediate or in not more than 15 years) on the termination of the defendant's current tenancy and who is likely to be affected by the grant of a new tenancy; or
  (b) if the defendant does not know of anyone specified by sub-paragraph (4)(a), anyone who has a freehold interest in the property; and

(5) whether, if a new tenancy is granted, the defendant objects to any of the terms proposed by the claimant and, if so—
  (a) the terms to which he objects; and
  (b) the terms that he proposes in so far as they differ from those proposed by the claimant.

Acknowledgment of service and defence where the claim is an opposed claim and where the claimant is the tenant

3.12 Where the claim is an opposed claim and the claimant is the tenant— **56PD.7D**

(1) the acknowledgment of service is to be in form N9; and

(2) in his defence the defendant must state with particulars—
(a) the defendant's grounds of opposition;
(b) full details of those grounds of opposition;
(c) whether, if a new tenancy is granted, the defendant objects to any of the terms proposed by the claimant and if so—
(i) the terms to which he objects; and
(ii) the terms that he proposes in so far as they differ from those proposed by the claimant;
(d) whether the defendant is a tenant under a lease having less than 15 years unexpired at the date of the termination of the claimant's current tenancy and, if so, the name and address of any person who, to the knowledge of the defendant, has an interest in the reversion in the property expectant (whether immediately or in not more than 15 years from that date) on the termination of the defendant's tenancy;
(e) the name and address of any person having an interest in the property who is likely to be affected by the grant of a new tenancy; and
(f) if the claimant's current tenancy is one to which section 32(2) of the 1954 Act applies, whether the defendant requires that any new tenancy shall be a tenancy of the whole of the property comprised in the claimant's current tenancy.

Acknowledgment of service and defence where the claimant is the landlord making an application for the termination of a tenancy under section 29(2) of the 1954 Act

56PD.7E **3.13** Where the claim is an opposed claim and the claimant is the landlord—
(1) the acknowledgment of service is to be in form N9; and
(2) in his defence the defendant must state with particulars—
(a) whether the defendant relies on section 23(1A), 41 or 42 of the 1954 Act and, if so, the basis on which he does so;
(b) whether the defendant relies on section 31A of the 1954 Act and, if so, the basis on which he does so; and
(c) the terms of the new tenancy that the defendant would propose in the event that the claimant's claim to terminate the current tenancy fails.

Evidence in an opposed claim

56PD.7F **3.14** Where the claim is an opposed claim, evidence (including expert evidence) must be filed by the parties as the court directs and the landlord shall be required to file his evidence first.

Evidence in an opposed claim

56PD.7G **3.15** Where the claim is an opposed claim, evidence (including expert evidence) must be filed by the parties as the court directs and the landlord shall be required to file his evidence first.

Grounds of opposition to be tried as a preliminary issue

56PD.7H **3.16** Where proceedings have already been commenced for the grant of a new tenancy or the termination of an existing tenancy, the claim for interim rent under section 24A of the 1954 Act shall be made in those proceedings by—

Applications for interim rent under section 24A to 24D of the 1954 Act

3.17 Unless in the circumstances of the case it is unreasonable to do so, any grounds of opposition shall be tried as a preliminary issue. **56PD.7I**

(1) the claim form;
(2) the acknowledgment of service or defence; or
(3) an application on notice under Part 23.

3.18 Any application under section 24D(3) of the 1954 Act shall be made by an application on notice under Part 23 in the original proceedings.

3.19 Where no other proceedings have been commenced for the grant of a new tenancy or termination of an existing tenancy or where such proceedings have been disposed of, an application for interim rent under section 24A of the 1954 Act shall be made under the procedure in Part 8 and the claim form shall include details of—

(1) the property to which the claim relates;
(2) the particulars of the relevant tenancy (including date, parties and duration) and the current rent (if not the original rent);
(3) every notice or request given or made under sections 25 or 26 of the 1954 Act;
(4) if the relevant tenancy has terminated, the date and mode of termination; and
(5) if the relevant tenancy has been terminated and the landlord has granted a new tenancy of the property to the tenant—
   (a) particulars of the new tenancy (including date, parties and duration) and the rent; and
   (b) in a case where section 24C(2) of the 1954 Act applies but the claimant seeks a different rent under section 24C(3) of that Act, particulars and matters on which the claimant relies as satisfying section 24C(3).

PART 57

PROBATE AND INHERITANCE

Procedure for claims under section 1 of the Act

For "The time" substitute:

57.16—(4) Subject to paragraph (4A), the time **57.16**

Add new rule 57.16(4A):

(4A) **If the claim form is served out of the jurisdiction under rule 6.19, the period for filing an acknowledgment of service and any written evidence is 7 days longer than the relevant period specified in rule 6.22 or the practice direction supplementing Section III of Part 6.**

PART 65

PROCEEDINGS RELATING TO ANTI–SOCIAL BEHAVIOUR AND HARASSMENT

Add new Part 65:

65.0.1 Contents

I. Housing Act 1996 Injunctions

II. Applications by Local Authorities for Power of Arrest to be Attached to an Injunction

III. Demotion Claims and Proceedings Relating to Demoted Tenancies

IV. Anti–Social Behaviour Orders under the Crime and Disorder Act 1998

Editorial Introduction

Add new paragraphs 65.0.2 to 65.0.4:

65.0.2 Part 65 and its Practice Direction were introduced by the Civil Procedure (Amendment) Rules 2004 (see the 35th Update to the Civil Procedure Rules). They came into effect on June 30, 2004. Their main purpose is to update procedure to allow claims for anti–social behaviour injunctions and demotion of tenancies in the light of the amendments to substantive law (especially Housing Act 1996—see para. 3A–916) introduced by the Anti–social Behaviour Act 2003. However they also deal with anti–social behaviour orders (ASBOs) and injunctions under the Protection from Harassment Act 1997.

Related Sources

65.0.3

- PD 2B (Allocation of cases to levels of judiciary)
- Part 7 (How to start proceedings – the claim form)
- Part 8 (Alternative Procedure for claims)
- Part 10 (Acknowledgement of Service)
- Part 12 (Default Judgment)
- Part 16 (Statements of Case)
- Part 19 (Parties and Group Litigation)
- Part 23 (General Rules about Applications for Court Orders)
- Part 55 (Possession Claims)
- RSC Order 52
- CCR Order 29
- Housing Act 1996, as amended by Anti–Social Behaviour Act 2003
- Protection from Harassment Act 1997
- Crime and Disorder Act 1998 (as amended by Police Reform Act 2002 and the Anti–Social Behaviour Act 2003)

Forms

65.0.4

- **N6** Claim form for demotion of tenancy
- **N7D** Notes for defendant to a demotion claim
- **N11D** Defence form to a claim for a demotion order, and
- N16 Injunction Order
- N16A Application for injunction (general form)
- N110A Anti–social behaviour injunction power of arrest
- N113 (Anti–social behaviour order)
- **N122** Particulars of claim for demotion order
- N142 Guardianship Order (Housing Act 1996, Mental Health Act 1983)
- N143 Interim Hospital Order (Housing Act 1996, Mental Health act 1983)
- N206D Notice of Issue (demotion claim)
- **N244** (Application Notice)

Scope of this Part

65.1 **65.1 This Part contains rules—**

(a) **in Section I, about injunctions under the Housing Act 1996**[1]

(b) **in Section II, about applications by local authorities under section 91(3) of the Anti–social Behaviour Act 2003**[2] **for a power of arrest to be attached to an injunction;**

(c) **in Section III, about claims for demotion orders under the Housing Act 1985**[3] **and Housing Act 1988**[4] **and proceedings relating to demoted tenancies;**

(d) **in Section IV, about anti–social behaviour orders under the Crime and Disorder Act 1998**[5]**;**

(e) **in Section V, about claims under section 3 of the Protection from Harassment Act 1997**[6]

Add new paragraph 65.1.1:

65.1.1 **injunctions under the Housing Act 1996** See para. 3A–1117.
applications by local authorities under section 91(3) of the Anti–social Behaviour Act 2003 for a power of arrest See para. 3A–1129.
claims for demotion orders See paras 3A–356 and 3A–697.
proceedings relating to demoted tenancies See para. 3A–1028.
anti–social behaviour orders under the Crime and Disorder Act 1998 See 3A–1401.1

I. HOUSING ACT 1996 INJUNCTIONS

Scope of this Section and interpretation

65.2 **65.2—(1) This Section applies to applications for an injunction and other related proceedings under Chapter III of Part V of the Housing Act 1996 (injunctions against anti–social behaviour).**

(2) **In this Section "the 1996 Act" means the Housing Act 1996.**

Injunctions under the Housing Act 1996

Add new paragraph 65.2.1:

65.2.1 See para. 3A–1117. In particular Housing Act 1996, s.153A gives "relevant landlords" (as defined in s.153E) power to apply for free–standing anti–social behaviour injunctions irrespective of whether or not there is any other common law or statutory cause of action. The court has power to grant such an anti–social behaviour injunction to restrain conduct

(a) which is capable of causing nuisance or annoyance to any person; or
(b) which directly or indirectly relates to or affects the housing management functions of a relevant landlord.

Applications for an injunction

65.3 **65.3—(1) An application for an injunction under Chapter III of Part V of the 1996 Act**[7] **shall be subject to the Part 8 procedure as modified by this rule and the relevant practice direction.**

(2) **The application must be—**

(a) **made by a claim form in accordance with the relevant practice direction;**

---

[1] 1996 c. 52
[2] 2003 c. 38
[3] 1985 c. 68
[4] 1988 c. 50
[5] 1998 c. 37
[6] 1997 c. 40
[7] 1996 c. 52. These sections were inserted by section 13 of the Anti–social Behaviour Act 2003.

(b) commenced in the court for the district in which the defendant resides or the conduct complained of occurred; and

(c) supported by a witness statement which must be filed with the claim form.

(3) The claim form must state—

(a) the matters required by rule 8.2; and

(b) the terms of the injunction applied for.

(4) An application under this rule may be made without notice and where such an application without notice is made—

(a) the witness statement in support of the application must state the reasons why notice has not been given; and

(b) the following rules do not apply—

(i) 8.3;

(ii) 8.4;

(iii) 8.5(2) to (6);

(iv) 8.6(1);

(v) 8.7; and

(vi) 8.8.

(5) In every application made on notice, the application notice must be served, together with a copy of the witness statement, by the claimant on the defendant personally.

(6) An application made on notice may be listed for hearing before the expiry of the time for the defendant to file an acknowledgement of service under rule 8.3, and in such a case—

(a) the claimant must serve the application notice and witness statement on the defendant not less than two days before the hearing; and

(b) the defendant may take part in the hearing whether or not he has filed an acknowledgment of service.

Editorial Introduction

Add new paragraphs 65.3.1 to 65.3.7:

65.3.1 Applications for injunctions under ss.153A, 153B or 153D must be made in Form N16A and follow the Part 8 procedure. They must be made in the court for the district in which the defendant resides or the conduct complained of occurred (CPR, r.65.3; PD65, para.1). All applications must state the terms of the injunction applied for and be supported by written evidence. They must be made on two days notice unless the court otherwise directs (see CPR, r.65.3(6)(a)). The defendant must be served personally. If the application is made without notice the affidavit should explain why notice has not been given (CPR, r.65.3(4)(a)). Unless otherwise directed applications made on notice should be heard in public (CPR, r.39.2) Applications for injunctions must be made in Form N16A (PD65, para.1). Injunctions should be in Form N16. Wherever possible the claimant should file a draft of the order sought with the application and a disc with the draft order should be available to the court (PD25, para.2.4). Injunctions must be "framed in terms appropriate and proportionate to the facts of the case". If there is a risk of significant harm to a particular person or persons it is usually appropriate for the injunction to identify that person or those persons. However, in order to justify granting a wider injunction, restraining someone from causing a nuisance or annoyance to "a person of a similar description", it is normally necessary for the judge to make a finding that there has been use or threats of violence to persons of a similar description, and that there is a risk of significant harm to persons of a similar description if an injunction is not granted in respect of them (*Manchester City Council v. Lee* [2003] EWCA Civ 1256; [2004] 1 W.L.R. 349).

Application for an injunction under section 153A, 153B or 153D

65.3.2 See paras 3A–1117, 3A–1123, 3A–1129 and 3A–1134.

Claim form

65.3.3 See Form N16A which, under Part 65, is to be treated as the Part 8 claim form (PD65.1). In particular, the claimant must state the remedy sought, the legal basis for the claim to that remedy and the enactment under which the remedy is sought.

Court for the district in which the defendant resides or the conduct complained of occurred

65.3.4 *c.f.* CPR, r.55.3 and r.56.2. In the light of CPR, r.3.10, issue in the wrong court is likely to be seen as an error of procedure which does not invalidate the step taken. In most cases judges would correct the error by transferring to the appropriate court. See, in another context, *Gwynedd CC v. Grunshaw* [2000] 1 W.L.R. 494, CA.

The following rules do not apply

65.3.5 Unlike most Part 8 claims,

(a) there is no requirement for an acknowledgement of service (*c.f.* CPR, r.8.3 and 8.4);

(b) the normal Part 8 provisions for filing of evidence do not apply (*i.e.* Part 8.5(2) to (6) and 8.6(1)), but N.B. the requirement for affidavit evidence in CPR, r.65.3(2)(b); and

(c) the procedure for objecting to the Part 8 procedure does not apply (*c.f.* Part 8.8).

Application notice and affidavit

65.3.6 See Form N16A (PD65.1). If the application for an injunction is made without notice, the affidavit in support of the application must state the reasons why notice has not been given.

Jurisdiction

65.3.6 See PD 2B as amended. The former position was that the jurisdiction of the court under repealed ss.152 and 153 could be exercised by district judges as well as circuit judges. PD 2B, paras 8.1 and 8.3, as amended, make it clear that district and deputy district judges have jurisdiction to grant anti–social behaviour injunctions and to commit for contempt. There is no longer any requirement that district judges and deputy district judges have to have had appropriate training before exercising the jurisdiction (*c.f.* the Practice Direction made by the Lord Chancellor on August 28, 1997 which has been revoked and not replaced.) Notwithstanding the suggestion in some quarters that the former rule giving district judges jurisdiction was ultra vires, it is now accepted that this is not the case—see County Courts Act 1984, s.75(3)(d), repealed by Civil Procedure Act 1997, Sched 2, but Sched 1 of that Act provides that the Civil Procedure Rules may deal with the subjects contained in the former rules.

Injunction containing provisions to which a power of arrest is attached

65.4 **65.4—(1) In this rule "relevant provision" means a provision of an injunction to which a power of arrest is attached.**

(Sections 153C(3) and 153D(4) of the 1996 Act[1] confer powers to attach a power of arrest to an injunction)

(2) **Where an injunction contains one or more relevant provisions—**

(a) **each relevant provision must be set out in a separate paragraph of the injunction; and**

(b) **subject to paragraph (3), the claimant must deliver a copy of the relevant provisions to any police station for the area where the conduct occurred.**

(3) **Where the injunction has been granted without notice, the claimant must not deliver a copy of the relevant provisions to any police station for the area where the conduct occurred before the defendant has been served with the injunction containing the relevant provisions.**

(4) **Where an order is made varying or discharging any relevant provision, the claimant must—**

[1] 1996 c. 52. These sections were inserted by section 13 of the Anti–social Behaviour Act 2003.

(a) **immediately inform the police station to which a copy of the relevant provisions was delivered under paragraph (2)(b); and**

(b) **deliver a copy of the order to any police station so informed.**

Power of arrest

Add new paragraph 65.4.1:

65.4.1 See Housing Act 1996, ss.153C and 153D at paras 3A–1129 and 3A–1134. A power of arrest should made be in Form N110A. If a power of arrest is sought, each provision which is to be subject to the power of arrest must be set out in a separate clause of the injunction (CPR, r.65.4). Powers of arrest may be sought in claim forms, acknowledgements of service or Part 23 applications. They must be supported by written evidence. If made on notice, not less than two days notice must be given (CPR, r.65.9). It is important to spell out in the injunction the specific activities which are forbidden and confine the power of arrest to those specific activities alone. Under ECHR law, citizens must be able, if necessary with appropriate advice, to foresee to a reasonable degree the consequences that a given action may produce (*Silver v. UK* (1983) 5 EHHR 347, at paras 87–8). Summary arrest and detention are clearly an extremely serious interference with a person's private life, which can only be justified by an order which is "particularly precise" (*Kopp v. Switzerland* (1991) 27 EHRR 91, at para.72). See too *Manchester CC v. Lee* [2003] EWCA Civ 1256; [2004] 1 W.L.R. 349 and, in a domestic violence context, *Hale v. Tanner* [2000] 1 W.L.R. 2377, CA, which suggests a power of arrest be attached only to paragraphs prohibiting violence or physical proximity. This is confirmed by s.153C.

The claimant must deliver a copy an injunction with a Power of Arrest to any police station for the area where the conduct occurred—but if it was granted without notice, only after service on the defendant (CPR, r.65.4). The claimant must immediately inform the police station if an injunction containing a power of arrest is varied or discharged.

Application for warrant of arrest under section 155(3) of the 1996 Act[1]

65.5 **65.5—(1) An application for a warrant of arrest under section 155(3) of the 1996 Act must be made in accordance with Part 23 and may be made without notice.**

(2) An applicant for a warrant of arrest under section 155(3) of the 1996 Act must—

(a) **file an affidavit setting out grounds for the application with the application notice; or**

(b) **give oral evidence as to the grounds for the application at the hearing.**

Housing Act 1996, s.155

Add new paragraphs 65.5.1 and 65.5.2:

65.5.1 See para. 3A–1144.

Warrant

65.5.2 A warrant of arrest under s.155(3) shall not be issued unless the application is substantiated on oath and the judge has reasonable grounds for believing that the defendant has failed to comply with the injunction (see PD65, para.2.1).

Proceedings following arrest

65.6 **65.6—(1) This rule applies where a person is arrested pursuant to—**

(a) **a power of arrest attached to a provision of an injunction; or**

(b) **a warrant of arrest.**

[1] 1996 c. 52. This section was amended by section 13 of the Anti–social Behaviour Act 2003.

(2) The judge before whom a person is brought following his arrest may—

(a) deal with the matter; or

(b) adjourn the proceedings.

(3) Where the proceedings are adjourned the judge may remand the arrested person in accordance with section 155(2)(b) or (5) of the 1996 Act.

(4) Where the proceedings are adjourned and the arrested person is released—

(a) the matter must be dealt with (whether by the same or another judge) within 28 days of the date on which the arrested person appears in court; and

(b) the arrested person must be given not less than 2 days' notice of the hearing.

(5) An application notice seeking the committal for contempt of court of the arrested person may be issued even if the arrested person is not dealt with within the period mentioned in paragraph (4)(a).

(6) CCR Order 29, rule 1 shall apply where an application is made in a county court to commit a person for breach of an injunction, as if references in that rule to the judge included references to a district judge.

(For applications in the High Court for the discharge of a person committed to prison for contempt of court see RSC Order 52, rule 8. For such applications in the county court see CCR Order 29, rule 3).

Power of arrest

Add new paragraphs 65.6.1 to 65.6.5:

65.6.1 See Housing Act 1996, ss.153C and 153D at paras 3A–1129 and 3A–1134 and CPR, r.65.4 above.

Warrant of arrest

65.6.2 See CPR, r.65.5 above.

Dealing with breaches of anti-social behaviour injunctions

65.6.3 The judge before whom an arrested person is brought may deal with the matter or adjourn proceedings (CPR, r.65.6). In such circumstances the arrested person may be remanded or released. If the person is released, the matter shall be dealt with by the same or another judge within 28 days of the date the arrested person appears in court. At least two days notice of the adjourned hearing must be given (CPR, r.65.6).

Applications for bail

65.6.4 An application for bail made by a person arrested under a power of arrest attached to an injunction or a warrant of arrest issued under s.155(3) may be made either orally or in an application notice. An application notice seeking bail must contain (1) the full name of the person making the application; (2) the address of the place where the person making the application is detained; (3) the address where s/he would reside if bail were granted; (4) the amount of any proposed recognizance; and (5) the grounds for the application and, where a previous application has been refused, full details of any change in circumstances which has occurred since that refusal. A copy of the application notice must be served on the person who obtained the injunction (PD 65, para. 3). If a person is bailed, subject to a recognizance, the recognizance may subsequently be taken by a judge, a justice of the peace, a justice's clerk, a senior police officer or the governor of a prison (CPR, r.65.7).

Jurisdiction

65.6.5 See PD2B as amended. The former position was that the jurisdiction of the court under repealed ss.152 and 153 could be exercised by district judges as well as circuit judges. The amendment to PD2B makes it clear that district and deputy district judges have jurisdiction to grant anti–social behaviour injunctions and to commit for contempt. There is no longer any requirement that district judges and deputy district judges have to have had appropriate training before exercising the jurisdiction (*c.f.* the Practice Direction made by the Lord Chancellor on August 28, 1997 which has been revoked and not replaced). Notwithstanding the suggestion in some quarters that the former rule giving district judges jurisdiction was ultra vires, it is now accepted that this is not the case—see County Courts Act 1984, s.75(3)(d), repealed by Civil Procedure Act 1997 Sched 2, but Sched 1 of that Act provides that the Civil Procedure Rules may deal with the subjects contained in the former rules. See too CPR, r.65.6(6) which provides that CCR O.29, r.1 applies on an application to commit for breach of an anti–social behaviour injunction, as if references in that rule to the judge included references to a district judge.

Recognizance

65.7

65.7—(1) Where, in accordance with paragraph 2(2)(b) of Schedule 15 to the 1996 Act, the court fixes the amount of any recognizance with a view to it being taken subsequently, the recognizance may be taken by—

(a) **a judge;**
(b) **a justice of the peace;**
(c) **a justices' clerk;**
(d) **a police officer of the rank of inspector or above or in charge of a police station; or**
(e) **where the arrested person is in his custody, the governor or keeper of a prison,**

with the same consequences as if it had been entered into before the court.

(2) **The person having custody of an applicant for bail must release him if satisfied that the required recognizances have been taken.**

Housing Act 1996, Sched.15

Add new paragraphs 65.7.1 and 65.7.2:

65.7.1

See para. 3A–1397.

Recognizance

65.7.2

See commentary to CPR, r.65.6, above.

II. APPLICATIONS BY LOCAL AUTHORITIES FOR POWER OF ARREST TO BE ATTACHED TO AN INJUNCTION

Scope of this Section and interpretation

65.8

65.8—(1) This Section applies to applications by local authorities under section 91(3) of the Anti–social Behaviour Act 2003[1] for a power of arrest to be attached to an injunction. (Section 91 of the 2003 Act applies to proceedings in which a local authority is a party by virtue of section 222 of the Local Government Act 1972[2] (power of local authority to bring, defend or appear in proceedings for the promotion or protection of the interests of inhabitants in their area)

(2) **In this Section "the 2003 Act" means the Anti–social Behaviour Act 2003.**

[1] 2003 c. 38
[2] 1972 c. 70

Editorial Introduction

Add new paragraph 65.8.1:

65.8.1 Local Government Act 1972, s.222, gives local authorities power to bring civil proceedings "for the promotion or protection of the interests of the inhabitants of their area". In *Nottingham City Council v. Zain* [2001] EWCA Civ 1248; [2002] 1 W.L.R. 607, the Court of Appeal held that a local authority has the power to institute proceedings under s.222 in its own name for injunctive relief to restrain a public nuisance provided that it considers it expedient for the promotion and protection of the interests of the inhabitants of its area. Anti-social Behaviour Act 2003, s.91 provides that if the court grants a s.222 injunction which prohibits conduct which is capable of causing nuisance or annoyance, it may attach a power of arrest to any provision of the injunction if the court thinks that either the conduct consists of or includes the use or threatened use of violence, or there is a significant risk of harm to the person mentioned in that subsection. Harm includes serious ill-treatment or abuse (whether physical or not).

Applications under section 91(3) of the 2003 Act for a power of arrest to be attached to any provision of an injunction

65.9 **65.9—(1) An application under section 91(3) of the 2003 Act for a power of arrest to be attached to any provision of an injunction must be made in the proceedings seeking the injunction by—**

(a) the claim form;

(b) the acknowledgment of service;

(c) the defence or counterclaim in a Part 7 claim; or

(d) application under Part 23.

(2) Every application must be supported by written evidence.

(3) Every application made on notice must be served personally, together with a copy of the written evidence, by the local authority on the person against whom the injunction is sought not less than 2 days before the hearing.

(Attention is drawn to rule 25.3(3)—applications without notice)

Anti-social Behaviour Act 2003, s.91

Add new paragraphs 65.9.1 and 65.9.2:

65.9.1 See commentary to CPR, r.65.8.

Power of arrest

65.9.2 See commentary at para. 65.8.1.

Injunction containing provisions to which a power of arrest is attached

65.10 **65.10—(1) Where a power of arrest is attached to a provision of an injunction on the application of a local authority under section 91(3) of the 2003 Act, the following rules in Section I of this Part shall apply—**

(a) rule 65.4; and

(b) paragraphs (1), (2), (4) and (5) of rule 65.6.

(2) CCR Order 29, rule 1 shall apply where an application is made in a county court to commit a person for breach of an injunction.

Anti-social Behaviour Act 2003, s.91

Add new paragraphs 65.10.1 to 65.10.2:

65.10.1 See commentary to CPR, r.65.8.

Power of arrest

65.10.2 See the commentary to CPR, r.65.4 and r.65.6 above.

Jurisdiction

65.10.3 See commentary at para. 65.3.6 and para. 65.6.5 above.

III. DEMOTION CLAIMS AND PROCEEDINGS RELATING TO DEMOTED TENANCIES

Scope of this Section and interpretation

65.11 **65.11—(1) This Section applies to—**

(a) claims by a landlord for an order under section 82A of the Housing Act 1985[1] or under section 6A of the Housing Act 1988[2] ("a demotion order"); and

(b) proceedings relating to a tenancy created by virtue of a demotion order.

(2) In this Section—

(a) "a demotion claim" means a claim made by a landlord for a demotion order; and

(b) "a demotion tenancy" means a tenancy created by virtue of a demotion order.

Housing Act 1985, s.82A

Add new paragraphs 65.11.1 to 65.11.3:

65.11.1 See para. 3A–356.

Housing Act 1985, s.6A

65.11.2 See para. 3A–697.

Editorial Introduction

65.11.3 The Anti–Social Behaviour Act 2003 amended the Housing Acts 1985, 1988 and 1996 to give county courts power to change secure or assured tenancies into demoted tenancies, lacking the rights that are associated with secure and assured tenancies. Applications for demoted tenancies may be made by local housing authorities, housing action trusts and registered social landlords. The court can only grant a demotion order if—

(a) a notice seeking a demotion order has been served or it is just and equitable to dispense with that requirement;

(b) it is satisfied that the tenant or a person residing in or visiting the dwelling–house has engaged or has threatened to engage in conduct to which Housing Act 1996, s.153A or s.153B (anti–social behaviour or use of premises for unlawful purposes) applies, and

(c) it is reasonable to make the order.

A demotion order—

(a) terminates the secure or assured tenancy with effect from the date specified in the order;

(b) if the tenant remains in occupation, creates a demoted tenancy; and

(c) makes it a term of the demoted tenancy that any arrears of rent payable at the termination of the secure tenancy become payable under the demoted tenancy. A demoted tenancy lacks security of tenure but before bringing a possession claim, a local authority landlord of a former secure demoted tenant must serve on the tenant a notice of proceedings which—

(i) states that the court will be asked to make a possession order;

(ii) sets out the reasons for the landlord's decision to apply for the order; and

(iii) specifies the date after which proceedings for the possession of the dwelling–house may be begun.

Housing Act 1996, s.143F provides a procedure for an internal review of the decision to seek possession.

If the former tenancy was an assured tenancy, the tenant becomes a demoted assured

---

[1] 1985 c. 68. This section was inserted by section 14 of the Anti–social Behaviour Act 2003

[2] 1988 c. 50. This section was inserted by section 14 of the Anti–social Behaviour Act 2003

shorthold tenant. If the landlord wishes to recover possession, it need only comply with Housing Act 1988, s.21 (para. 3A–819). There is no right to a review.

Demotion claims made in the alternative to possession claims

65.12 **65.12 Where a demotion order is claimed in the alternative to a possession order, the claimant must use the Part 55 procedure and Section I of Part 55 applies, except that the claim must be made in the county court for the district in which the property to which the claim relates is situated.**

A demotion order

Add new paragraphs 65.12.1 to 65.12.3:

65.12.1 See CPR, r.65.11.

Part 55 procedure

65.12.2 A demotion claim may be sought as an alternative to possession. In those circumstances, Part 55, the normal procedure for possession claims, applies. See CPR, r.55.3, the paragraphs which follow and the commentary thereto. If the landlord only seeks demotion, Part 65 applies—see below—although the procedure is very similar to that provided for by Part 55.

The county court for the district in which the property to which the claim relates is situated

65.12.3 CPR, r.55.3 gives a landlord the option of starting a possession claim in the High Court in certain circumstances. That option is disapplied in relation to demotion claims by CPR, r.62.12.

Other demotion claims

65.13 **65.13 Where a demotion claim is made other than in a possession claim, rules 65.14 to 65.19 apply.**

Demotion claim

Add new paragraph 65.13.1:

65.13.1 See CPR, r.65.11. If demotion is sought as an alternative to possession, CPR Pt 55, the normal procedure for possession claims, applies. If the landlord only seeks demotion, Part 65 applies, although the procedure is very similar to that provided for by Part 55.

Starting a demotion claim

65.14 **65.14—(1) The demotion claim must be made in the county court for the district in which the property to which the claim relates is situated.**

(2) The claim form and form of defence sent with it must be in the forms set out in the relevant practice direction.

(The relevant practice direction and Part 16 provide details about the contents of the particulars of claim)

Demotion claim

Add new paragraphs 65.14.1 and 65.14.2:

65.14.1 See CPR, r.65.11.

Court for the district in which the defendant resides or the conduct complained of occurred

65.14.2 See too PD65, para.6.1; *c.f.* CPR, rr.55.3, 56.2 and 65.3. In the light of CPR, r.3.10, issue in the wrong court is likely to be seen as an error of procedure which does not invalidate the step taken. In most cases judges would correct the error by transferring to the appropriate court. See, in another context, *Gwynedd CC v. Grunshaw* [2000] 1 W.L.R. 494, CA.

Particulars of claim

65.15 The particulars of claim must be filed and served with the claim form. **65.15**

Claim form

Add new paragraphs 65.15.1 and 65.15.2:

See PD65, para.6.2 and Form N6. **65.15.1**

Particulars of claim

See PD65, para.6.2 and Form N122. PD65, para.7.1 provides that the particulars of claim must— **65.15.2**

(1) state whether the demotion claim is made under Housing Act 1985, s.82A(2) or Housing Act 1988, s.6A(2);
(2) state whether the claimant is a local housing authority, a housing action trust or a registered social landlord;
(3) identify the property to which the claim relates;
(4) provide details about the tenancy, including the parties, the period of the tenancy, the rent, the dates on which the rent is payable and any statement of express terms of the tenancy served on the tenant under s.82A(7) or under s.6A(10); and
(5) state details of the conduct alleged.

PD65, para.9.1 provides that each party should wherever possible include all the evidence he or she wishes to present in his statement of case, verified by a statement of truth.

Hearing date

65.16—(1) The court will fix a date for the hearing when it issues the claim form. **65.16**

(2) The hearing date will be not less than 28 days from the date of issue of the claim form.

(3) The standard period between the issue of the claim form and the hearing will be not more than 8 weeks.

(4) The defendant must be served with the claim form and the particulars of claim not less than 21 days before the hearing date.

(Rule 3.1(2)(a) provides that the court may extend or shorten the time for compliance with any rule and rule 3.1(2)(b) provides that the court may adjourn or bring forward a hearing)

Hearing date

Add new paragraph 65.16.1:

These provisions are exactly the same as the comparable provisions which apply to possession claims—see CPR, r.55.5(1) and (3) and the commentary at para. 55.5.3. Note that PD65, para.8.2 provides that particular consideration should be given to abridging time between service and the hearing if— **65.16.1**

(1) the defendant has assaulted or threatened to assault the claimant, a member of the claimant's staff or another resident in the locality;
(2) there are reasonable grounds for fearing such an assault; or
(3) the defendant has caused serious damage or threatened to cause serious damage to the property or to the home or property of another resident in the locality.

Defendant's response

65.17—(1) An acknowledgement of service is not required and Part 10 does not apply. **65.17**

(2) Where the defendant does not file a defence within the time specified in rule 15.4 he may take part in any hearing but the court may take his failure to do so into account when deciding what order to make about costs.

(3) Part 12 (default judgment) does not apply in a demotion claim.

Defence

Add new paragraph 65.17.1:

65.17.1 See Form N11D. These provisions are exactly the same as the comparable provisions which apply to possession claims—see CPR, r.55.7(1) and (3) and the commentary at para. 55.7.4.

The hearing

65.18 **65.18—(1) At the hearing fixed in accordance with rule 65.16(1) or at any adjournment of that hearing the court may—**

(a) decide the demotion claim; or

(b) give case management directions.

(2) Where the demotion claim is genuinely disputed on grounds which appear to be substantial, case management directions given under paragraph (1)(b) will include the allocation of the demotion claim to a track or directions to enable it to be allocated.

(3) Except where—

(a) the demotion claim is allocated to the fast track or the multi-track; or

(b) the court directs otherwise,

any fact that needs to be proved by the evidence of witnesses at a hearing referred to in paragraph (1) may be proved by evidence in writing.

(Rule 32.2(1) sets out the general rule about evidence. Rule 32.2(2) provides that rule 32.2(1) is subject to any provision to the contrary).

(4) All witness statements must be filed and served at least two days before the hearing.

(5) Where the claimant serves the claim form and particulars of claim, he must produce at the hearing a certificate of service of those documents and rule 6.14(2)(a) does not apply.

Demotion claim

Add new paragraphs 65.18.1 to 65.18.4:

65.18.1 See CPR, r.65.11.

The hearing

65.18.2 These provisions are almost exactly the same as the comparable provisions which apply to possession claims—see CPR, r.55.8 and the commentary at para. 55.8.7.

Jurisdiction

65.18.3 District judges have jurisdiction to try demotion claims—see PD2B, para.11.1(b).

Evidence

65.18.4 See PD65, para.6.3. The claimant's evidence should include details of the conduct alleged.

Allocation

65.19 **65.19 When the court decides the track for a demotion claim, the matters to which it shall have regard include—**

(a) **the matters set out in rule 26.8; and**
(b) **the nature and extent of the conduct alleged.**

Demotion claim

Add new paragraphs 65.19.1 and 65.19.2:

65.19.1 See CPR, r.65.11.

Allocation

65.19.2 *c.f.* CPR, r.55.9. See the commentary at para. 26.8.4.

Proceedings relating to demoted tenancies

65.20 **65.20 A practice direction may make provision about proceedings relating to demoted tenancies.**

Demoted tenancy

Add new paragraphs 65.20.1 and 65.20.2:

65.20.1 See CPR, r.65.11.

A practice direction

65.20.2 PD65, para.11.1 provides that proceedings as to whether a statement supplied in pursuance to Housing Act 1996, s.143M(4)(b) (see para. 3A-1088—written statement of certain terms of tenancy) is accurate must be brought under the Part 8 procedure.

IV. ANTI-SOCIAL BEHAVIOUR ORDERS UNDER THE CRIME AND DISORDER ACT 1998

Scope of this Section and interpretation

65.21 **65.21—(1) This Section applies to applications in proceedings in a county court under sub-sections (2), (3) or (3B) of section 1B of the Crime and Disorder Act 1998[1] by a relevant authority, and to applications for interim orders under section 1D of that Act.**

(2) **In this Section—**

(a) **"the 1998 Act" means the Crime and Disorder Act 1998;**
(b) **"relevant authority" has the same meaning as in section 1(1A) of the 1998 Act; and**
(c) **"the principal proceedings" means any proceedings in a county court.**

Crime and Disorder Act 1998, s.1B

Add new paragraphs 65.21.1 to 65.21.5:

65.21.1 See 3A-1401.1.

Editorial introduction

65.21.2 Part I of the Crime and Disorder Act 1998 included provisions which enable Magistrates Courts to grant anti-social behaviour orders ("ASBOs"), parenting orders and child safety orders. Among the grounds for the grant of an ASBO is a finding that "the person has acted in an anti-social manner, that is to say, in a manner that caused or was likely to cause harassment, alarm or distress to two or more persons not of the same household as himself". An ASBO may only be granted if such an order is necessary to protect relevant persons from further anti-social acts (s.1(1)). When considering whether a person's conduct has caused or is likely to cause harassment, alarm or distress to others within the meaning of Crime and Disorder Act 1998, s.1(1)(a) "likely" means "more probable than not". The

[1] 1998 c. 37. Sections 1(1A) and 1B were amended by section 85 of the Anti-social Behaviour Act 2003 (c. 38).

likelihood has to be proved to the criminal standard (see *Chief Constable of Lancashire v. Potter* [2003] EWHC 2272 (Admin) and *R. (on the application of McCann) v. Manchester Crown Court* [2002] UKHL 39; [2003] 1 A.C. 787; [2002] 3 W.L.R. 1313). An ASBO may prohibit the defendant from doing anything described in the order. The prohibitions that may be imposed by an ASBO are "those necessary for the purpose of protecting persons (whether relevant persons or persons elsewhere in England and Wales) from further anti-social acts by the defendant" (s.1(4) and (6)). ASBOs have effect for the period (not less than two years) specified in the order or until further order (s.1(7)). Breach of an ASBO may be punished on summary conviction by imprisonment for a term not exceeding six months or a fine or both; or on conviction on indictment, by imprisonment for a term not exceeding five years or to a fine, or to both (s.1(10)). Breach of such orders amounts to a criminal offence.

The power to grant ASBOs has been extended to county courts since April 1, 2003—see Police Reform Act 2002, s.63, inserting s.1B into the Crime and Disorder Act 1998 and the Police Reform Act 2002 (Commencement No.4) Order 2003, S.I. 2003 No. 808. Anti-social Behaviour Act 2003, s.85 also amends s.1B to allow a relevant authority which considers that a person who is not a party to county court proceedings has acted in an anti-social manner, and that those anti-social acts are material to the proceedings, to apply for that person to be joined to the county court proceedings so that the county court may make an ASBO. A relevant authority may also apply to be joined to county court proceedings if it is not already a party so that it may apply for an ASBO. These changes came into effect on March 31, 2004.

A relevant authority

65.21.3 See the Crime and Disorder Act 1998, s.1(1A), namely the council for a local government area, a county council, the chief officer of police of any police force maintained for a police area, the chief constable of the British Transport Police Force, a social landlord who provides or manages any houses or hostel which is registered under Housing Act 1996, s.1 or a housing action trust (see Housing Act 1988, s.62).

Service

65.21.4 PD65, para.13.1 provides that an ASBO made under s.1B(4) or an interim order under s.1D must be served personally on the defendant.

Jurisdiction

65.21.5 PD2B, para.8.1A provides that district judges have jurisdiction to make ASBOs under s.1B and interim ASBOs under s.1D.

Application where the relevant authority is a party in principal proceedings

65.22 **65.22—(1) Subject to paragraph (2)—**

(a) **where the relevant authority is the claimant in the principal proceedings, an application under section 1B(2) of the 1998 Act for an order under section 1B(4) of the 1998 Act must be made in the claim form; and**

(b) **where the relevant authority is a defendant in the principal proceedings, an application for an order must be made by application notice which must be filed with the defence.**

(2) **Where the relevant authority becomes aware of the circumstances that lead it to apply for an order after its claim is issued or its defence filed, the application must be made by application notice as soon as possible thereafter.**

(3) **Where the application is made by application notice, it should normally be made on notice to the person against whom the order is sought.**

Relevant Authority

Add new paragraphs 65.22.1 to 65.22.3:

65.22.1 See CPR, r.65.21 and the Crime and Disorder Act 1998, s.1(1A) (para. 3A–1401.1), namely the council for a local government area, a county council, the chief officer of police of any police force maintained for a police area, the chief constable of the British Transport Police Force, a social landlord who provides or manages any houses or hostel which is registered under Housing Act 1996, s.1 or a housing action trust (see Housing Act 1988, s.62).

Principal proceedings

65.22.2 See Crime and Disorder Act 1998, s.1B (para. 3A–1401.8) and CPR, r.65.21— *i.e.* any proceedings in a county court.

Application notice

65.22.3 See CPR, r.23.3 and Form N244. An application must be made as soon as possible after the authority becomes aware of the circumstances that lead it to apply for an order—see CPR, r.65.22(2). Such an application should normally be made on notice in accordance with CPR, r.23.7— *i.e.* at least three days before the court is to deal with the application—but see CPR, r.23.4.

Application by a relevant authority to join a person to the principal proceedings

65.23 **65.23—(1) An application under section 1B(3B) of the 1998 Act by a relevant authority which is a party to the principal proceedings to join a person to the principal proceedings must be made—**

(a) in accordance with Section I of Part 19;

(b) in the same application notice as the application for an order under section 1B(4) of the 1998 Act against the person; and

(c) as soon as possible after the relevant authority considers that the criteria in section 1B(3A) of the 1998 Act are met.

(2) The application notice must contain—

(a) the relevant authority's reasons for claiming that the person's anti–social acts are material in relation to the principal proceedings; and

(b) details of the anti–social acts alleged.

(3) The application should normally be made on notice to the person against whom the order is sought.

Part 19

Add new paragraphs 65.23.1 to 65.23.4:

65.23.1 See in particular CPR, r.19.4.

Relevant authority

65.23.2 See CPR, r.65.21 and the Crime and Disorder Act 1998, s.1(1A), namely the council for a local government area, a county council, the chief officer of police of any police force maintained for a police area, the chief constable of the British Transport Police Force, a social landlord who provides or manages any houses or hostel which is registered under Housing Act 1996, s.1 or a housing action trust (see Housing Act 1988, s.62).

Principal proceedings

65.23.3 See Crime and Disorder Act 1998, s.1B and CPR, r.65.21— *i.e.* any proceedings in a county court.

Application to join a person

65.23.4 See Crime and Disorder Act 1998, s.1B(3C) at 3A–1401.8. A person may only be joined if his or her anti–social acts are material in relation to the principal proceedings. The application should be made in Form N244 and must contain the relevant authority's reasons for claiming that the person's anti–social acts are material in relation to the principal proceedings and details of the anti–social acts alleged. Such applications should normally be made on notice in accordance with CPR, r.23.7— *i.e.* at least three days before the court is to deal with the application—but see CPR, r.23.4.

Application where the relevant authority is not party in principal proceedings

65.24 **65.24—(1) Where the relevant authority is not a party to the principal proceedings—**

(a) **an application under section 1B(3) of the 1998 Act to be made a party must be made in accordance with Section I of Part 19; and**

(b) **the application to be made a party and the application for an order under section 1B(4) of the 1998 Act must be made in the same application notice.**

(2) **The applications—**

(a) **must be made as soon as possible after the authority becomes aware of the principal proceedings; and**

(b) **should normally be made on notice to the person against whom the order is sought.**

Relevant authority

Add new paragraphs 65.24.1 to 65.24.4:

65.24.1 See CPR, r.65.21 and the Crime and Disorder Act 1998, s.1(1A), namely the council for a local government area, a county council, the chief officer of police of any police force maintained for a police area, the chief constable of the British Transport Police Force, a social landlord who provides or manages any houses or hostel which is registered under Housing Act 1996, s.1 or a housing action trust (see Housing Act 1988, s.62).

Principal proceedings

65.24.2 See Crime and Disorder Act 1998, s.1B and CPR, r.65.21— *i.e.* any proceedings in a county court.

Part 19

65.24.3 See in particular CPR, r.19.4.

Application to be joined

65.24.4 See Crime and Disorder Act 1998 s.1B(3) at para. 3A–1401.8. The application should be made in Form N244. It should normally be made on notice in accordance with CPR, r.23.7— *i.e.* at least three days before the court is to deal with the application—but see CPR, r.23.4.

Evidence

65.25 **65.25 An application for an order under section 1B(4) of the 1998 Act must be accompanied by written evidence, which must include evidence that section 1E of the 1998 Act has been complied with.**

Written evidence

Add new paragraphs 65.25.1 to 65.25.3:

65.25.1 This may either be contained in Part C of the application notice in Form N244 or in a separate witness statement.

An order under Crime and Disorder Act 1998, s.1B(4)

65.25.2 *i.e.* an ASBO. See 3A–1401.8.

Crime and Disorder Act 1998, s.1E

65.25.3 Section 1E imposes consultation requirements—see para. 3A–1401.19 and *McC v. Wigan MBC*, October 30, 2003 where the lead role in seeking ASBOs was taken by a management company, which, although solely owned by the council, was a separate entity to the council. As such, in the absence of authorisation from the council, it was not authorised to consult. It was also apparent that there was a lack of knowledge on the part of the tenancy relations manager about the Home Office Guidance and an unstructured approach to the process. However these failings did not result in a substantial failure to comply with the consultation requirements. The requirement for consultation between the police and local authority in s.1E is fulfilled by substantial compliance, even though there may not have been full compliance. Information had been exchanged before making the application.

Application for an interim order

65.26—(1) An application for an interim order under section 1D of the 1998 Act must be made in accordance with Part 25. **65.26**

(2) **The application should normally be made—**

(a) **in the claim form or application notice seeking the order; and**

(b) **on notice to the person against whom the order is sought.**

Interim order

Add new paragraphs 65.26.1 to 65.26.3:

65.26.1 See Crime and Disorder Act 1998, s.1D. The court may make an interim ASBO if it considers that it is just to make such an order pending the determination of the main application. Interim ASBOs should be made for a fixed period, but may be varied, renewed or discharged.

Jurisdiction

65.26.2 PD2B, para.8.1A provides that district judges have jurisdiction to make an interim ASBO under s.1D.

Service

65.26.3 PD65, para.13.1 provides that an order under s.1B(4) or an interim order under s.1D must be served personally on the defendant.

V. PROCEEDINGS UNDER THE PROTECTION FROM HARASSMENT ACT 1997

Scope of this Section

65.27 This Section applies to proceedings under section 3 of the Protection from Harassment Act 1997[1] ("the 1997 Act"). **65.27**

Editorial introduction

Add new paragraph 65.27.1:

65.27.1 Protection from Harassment Act 1997, s.1(1) provides that a person must not pursue a course of conduct (a) which amounts to harassment of another, and (b) which he knows or ought to know amounts to harassment of the other— *i.e.* if a reasonable person in possession of the same information would think the course of conduct amounted to harassment of the other. Such conduct is a criminal offence. In addition county courts may grant injunctions and award damages. Breach of an injunction is an arrestable criminal offence.

Claims under section 3 of the 1997 Act

65.28 A claim under section 3 of the 1997 Act— **65.28**

(a) **shall be subject to the Part 8 procedure; and**

(b) **must be commenced—**

(i) **if in the High Court, in the Queen's Bench Division;**

[1] 1997 c. 40

(ii) **if in the county court, in the court for the district in which the defendant resides or carries on business or the court for the district in which the claimant resides or carries on business.**

Subject to the Part 8 procedure

Add new paragraphs 65.28.1 and 65.28.2:

65.28.1 One effect of this is that claims must be issued in Form N208. They are automatically allocated to the multi–track. However PD2B, para.8.1 provides that district judges have jurisdiction to grant injunctions under Protection from Harassment Act 1997, s.3. However they do not have jurisdiction to make orders committing a person to prison for breach of a Protection from Harassment Act 1997 injunction. See PD2B, para.8.3 and CCR O.29, r.1. In that context "judge" means "circuit judge".

Court for the district in which the defendant or claimant resides or carries on business

65.28.2 *c.f.* CPR, rr.55.3 and 56.2. In the light of CPR, r.3.10, issue in the wrong court is likely to be seen as an error of procedure which does not invalidate the step taken. In most cases judges would correct the error by transferring to the appropriate court. See, in another context, *Gwynedd CC v. Grunshaw* [2000] 1 W.L.R. 494, CA.

Applications for issue of a warrant of arrest under section 3(3) of the 1997 Act

65.29 **65.29—(1) An application for a warrant of arrest under section 3(3) of the 1997 Act—**

(a) **must be made in accordance with Part 23; and**
(b) **may be made without notice.**

(2) **The application notice must be supported by affidavit evidence which must—**

(a) **set out the grounds for the application;**
(b) **state whether the claimant has informed the police of the conduct of the defendant as described in the affidavit; and**
(c) **state whether, to the claimant's knowledge, criminal proceedings are being pursued.**

Warrant

Add new paragraph 65.29.1:

65.29.1 PD65, para.14.1 provides that a warrant of arrest under s.3(3) may only be issued if the application is substantiated on oath and the judge has reasonable grounds for believing that the defendant has done anything prohibited by the injunction.

Proceedings following arrest

65.30 **65.30—(1) The judge before whom a person is brought following his arrest may—**

(a) **deal with the matter; or**
(b) **adjourn the proceedings.**

(2) **Where the proceedings are adjourned and the arrested person is released—**

(a) **the matter must be dealt with (whether by the same or another judge) within 28 days of the date on which the arrested person appears in court; and**
(b) **the arrested person must be given not less than 2 days' notice of the hearing.**

Jurisdiction

Add new paragraph 65.30.1:

District judges do not have jurisdiction to make orders committing a person to prison for breach of a Protection from Harassment Act 1997 injunction. See PD2B, para.8.3 and CCR O.29, r.1. In that context "judge" means "circuit judge". **65.30.1**

PRACTICE DIRECTION—ANTI-SOCIAL BEHAVIOUR AND HARASSMENT

This Practice Direction supplements CPR Part 65 **65PD.1**

Add new Practice Direction 65:

I. HOUSING ACT 1996 INJUNCTIONS

Issuing the Claim

1.1 An application for an injunction under section Chapter III of Part V of the 1996 Act must be made by form N16A and for the purposes of applying the practice direction that supplements Part 8 to applications under Section I of Part 65, form N16A shall be treated as the Part 8 claim form.

Warrant of Arrest on an Application under Section 155(3) of the 1996 Act

2.1 In accordance with section 155(4) of the 1996 Act, a warrant of arrest on an application under section 155(3) of that Act shall not be issued unless— **65PD.2**

(1) the application is substantiated on oath; and

(2) the judge has reasonable grounds for believing that the defendant has failed to comply with the injunction.

Application for Bail

3.1 An application for bail by a person arrested under— **65PD.3**

(1) a power of arrest attached to an injunction under Chapter III of Part V of the 1996 Act; or

(2) a warrant of arrest issued on an application under section 155(3) of that Act,

may be made either orally or in an application notice.

3.2 An application notice seeking bail must contain—

(1) the full name of the person making the application;

(2) the address of the place where the person making the application is detained at the time when the application is made;

(3) the address where the person making the application would reside if he were to be granted bail;

(4) the amount of the recognizance in which he would agree to be bound; and

(5) the grounds on which the application is made and, where previous application has been refused, full details of any change in circumstances which has occurred since that refusal.

3.3 A copy of the application notice must be served on the person who obtained the injunction.

Remand for Medical Examination and Report

4.1 Section 156(4) of the 1996 Act provides that the judge has power to make an order under section 35 of the Mental Health Act 1983 in **65PD.4**

certain circumstances. If he does so attention is drawn to section 35(8) of that Act, which provides that a person remanded to hospital under that section may obtain at his own expense an independent report on his mental condition from a registered medical practitioner chosen by him and apply to the court on the basis of it for his remand to be terminated under section 35(7).

III. DEMOTION CLAIMS

Demotion Claims Made in the Alternative to Possession Claims

65PD.5 **5.1** If the claim relates to residential property let on a tenancy and if the claim includes a demotion claim, the particulars of claim must—

(1) state whether the demotion claim is a claim under section 82A(2) of the 1985 Act or under section 6A(2) of the 1988 Act;
(2) state whether the claimant is a local housing authority, a housing action trust or a registered social landlord;
(3) provide details of any statement of express terms of the tenancy served on the tenant under section 82A(7) of the 1985 Act or under section 6A(10) of the 1988 Act, as applicable; and
(4) state details of the conduct alleged.

Other Demotion Claims

65PD.6 **6.1** Demotion claims must be made in the county court for the district in which the property to which the claim relates is situated.

6.2 The claimant must use the appropriate claim form and particulars of claim form set out in Table 1 to the Part 4 practice direction. The defence must be in form N11D as appropriate.

6.3 The claimant's evidence should include details of the conduct alleged.

Particulars of claim

65PD.7 **7.1** In a demotion claim the particulars of claim must—

(1) state whether the demotion claim is an claim under section 82A(2) of the 1985 Act or under section 6A(2) of the 1988 Act;
(2) state whether the claimant is a local housing authority, a housing action trust or a registered social landlord;
(3) identify the property to which the claim relates;
(4) provide the following details about the tenancy to which the demotion claim relates—
  (a) the parties to the tenancy;
  (b) the period of the tenancy;
  (c) the amount of the rent;
  (d) the dates on which the rent is payable; and
  (e) any statement of express terms of the tenancy served on the tenant under section 82A(7) of the 1985 Act or under section 6A(10) of the 1988 Act, as applicable; and
(5) state details of the conduct alleged.

Hearing Date

65PD.8 **8.1** The court may use its powers under rules 3.1(2)(a) and (b) to shorten the time periods set out in rules 65.16(2), (3) and (4).

8.2 Particular consideration should be given to the exercise of this power if—

(1) the defendant, or a person for whom the defendant is responsible, has assaulted or threatened to assault—

(a) the claimant;

(b) a member of the claimant's staff; or

(c) another resident in the locality;

(2) there are reasonable grounds for fearing such an assault; or

(3) the defendant, or a person for whom the defendant is responsible, has caused serious damage or threatened to cause serious damage to the property or to the home or property of another resident in the locality.

8.3 Where paragraph 8.2 applies but the case cannot be determined at the first hearing fixed under rule 65.16, the court will consider what steps are needed to finally determine the case as quickly as reasonably practicable.

The Hearing

65PD.9 **9.1** Attention is drawn to rule 65.18(3). Each party should wherever possible include all the evidence he wishes to present in his statement of case, verified by a statement of truth.

9.2 The claimant's evidence should include details of the conduct to which section 153A or 153B of the 1996 Act applies and in respect of which the demotion claim is made.

9.3 If—

(1) the maker of a witness statement does not attend a hearing; and

(2) the other party disputes material evidence contained in the statement,

the court will normally adjourn the hearing so that oral evidence can be given.

III. PROCEEDINGS RELATING TO DEMOTED TENANCIES

Proceedings for the Possession of a Demoted Tenancy

65PD.10 **10.1** Proceedings against a tenant of a demoted tenancy for possession must be brought under the procedure in Part 55 (Possession Claims).

Proceedings in Relation to a Written Statement of Demoted Tenancy Terms

65PD.11 **11.1** Proceedings as to whether a statement supplied in pursuance to section 143M(4)(b) of the 1996 Act (written statement of certain terms of tenancy) is accurate must be brought under the procedure in Part 8.

Recovery of Costs

65PD.12 **12.1** Attention is drawn to section 143N(4) of the 1996 Act which provides that if a person takes proceedings under Chapter 1A of the 1996 Act in the High Court which he could have taken in the county court, he is not entitled to recover any costs.

IV. ANTI-SOCIAL BEHAVIOUR ORDERS UNDER THE CRIME AND DISORDER ACT 1998

Service of an Order under Sections 1B(4) or 1D of the 1998 Act

65PD.13 **13.1** An order under section 1B(4) or an interim order under section 1D of the 1998 Act must be served personally on the defendant.

13.2 Application to join a person to the principal proceedings

Except as provided in paragraph 13.3, an application by a relevant authority under section 1B(3B) of the 1998 Act to join a person to the principal proceedings may only be made against a person aged 18 or over.

13.3 Pilot scheme : application to join a child to the principal proceedings

(1) A pilot scheme shall operate from 1st October 2004 to 31st March 2006 in the county courts specified below, under which a relevant authority may—
  (a) apply under section 1B(3B) of the 1998 Act to join a child to the principal proceedings; and
  (b) if that child is so joined, apply for an order under section 1B(4) of the 1998 Act against him.

(2) In this paragraph, "child" means a person aged under 18.

(3) The county courts in which the pilot scheme shall operate are Bristol, Central London, Clerkenwell, Dewsbury, Huddersfield, Leicester, Manchester, Oxford, Tameside, Wigan and Wrexham.

(4) Attention is drawn to the provisions of Part 21 and its practice direction: in particular as to the requirement for a child to have a litigation friend unless the court makes an order under rule 21.2(3), and as to the procedure for appointment of a litigation friend. The Official Solicitor may be invited to act as litigation friend where there is no other willing and suitable person.

(5) Rule 21.3(2)(b) shall not apply to an application under the pilot scheme, and sub-paragraph (6) shall apply instead.

(6) A relevant authority may not, without the permission of the court, take any step in an application to join a child to the principal proceedings, except
  (a) filing and serving its application notice; and
  (b) applying for the appointment of a litigation friend under rule 21.6, unless the child has a litigation friend.

V. PROCEEDINGS UNDER THE PROTECTION FROM HARASSMENT ACT 1997

Warrant of Arrest on Application under Section 3(3) of the 1997 Act

65PD.14 **14.1** In accordance with section 3(5) of the 1997 Act, a warrant of arrest on an application under section 3(3) of that Act may only be issued if—

(1) the application is substantiated on oath; and

(2) the judge has reasonable grounds for believing that the defendant has done anything which he is prohibited from doing by the injunction.

PART 69

COURT'S POWER TO APPOINT A RECEIVER

Editorial Introduction

69.0.2 *In the third paragraph, add after "for the purpose of preserving property":*

during the course of litigation

Application for discharge of receiver

Existing rule 69.10 is renumbered 69.10(1).

69.10—(1) **A receiver or any party may apply for the receiver to be discharged on completion of his duties.** **69.10**

Add new rule 69.10(2):

(2) **The application notice must be served on the persons who were required under rule 69.4 to be served with the order appointing the receiver.**

PART 70

GENERAL RULES ABOUT ENFORCEMENT OF JUDGMENTS AND ORDERS

Enforcement of High Court judgment or order in a county court—rule 70.3

Paragraph 3 is renumbered 3.1.

In sub–paragraph 3.1(3), for "sheriff's return" substitute: **70PD.3**

(3) relevant enforcement officer's return

Add new paragraph 3.2:

In this paragraph and paragraph 7—

(1) "enforcement officer" means an individual who is authorised to act as an enforcement officer under the Courts Act 2003; and

(2) "relevant enforcement officer" means—

(a) in relation to a writ of execution which is directed to a single enforcement officer, that officer;

(b) in relation to a writ of execution which is directed to two or more enforcement officers, the officer to whom the writ is allocated.

Payment of debt after issue of enforcement proceedings

In paragraph 7.2, for "Sheriff's Office" substitute:

7.2 relevant enforcement officer **70PD.7**

PART 71

ORDERS TO OBTAIN INFORMATION FROM JUDGMENT DEBTORS

Judgment creditor's affidavit

Rule 71.5(1)(c) was previously omitted:

71.5—(1) (c) **stating how much of the judgment debt remains unpaid.** **71.5**

PART 74

ENFORCEMENT OF JUDGMENTS IN DIFFERENT JURISDICTIONS

Protection of Trading Interests Act 1980

Add new paragraph 74.11.19.1:

74.11.19.1 Section 5 of the Act prohibits the recovery of multiple damages pursuant to a foreign judgment. However, the prohibition does not prevent the recovery of ordinary compensatory damages for private causesof action similar to those available under English law: *Lewis v. Eliades* [2003] EWCA Civ 1758; [2004] 1 W.L.R. 692.

Chancery Division

Delete paragraph 74.13.4.

74.13.4

SCHEDULE 1

RSC ORDER 45 – ENFORCEMENT OF JUDGMENTS AND ORDERS: GENERAL

Amendment

Existing title is amended. Delete exisiting text of paragraph sc45.0.5 and substitute:

sc45.0.5 The amendment foreshadowed in this paragraph in the main work duly came into force on April 1, 2004. High Court Enforcement Officers (and not the Sheriff) are now responsible for the execution of High Court writs of enforcement.The forms of the various writs (but not their numbers) have changed accordingly and are addressed to the HCEO. For the relevant regulations see the next paragraph.

Add The High Court Enforcement Officers Regulations 2004 (S.I. 2004 No. 400):

sc45.0.6

The High Court Enforcement Officers Regulations 2004

S.I. 2004 No. 400

PART 1

INTRODUCTION

Citation and commencement

1. These Regulations may be cited as the High Court Enforcement Officers Regulations 2004 and shall come into force on 15th March 2004.

Interpretation

sc45.0.7 **2.**—(1) In these Regulations—

(a) "application" means an application by an individual for authorisation to act as an enforcement officer;

(b) "district" means a district set out in Schedule 1 to these Regulations;

(c) "enforcement officer" means an individual authorised by the Lord Chancellor under Schedule 7 to act as such;

(d) "Schedule 7" means Schedule 7 to the Courts Act 2003.

(2) References in these Regulations to—

(a) the Lord Chancellor shall include a person acting on his behalf under Schedule 7;

(b) a writ of execution shall not include—

(i) a writ of sequestration; or

(ii) a writ relating to ecclesiastical property.

Districts for enforcement of writs of execution by enforcement officers

3.—(1) For the purposes of Schedule 7 and these Regulations, England and Wales is to be divided into 105 districts. **sc45.0.8**

(2) Such districts correspond with the postal areas for England and Wales and are listed in Schedule 1 to these Regulations.

PART 2

AUTHORISATION OF ENFORCEMENT OFFICERS

Conditions to be satisfied

4.—(1) An individual will not be authorised to act as an enforcement officer unless the conditions in paragraph (2) are satisfied. **sc45.0.9**

(2) The individual must not —

(a) have been convicted of any criminal offence—
 (i) for which he received a custodial sentence; or
 (ii) involving dishonesty or violence;
(b) be liable for any unpaid fines;
(c) be liable for any court judgment granted within the last 6 years which remains unsatisfied;
(d) be an undischarged bankrupt;
(e) have been disqualifed from acting as a director of a company within the last 6 years;
(f) carry on or be involved in any business relating to or including the purchase or sale of debts.

Application procedure

5.—(1) An application for authorisation to act as an enforcement officer may only be made by an individual and must— **sc45.0.10**

(a) be made in writing; and
(b) contain a statement signed and dated by the individual certifying that the contents of the application are true.

(2) The application must contain the following information about the individual—

(a) his name, address and date of birth;
(b) whether he has been convicted of any criminal offence, whether or not punishable by imprisonment, and if so details of each offence and conviction;
(c) whether he is liable for any unpaid fines and if so appropriate details;
(d) whether he is or has been liable for any court judgment and if so appropriate details including whether any judgment remains unsatisfied;
(e) whether he is or has ever been subject to any of the following proceedings and if so with what result—
 (i) bankruptcy proceedings;
 (ii) an administration order under section 112 of the County Courts Act 1984;
 (iii) a deed of arrangement under the Deeds of Arrangement Act 1914 or an individual voluntary arrangement under Part VIII of the Insolvency Act 1986;

(iv) proceedings under the Company Directors Disqualification Act 1986;
(v) insolvency proceedings in relation to any partnership in which he was a partner or any company of which he was a director; or
(vi) any other proceedings under the Insolvency Act 1986.

(3) The application shall also—
(a) specify to which district or districts the applicant is requesting assignment; and
(b) include details and documentation giving evidence of—
(i) any relevant insurance policies held by the applicant;
(ii) any licence held by the applicant under the Consumer Credit Act 1974;
(iii) any notification given by the applicant to the Information Commissioner under section 18 of the Data Protection Act 1998;
(iv) any current membership held by the applicant of a professional body which is listed in Schedule 2 to these Regulations as a professional body recognised by the Lord Chancellor;
(v) the bank account or accounts held by the applicant through which it is proposed that monies recovered on behalf of judgment debtors are to be collected and paid;
(vi) the applicant's relevant experience;
(vii) the applicant's knowledge of the laws and the practice and procedure of the High Court in relation to enforcement of debts;
(viii) the applicant's business plan including any person whom the applicant is proposing to engage to act on his behalf to assist with his work as an enforcement officer;
(ix) the applicant's policies in relation to the selection and employment of staff; and
(x) any existing or previous businesses of the applicant.

(4) Where the applicant has an existing business, the application shall be accompanied by audited or certified accounts of the applicant and of any company associated with the applicant for the preceding 3 years, or for the period of trading if this is shorter.

(5) In the case of any application, the Lord Chancellor may require further details of information already given or any additional information or documentation which seems to him to be necessary.

(6) For the purposes of this regulation and regulation 8, "relevant insurance policies" means—
(a) professional indemnity insurance;
(b) public liability insurance;
(c) employers liability insurance, where the individual is an employer; and
(d) goods in transit insurance, where the individual will be conducting his own removals.

Authorisation and assignment

sc45.0.11 **6.**—(1) The Lord Chancellor may take account, in deciding whether to authorise an individual to act as an enforcement officer, of—
(a) the information contained in or provided with the individual's application; and

(b) any other relevant information available to him.

(2) Upon being authorised to act as an enforcement officer, an individual may be assigned to—

(a) any or all of the districts to which he has requested assignment; and

(b) any other district or districts, if the Lord Chancellor considers it necessary or expedient in order to ensure that sufficient enforcement officers are assigned to each district.

PART 3

POST AUTHORISATION

Duty to execute writs

7. Once assigned to a district or a number of districts, the enforcement officer must undertake enforcement action for all writs of execution received which are to be executed at addresses which fall within his assigned district. **sc45.0.12**

Conditions to be satisfied following authorisation

8. Every enforcement officer is under a continuing duty to— **sc45.0.13**

(a) successfully complete any required training;

(b) comply with any requirements set by the Lord Chancellor for his continuous professional development;

(c) hold current relevant insurance policies;

(d) hold a bank account through which monies recovered on behalf of judgment debtors are to be collected and paid;

(e) produce to the Lord Chancellor—

(i) annual audited or certified accounts;

(ii) performance statistics when requested; and

(iii) such other information or documentation relevant to his work as an enforcement officer as may be required.

Change of details

9. An enforcement officer must immediately give the Lord Chancellor written notification of any change in— **sc45.0.14**

(a) his name;

(b) his address;

(c) the bank account or accounts held by him through which monies recovered on behalf of judgment debtors are collected and paid; or

(d) the information or documentation contained in his application for authorisation to act as an enforcement officer.

Changes to assignment

10.—(1) An enforcement officer may at any time apply to the Lord Chancellor to change the districts to which he is assigned. **sc45.0.15**

(2) An application under paragraph (1) must be made in writing and must include a declaration of any changes in the information and documentation contained in the individual's application for authorisation to act as an enforcement officer.

(3) An enforcement officer may at any time be assigned to an additional district or districts without having applied for such assignment, if the

Lord Chancellor considers it necessary or expedient in order to ensure that sufficient enforcement officers are assigned to each district.

Resignation

sc45.0.16 **11.** If an enforcement officer wishes to resign from his appointment he must provide the Lord Chancellor with at least 28 days' written notice of his intended resignation.

Termination of authorisation or assignment

sc45.0.17 **12.**—(1) The Lord Chancellor may at any time terminate—

(a) the authorisation of an individual to act as an enforcement officer; or

(b) the assignment of an enforcement officer to any one or more of the districts to which he is assigned,

on any of the grounds in paragraph (2).

(2) The grounds are that—

(a) it would be in the public interest to do so;

(b) any of the—

(i) information provided in the application for authorisation; or

(ii) documentation supplied,

under regulation 5 is found to be incomplete or untrue;

(c) the enforcement officer or any person acting on his behalf who assists with his work as an enforcement officer has behaved in a manner which the Lord Chancellor reasonably considers to be unprofessional or unacceptable; or

(d) the enforcement officer has failed to satisfy one or more of the conditions of regulation 8.

(3) Where practicable, the Lord Chancellor when considering whether to terminate the authorisation or assignment of an enforcement officer shall firstly notify the enforcement officer of the reasons and provide the enforcement officer with a reasonable opportunity to—

(a) make representations about the Lord Chancellor's reasons for proposing to terminate his authorisation or assignment; and

(b) remedy the circumstances giving rise to the Lord Chancellor's proposal to terminate his authorisation or assignment.

PART 4

MISCELLANEOUS

Fees

sc45.0.18 **13.**—(1) Schedule 3 to these Regulations sets out the fees that may be charged by enforcement officers.

(2) Where the execution of a writ of fieri facias is completed by sale, fees 1, 2, 3, 4, 5, 6 (1) and 7 under Schedule 3 may be levied by deducting them from the proceeds of sale.

(3) Where a writ is withdrawn or satisfied or its execution is stopped, the fees set out under Schedule 3 must be paid by—

(a) the person upon whose application the writ was issued; or

(b) the person at whose instance the execution is stopped,

as the case may be.

(4) An enforcement officer or a party liable to pay any fees under

Schedule 3 may apply to a costs judge or a district judge of the High Court for an assessment of the amount payable, by the detailed assessment procedure in accordance with the Civil Procedure Rules 1998 .

Directories

14. Directories containing details of all current enforcement officers, the districts to which they have been assigned and the addresses to which writs of execution issued from the High Court to enforcement officers are to be sent shall be published and available for inspection at— **sc45.0.19**

(a) the Royal Courts of Justice;
(b) district registries of the High Court; and
(c) county courts,

during the hours when the offices of such courts are open.

Walking possession agreement

15. Schedule 4 to these Regulations sets out the form of an agreement under which an enforcement officer may take walking possession of goods. **sc45.0.20**

REGULATION 3

SCHEDULE 1

DISTRICTS FOR WRITS OF EXECUTION ENFORCED BY ENFORCEMENT OFFICERS

sc45.0.21

District	*Postal Area*
Bath	BA
Birmingham	B
Blackburn	BB
Bolton	BL
Bournemouth	BH
Bradford	BD
Brighton	BN
Bristol	BS
Bromley	BR
Cambridge	CB
Canterbury	CT
Cardiff	CF
Carlisle	CA
Chelmsford	CM
Chester	CH
Cleveland (Teesside)	TS
Colchester	CO
Coventry	CV
Crewe	CW
Croydon	CR
Darlington	DL
Dartford	DA
Derby	DE
Doncaster	DN
Dorchester	DT
Dudley	DY
Durham	DH
Enfield	EN

District	*Postal Area*
Exeter	EX
Fylde (Blackpool)	FY
Gloucester	GL
Guildford	GU
Halifax	HX
Harrogate	HG
Harrow	HA
Hemel Hempstead	HP
Hereford	HR
Huddersfield	HD
Hull	HU
Ilford	IG
Ipswich	IP
Kingston upon Thames	KT
Lancaster	LA
Leeds	LS
Leicester	LE
Lincoln	LN
Liverpool	L
Llandridnod Wells	LD
Llandudno	LL
London East	E
London East Central	EC
London North	N
London North West	NW
London South East	SE
London South West	SW
London West	W
London West Central	WC
Luton	LU
Manchester	M
Medway	ME
Milton Keynes	MK
Newcastle	NE
Newport	NP
Northampton	NN
Norwich	NR
Nottingham	NG
Oldham	OL
Oxford	OX
Peterborough	PE
Plymouth	PL
Portsmouth	PO
Preston	PR
Reading	RG
Redhill	RH
Romford	RM
Salisbury	SP

District	*Postal Area*
Sheffield	S
Shrewsbury	SY
Slough	SL
Southall (Uxbridge)	UB
Southampton	SO
Southend on Sea	SS
St. Albans	AL
Stevenage	SG
Stockport	SK
Stoke on Trent	ST
Sunderland	SR
Sutton	SM
Swansea	SA
Swindon	SN
Taunton	TA
Telford	TF
Tonbridge	TN
Torquay	TQ
Truro	TR
Tweeddale (Berwick upon Tweed)	TD
Twickenham	TW
Wakefield	WF
Walsall	WS
Warrington	WA
Watford	WD
Wigan	WN
Wolverhampton	WV
Worcester	WR
York	YO

REGULATION 5

SCHEDULE 2

PROFESSIONAL BODIES RECOGNISED BY THE LORD CHANCELLOR

The Lord Chancellor recognises the following as professional bodies: **sc45.0.22**

- High Court Enforcement Officers Association

REGULATION 13

SCHEDULE 3

FEES CHARGEABLE BY ENFORCEMENT OFFICERS

sc45.0.23 The fees chargeable by enforcement officers on execution of writs are as follows. Value Added Tax, if payable, may be added to the fees specified.

A. Fees chargeable on execution of writs of fieri facias	
1. Percentage of amount recovered	
For executing a writ of fieri facias, the following percentages of the amount recovered:	
(a) on the first £100	5 per cent
(b) above £100	2.5 per cent
2. Mileage	
Mileage from the enforcement officer's business address to the place of execution and return, in respect of one journey to seize goods and, if appropriate, one journey to remove the goods	

	29.2 pence per mile, up to a maximum of £50.00 in total
3. Seizure of goods	
For each building or place at which goods are seized	£2.00
4. Making enquiries or dealing with claims for rent or to the goods	
(1) For making enquiries as to claims for rent or to goods, including giving notice to parties of any such claims	a sum not exceeding £2.00
(2) For all expenses actually and reasonably incurred in relation to such work including any postage, telephone, fax and e–mail charges	a further sum not exceeding £2.00
5. Taking possession, removal and storage of goods	
(1) Where a person is left in physical possession of goods seized	£3.00 per person per day
(2) Where an enforcement officer takes walking possession under a walking possession agreement in the form set out in Schedule 4 to these Regulations	£0.25 per day
(Fees 5(1) and 5(2) are payable in respect of the day on which execution is levied, but fee 5(1) may not be charged where a walking possession agreement is signed at the time of levy. Fees 5(1) and 5(2) may not be charged after the goods have been removed.)	
(3) For— (a) the removal of goods; (b) the storage of goods which have been removed; and (c) where animals have been seized, their upkeep while in the custody of the enforcement officer, whether before or after removal	
	the sums actually and reasonably paid
6. Sale of goods by auction	
(1) To cover the auctioneer's commission and expenses, where goods are sold by auction or work has been done with a view to sale by auction: (a) when goods are sold by auction on the auctioneer's premises, the following percentages of the sum realised—	
(i) on the first £100	15 per cent
(ii) on the next £900	12.5 per cent
(iii) above £1,000	10 per cent
(b) when goods are sold by auction on the debtor's premises, 7.5 per cent of the sum realised plus expenses actually and reasonably incurred.	
(2) When no sale takes place either by auction or private contract, but work has been done by the auctioneer or enforcement officer in preparing for a sale by auction, including the preparation of a detailed inventory of the goods seized— (a) if the goods have been removed to the auctioneer's premises, 10 per cent of the value of the goods; (b) if the goods have not been removed from the debtor's premises, 5 per cent of the value of the goods plus expenses actually and reasonably incurred.	
7. Sale of goods by private contract	
Where an enforcement officer sells goods by private contract— (a) the following percentages of the proceeds of sale—	
(i) on the first £100	7.5 per cent
(ii) on the next £900	6.25 per cent
(iii) above £1,000	5 per cent; and
(b) when work has been done in preparing for a sale by auction, including the preparation of a detailed inventory of the goods seized, an additional sum not exceeding 2.5 per cent of the value of the goods plus expenses actually and reasonably incurred.	
B. Fees chargeable on executing writs of possession or delivery	
8. Mileage	

Mileage from the enforcement officer's business address to the place of execution and return, in respect of one journey	29.2 pence per mile, up to a maximum of £25.00 in total
9. Writs of possession	
(1) Where an enforcement officer executes a writ of possession of domestic property within the meaning of section 66 of the Local Government Finance Act 1988, 3 per cent of the net annual value for rating shown in the valuation list in force immediately before 1st April 1990 in respect of the property seized, subject to paragraph (3). (2) Where an enforcement officer executes a writ of possession to which paragraph (1) does not apply, 0.4 per cent of the net annual value for rating of the property seized, subject to paragraph (4). (3) For the purposes of paragraph (1), where the property does not consist of one or more hereditament which, immediately before 1st April 1990— (a) had a separate net annual value for rating shown on the valuation list then in force; and (b) was domestic property within the meaning of section 66 of the Local Government Finance Act 1988, the property or such part of it as does not so consist shall be taken to have had such a value for rating equal to two–fifteenths of its value by the year when seized. (4) For the purposes of paragraph (2), where the property does not consist of one or more hereditaments having a separate net annual value for rating, the property or such part of it as does not so consist shall be taken to have such a value equal to its value by the year when seized.	
10. Writs of delivery	
For executing a writ of delivery, 4 per cent of the value of the goods as stated in the writ or judgment.	
C. General fees	
11. Copies of returns	
For a copy of any return indorsed by the enforcement officer on a writ of execution	£5.00
12. Miscellaneous	
For any matter not otherwise provided for, such sum as a Master, district judge or costs judge may allow upon application.	

REGULATION 15

SCHEDULE 4

sc45.0.24

WALKING POSSESSION AGREEMENT

In the High Court of Justice
..........Division
..........District Registry
High Court Claim number ....
[County Court Claim number ....]
[Sent from the .... County Court by Certificate dated ....]
Claimant ....
Defendant ....

To .... an enforcement officer authorised to execute writs of execution issued from the High Court

I request that you will not leave a possession man on my premises in close possession of the goods which you have seized under the writ of execution issued in this claim.

If this request is allowed to me, I undertake, pending withdrawal or satisfaction of the writ—

(a) not to remove the goods or any part of them nor to permit their removal by any person not authorised by you;

(b) to inform any person who may visit my premises for the purpose of levying any other execution or distress that you are already in possession of my goods under the writ;

(c) to notify you immediately of any such visit.

AND I authorise you or a person acting on your behalf, pending the withdrawal or satisfaction of the writ, to re–enter my premises at any time and as often as you may consider necessary for the purpose of inspecting the goods or completing the execution of the writ.

Dated this ....day of .... 20 ....

Signed .... Judgment Debtor

High Court Enforcement Officers

Add new paragraph sc45.1A.1:

sc45.1A.1 By s.99 and Sched.7 Courts Act 2003, Sheriffs are no longer responsible for enforcement of High Court writs of execution. Enforcement is now undertaken by High Court Enforcement Officers. (See further para. sc45.0.6.) One important change is that the judgment creditor (rather than, as formerly, the Under–Sheriff) can choose which HCEO to instruct to enforce the writ. No doubt, over time, solicitors will develop a working relationship with particular HCEOs. The HCEO is no longer confined to a particular bailiwick. Bailiwicks are abolished and the country is divided into areas by post–code but the jurisdiction of a HCEO is not confined to a particular area. On issue, the writ can be addressed to a particular HCEO for the relevant post–code of the judgment debtor.

A complete list of HCEOs appears in this Supplement at Para 10–72.

The High Court Enforcement Officers Association website at www.hceoa.org.uk has a search facility by name of HCEO and by post code. All Court Offices have a copy of the Directory of HCEOs but court officerst cannot give advice or recommend a particular HCEO. There is an option of putting the postal area on the writ instead of the name of a particular HCEO in which case the writ will be allocated in strict rotation through the HCEOA's central database. However, already it is clear that HCEOs are accepting work at a greater distance than was formerly the case and it is often worthwhile enquiring of a HCEOwho is known.

RSC ORDER 46 – WRITS OF EXECUTION: GENERAL

Enforcement of money judgements by writ of fi. fa.

Duties of sheriff

Add at end:

sc46.1.6 The duties of the sheriff for enforcement purposes have now passed to High Court Enforcement Officers. See further paras sc45.0.5; sc45.0.6; and sc45.1A above.

Sale by sheriff without notice of claim

Add at end:

sc46.1.7 See para sc46.1.6 above.

Wrongful seizure by sheriff

Add at end:

sc46.1.11 See para sc46.1.6 above.

High Court Enforcement Officers

Amend existing title and delete paragraphs sc46.1.50 and sc46.1.51 and substitute:

sc46.1.50 By s.99 and Sched. 7 Courts Act 2003 the former responsibilities of the Sheriff for executing High Court writs of enforcement now vest in High Court Enforcement Officers. The Directory of these officers is in this Supplement at para. 10–72. See further para.sc45.1A.1.

Any High Court judgment and any county court judgment for over £600 (except where the judgment arises from a regulated agreement under the Consumer Credit Act 1974) can be enforced in the High Court. A county court judgment needs to be transferred to the High Court for enforcement purposes (use Form N293A). Many of the larger HCEO offices offer a transfer up service to assist judgment creditors to turn their county court judgment into a writ for enforcement in the High Court. Enquiries can be made of the HCEO where the writ of execution is to be sent; many arrange transfer up without charge (there is a court fee). Those not wanting to issue writs themselves and wishing to use a transfer up service can speed things up by getting the certificate of judgment stamped by the appropriate county court on Part 2 of the N293A before sending it to the transfer up service provider.

As ever, any practical information about assets available for seizure should be provided to the HCEO. For example, while it is correct to use a registered office to serve a company this may be useless for enforcement purposes and a trading address is required.

RSC ORDER 47 - WRITS OF FIERI FACIAS

Amendment

Delete existing paragraph sc47.0.5 and substitute:

sc47.0.5 See paras sc45.0.5; sc45.0.6 and sc45.1A.

Entitlement of sheriff to his fees and poundage

Add at end:

sc47.4.2 The former responsibilities of sheriffs are now those of High Court Enforcement Officers. See further paras sc45.0.5; sc45.0.6 and sc45.1A.

Sheriff's fees, etc.

Add at end:

sc47.4.4 The former responsibilities of sheriffs are now those of High Court Enforcement Officers. See further paras sc45.0.5; sc45.0.6 and sc45.1A.

Sale of goods by sheriff

Add at end:

sc47.6.2 The former responsibilities of sheriffs are now those of High Court Enforcement Officers. See further paras sc45.0.5; sc45.0.6 and sc45.1A.

Protection of sheriff—Supreme Court Act 1981, s.138B

Add at end:

sc47.6.4 The former responsibilities of sheriffs are now those of High Court Enforcement Officers. See further paras sc45.0.5; sc45.0.6 and sc45.1A.

RSC ORDER 52 - COMMITTAL

Civil and criminal contempts

Add at end:

sc52.1.2 Where a party alleges a failure to comply with an undertaking or order, the burden of proof will lie on that party. The standard of proof however will depend on the purpose for which the allegation is made. Where it is for the purpose of establishing a fresh allegation of contempt and a fresh committal it will be to the criminal standard, but if it is for some other purpose it will be to the civil standard: *Phillips v. Symes* [2003] EWCA Civ 1769 (Waller, Hale and Carnwath L.JJ.)

M. Acts calculated to prejudice the due course of justice

Add at end:

sc52.1.20 Illegal photography in court has the potential gravely to prejudice the administration of criminal justice. The taking of photographs using mobile phones in court had become a major problem in both Magistrates Courts and the Crown Court, and was also a matter of concern in civil courts. In an appropriate case an immediate sentence of imprisonment was likely: *Regina v. D (Contempt of Court; illegal photography), The Times*, May 13, 2004 (Lord Woolf C.J., Aikens and Fulford JJ.).

Effect of party being in contempt

At the end of the first paragraph add:

sc52.1.30 It is now recognised that there is no general rule that a Court will not hear an application for a contemnor's own benefit unless he has first purged his contempt. It was wrong for a judge to proceed with an effective hearing of an application to commit, where he knew that the contemnor wished to be heard in person but was prevented from attending for reasons over which he had no control. *Raja v. Van Hoogstraten* [2004] EWCA Civ 968 (Pill, Chadwick and May LJ.J.).

Appeal

Add at end:

sc52.1.42 An application for habeas corpus is not the appropriate remedy to challenge a committal for contempt (*Rayne, Re* [2004] EWCA Civ 543 (Tuckey and Laws LJJ)).

Personal service

Add at end:

sc52.3.2 Where a contemnor had been shown every latitude, but his attitude remained one of contumacious defiance and he had deliberately stayed away from the committal proceedings, there was no failure of due process giving rise to such injustice or unfairness as would warrant the exercise of the court's appellate power under s.13 of the 1960 Act. *Scriven, Re* [2004] EWCA Civ 683 (Clarke and Sedley LJ.J).

Early release

Add at end:

sc52.8.2 In imposing a sentence of imprisonment for contempt a court has therefore no power to direct that the contemnor should not be released until a specified date, since the early release provisions of s.33 Criminal Justice Act 1991 will apply in such a case, where the sentence is one of 12 months or less. *Thompson v. Mitchell The Times*, September 13, 2004 (Keene and Wall LJ.J).

RSC ORDER 81 – PARTNERS

Note

Add after "If the notice is not complied with the defendant may apply":

sc81.2.1 by Pt 23 application notice

Service

Acknowledgement of service

In the second paragraph under 'Acknowledgement of service', add at end:

sc81.4.1 Para. 4.4 of the PD to Pt 10 provides that where the defendant is a partnership, the acknowledgment of service may be signed by any of the partners or by a person having the control or management of the partnership business.

RSC ORDER 94 – APPLICATIONS AND APPEALS TO HIGH COURT UNDER VARIOUS ACTS: QUEEN'S BENCH DIVISION

Applications under s.42, Supreme Court Act 1981, generally

Add at end:

sc94.15.3 Following *Attorney General v. Vernazza* [1959] 1 W.L.R. 622, the Court will look at the whole history of the matter, which is not to be determined by whether the pleadings disclose a cause of action. Moreover it is not the task of the Court to reconsider the merits of the underlying actions. The Court was entitled to rely on the conclusions reached by the judges in those proceedings (see *Attorney General v. Jones* [1990] W.L.R. 859). Claims where private individuals are subjected to trouble, harassment and expense by the abuse of the legal system are of particular concern. Those who indulge in habitual, persistent, vexatious abuse of the Court's processes should take note that the Court is very ready to make orders under s.42 of the Act when such cases are brought before it. In appropriate cases the Court will make an interim, as in *Blackstone, Re* [1995] C.O.D. 105; *HM Attorney General v. Mahon* [2003] EWHC 2435 (Admin) (Brooke L.J. and Sullivan J.).

Proceedings under the Protection from Harassment Act 1997

Rule 16 is revoked by the 35th Update of the Civil Procedure Rules.

sc94.16 16. [Revoked]

General approach

In the first sentence, for "Harassment Act 1996" substitute:

Protection from Harassment Act 1997 **sc94.16.1**

Add at end:

A company cannot be the victim of harassment under the Act and cannot bring a claim under it. However individuals who were non–corporate claimants, such as directors and employees, could be entitled to the protection of the Act and may institute proceedings: *Daiichi UK Ltd v. Stop Huntingdon Animal Cruelty* [2003] EWHC 2337 (Owen J).

A director of a company may bring proceedings on behalf of employees of the company as being the most convenient and expeditious way of enabling the Court to protect their interests: *Emerson Developments v. Avery* [2004] EWHC 194 (QB) (Field J.).

RSC ORDER 98 – LOCAL GOVERNMENT FINANCE ACT 1982, PART III

RSC Order 98 is revoked by the Civil Procedure Rules 2004 (S.I. 2004 No. 1306).

[Revoked] **sc98.1**

RSC ORDER 112 – APPLICATIONS FOR USE OF SCIENTIFIC TESTS IN DETERMINING PARENTAGE

Fees

Delete regulation 12 and substitute:

12. (1) A sampler may charge £27.50 for making the arrangements to take a sample. (2) The charge in paragraph (1) is payable whether or not a sample is taken. **sc112.6.24**

Delete Schedule 2

Effect of rule

For "the sheriff not the bailiff" substitute:

a High Court Enforcement Officer not a county court bailiff **cc16.7.2**

CCR ORDER 25 – ENFORCEMENT OF JUDGMENTS AND ORDERS: GENERAL

Editorial Introduction

Delete the last two paragraphs and substitute:

Where the sum which it is sought to enforce wholly or partially by execution against goods is £5000 or more it can be enforced only in the High Court: where that sum is less than £600 it can be enforced only in a county court (save that all county court judgments arising out of agreements regulated by the Consumer Credit Act 1974 must be enforced in a county court).For judgments in between there is a choice and either court can be used. In the High Court, judgments are enforced by independent High Court Enforcement Officers (see further, para. sc46.1.50 in this Supplement) whereas enforcement in the county court is undertaken by the county court's own bailiffs. **cc25.0.2**

Delete paragraph cc25.0.5

Procedure on Transfer

Amend existing title. Delete the whole of paragraph cc25.13.2 and substitute:

The procedure on transfer to the High Court for enforcement is very simple and is governed by CCR Ord 22 r.8. The relevant form to use depends on the purpose of the transfer as set out in that rule. Form N293A is a "Combined Certificate of Judgment and request for writ of fi–fa". After transfer, two copies should be filed at the District Registry (or, at the RCJ in Room E17). Some High Court Enforcement Officers will also arrange transfer up prior to execution (see further para. sc46.1.50 in this Supplement). **cc25.13.2**

CCR ORDER 26 – WARRANTS OF EXECUTION, DELIVERY AND POSSESSION

High Court Enforcement Officers

Amend existing title. Delete paragraph and substitute:

cc26.0.5 See paras sc46.1.48 and sc46.1.50.

CCR ORDER 29 – COMMITTAL FOR BREACH OF ORDER OR UNDERTAKING

Family Proceedings

Add at end:

cc29.1.4 Where there was a non violent breach of a non molestation order the primary purpose should be to try to secure future compliance. The appellant's silly conduct had been a nuisance but had involved no violence. A six months sentence was excessive and would be reduced to three months. The applicable principles had been laid down in *Hale v. Tanner* [2000] 1 W.L.R. 2377; in general the court would not tinker with such sentences; the judge's discretion was wide but the cardinal principle was to strike the right balance between a coercive and punitive approach: *Aquillina v. Aquillina, The Times*, April 15, 2004 (Ward and Clarke L.JJ.).

Contempt procedure

Add at end:

cc29.1.5 Where a young person was in breach of a county court order excluding him from a specified area the imposition of a committal for two years was not appropriate because (1) the maximum sentence of two years should be reserved for the worst case and (2) in the circumstances the sentence was excessive. County Courts should pay particular regard to the requirement in para. 4.2. of the Practice Direction that the hearing date for the committal application should not be less than 14 days after service of the notice: *Turnbull v. Middlesbrough BC* [2003] EWCA Civ 1327 (Kennedy and Peter Gibson L.JJ.).

A sentence for contempt under s.42 of the Family Law Act 1996, for breaching injunctions, will not be increased on appeal unless it can be shown that it is not merely lenient, but unduly lenient. Moreover the Court of Appeal would also reflect the element of double jeopardy when determining the appropriate sentence: *Lomas v. Parle* [2004] 1 W.L.R. 1642 (Dame Elizabeth Butler–Sloss, P. Thorpe and Mance L.JJ.).

CCR ORDER 47 – DOMESTIC AND MATRIMONIAL PROCEEDINGS

Related Sources

Add after "(S.I. 1971 No. 1861)":

cc47.0.3
- as amended by the Blood Tests (Evidence of Paternity) (Amendment) Regulations 1992, 2001 and 2004 (S.I. 1992 No. 1369; S.I. 2001 No. 773 and S.I. 2004 No.596).

CCR ORDER 49 – MISCELLANEOUS STATUTES

Delete CCR Ord 49 and substitute:

cc49.0.1 **Contents**

Editorial Introduction

cc49.0.2 For many years when Parliament created a new right or remedy (*e.g.* under the Access to Neighbouring Land Act 1992 or under the Race Relations Act 1976) the practice has been to confer jurisdiction on the county courts. This usually resulted in a new rule being added to CCR O.49. Unfortunately and inevitably, CCR O.49 became unweildy and dealt with many diverse "Miscellaneous Statutes"; some very important and others of minor, or even trivial significance. The statutes are so diverse that no meaningful generalisations can be made for O.49. At least each statute had its own rule within O.49 and the strange rule numbering can be explained by the fact that the "miscellaneous statutes"are arranged alphabetically.

The process of tidying up O.49 continues. CPR Part 56, "Landlord and Tenant Claims and Miscellaneous Provisions about Land", deals with many statutes formerly governed by O.49. CPR Part 65, "Proceedings relating to Anti-Social Behaviour and Harassment" replaced O.49, r.6B as from June 30, 2004. Indeed, O.49 has been amended so many times that it is convenient to print the rump that remains in full in this Supplement.

Related Sources

cc49.0.3

- See the statutes listed in the contents list above.
- High Court and County Courts Jurisdiction Order 1991 (see Vol. 2, Section 9B)
- Part 56 Landlord and Tenant Claims and Micellaneous Provisions about Land
- Part 65 Proceedings relating to Anti-Social Behaviour and Harassment

Housing Act 1996: injunctions

Rule 6B is revoked by Civil Procedure (Amendment) Rules 2004 (S.I. 2004 No. 1306)

6B. [Revoked] **cc49.6B**

History of rule

Add at end:

cc49.6B.1

CCR Ord. 49 r.6B was revoked as from June 30, 2004 by the Civil Procedure (Amendment) Rules 2004 (S.I. 2004 No. 1306) but continue to have effect in applications for an injunction under Chaper III of Part V of the Housing Act 1996 issued before June 30, 2004. The full text can be found in Volume I of the Main Work. For cases issued on or after June 30, 2004, see CPR Part 65

Injunctions to prevent environmental harm: Town and Country Planning Act 1990 etc.

cc49.7

7.—(1) An injunction under—

(a) section 187B or 214A of the Town and Country Planning Act 1990;

(b) section 44A of the Planning (Listed Buildings and Conservation Areas) Act 1990; or

(c) section 26AA of the Planning (Hazardous Substances) Act 1990,

may be granted against a person whose identity is unknown to the applicant; and in the following provisions of this rule such an injunction against such a person is referred to as "an injunction under paragraph (1)", and the person against whom it is sought is referred to as "the respondent".

(2) A applicant for an injunction under paragraph (1) shall describe the respondent by reference to—

(a) a photograph;

(b) a thing belonging to or in the possession of the respondent; or

(c) any other evidence,

with sufficient particularity to enable service to be effected, and the form of the claim form used shall be modified accordingly.

(3) An applicant for an injunction under paragraph (1) shall file evidence by witness statement or affidavit—

(a) verifying that he was unable to ascertain, within the time reasonably available to him, the respondent's identity.

(b) setting out the action taken to ascertain the respondent's identity and

(c) verifying the means by which the respondent has been described in the claim form and that the description is the best that the applicant is able to provide.

(4) Paragraph (2) is without prejudice to the power of the court to make an order in accordance with CPR Part 6 for service by an alternative method or dispensing with service.

Related Sources

cc49.7.1

- Town and Country Planning Act 1990
- Planning (Listed Buildings and Conservation Areas) Act 1990
- Planning (Hazardous Substances) Act 1990
- Sched.1, RSC O.110—Environmental Control Proceedings
- Sched.2, CCR O.29—Committal

Form

cc49.7.2

- **N16** General Form of Injunction

Mental Health Act 1983

cc49.12

12.—(1) In this rule—

a section referred to by number means the section so numbered in the Mental Health Act 1983 and "Part II" means Part II of that Act;

"place of residence" means, in relation to a patient who is receiving treatment as an in–patient in a hospital or other institution, that hospital or institution;

"hospital authority" means the managers of a hospital as defined in section 145(1).

(2) An application to a county court under Part II shall be made by a claim form filed in the court for the district in which the patients' place of residence is situated or, in the case of an application made under section 30 for the discharge or variation of an order made under section 29, in that court or in the court which made the order.

(3) Where an application is made under section 29 for an order that the functions of the nearest relative of the patient shall be exercisable by some other person—

(a) the nearest relative shall be made a respondent to the application unless the application is made on the grounds set out in subsection (3)(a) of the said section or the court otherwise orders; and

(b) the court may order that any other person, not being the patient, shall be made a respondent.

(4) On the hearing of the application the court may accept as evidence of the facts stated therein any report made by a medical practitioner and any report made in the course of his official duties by—

(a) a probation officer; or

(b) an officer of a local authority or of a voluntary organisation exercising statutory functions on behalf of a local authority; or

(c) an officer of a hospital authority,

provided that the respondent shall be told the substance of any part of the report bearing on his fitness or conduct which the judge considers to be material for the fair determination of the application.

(5) Unless otherwise ordered, an application under Part II shall be heard and determined by the court sitting in private.

(6) For the purpose of determining the application the judge may interview the patient either in the presence of or separately from the parties and either at the court or elsewhere, or may direct the district judge to interview the patient and report to the judge in writing.

Editorial Note

cc49.12.1 See the various sections in the Mental Health Act 1983 referred to in the rule. The procedure under Sched.2, CCR O.49, r.12 is now by claim form (r.12(2)) and is heard in private (r.12(5)). Note the provisions as to evidence in r.12(3), and the provision to interview the patient in r.12(6). A report by the district judge is in Form **N437**.

Postal Services Act 2000

cc49.15 15.—(1) An application under section 92 of the Postal Services Act 2000 for permission to bring proceedings in the name of the sender or addressee of a postal packet or his personal representatives shall be made by a claim form.

(2) The respondents to the application shall be the universal service provider and the person in whose name the applicant seeks to bring proceedings.

Sex Discrimination Act 1975, Race Relations Act 1976, Disability Discrimination Act 1995 and Disability Rights Commission Act 1999

cc49.17 17.—(1) In this rule—

(a) "the Act of 1975", "the Act of 1976", "the Act of 1995", and "the Act of 1999" mean respectively the Sex Discrimination Act 1975and the Race Relations Act 1976, the Disability Discrimination Act 1995 and the Disability Rights Commission Act 1999;

(aa) "the Religion or Belief Regulations" means the Employment Equality (Religion or Belief) Regulations 2003 and "the Sexual Orientation Regulations" means the Employment Equality (Sexual Orientation) Regulations 2003;

(b) in relation to proceedings under any of those Acts or Regulations, expressions which are used in the Act or Regulations concerned have the same meanings in this rule as they have in that Act or those Regulations;

(c) in relation to proceedings under the Act of 1976 "court" means a designated county court and "district" means the district assigned to such a court for the purposes of that Act.

(2) A claimant who brings a claim under section 66 of the Act of 1975 or section 57 of the Act of 1976 shall forthwith give notice to the Commission of the commencement of the proceedings and file a copy of the notice.

(3) CPR Rule 35.15 shall have effect in relation to an assessor who is to be appointed in proceedings under section 66(1) of the Act of 1975.

(4) Proceedings under section 66, 71 or 72 of the Act of 1975, section 57, 62 or 63 of the Act of 1976, regulation 31 of the Religion or Belief Regulations or regulation 31 of the Sexual Orientation Regulations, section 17B or 25 of the Act of 1995 or section 6 of the Act of 1999 may be commenced—

(a) in the court for the district in which the defendant resides or carries on business; or

(b) in the court for the district in which the act or any of the acts in respect of which the proceedings are brought took place.

(5) An appeal under section 68 of the Act of 1975 or section 59 of the Act of 1976 against a requirement of a non–discrimination notice shall be brought in the court for the district in which the acts to which the requirement relates were done.

(6) Where the claimant in any claim alleging discrimination has questioned the defendant under section 74 of the Act of 1975, section 65 of the Act of 1976, regulation 33 of the Religion or Belief Regulations or regulation 33 of the Sexual Orientation Regulations—

(a) either party may make an application to the court in accordance with CPR Part 23 to determine whether the question or any reply is admissible under that section; and

(b) CPR Rule 3.4, shall apply to the question and any answer as it applies to any statement of case.

(7) Where in any claim the Commission claim a charge for expenses incurred by them in providing the claimant with assistance under section 75 of the Act of 1975, section 66 of the Act of 1976, or section 7 of the Act of 1999—

(a) the Commission shall, within 14 days after the determination of the claim, give notice of the claim to the court and the claimant and thereafter no money paid into court for the benefit of the claimant, so far as it relates to any costs or expenses, shall be paid out except in pursuance of an order of the court; and

(b) the court may order the expenses incurred by the Commission to be assessed whether by the summary or detailed procedure as if they were costs payable by the claimant to his own solicitor for work done in connection with the proceedings.

(8) Where an application is made for the removal or modification of any term of a contract to which section 77(2) of the Act of 1975, section 72(2) of the Act of 1976, section 26 or Schedule 3A to the Act of 1995, paragraph 1(1) or (2) of Schedule 4 to the Religion or Belief Regulations or paragraph 1(1) or (2) of Schedule 4 to the Sexual Orientation Regulations applies, all persons affected shall be made respondents to the application, unless in any particular case the court otherwise directs, and the proceedings may be commenced—

(a) in the court for the district in which the respondent or any of the respondents resides or carries on business, or

(b) in the court for the district in which the contract was made.

Editorial Note

cc49.17.1 Only county courts designated by the Lord Chancellor by Order pursuant to s.67 of the County Courts Act 1984 have jurisdiction in Race Relations cases. However, the districts of courts not so designated are assigned to a county court which is so designated. The judge hearing the case sits with assessors unless the parties agree to dispense with them. Note the requirement in r.17(2) to give notice to the Commission. In practice it is better to contact the Commission prior to the issue of proceedings for explanatory leaflets and advice.

Telecommunications Act 1984

cc49.18A 18A.—(1) CPR Rule 35.15 applies to proceedings under paragraph 5 of Schedule 2 to the Telecommunications Act 1984.

Related Source

cc49.18A.1
- CPR, r.35.15—Assessors

Trade Union and Labour Relations Consolidation Act 1992

19.—(1) Where a complainant desires to have an order of the Certification Officer under section 82 of the Trade Union and Labour Relations Consolidation Act 1992 recorded in the county court, he shall produce the order and a copy thereof to the court for the district in which he resides or the head or main office of the trade union is situate. **cc49.19**

(2) The order shall be recorded by filing it, and the copy shall be sealed and dated and returned to the complainant.

(3) The sealed copy shall be treated as if it were the notice of issue in a claim begun by the complainant.

(4) The costs, if any, allowed for recording the order shall be recoverable as if they were payable under the order.

(5) The order shall not be enforced until proof is given to the satisfaction of the court that the order has not been obeyed and, if the order is for payment of money, of the amount remaining unpaid.

PRACTICE DIRECTION—HOUSING ACT 1996: INJUNCTION

Delete Practice Direction—Housing Act 1996: Injunction

SECTION B

ccpd49.1

PRACTICE DIRECTIONS AND PRACTICE STATEMENTS

Editorial Note

Use of Pt 8 procedure

Delete the full stop at the end of the sentence that begins "However, use of the Pt 7 procedure with statements of case" and add:

(though the courts have recognised that the evidence in support of the application "has of necessity something of the character of a pleading": Laddie J. in *Re Finelist* [2003] EWHC 1780 (Ch) at [14]. **B1–004.1**

Cross–examination

Add new second paragraph:

It should be noted that the court's power to control cross–examination can be invoked. This power is part of the court's inherent jurisdiction, as well as being set out in CPR, r. 32.1(3). See *Secretary of State for Trade and Industry v. Gill* [2004] EWHC 175 where, after refusing an application by the Secretary of State for permission to amend an allegation shortly before trial, Blackburn J. that cross–examination of the defendants' witnesses "must be properly confined to the complaint as it presently stands". **B1–010.4**

PRACTICE DIRECTION—APPLICATION FOR WARRANT UNDER THE COMPETITION ACT 1998

Delete existing Practice Direction and substitute:

1. Interpretation **B3–001**

In this practice direction—

(1) 'the Act' means the Competition Act 1998;

(2) 'the Commission' means the European Commission;

(3) 'Commission official' means a person authorised by the Commission for any of the purposes set out in section 62(10), 62A(12) or 63(10) of the Act;

(4) 'the OFT' means the Office of Fair Trading;

(5) 'officer' means an officer of the OFT;

(6) 'named officer' means the person identified in a warrant as the principal officer in charge of executing that warrant, and includes a named authorised officer under section 63 of the Act; and

(7) 'warrant' means a warrant under section 28, 28A, 62, 62A, 63, 65G or 65H of the Act.

1.2 In relation to an application for a warrant by a regulator entitled pursuant to section 54 and Schedule 10 of the Act to exercise the functions of the OFT, references to the OFT shall be interpreted as referring to that regulator.

Application for a warrant

B3–002 **2.1** An application by the Director for a warrant must be made to a High Court judge using the Part 8 procedure as modified by this practice direction.

2.2 The application should be made to a judge of the Chancery Division at the Royal Courts of Justice (if available).

2.3 The application is made without notice and the claim form may be issued without naming a defendant. Rules 8.1(3), 8.3, 8.4, 8.5(2)–(6), 8.6(1), 8.7 and 8.8 do not apply.

Confidentiality of court documents

B3–003 **3.1** The court will not effect service of any claim form, warrant, or other document filed or issued in an application to which this practice direction applies, except in accordance with an order of the judge hearing the application.

3.2 CPR rule 5.4 does not apply, and paragraphs 3.3 and 3.4 have effect in its place.

3.3 When a claim form is issued the court file will be marked 'Not for disclosure' and, unless a High Court judge grants permission, the court records relating to the application (including the claim form and documents filed in support and any warrant or order that is issued) will not be made available by the court for any person to inspect or copy, either before or after the hearing of the application.

3.4 An application for permission under paragraph 3.3 must be made on notice to the Director in accordance with Part 23.

(Rule 23.7(1) requires a copy of the application notice to be served as soon as practicable after it is filed, and in any event at least 3 days before the court is to deal with the application.)

Contents of claim form, affidavit and documents in support

B3–004 **4.1** The claim form must state—

(1) the section of the Act under which the OFT is applying for a warrant;

(2) the address or other identification of the premises to be subject to the warrant; and

(3) the anticipated date or dates for the execution of the warrant.

4.2 The application must be supported by affidavit evidence, which must be filed with the claim form.

4.3 The evidence must set out all the matters on which the OFT relies in support of the application, including all material facts of which the court should be made aware. In particular it must state—

(1) the subject matter (*i.e.* the nature of the suspected infringement of the Chapter I or II prohibitions in the Act, or of Articles 81 or 82 of the Treaty establishing the European Community) and purpose of the investigation to which the application relates;

(2) the identity of the undertaking or undertakings suspected to have committed the infringement;

(3) the grounds for applying for the issue of the warrant and the facts relied upon in support;

(4) details of the premises to be subject to the warrant and of the possible occupier or occupiers of those premises;

(5) the connection between the premises and the undertaking or undertakings suspected to have committed the infringement;

(6) the name and position of the officer who it is intended will be the named officer;

(7) if it is intended that the warrant may pursuant to a relevant provision of the Act authorise any person (other than an officer or a Commission official) to accompany the named officer in executing the warrant, the name and job title of each such person and the reason why it is intended that he may accompany the named officer.

4.4 There must be exhibited to an affidavit in support of the application—

(1) the written authorisation of the OFT containing the names of—
 (a) the officer who it is intended will be the named officer;
 (b) the other persons who it is intended may accompany him in executing the warrant; and

(2) in the case of an application under section 62, 62A or 63 of the Act, if it is intended that Commission officials will accompany the named officer in executing the warrant, the written authorisations of the Commission containing the names of the Commission officials.

4.5 There must also be filed with the claim form—

(1) drafts of—
 (a) the warrant; and
 (b) an explanatory note to be produced and served with it; and

(2) the written undertaking by the named officer required by paragraph 6.2 of this practice direction.

(Examples of forms of warrant under sections 28 and 62 of the Act, and explanatory notes to be produced and served with them, are annexed to this practice direction. These forms and notes should be used with appropriate modifications in applications for warrants under other sections of the Act.)

4.6 If possible the draft warrant and explanatory note should also be supplied to the court on disk in a form compatible with the word processing software used by the court.

Listing

B3–005 **5.** The application will be listed by the court on any published list of cases as 'An application by D'.

Hearing of the application

B3–006 **6.1** An application for a warrant will be heard and determined in private, unless the judge hearing it directs otherwise.

6.2 The court will not issue a warrant unless there has been filed a written undertaking, signed by the named officer, to comply with paragraph 8.1 of this practice direction.

The warrant

B3–007 **7.1** The warrant must—

(2) state the address or other identification of the premises to be subject to the warrant;

(3) state the names of—
  (a) the named officer; and
  (b) any other officers, Commission officials or other persons who may accompany him in executing the warrant;

(4) set out the action which the warrant authorises the persons executing it to take under the relevant section of the Act;

(5) give the date on which the warrant is issued;

(6) include a statement that the warrant continues in force until the end of the period of one month beginning with the day on which it issued; and

(7) state that the named officer has given the undertaking required by paragraph 6.2.

7.2 Rule 40.2 applies to a warrant.

(Rule 40.2 requires every judgment or order to state the name and judicial title of the person making it, to bear the date on which it is given or made, and to be sealed by the court.)

7.3 Upon the issue of a warrant the court will provide to the OFT—

(1) the sealed warrant and sealed explanatory note; and

(2) a copy of the sealed warrant and sealed explanatory note for service on the occupier or person in charge of the premises subject to the warrant.

Execution of warrant

B3–008 **8.1** A named officer attending premises to execute a warrant must, if the premises are occupied—

(1) produce the warrant and an explanatory note on arrival at the premises; and

(2) as soon as possible thereafter personally serve a copy of the warrant and the explanatory note on the occupier or person appearing to him to be in charge of the premises.

8.2 The named officer must also comply with any order which the court may make for service of any other documents relating to the application.

8.3 Unless the court otherwise orders—

(1) the initial production of a warrant and entry to premises under

the authority of the warrant must take place between 9.30 a.m. and 5.30 p.m. Monday to Friday; but

(2) once persons named in the warrant have entered premises under the authority of a warrant, they may, whilst the warrant remains in force—

(a) remain on the premises; or

(b) re-enter the premises to continue executing the warrant,

outside those times.

8.4 If the persons executing a warrant propose to remove any items from the premises pursuant to the warrant they must, unless it is impracticable—

(1) make a list of all the items to be removed;

(2) supply a copy of the list to the occupier or person appearing to be in charge of the premises; and

(3) give that person a reasonable opportunity to check the list before removing any of the items.

Application to vary or discharge warrant

B3–009

9.1 The occupier or person in charge of premises in relation to which a warrant has been issued may apply to vary or discharge the warrant.

9.2 An application under paragraph 9.1 to stop a warrant from being executed must be made immediately upon the warrant being served.

9.3 A person applying to vary or discharge a warrant must first inform the named officer that he is making the application.

9.4 The application should be made to the judge who issued the warrant, or, if he is not available, to another High Court judge.

Application under s.59 Criminal Justice and Police Act 2001

B3–010

10.1 Attention is drawn to section 59 of the Criminal Justice and Police Act 2001, which makes provision about applications relating to property seized in the exercise of the powers conferred by (among other provisions) section 28(2) of the Act.

Warrant

B3–011 IN THE HIGH COURT OF JUSTICE CLAIM No. of 20
CHANCERY DIVISION

CLAIMANT:

OFFICE OF FAIR TRADING
[insert address]

PREMISES TO WHICH THIS WARRANT RELATES:

[insert address]

WARRANT TO ENTER PREMISES AND EXERCISE POWERS UNDER SECTIONS 62 AND 64 COMPETITION ACT 1998

To *[insert name of undertaking]* who is believed to be the occupier of the premises described above ("the premises") and to any undertaking in charge of, or operating at or from, the premises:

You should read the terms of this Warrant and the accompanying Explanatory Note very carefully. You are advised to consult a Solicitor as soon as possible. If you intentionally obstruct any person in the exercise of his powers under the Warrant, you will have committed a criminal offence under section 65 of the Competition Act 1998, the relevant terms of which are set out in Schedule C to this Warrant.

An application was made on *[insert date]* by Counsel for the Office of Fair Trading ("the OFT") to The Honourable Mr Justice *[insert name]*("the Judge"), for a warrant under section 62(1) of the Competition Act 1998 ("the Act") on the grounds that *[insert the text of the relevant subsections (1) and (2), (3) or (4) as appropriate]*

The Judge read the evidence in support of the application and was satisfied that the grounds in section 62(1) and *[insert the relevant subsection (2), (3) or (4) as appropriate]* of the Act have been met and accepted the undertakings by *[insert name]*, an officer of the OFT authorised to act as the "named officer", set out in Schedule A to this Warrant. The named officer is the principal officer of the OFT in charge of executing this Warrant.

As a result of the application, this Warrant in relation to the premises was issued by the Judge on *[insert date]*.

1. This Warrant is issued in respect of an inspection by the European Commission ordered by its Decision *[insert Decision number]* dated *[insert date]* into *[set out the subject matter and purpose of the inspection]*

2. This Warrant continues in force until the end of the period of one month beginning with the day on which it is issued and may be executed on any one or more days within that period.

3. By this Warrant the persons named in Schedule B are authorised to produce the Warrant between 9:30am and 5:30pm on a weekday *[unless the Judge has ordered otherwise]*and on producing the Warrant:

   (a) to enter the premises using such force as is reasonably necessary for the purpose;

   (b) to search for books and records which a Commission official has power to examine, using such force as is reasonably necessary for the purpose;

   (c) to take or obtain copies of or extracts from such books and records; and

   (d) to seal the premises, any part of the premises or any books or records which a Commission official has power to seal, for the period and to the extent necessary for the inspection.

4. Any person entering the premises by virtue of this Warrant may take with him such equipment as appears to him to be necessary.

5. If there is no one at the premises when the named officer proposes to execute this Warrant he must, before executing it -

   (a) take such steps as are reasonable in all the circumstances to inform the occupier of the intended entry; and

   (b) if the occupier is so informed, afford him or his legal or other representative a reasonable opportunity to be present when the Warrant is executed.

6. If the named officer is unable to inform the occupier of the intended entry he must, when executing this Warrant, leave a copy of it in a prominent place on the premises.

7. On leaving the premises, the named officer must, if they are unoccupied or the occupier is temporarily absent, leave them as effectively secured as he found them.

8. Terms used in this Warrant have the following meanings in accordance with the Act:

   "books and records" includes books and records stored on any medium;

   "Commission official" means any of the persons authorised by the European Commission to conduct the inspection ordered by the Decision specified in paragraph 1 of this Warrant and whose name is set out in Schedule B;

"occupier" means any person whom the named officer reasonably believes is the occupier of the premises; and

"premises" means any premises (and includes any land or means of transport) of an undertaking or association of undertakings which a Commission official has power to enter in the course of the inspection ordered by the Decision specified in paragraph 1 of this Warrant; and for the avoidance of doubt, "premises" does not include the homes of directors, managers or other members of staff of the undertaking or association of undertakings concerned.

SCHEDULE A

UNDERTAKINGS GIVEN TO THE COURT BY THE NAMED OFFICER

If the premises are occupied when the Warrant is to be executed:

1. To produce the Warrant and an Explanatory Note on arrival at the premises; and

2. As soon as possible thereafter to serve personally a copy of the Warrant and of the Explanatory Note on the occupier or person appearing to him to be in charge of the premises.

The Explanatory Note was produced to the Court with the application for the Warrant.

SCHEDULE B

NAMES OF PERSONS AUTHORISED TO EXECUTE THE WARRANT

[insert name of the named officer] who is the OFT's officer authorised in writing by the OFT to be the named officer.

[insert name of each of the other officers] who are the OFT's other officers authorised in writing by the OFT to accompany the named officer.

*[insert name of each of the other person(s)]*who is *[insert job title of each person]* and who [is/are] authorised in writing by the OFT to accompany the named officer. *[This paragraph shall be included if the Judge so orders pursuant to section 62(5A).]*

[insert name of each of the Commission officials] who are the persons authorised by the European Commission to conduct the inspection ordered by the Decision specified in paragraph 1 of this Warrant.

SCHEDULE C

OFFENCE CREATED BY SECTION 65 OF THE ACT

The offence created by section 65 of the Act in connection with the execution of a warrant under section 62 is set out below. Text marked as [...] denotes the omission of provisions that are not relevant for section 62 purposes.

65.-(1) A person is guilty of an offence if he intentionally obstructs any person in the exercise of his powers under a warrant issued under section 62 [...].

(2) A person guilty of an offence under subsection (1) is liable –
(a) on summary conviction, to a fine not exceeding the statutory maximum;
(b) on conviction on indictment, to imprisonment for a term not exceeding two years or to a fine or to both.

The statutory maximum fine on summary conviction is currently £5,000. The fine on conviction on indictment is unlimited.

SECTION 72 OF THE ACT

The text of section 72 is set out below. Text marked as [...] denotes the omission of provisions that are not relevant for section 62 purposes.

72.- (1) This section applies to an offence under [...] section [...] 65.

(2) If an offence committed by a body corporate is proved –
(a) to have been committed with the consent or connivance of an officer, or
(b) to be attributable to any neglect on his part,

the officer as well as the body corporate is guilty of the offence and liable to be proceeded against and punished accordingly.

(3) In subsection (2) "officer", in relation to a body corporate, means a director, manager, secretary or other similar officer of the body, or a person purporting to act in any such capacity.

(4) If the affairs of a body corporate are managed by its members, subsection (2) applies in relation to the acts and defaults of a member in connection with his functions of management as if he were a director of the body corporate.

(5) If an offence committed by a partnership in Scotland is proved –
(a) to have been committed with the consent or connivance of a partner, or
(b) to be attributable to any neglect on his part,

the partner as well as the partnership is guilty of the offence and liable to be proceeded against and punished accordingly.

(6) In subsection (5) "partner" includes a person purporting to act as a partner.

DATED this [ ] day of [ ] 20
THE HONOURABLE MR JUSTICE [ ]

Warrant

B3–012

IN THE HIGH COURT OF JUSTICE CLAIM No. of 20
CHANCERY DIVISION

CLAIMANT:

OFFICE OF FAIR TRADING
[insert address]

PREMISES TO WHICH THIS WARRANT RELATES:

[insert address]

WARRANT TO ENTER PREMISES AND EXERCISE POWERS UNDER SECTIONS 62 AND 64 COMPETITION ACT 1998

To *[insert name of undertaking]* who is believed to be the occupier of the premises described above ("the premises") and to any undertaking in charge of, or operating at or from, the premises:

You should read the terms of this Warrant and the accompanying Explanatory Note very carefully. You are advised to consult a Solicitor as soon as possible. If you intentionally obstruct any person in the exercise of his powers under the Warrant, you will have committed a criminal offence under section 65 of the Competition Act 1998, the relevant terms of which are set out in Schedule C to this Warrant.

An application was made on *[insert date]* by Counsel for the Office of Fair Trading ("the OFT") to The Honourable Mr Justice *[insert name]*("the Judge"), for a warrant under section 62(1) of the Competition Act 1998 ("the Act") on the grounds that *[insert the text of the relevant subsections (1) and (2), (3) or (4) as appropriate]*

The Judge read the evidence in support of the application and was satisfied that the grounds in section 62(1) and *[insert the relevant subsection (2), (3) or (4) as appropriate]* of the Act have been met and accepted the undertakings by *[insert name]*, an officer of the OFT authorised to act as the "named officer", set out in Schedule A to this Warrant. The named officer is the principal officer of the OFT in charge of executing this Warrant.

As a result of the application, this Warrant in relation to the premises was issued by the Judge on *[insert date]*.

1. This Warrant is issued in respect of an inspection by the European Commission ordered by its Decision *[insert Decision number]* dated *[insert date]* into *[set out the subject matter and purpose of the inspection]*

8

2. This Warrant continues in force until the end of the period of one month beginning with the day on which it is issued and may be executed on any one or more days within that period.

3. By this Warrant the persons named in Schedule B are authorised to produce the Warrant between 9:30am and 5:30pm on a weekday *[unless the Judge has ordered otherwise]* and on producing the Warrant:

   (a) to enter the premises using such force as is reasonably necessary for the purpose;

   (b) to search for books and records which a Commission official has power to examine, using such force as is reasonably necessary for the purpose;

   (c) to take or obtain copies of or extracts from such books and records; and

   (d) to seal the premises, any part of the premises or any books or records which a Commission official has power to seal, for the period and to the extent necessary for the inspection.

4. Any person entering the premises by virtue of this Warrant may take with him such equipment as appears to him to be necessary.

5. If there is no one at the premises when the named officer proposes to execute this Warrant he must, before executing it -

   (a) take such steps as are reasonable in all the circumstances to inform the occupier of the intended entry; and

   (b) if the occupier is so informed, afford him or his legal or other representative a reasonable opportunity to be present when the Warrant is executed.

6. If the named officer is unable to inform the occupier of the intended entry he must, when executing this Warrant, leave a copy of it in a prominent place on the premises.

7. On leaving the premises, the named officer must, if they are unoccupied or the occupier is temporarily absent, leave them as effectively secured as he found them.

8. Terms used in this Warrant have the following meanings in accordance with the Act:

   "books and records" includes books and records stored on any medium;

   "Commission official" means any of the persons authorised by the European Commission to conduct the inspection ordered by the Decision specified in paragraph 1 of this Warrant and whose name is set out in Schedule B;

9

"occupier" means any person whom the named officer reasonably believes is the occupier of the premises; and

"premises" means any premises (and includes any land or means of transport) of an undertaking or association of undertakings which a Commission official has power to enter in the course of the inspection ordered by the Decision specified in paragraph 1 of this Warrant; and for the avoidance of doubt, "premises" does not include the homes of directors, managers or other members of staff of the undertaking or association of undertakings concerned.

SCHEDULE A

UNDERTAKINGS GIVEN TO THE COURT BY THE NAMED OFFICER

If the premises are occupied when the Warrant is to be executed:

1. To produce the Warrant and an Explanatory Note on arrival at the premises; and
2. As soon as possible thereafter to serve personally a copy of the Warrant and of the Explanatory Note on the occupier or person appearing to him to be in charge of the premises.

The Explanatory Note was produced to the Court with the application for the Warrant.

SCHEDULE B

NAMES OF PERSONS AUTHORISED TO EXECUTE THE WARRANT

[insert name of the named officer] who is the OFT's officer authorised in writing by the OFT to be the named officer.

[insert name of each of the other officers] who are the OFT's other officers authorised in writing by the OFT to accompany the named officer.

*[insert name of each of the other person(s)]*who is *[insert job title of each person]* and who [is/are] authorised in writing by the OFT to accompany the named officer. *[This paragraph shall be included if the Judge so orders pursuant to section 62(5A).]*

[insert name of each of the Commission officials] who are the persons authorised by the European Commission to conduct the inspection ordered by the Decision specified in paragraph 1 of this Warrant.

SCHEDULE C

OFFENCE CREATED BY SECTION 65 OF THE ACT

The offence created by section 65 of the Act in connection with the execution of a warrant under section 62 is set out below. Text marked as […] denotes the omission of provisions that are not relevant for section 62 purposes.

65.-(1) A person is guilty of an offence if he intentionally obstructs any person in the exercise of his powers under a warrant issued under section 62 […].

(2) A person guilty of an offence under subsection (1) is liable –
(a) on summary conviction, to a fine not exceeding the statutory maximum;
(b) on conviction on indictment, to imprisonment for a term not exceeding two years or to a fine or to both.

The statutory maximum fine on summary conviction is currently £5,000. The fine on conviction on indictment is unlimited.

SECTION 72 OF THE ACT

The text of section 72 is set out below. Text marked as […] denotes the omission of provisions that are not relevant for section 62 purposes.

72.- (1) This section applies to an offence under […] section […] 65.

(2) If an offence committed by a body corporate is proved –
(a) to have been committed with the consent or connivance of an officer, or
(b) to be attributable to any neglect on his part,

the officer as well as the body corporate is guilty of the offence and liable to be proceeded against and punished accordingly.

(3) In subsection (2) "officer", in relation to a body corporate, means a director, manager, secretary or other similar officer of the body, or a person purporting to act in any such capacity.

(4) If the affairs of a body corporate are managed by its members, subsection (2) applies in relation to the acts and defaults of a member in connection with his functions of management as if he were a director of the body corporate.

(5) If an offence committed by a partnership in Scotland is proved –
(a) to have been committed with the consent or connivance of a partner, or
(b) to be attributable to any neglect on his part,

the partner as well as the partnership is guilty of the offence and liable to be proceeded against and punished accordingly.

(6) In subsection (5) "partner" includes a person purporting to act as a partner.

DATED this [ ] day of [ ] 20
THE HONOURABLE MR JUSTICE [ ]

PRACTICE DIRECTION – ANTI-SOCIAL BEHAVIOUR (ORDERS UNDER SECTION 1B(4) OF THE CRIME AND DISORDER ACT 1998)

B10–001 *Practice Direction – Anti-Social Behaviour (Orders Under Section 1B(4) Of the Crime And Disorder Act 1998) is revoked by the Civil Procedure Rules 2004 (S.I. 204 no. 1306).*

PRACTICE DIRECTION—COMPETITION LAW—CLAIMS RELATING TO THE APPLICATION OF ARTICLES 81 AND 82 OF THE EC TREATY AND CHAPTERS I AND II OF PART I OF THE COMPETITION ACT 1998

Delete existing Practice Direction and substitute:

Scope and Interpretation

B12–001

1.1 This practice direction applies to any claim relating to the application of—

(a) Article 81 or Article 82 of the Treaty establishing the European Community; or

(b) Chapter I or Chapter II of Part I of the Competition Act 1998.

1.2 In this practice direction—

(a) 'the Act' means the Competition Act 1998;

(b) 'the Commission' means the European Commission;

(c) 'the Competition Regulation' means Council Regulation (EC) No 1/2003 of 16 December 2002 on the implementation of the rules on competition laid down in Articles 81 and 82 of the Treaty;

(d) 'national competition authority' means—

(i) the Office of Fair Trading; and

(ii) any other person or body designated pursuant to Article 35 of the Competition Regulation as a national competition authority of the United Kingdom;

(d) 'the Treaty' means the Treaty establishing the European Community.

Venue

B12–002

2.1 A claim to which this Practice Direction applies—

(a) must be commenced in the High Court at the Royal Courts of Justice; and

(b) will be assigned to the Chancery Division.

2.2 Any party whose statement of case raises an issue relating to the application of Article 81 or 82 of the Treaty, or Chapter I or II of Part I of the Act, must—

(a) state that fact in his statement of case; and

(b) apply for the proceedings to be transferred to the Chancery Division at the Royal Courts of Justice, if they have not been commenced there.

2.3 Rule 30.8 provides that where proceedings are taking place in the

Queen's Bench Division, a district registry of the High Court or a county court, the court must transfer the proceedings to the Chancery Division at the Royal Courts of Justice if the statement of case raises an issue relating to the application of Article 81 or 82, or Chapter I or II.

2.4 Where proceedings are commenced in or transferred to the Chancery Division at the Royal Courts of Justice in accordance with this paragraph, that court may transfer the proceedings or any part of the proceedings to another court if—

(a) the issue relating to the application of Article 81 or 82, or Chapter I or II, has been resolved; or

(b) the judge considers that the proceedings or part of the proceedings to be transferred does not involve any issue relating to the application of Article 81 or 82, or Chapter I or II.

(Rule 30.3 sets out the matters to which the court must have regard when considering whether to make a transfer order.)

Notice of proceedings

B12–003 **3** Any party whose statement of case raises or deals with an issue relating to the application of Article 81 or 82, or Chapter I or II, must serve a copy of the statement of case on the Office of Fair Trading at the same time as it is served on the other parties to the claim (addressed to the Director of Competition Policy Co–ordination, Office of Fair Trading, Fleetbank House, 2–6 Salisbury Square, London EC4Y 8JX).

Case management

B12–004 **4.1** Attention is drawn to the provisions of article 15.3 of the Competition Regulation (co–operation with national courts), which entitles competition authorities and the Commission to submit written observations to national courts on issues relating to the application of Article 81 or 82 and, with the permission of the court in question, to submit oral observations to the court.

4.1A A national competition authority may also make written observations to the court, or apply for permission to make oral observations, on issues relating to the application of Chapter I or II.

4.2 If a national competition authority or the Commission intends to make written observations to the court, it must give notice of its intention to do so by letter to Chancery Chambers at the Royal Courts of Justice (including the claim number and addressed to the Court Manager, Room TM 6.06, Royal Courts of Justice, Strand, London WC2A 2LL) at the earliest reasonable opportunity.

4.3 An application by a national competition authority or the Commission for permission to make oral representations at the hearing of a claim must be made by letter to Chancery Chambers (including the claim number and addressed to the Court Manager, Room TM 6.06, Royal Courts of Justice, Strand, London WC2A 2LL) at the earliest reasonable opportunity, identifying the claim and indicating why the applicant wishes to make oral representations.

4.4 If a national competition authority or the Commission files a notice under paragraph 4.2 or an application under paragraph 4.3, it must at the same time serve a copy of the notice or application on every party to the claim.

4.5 Any request by a national competition authority or the Commission for the court to send it any documents relating to a claim should be made at the same time as filing a notice under paragraph 4.2 or an application under paragraph 4.3.

4.6 Where the court receives a notice under paragraph 4.2 it may give case management directions to the national competition authority or the Commission, including directions about the date by which any written observations are to be filed.

4.7 The court will serve on every party to the claim a copy of any directions given or order made—

(a) on an application under paragraph 4.3; or

(b) under paragraph 4.6.

4.8 In any claim to which this practice direction applies, the court shall direct a pre–trial review to take place shortly before the trial, if possible before the judge who will be conducting the trial.

Avoidance of conflict with Commission decisions

5.1 In relation to claims which raise an issue relating to the application of Article 81 or 82 of the Treaty, attention is drawn to the provisions of article 16 of the Competition Regulation (uniform application of Community competition law). **B12–005**

5.2 Every party to such a claim, and any national competition authority which has been served with a copy of a party's statement of case, is under a duty to notify the court at any stage of the proceedings if they are aware that—

(a) the Commission has adopted, or is contemplating adopting, a decision in relation to proceedings which it has initiated; and

(b) the decision referred to in (a) above has or would have legal effects in relation to the particular agreement, decision or practice in issue before the court.

5.3 Where the court is aware that the Commission is contemplating adopting a decision as mentioned in paragraph 5.2(a), it shall consider whether to stay the claim pending the Commission's decision.

Judgments

6 Where any judgment is given which decides on the application of Article 81 or Article 82 of the Treaty, the judge shall direct that a copy of the transcript of the judgment shall be sent to the Commission. **B12–006**

At the end of paragraph 6 add:

Judgments may be sent to the Commission electronically to comp–amicus@.eu.int or by post to the European Commission–DG Competition, B–1049, Brussels.

Note

For first sentence substitute:

This Practice Directions came into force on June 1, 2004. **B12–007**

SECTION C

PRE–ACTION PROTOCOL

PRE–ACTION PROTOCOLS—EDITORIAL

Future developments

For "six" substitute:

C1A–006 eight

Delete last two sentences.

Compliance with the Practice Direction and Protocols: The Court's Role

Add at end:

C1A–010 Very few cases are reported in relation to the Construction and Engineering protocol. In *Daejan Investments Ltd v. Park West Club Ltd* (Part 20 Buxton Associates) [2003] EWHC 2872a dispute about allegedly defective waterproofing, the claimant issued proceedings without properly investigating the situation or taking advice from a waterproofing expert. The nature of their claim changed several times. When applying to significantly amend their statement of case they were ordered to pay all the costs of the Part 20 party to date for non–compliance with the protocol.

Pre–Action Disclosure of Documents CPR 31.16 - see also editorial to Part 31

Add after penultimate paragraph:

C1A–012 In *Rose v. Lynx Express Ltd* [2004] EWCA Civ 447 the Court of Appeal reversed a first instance decision to refuse preaction disclosure as the judge had prematurely decided that the applicant's cause of action in a potential claim concerning the transfer of shares was not made out: they said that it would normally be sufficient to found an application under CPR, r.31.16(3) for the substantive claim to be "properly arguable" and to have a real prospect of success.

In *Marshall v. Allots (a firm)* 2004 unrep. preaction disclosure of documents relating to the valuation of shares was ordered in a professional negligence dispute as they would enable the case to be pleaded in a more focussed way.

In the final paragraph, delete final bullet point paragraph.

Add at end:

The Chancery Division and Commercial Court perhaps show greater reluctance to make orders for preaction disclosure, including where the documents requested would be disclosed at a slightly later stage under a preaction protocol.

In *Inland Revenue Commissioners v. Blueslate Ltd* [2003] EWHC 2022, ChD, the commissioners' application for disclosure of documents by the company to enable the Commissioners to decide whether to start misfeasance proceedings against the company directors and the liquidator was refused on the grounds that disclosure in advance of the precise identification of issues would militate against efficient case management of the potential proceedings.

Steamship Mutual Underwriting Association Trustees (Bermuda Ltd) v. Baring Asset Management Ltd [2004] EWHC 202 was a professional negligence claim about the alleged mismanagement of a fund, to which that preaction protocol applied. The Trustees application for disclosure of documents to enable them to draft the letter of claim was refused because the protocol provided for disclosure with the letter of response and a letter of claim could be written without documents.

In *Snowstar Shipping Co. Ltd v. Craig Shipping Plc* [2003] EWHC 1367 (Comm.), Morison J. said for an order to be made the documents requested must be "decisive on the conduct or even the existence of the potential litigation" and any order would be "limited to what is strictly necessary".

In *Phoenix Natural Gas Ltd v. British Gas Trading Ltd* [2004] EWHC 451, Cooke J. said that an applicant had to show "exceptional circumstances" to obtain an order for preaction disclosure. The case concerned a supply contract which included a provision for British Gas to reopen the price on service of a notice if certain conditions were fulfilled. A notice was served which Phoenix wanted to challenge and the documents they requested were those which British Gas were relying upon to justify that the conditions in the contract had been met.

Commencement

For table in paragraph 5.1 substitute:

C1–005

Protocol	Coming into force	Publication
Personal Injury	26 April 1999	January 1999
Clinical Negligence	26 April 1999	January 1999
Construction and Engineering Disputes	2 October 2000	September 2000
Defamation	2 October 2000	September 2000
Profesional Negligence	16 July 2001	May 2001
Judicial Review	4 March 2002	3 December 2001
Disease and Illness	8th December 2003	September 2003
Housing Disrepair	8th December 2003	September 2003

Other points of difficulty

Pre–action admissions

Add at end:

C2A–005 And in *Hamilton v.Hertfordshire CC* [2003] EWHC 3018, QB the defendant was allowed to withdraw an admission of liability for an accident to a teaching assistant involved in lifting a disabled child from a school swimming pool because she had given three different accounts of the incident in the letter of claim and witness statements. *Mallia v. Islington London Borough Council* [2004] 1 C.L. 40 permission was refused to resile from the admission when the time lapse between the admission and the application to resile was 20 months and when no reason was given for the change of mind. *Ali v. Car Nation* [2004] 5 C.L. 48 was decided similarly when the time lapse was 11 months and the defendant sought to rely on an expert's report received after the admission was given but six months before the application was made– the court said the claimant would be prejudiced and the application was not made promptly.

SECTION D

PROCEDURAL GUIDES

EXECUTION

Add after the heading 'Guide No. 12.6':

D1–031 CCR Order 29 rule 1(5A) provides that a warrant of committal shall not, without further order of the court, be enforced more than 2 years after the date on which the warrant is issued.

Add after the heading 'Guide No. 12.7':

D1–032 RSC Order 52, rule 7A provides that a warrant for the arrest of a person against whom an order of committal has been made shall not, without further order of the court, be enforced more than 2 years after the date on which the warrant is issued.

Add after the heading 'Guide No. 12.8':

D1–033 With effect from April 1, 2004, please note that references to "Sheriffs" in CCR O.16 and CCR O.17, should be interpreted as including references to an individual authorised to act as an enforcement officer under the Courts Act 2003. (See CCR O.16, r.7(1A) and CCR O.17, r.1(2).) See also the Courts Act 2003, s.99 and Schedule 7, which abolish any rule of law requiring a writ of execution issued from the High Court to be directed to a sheriff and provide for the authorisation of High Court enforcement officers.

APPEALS

Delete existing text under the heading 'Documents to be filed with the Appellant's Notice' and substitute:

D1–035 Save in appeals from the small claims track, the documents to be filed with the Appellant's Notice are listed at PD52 para. 5.6. (For small claims see PD52 para. 5.8A).

In the second paragraph under the heading 'Procedure after permission is obtained, or if permission is not required', for "(PD52 6.2)" substitute:

(PD52 para. 6.3)

In the first paragraph under the heading 'Documents to be filed with the Respondent's Notice', for "no later than 21 days" substitute:

D1–036 no later than **14** days

In the second paragraph under the heading 'Miscellaneous matters', for "see PD52 15.3 to 15.6" substitute:

see CPR, r.52.15

In the third paragraph under the heading 'Miscellaneous matters', for "PD52 15.1 to 15.14" substitute:

PD52 15.1 to 15.19

COSTS

Add after the heading 'Guide No. 14.1':

D1–038 Note: from January 6, 2004 for a limited period, a pilot scheme for detailed assessment by the Supreme Court Costs Office of costs of civil proceedings in London County Courts is in force. Please refer to "Practice direction—Pilot scheme for detailed assessment by the Supreme Court Costs Office of costs of civil proceedings in London county courts" which supplements CPR Part 47 to check whether the pilot scheme applies to any particular case.

VOLUME 2

CIVIL PROCEDURE RULES

SECTION 2

SPECIALIST PROCEEDINGS UNDER PART 49 OF THE CIVIL PROCEDURE RULES

2C PROCEEDINGS IN THE TECHNOLOGY & CONSTRUCTION COURT

PART 60—TECHNOLOGY AND CONSTRUCTION COURT CLAIMS

Transfer of proceedings

In rule 5.2, for "(Room 30.5(3) provides" substitute:

5.2 (Rule 30.5(3) provides **2C–15**

2D ADMIRALTY JURISDICTION AND PROCEEDINGS

PART 61—ADMIRALTY CLAIMS AND THE PRACTICE DIRECTION—ADMIRALTY CLAIMS

Limitation Claim

Delete the full stop at the end of the fourth paragraph and add:

(para. 13). **2D–71**

Delete the full stop at the end of the fifth paragraph and add:

(*ibid*, para. 17).

Delete the full stop at the end of the sixth paragraph and add:

(*ibid*, para. 18).

Add at end:

Article 2.1(a) of the 1976 Convention does not extend the right to limit to a claim for damage to the vessel by reference to the tonnage of which limitation is to be calculated, see *CMA CGM SA v. Classica Shipping Co. Ltd (The CMA Djakarta)* [2004] EWCA Civ 114; [2004] 1 Lloyd's Rep. 460, CA. Nor does the Convention provide for a limitation on liablity for the costs of litigation, see *Thompson v. Masterton* [2004] 1 Lloyd's Rep 304 [Roy. Ct. Guernsey]. See too *Newcastle Port Corp v. Pevitt (The Robert Whitmore)* [2004] 2 Lloyd's Rep. 47(NSWSC), fund is exclusive of costs.

Service

Add at end:

2D–73 In the *ICL Shipping Ltd v. Chin Tai Steel Enterprise Co Ltd (The ICL Vikraman)* [2003] EWHC 2320; [2004] 1 W.L.R. 2254 the Court held that in CPR, r.61.11(5)(c) the "claim" referred to is the claim to limit rather than any underlying claim and the words "any applicable convention" should be construed as covering the 1976 Convention. This case also concerns the construction and scope of Articles 11 and 13 of the 1976 Convention.

Charterers

For the last sentence substitute:

2D–76 See further *CMA CGM SA v. Classica Shipping Co. Ltd (The CMA Djakarta)* [2004] EWCA Civ 114; [2004] 1 Lloyd's Rep. 460, CA. The term charterers is to be given its ordinary meaning. Accordingly, the charterer's ability to limit will depend on the type of claim brought against him and not the capacity (*e.g.* qua owner) in which he was acting when his liability was incurred.

PRACTICE DIRECTION—ADMIRALTY CLAIMS

Withdrawal of cautions

For "Form ADM12A (see para. 7.4 above)." substitute:

2D–103 Form **ADM12A** (see para. 7.5 above).

Limitation fund and interest

Delete the full stop at the end of the first paragraph and add:

2D–108 and the Merchant Shipping (Liability of Shipowners and Others) (New Rate of Interest) Order 2004 (S.I. 2004 No. 931) effective April 28, 2004.

For the last paragraph substitute:

The prescribed rate is defined as one per cent more than the base rate quoted from time to time by the Bank of England or the rate of interest set by any body which may supercede it and, where there is for the time being more than one such rate, the lowest of them (Article 2 of the S.I. 2004 No. 931).

2E ARBITRATION PROCEEDINGS

PART 62—ARBITRATION CLAIMS

Note

Delete existing text and substitute:

2E–16.1 In *Moscow City Council v. Bankers Trust Co.* [2004] EWCA Civ 314; [2004] 2 Lloyd's Rep. 179, the Court of Appeal reviewed the several considerations material to deciding whether the hearing of an arbitration claim should be in public or in private and whether publication of any judgment given or order made should be restricted or not. At paragraph 34, Mance L.J. said:

"The consideration that parties have elected to arbitrate confidentially and privately cannot dictate the position is respect of arbitration claims brought to court under CPR 62.10. CPR 62.10 therefore only represents a starting point. Such proceedings are no longer consensual. The possibility of pursuing them exists in the public interest . The courts, when called upon to exercise the supervisory role assigned to them under the Arbitration Act 1996, are acting as a branch of the state, not as a mere extension of the consensual arbitral process. Nevertheless, they are acting in the public interest to facilitate the fairness and well–being of a consensual method of dispute resolution, and both the Rule Committee and the courts can still take into account the parties' expectations regarding privacy and confidentiality when agreeing to arbitrate."

And at paragraphs 38 and 39:

"...In arbitration claims relating to such arbitrations, the starting point may easily give way to a public hearing. In every case, while it will be appropriate to start the hearing in private as contemplated by CPR 62.10, the court should be ready to hear representations from one or other party that the hearing should be continued in public, and should anyway if appropriate raise this possibility with the parties, as Lord Woolf stressed in *ex p. Kaim Todner*.

Further, even though the hearing may have been in private, the court should, when preparing and giving judgment, bear in mind that any judgment should be given in public, where this can be done without disclosing significant confidential information."

And at paragraph 42:

"...It is, I think, better to describe CPR 62.10 and indeed 39.2 as establishing starting points, rather than as presumptions. If neither the parties nor the judge of his or her own motion raises any question about the appropriateness of private hearing, where that is the starting position, then the hearing will remain private. But, once the question of publication is raised, the judge's task is to weigh all relevant circumstances; and even where it is not raised by the parties, he or she may if appropriate raise it of his own motion."

THE ARBITRAL PROCEEDINGS

Section 39 – Power to make provisional awards

Note

Add new paragraph 2E–168.1:

2E–168.1 Under this provision an arbitrator has power to make a freezing order on a provisional basis if the parties have so agreed, see *Kastner v. Jason* [2004] EWHC 592; [2004] 2 lloyd's Rep. 233(Ch).

POWERS OF COURT IN RELATION TO ARBITRAL PROCEEDINGS

Section 43 – Securing the attendance of witnesses

Note

Add new paragraph 2E–180.1:

2E–180.1 There is no power under s.43 for a Court to order disclosure against a third party as opposed to issuing a witness summons for the production in evidence of specific documents. Nor are the Courts powers under CPR, r.31.17 to be translated into the context of arbitration, see *BNP Paribas v. Deloitte and Touch LLP* [2003] EWHC 2874 (Comm); [2004] 1 Lloyd's Rep. 233.

Section 44 – Court powers exercisable in support of arbitral proceedings

Interim Injunctions

Add at end:

2E–183.1 In determining the Court's jurisdiction under s.44(2)(e) it is necessary to consider subsections (3), (4) and (5) viewing subsection (3) as permissive and not prohibitive in its effect, see *Hiscox Underwriting Ltd v. Dickson Manchester & Co Ltd* [2004] EWHC 479; [2004] 1 All E.R. (Comm) 753.

POWERS OF THE COURT IN RELATION TO AWARD

Section 67 – Challenging the award: substantive jurisdiction

Note

Add at end:

2E–239 A challenge under this section involves a re–hearing rather than a review, see *Azov Shipping Co. v. Baltic Shipping Co. (No.1)* [1999] 1 All E.R. 476; [1999] 1 Lloyd's Rep. 68; *Peterson Farms Inc. v. C&M Farming Ltd* [2004] EWHC 121 (Comm); [2004] 1 Lloyd's Rep. 603.

The identification of parties to an arbitration agreement is a matter of substantive not procedural law, see *Peterson Farms Inc. v. C&M Farming Ltd* above in which award in favour of non–parties which were within the same group of companies as the company named in the arbitration agreement held to have been made without jurisdiction.

Section 70 – Challenge or appeal: supplementary provisions

Section 70(7)

Add new paragraph 2E–252.1:

2E–252.1 In *Peterson Farms Inc v. C & M Farming Ltd* [2003] EWHC 2298; [2004] 1 Lloyd's Rep. 614 the Court considered factors material to the exercise of its discretion under s.70(7) holding inter alia that in most cases, it is likely that demonstration by the party against whom the jurisdictional challenge is made that the challenge is flimsy or otherwise lacks substance is likely to be regarded as a threshold requirement for the court's consideration whether in all the circumstances it is appropriate to require, as a condition of proceeding under s.67, that money payable under the award shall be brought into Court or otherwise secured pending the determination of the application.

2F INTELLECTUAL PROPERTY PROCEEDINGS

I. PROVISIONS ABOUT PATENTS AND REGISTERED DESIGNS

Jurisdiction of Masters

In sub–paragraph 8.1(4), delete "and".

2F–90 *Add new sub–paragraph 8.1(6):*

(6) enforcement of money judgments.

2G APPLICATIONS UNDER THE COMPANIES ACT 1985

Para. (f) Applications to sanction a compromise or arrangement (s.425 et seq.)

In the second paragraph, for "Re Inpower Ltd [2003] EWHC 2743 (Ch)" substitute:

2G–38 *Re InPower Ltd* [2004] 1 All E.R. 903.

SECTION 3

OTHER PROCEEDINGS

3A RESIDENTIAL TENANCIES

NATIONAL ASSISTANCE ACT 1948

PART III – LOCAL AUTHORITY SERVICES

PROVISION OF ACCOMODATION

Section 21 – Duty of local authorities to provide accommodation

Editorial Introduction

In "A and W v. Lambeth LBC; G v. Barnet LBC (also reported as R.(on the application of G) v. Barnet LBC)", for "[2003] UKHL 57; [2003] 3 W.L.R. 1194; The Times, October 24, 2003" substitute:

3A–32 *A and W v. Lambeth LBC*; *G v. Barnet LBC* (also reported as *R.(on the application of G) v. Barnet LBC*) [2003] UKHL 57; [2003] 3 W.L.R. 1194; [2004] 1 All E.R. 97

Asylum Seekers

In the second paragraph, add at the end after "solely because of destitution.":

3A–38 Where a destitute 'asylum–seeker' within the terms of Asylum and Immigration Act 1999, s.94(1) with children requires accommodation, a local authority's duty does not extend to accommodating the children. Responsibility for them falls on NASS rather than on the local authority and they are to be treated as "destitute" even though actually sheltered with their parent. In such circumstances, the appropriate practical solution is for the council to accommodate the whole family with NASS meeting the cost of accommodating the children (*R.(on the application of O) v. Haringey LBC* [2004] EWCA Civ 535).

In "R (Mani) v. Lambeth LBC", for "[2003] EWCA Civ 836; The Times, July 23, 2003" substitute:
R.(Mani) v. Lambeth LBC [2003] EWCA Civ 836; [2004] H.L.R. 5

discharge of duty

In "Anufrijeva v. Southwark LBC", for "[2003] EWCA Civ 1406; The Times, October 17, 2003" substitute:

3A-39 *Anufrijeva v. Southwark LBC* [2003] EWCA Civ 1406; [2004] 2 W.L.R. 603; [2004] 1 All E.R. 833

PROTECTION FROM EVICTION ACT 1977

PART I - UNLAWFUL EVICTION AND HARASSMENT

UNLAWFUL EVICTION AND HARASSMENT

Section 3- Prohibition of eviction without due process of law

Prohibition of eviction without due process of law

Delete from "It does not apply to:" to "Breach of this section is an actionable tort." and substitute:

3A-88 It applies to occupiers who are not statutorily protected (*i.e.* those who lack full security of tenure as defined in s.8(1), *i.e.* under Rent Act 1977, Rent (Agriculture) Act 1976, Landlord and Tenant Act 1954 Part II, Agricultural Holdings Act 1986, Housing Act 1988 and Agricultural Tenancies Act 1995). Eviction of such tenants without a court order is unlawful.

It does not however apply to excluded tenants (see s.3A below). Excluded occupiers can be evicted without court orders.

Breach of section 3 is an actionable tort.

Section 3A - Excluded tenancies and licences

Excluded tenancies

Delete the full stop at the end and add:

3A-91 , and for a case where Elias J. considered whether premises were "a hostel" (s.3A(8)), see *Rogerson v. Wigan MBC* [2004] EWHC 1677, QB (residents allocated bedrooms with their own locks in flat but shared the facilities with other residents, warden with master key and terms of occupation including a nightly curfew, a prohibition on alcohol and drugs. The premises met the statutory definition of a "hostel" in Housing Act 1985, s.622 in that they provided residential accommodation with facilities for preparation of food "otherwise than in separate or self contained accommodation"). See too *Mohamed v. Manek and Kensington and Chelsea RLBC* (1995) 27 H.L.R. 439, CA.

RENT ACT 1977

PART VII - SECURITY OF TENURE

LIMITATIONS ON RECOVERY OF POSSESSION OF DWELLING-HOUSES LET ON PROTECTED TENANCIES OR SUBJECT TO STATUTORY TENANCIES

Section 98 - Grounds for possession of certain dwelling-houses

ECHR Art 8 and reasonableness

Add at end:

3A-203 See too *Newham LBC v. Kibata* [2003] EWCA Civ 1785; [2004] HLR 28 and *Bradney v. Birmingham CC; Birmingham CC v. McCann* [2003] EWCA Civ 1783; [2004] HLR 27.

SCHEDULES

SCHEDULE 1 – STATUTORY TENANCIES

Part II – Relinquishing Tenancies and Changing Tenants

No pecuniary consideration to be required on change of tenant under paragraph 13

Member of the original tenant's family

For "The Court of Appeal has held" substitute:

3A-251 The House of Lords has held

In "Ghaidan v. Mendoza" for "[2002] EWCA Civ 1533; [2003] Ch 380; [2003] 1 W.L.R. 684; The Times, November 14, 2002" substitute:

Ghaidan v. Mendoza [2004] UKHL 30; [2004] 3 W.L.R. 113

HOUSING ACT 1980

PART IV – JURISDICTION AND PROCEDURE

JURISDICTION AND PROCEDURE

Section 89 – Restriction on discretion of court in making orders for possession of land

Restriction on discretion of court in making orders for possession of land

In "Hackney LBC v. Side by Side (Kids) Ltd", for "[2003] EWHC 1813 (QBD); The Times, August 5, 2003" substitute:

3A-301 *Hackney LBC v. Side by Side (Kids) Ltd* [2003] EWHC 1813 (QBD); [2004] 1 W.L.R. 363

SECURITY OF TENURE

Section 79 – Secure tenancies

Sub-tenancies

Add new paragraph 3A-338.1:

3A-338.1 A secure tenancy for the purpose of s.79 is one in which there is a direct landlord and tenant relationship between a landlord, satisfying the landlord condition in s.80, and a tenant, satisfying the tenant condition in s.81. If a local housing authority grants a lease to a charitable housing trust which in turn grants a sub-tenancy to an individual who lives in the property, the occupier's secure sub-tenancy persists while the intermediate lease continues, so long as the parties continue to meet the landlord and tenant conditions. As soon as either of them ceases to do so or the sub-lease in respect of which s.79 provided security ceases to exist, so also does the secure sub-tenancy (*Lambeth LBC v. Kay* [2004] EWCA Civ 926 and *Bruton v. London and Quadrant Housing Trust* [2000] 1 A.C. 406; [1999] 3 W.L.R. 150, HL).

Section 82 – Security of tenure

Security of tenure

For subsection 82(1) substitute:

3A-350 **82.**—(1) A secure tenancy which is either—

(a) a weekly or other periodic tenancy, or
(b) a tenancy for a term certain but subject to termination by the landlord,
cannot be brought to an end by the landlord except by obtaining an order mentioned in subsection (1A);

(1A) These are the orders—
(a) an order of the court for the possession of the dwelling–house;
(b) an order under subsection (3);
(c) a demotion order under section 82A.

Note

Delete existing text and substitute:

3A–351 Section 82 has been amended by Anti–social Behaviour Act 2003, s.14(1). This amendment was brought into force in England on June 30, 2004 by the Anti–social Behaviour Act 2003 (Commencement No.3 and Savings) Order 2004 S.I. 2004 No. 1502 (c.61). It does not have effect in relation to any proceedings for the possession of a dwelling–house begun before June 30, 2004. There will be a separate commencement order for Wales. The amendment allows a secure tenancy to be brought to an end by a demotion order.

Editorial note

In the first paragraph, for "It is not yet in force, but at the time that Civil Procedure 2004 went to press, it appeared likely that it would be implemented sometime during 2004. There will be separate commencement orders for England and Wales." substitute:

3A–357 This amendment was brought into force in England on June 30, 2004 by the Anti–social Behaviour Act 2003 (Commencement No.3 and Savings) Order 2004 S.I. 2004 No. 1502 (c.61). There will be a separate commencement order for Wales.

Section 83 – Proceedings for possession or termination: notice requirements

Proceedings for possession or termination: notice requirements

In subsection 83(1), for "the possession of a dwelling–house let under a secure tenancy or proceedings for the termination of a secure tenancy unless—" substitute:

3A–364 **83.**—(1) an order mentioned in section 82(1A) unless—

In subsection 83(2)(b), for "an order for the possession of the dwelling–house or for the termination of the tenancy" substitute:

(2)(b) the order

After subsection 83(4) add:

(4A) If the proceedings are for a demotion order under section 82A the notice—
(a) must specify the date after which the proceedings may be begun;
(b) ceases to be in force twelve months after the date so specified.

In subsection 83(5), for "subsection (3) or (4)" substitute:

(5) subsection (3), (4) or (4A)

Note

Delete existing text and substitute:

3A–365 Substituted by the Housing Act 1996, s.147.

Section 83 has been amended by Anti–social Behaviour Act 2003, s.14(3) and Schedule 1. The amendments were brought into force in England on June 30, 2004 by the Anti–social Behaviour Act 2003 (Commencement No.3 and Savings) Order 2004 S.I. 2004 No. 1502 (c.61). There will be a separate commencement order for Wales.

Proceedings for possession or termination: notice requirements

At the beginning of the second paragraph add:

3A–366 For the prescribed forms of notice, see the Secure Tenancies (Notices) Regulations 1987 S.I. 1987 No.775 (as amended by the Secure Tenancies (Notices) (Amendment) Regulations 1997 S.I. 1997 No. 71, the Secure Tenancies (Notices) (Amendment No.2) Regulations 1997 S.I. 1997 No. 377 and the Secure Tenancies (Notices) (Amendment) (England) Regulations 2004 S.I. 2004 No. 1627). Paragraph 2(1) of the Regulations states that the notice should be "substantially to the same effect" as that contained in the Regulations.

"the court considers it just and equitable to do dispense with the requirement of such a notice" (s.83(1)(b))

In the first line, delete "new".

3A–368 *In the first paragraph, add after "(cf. the Housing Act 1988, s.8(1)(b)).":*

It is "obviously only in relatively exceptional cases where the court should be prepared to dispense with a section 83 notice". (*Braintree DC v. Vincent* [2004] EWCA Civ 415—a case where the Court of Appeal held that a judge was entitled to dispense with the notice on unusual facts. A s.83 notice would have been of no benefit to the tenant—indeed it would have been to her disadvantage because it would have postponed the date for possession and added to her liability for rent.)

Section 84 – Grounds for orders for possession

ECHR Art 8 and reasonableness

Add at end:

3A–381 See too *Newham LBC v. Kibata* [2003] EWCA Civ 1785; [2004] HLR 28 and *Bradney v. Birmingham CC*; *Birmingham CC v. McCann* [2003] EWCA Civ 1783; [2004] HLR 27.

Disability Discrimination Act 1995

Add new paragraph 381.1:

3A–381.1 The effect of Disability Discrimination Act 1995, s.22(3)(c) is that it is unlawful to discriminate "by evicting [a] disabled person or subjecting him to any other detriment". Although unlawfulness under the Disability Discrimination Act is not a bar to a landlord seeking a possession order under the Housing Act, the fact that the eviction is unlawful and not justified is a highly relevant consideration for the s.7 discretion of whether or not to make a possession order. The Disability Discrimination Act contains its own code which requires a higher threshold than the Housing Act to justify an eviction (*North Devon Homes Ltd v. Brazier* [2003] EWHC 574 (QB)). In *Manchester CC v. Romano* [2004] EWCA (Civ) 834, the Court of Appeal, in a very thorough review of the legislation, stated that when a court considers the Disability Discrimination Act 1995 in the context of possession proceedings, the first matter which has to be determined is whether the person who complains about disability discrimination is a "disabled person" within the meaning of the Disability Discrimination (Meaning of Disability) Regulations 1996 S.I. 1996 No. 1455, Sched.1, ss.1–3, and the *Guidance on matters to be taking into account in determining questions relating to the definition of disability* issued by the Secretary of State. Secondly, the court should consider whether or not there has been discrimination— *i.e.* treating a disabled person less favourably for a reason which relates to the disabled person's disability. Thirdly, the court should consider whether the landlord's treatment of the tenant is justified. It is only justified if in the landlord's opinion the treatment (*viz*the decision to set in motion proceedings for possession) is necessary in order not to endanger the health or safety of any of the people living in neighbouring houses and it is reasonable, in all the circumstances, for the landlord to hold that opinion. The landlord must prove that if it does not take this action someone's health or safety would be endangered. It does not have to prove that that person's health or safety has actually been damaged. The 1995 Act does not explicitly provide a defence for disabled persons who wish to assert that the reason why their landlord brought possession proceedings related to disability. It is though open to such disabled persons to counterclaim for a declaration that they have been unlawfully discriminated against and/or to counterclaim for injunctive relief. Furthermore, if tenants can prove that the landlord's conduct amounts to unlawful discrimination, this is bound to be a relevant factor when the court is determining whether it is reasonable to make an order for possession. The Court of Appeal stated that it is preferable, in cases involving a secure tenancy or an assured tenancy, for tenants to assert that it is unreasonable for the court to make a possession order, rather than to complicate the proceedings by adding a formalistic counterclaim for a declaration or an injunction. Landlords whose tenants hold secure or assured tenancies must consider the position carefully before they decide to serve a notice seeking possession or to embark on possession proceedings against a tenant who is or might be mentally impaired. They should liase closely with local social services authorities at an early stage.

Section 85 – Extended discretion of court in certain proceedings for possession

Warrants and the ECHR

Delete full stop at the end of the first paragraph and add:

; *Newham LBC v. Kibata* [2003] EWCA Civ 1785; [2004] HLR 28 and *Bradney v. Birmingham CC; Birmingham CC v. McCann* [2003] EWCA Civ 1783; [2004] HLR 27. **3A–388**

Editorial note

For "It is not yet in force, but at the time that Civil Procedure 2004 went to press, it appeared likely that it would be implemented sometime during 2004. There will be separate commencement orders for England and Wales." substitute:

It was brought into force in England on June 30, 2004 by the Anti–social Behaviour Act 2003 (Commencement No.3 and Savings) Order 2004 S.I. 2004 No. 1502 (c.61). It does not have effect in relation to any proceedings for the possession of a dwelling–house begun before June 30, 2004. There will be a separate commencement order for Wales. **3A–390**

Section 87 – Persons qualified to succeed tenant

Persons qualified to succeed tenant

In the seventh paragraph, for "Ghaidan v. Mendoza [2002] EWCA Civ 1533; [2003] Ch. 380; [2003] 1 W.L.R. 684; The Times, November 14, 2002" substitute:

Ghaidan v. Mendoza [2004] UKHL 30; [2004] 3 W.L.R. 113 **3A–400**

Add at end:

A minor who satisfies the succession conditions may succeed to a secure tenancy. In that case a secure tenancy in equity vests in the minor. The Trusts of Land and Appointment of Trustees Act 1996, Sched.1 operates in such a way that the legal tenancy to which the minor succeeded is held on trust until the age of majority is reached (*Kingston–Upon–Thames RLBC v. Prince* (1999) 31 H.L.R. 794, CA and *Newham LBC v. Ria* [2004] EWCA Civ 41; January 15, 2004).

Section 89 – Succession to periodic tenancy

"member of the tenant's family"

For "R (Gangera) v. Hounslow LBC [2003] EWHC 794 Admin; April 11, 2003" substitute:

R. (on the application of Gangera) v. Hounslow LBC [2003] EWHC 794 Admin; [2003] H.L.R. 68 **3A–409**

Add at end:

See too *Newham LBC v. Kibata* [2003] EWCA Civ 1785; [2004] HLR 28 and *Bradney v. Birmingham CC; Birmingham CC v. McCann* [2003] EWCA Civ 1783; [2004] HLR 27.

Demoted tenancies

Add new section 1B:

1B. A tenancy is not a secure tenancy if it is a demoted tenancy within the meaning of section 143A of the Housing Act 1996. **3A–476.1**

Note

Delete full stop at the end of the first paragraph and add:

and by Anti–social Behaviour Act 2003, s.14(5) and Sched.1. **3A–489**

Delete from the third paragraph to the end and substitute:

Schedule 1 has been amended by Anti–social Behaviour Act 2003, s.14(5) and Sched.1. It was brought into force in England on June 30, 2004 by the Anti–social Behaviour Act 2003 (Commencement No.3 and Savings) Order 2004 S.I. 2004 No. 1502 (c.61). There will be a separate commencement order for Wales.

Sched.1, para. 4—accommodation for homeless persons

Add at end:

3A–493 Also *Newham LBC v. Kibata* [2003] EWCA Civ 1785; [2004] HLR 28 and *Bradney v. Birmingham CC; Birmingham CC v. McCann* [2003] EWCA Civ 1783; [2004] HLR 27.

Sched.2, Ground 5—tenancy obtained by false statement

In the second paragraph, add at end:

3A–520 See too *Waltham Forest LBC v. Roberts* [2004] EWCA Civ 940.

Proper working order

Add at end:

3A–536 The implied covenant to repair under s.11(1A)(b)(i) does not extend to installations located in parts of a building in which the lessor does not have an estate or interest, even if the lessor has an estate or interest in other parts of the same building (*Niazi Services Ltd v. Van der Loo* [2004] EWCA Civ 53; [2004] 1 W.L.R. 1254—inadequate water pressure in top floor flat caused by works in ground floor/basement restaurant in which the mesne lessor of the top floor had no interest).

Damages

Add at end:

3A–538 In *English Churches Housing Group v. Shine* [2004] EWCA Civ 434, the Court of Appeal stated that although the guidelines in *Wallace* "are not to be applied in a mechanistic or dogmatic way", and that there are cases "where the level of distress or inconvenience experienced by a tenant may require an award in excess of the level of rent payable" if an award is made in excess of the rent payable, "clear reasons need to be given". The Court referred to "a basic rule of thumb that—all other things being equal—the maximum award of damages should be the rental value of the premises." Where a global award of damages is made, it should be cross–checked against the annual rent to ensure that damages are neither too high nor too low.

Note

For "However that provision is not yet in force." substitute:

3A–568 As to implementation, see the Commonhold and Leasehold Reform Act 2002 (Commencement No.2 and Savings) (England) Order 2003 S.I. 2003 No. 1986 (C.82) and the Commonhold and Leasehold Reform Act 2002 (Commencement No.2 and Savings) (Wales) Order 2004 S.I. 2004 No. 669 (W.62) (C.25).

Note

Delete the last sentence and substitute:

3A–581 The new sections were brought into force on October 31, 2003 in England and on March 30, 2004 in Wales by the Commonhold and Leasehold Reform Act 2002 (Commencement No. 2 and Savings) (England) Order 2003 S.I. 2003 No. 1986 (C.82) and the Commonhold and Leasehold Reform Act 2002 (Commencement No.2 and Savings) (Wales) Order 2004 S.I. 2004 No. 669 (W.62) (C.25). However the new sections have no effect in relation to qualifying works begun before the commencement date.

Note

After "That new section is not yet in force," add:

3A–604 except to the extent that it provides for the making of regulations,

Delete full stop at the end and add:

3A–609 and the Commonhold and Leasehold Reform Act 2002 (Commencement No.2 and Savings) (Wales) Order 2004 S.I. 2004 No. 669 (W.62) (C.25).

Note

For "see the Commonhold and Leasehold Reform Act 2002 (Commencement No. 2 and Savings) (England) Order 2003 (S.I. 2003 No. 1986) (C.82)." substitute:

see the Commonhold and Leasehold Reform Act 2002 (Commencement No. 2 and Savings) (England) Order 2003 (S.I. 2003 No. 1986) (C.82) and the Commonhold and Leasehold Reform Act 2002 (Commencement No.2 and Savings) (Wales) Order 2004 S.I. 2004 No. 669 (W.62) (C.25). **3A–640**

Editorial note

For "It is not yet in force, but at the time that Civil Procedure 2004 went to press, it appeared likely that it would be implemented sometime during 2004. There will be separate commencement orders for England and Wales." substitute:

It was brought into force in England on June 30, 2004 by the Anti-social Behaviour Act 2003 (Commencement No.3 and Savings) Order 2004 S.I. 2004 No. 1502 (C.61). There will be a separate commencement order for Wales. **3A–698**

Orders for possession

Delete the full stop at the end of the first paragraph and add:

and *New Charter Housing (North) Ltd v. Ashcroft* [2004] EWCA Civ 310; March 8, 2004. **3A–708**

Disability Discrimination Act 1995

Add at end:

In *Manchester CC v. Romano* [2004] EWCA Civ 834, the Court of Appeal, in a very thorough review of the legislation, stated that when a court considers the Disability Discrimination Act 1995 in the context of possession proceedings, the first matter which has to be determined is whether the person who complains about disability discrimination is a "disabled person" within the meaning of the Disability Discrimination (Meaning of Disability) Regulations 1996 S.I. 1996 No. 1455, Sched.1, ss.1–3 and the *Guidance on matters to be taking into account in determining questions relating to the definition of disability* issued by the Secretary of State. Secondly, the court should consider whether or not there has been discrimination— *i.e.* treating a disabled person less favourably for a reason which relates to the disabled person's disability. Thirdly, the court should consider whether the landlord's treatment of the tenant is justified. It is only justified if in the landlord's opinion the treatment (*viz* the decision to set in motion proceedings for possession) is necessary in order not to endanger the health or safety of any of the people living in neighbouring houses and it is reasonable, in all the circumstances, for the landlord to hold that opinion. The landlord must prove that if it does not take this action someone's health or safety would be endangered. It does not have to prove that that person's health or safety has actually been damaged. The 1995 Act does not explicitly provide a defence for disabled persons who wish to assert that the reason why their landlord brought possession proceedings related to disability. It is though open to such disabled persons to counterclaim for a declaration that they have been unlawfully discriminated against and/or to counterclaim for injunctive relief. Furthermore, if tenants can prove that the landlord's conduct amounts to unlawful discrimination, this is bound to be a relevant factor when the court is determining whether it is reasonable to make an order for possession. The Court of Appeal stated that it is preferable, in cases involving a secure tenancy or an assured tenancy, for tenants to assert that it is unreasonable for the court to make a possession order, rather than to complicate the proceedings by adding a formalistic counterclaim for a declaration or an injunction. Landlords whose tenants hold secure or assured tenancies must consider the position carefully before they decide to serve a notice seeking possession or to embark on possession proceedings against a tenant who is or might be mentally impaired. They should liase closely with local social services authorities at an early stage. **3A–709**

ECHR art 8 and reasonableness

Delete closing bracket at end and add:

See too *Newham LBC v. Kibata* [2003] EWCA Civ 1785; [2004] HLR 28 and *Bradney v. Birmingham CC; Birmingham CC v. McCann* [2003] EWCA Civ 1783; [2004] HLR 27.) **3A–712**

"the court considers it just and equitable to dispense with the requirement of such a notice" (s.8(1)(b))

Add at the beginning of the second paragraph:

3A–725 It is "obviously only in relatively exceptional cases where the court should be prepared to dispense with a ... notice". (*Braintree DC v. Vincent* [2004] EWCA Civ 415—a case where the Court of Appeal held that a judge was entitled to dispense with a statutory notice on unusual facts. A notice would have been of no benefit to the tenant—indeed it would have been to her disadvantage because it would have postponed the date for possession and added to her liability for rent.)

Editorial note

For "It is not yet in force, but at the time that Civil Procedure 2004 went to press, it appeared likely that it would be implemented sometime during 2004. There will be separate commencement orders for England and Wales." substitute:

3A–740 It was brought into force in England on June 30, 2004 by the Anti-social Behaviour Act 2003 (Commencement No.3 and Savings) Order 2004 S.I. 2004 No. 1502 (C.61). There will be a separate commencement order for Wales.

Succession to assured periodic tenancy by spouse

In "Ghaidan v. Mendoza", for "[2002] EWCA Civ 1533; [2003] Ch. 380; [2003] 1 W.L.R. 684; The Times, November 14, 2002," substitute:

3A–790 *Ghaidan v. Mendoza* [2004] UKHL 30; [2004] 3 W.L.R. 113;

Editorial note

In the first paragraph, for "It is not yet in force, but at the time that Civil Procedure 2004 went to press, it appeared likely that it would be implemented sometime during 2004. There will be separate commencement orders for England and Wales." substitute:

3A–815 It was brought into force in England on June 30, 2004 by the Anti-social Behaviour Act 2003 (Commencement No.3 and Savings) Order 2004 S.I. 2004 No. 1502 (C.61). There will be a separate commencement order for Wales.

Recovery of possession on expiry or termination of assured shorthold tenancy

After subsection 21(5) add:

3A–819 **21.**—(5A) Subsection (5) above does not apply to an assured shorthold tenancy to which section 20B (demoted assured shorthold tenancies) applies.

Note

Delete from the second paragraph until the end and add:

3A–820 Section 21 has been amended by Anti-social Behaviour Act 2003, s.15(2). The amendment was brought into force in England on June 30, 2004 by the Anti-social Behaviour Act 2003 (Commencement No. 3 and Savings) Order 2004 S.I. 2004 No. 1502 (C.61). There will be a separate commencement order for Wales.

Recovery of possession on expiry or termination of assured shorthold tenancy

In the sixth paragraph, for "McDonald v. Fernandez [2003] EWCA Civ 1219; [2003] 42 E.G. 128; The Times, October 9, 2003" substitute:

3A–824 *McDonald v. Fernandez* [2003] EWCA Civ 1219; [2004] 1 W.L.R. 1027

For the seventh paragraph beginning "Accordingly, a notice served during a periodic assured shorthold tenancy..." substitute:

In order to be valid, a notice served upon a periodic assured shorthold tenant—

(1) must specify a date after which possession is required—either by inserting a particular date or by using a formula, as in *Lower Street Properties v. Jones* (above);

(2) give a date which is the last day of a period of the tenancy, and not any other day. The fact that the notice is too long does not save it from being defective. (*McDonald v. Fernandez* [2003] EWCA Civ 1219 (above));

(3) make it clear that possession is required after that date, not on it. This can be done either by stating "I require possession after [the date]" or by saying "This notice will

expire on [the date]. Proceedings cannot be commenced until after that date". It cannot be done by stating "I require possession on [the date]" because "on [the date]" and "after [the date]" are not the same thing.

Former demoted tenancies

Add new section 5A:

5A. An assured tenancy which ceases to be an assured shorthold tenancy by virtue of section 20B(2) or (4). **3A–944.1**

Note

Delete from the second paragraph until the end and add:

Section 21 has been amended by Anti–social Behaviour Act 2003, s.15(2). The amendment was brought into force in England on June 30, 2004 by the Anti–social Behaviour Act 2003 (Commencement No. 3 and Savings) Order 2004 S.I. 2004 No. 1502 (C.61). There will be a separate commencement order for Wales. **3A–948**

Restriction on termination of tenancy for failure to pay service charge

After the first paragraph add:

Courts are probably obliged to take s.81 into account even if it is not pleaded (*Mohammadi v. Anston Investments Ltd* [2003] EWCA Civ 981; [2004] H.L.R. 8). **3A–976**

Introductory tenancies

After the fifth paragraph add:

Where a landlord serves a Housing Act 1996, s.128 notice based upon the arrears, but then also relies upon allegations of nuisance, the correct procedure is normally for the landlord to serve an additional notice. However in a case where the tenant had not suffered any prejudice, and the same decision would have been reached, even without the allegations of nuisance, a tenant's challenge to the review process was dismissed (*R.(on the application of Laporte) v. Newham LBC* [2004] EWHC 227 (Admin); [2004] 2 All ER 874). **3A–993**

Add at beginning of new fourteenth paragraph, beginning "If the "trial period" ends before determination...":

In determining whether proceedings are started before the end of the trial period, proceedings are started by the issue of the claim form by the court (CPR, r.7.2 and PD7, para 5.1), not when the claim form is received by the court (*Salford City Council v. Garner* [2004] EWCA Civ 364; (2004) 148 S.J.L.B. 295).

Editorial note

For 'It is not yet in force, but at the time that Civil Procedure 2004 went to press, it appeared likely that it would be implemented sometime during 2004. There will be separate commencement orders for England and Wales." substitute:

It was brought into force in England on June 30, 2004 by the Anti–social Behaviour Act 2003 (Commencement No.3 and Savings) Order 2004 S.I. 2004 No. 1502 (C.61). There will be a separate commencement order for Wales. **3A–1029**

Editorial note

For 'It is not yet in force, but at the time that Civil Procedure 2004 went to press, it appeared likely that it would be implemented sometime during 2004. There will be separate commencement orders for England and Wales." substitute:

It was brought into force in England on June 30, 2004 by the Anti–social Behaviour Act 2003 (Commencement No.3 and Savings) Order 2004 S.I. 2004 No. 1502 (C.61). There will be a separate commencement order for Wales. **3A–1035**

Editorial note

For 'It is not yet in force, but at the time that Civil Procedure 2004 went to press, it appeared likely that it would be implemented sometime during 2004. There will be separate commencement orders for England and Wales." substitute:

It was brought into force in England on June 30, 2004 by the Anti–social Behaviour Act 2003 (Commencement No.3 and Savings) Order 2004 S.I. 2004 No. 1502 (C.61). There will be a separate commencement order for Wales. **3A–1039**

Editorial note

For "It is not yet in force, but at the time that Civil Procedure 2004 went to press, it appeared likely that it would be implemented sometime during 2004. There will be separate commencement orders for England and Wales." substitute:

3A–1048 It was brought into force in England on June 30, 2004 by the Anti–social Behaviour Act 2003 (Commencement No.3 and Savings) Order 2004 S.I. 2004 No. 1502 (C.61). There will be a separate commencement order for Wales.

Editorial note

For "It is not yet in force, but at the time that Civil Procedure 2004 went to press, it appeared likely that it would be implemented sometime during 2004. There will be separate commencement orders for England and Wales." substitute:

3A–1051 It was brought into force in England on June 30, 2004 by the Anti–social Behaviour Act 2003 (Commencement No.3 and Savings) Order 2004 S.I. 2004 No. 1502 (C.61). There will be a separate commencement order for Wales.

Editorial note

For "It is not yet in force, but at the time that Civil Procedure 2004 went to press, it appeared likely that it would be implemented sometime during 2004. There will be separate commencement orders for England and Wales." substitute:

3A–1055 It was brought into force in England on June 30, 2004 by the Anti–social Behaviour Act 2003 (Commencement No.3 and Savings) Order 2004 S.I. 2004 No. 1502 (C.61). There will be a separate commencement order for Wales.

Regulations

Delete existing text and substitute:

3A–1056 See the Demoted Tenancies (Review of Decisions) (England) Regulations 2004 S.I. 2004 No. 1679.

Editorial note

For "It is not yet in force, but at the time that Civil Procedure 2004 went to press, it appeared likely that it would be implemented sometime during 2004. There will be separate commencement orders for England and Wales." substitute:

3A–1060 It was brought into force in England on June 30, 2004 by the Anti–social Behaviour Act 2003 (Commencement No.3 and Savings) Order 2004 S.I. 2004 No. 1502 (C.61). There will be a separate commencement order for Wales.

Editorial note

For "It is not yet in force, but at the time that Civil Procedure 2004 went to press, it appeared likely that it would be implemented sometime during 2004. There will be separate commencement orders for England and Wales." substitute:

3A–1065 It was brought into force in England on June 30, 2004 by the Anti–social Behaviour Act 2003 (Commencement No.3 and Savings) Order 2004 S.I. 2004 No. 1502 (C.61). There will be a separate commencement order for Wales.

Editorial note

For "It is not yet in force, but at the time that Civil Procedure 2004 went to press, it appeared likely that it would be implemented sometime during 2004. There will be separate commencement orders for England and Wales." substitute:

3A–1071 It was brought into force in England on June 30, 2004 by the Anti–social Behaviour Act 2003 (Commencement No.3 and Savings) Order 2004 S.I. 2004 No. 1502 (C.61). There will be a separate commencement order for Wales.

Editorial note

For "It is not yet in force, but at the time that Civil Procedure 2004 went to press, it appeared likely that it would be implemented sometime during 2004. There will be separate commencement orders for England and Wales." substitute:

3A–1076 It was brought into force in England on June 30, 2004 by the Anti–social Behaviour Act 2003 (Commencement No.3 and Savings) Order 2004 S.I. 2004 No. 1502 (C.61). There will be a separate commencement order for Wales.

Editorial note

For 'It is not yet in force, but at the time that Civil Procedure 2004 went to press, it appeared likely that it would be implemented sometime during 2004. There will be separate commencement orders for England and Wales." substitute:

It was brought into force in England on June 30, 2004 by the Anti–social Behaviour Act 2003 (Commencement No.3 and Savings) Order 2004 S.I. 2004 No. 1502 (C.61). There will be a separate commencement order for Wales. Section 143K provides that a demoted tenancy cannot be assigned except in matrimonial proceedings or under Children Act 1989— *cf.* Housing Act 1985, s.91. There is no provision for mutual exchange— *cf.* Housing Act 1985, s.92. **3A–1081**

Editorial note

For 'It is not yet in force, but at the time that Civil Procedure 2004 went to press, it appeared likely that it would be implemented sometime during 2004. There will be separate commencement orders for England and Wales." substitute:

It was brought into force in England on June 30, 2004 by the Anti–social Behaviour Act 2003 (Commencement No.3 and Savings) Order 2004 S.I. 2004 No. 1502 (C.61). There will be a separate commencement order for Wales. **3A–1084**

Editorial note

For 'It is not yet in force, but at the time that Civil Procedure 2004 went to press, it appeared likely that it would be implemented sometime during 2004. There will be separate commencement orders for England and Wales." substitute:

It was brought into force in England on June 30, 2004 by the Anti–social Behaviour Act 2003 (Commencement No.3 and Savings) Order 2004 S.I. 2004 No. 1502 (C.61). There will be a separate commencement order for Wales. **3A–1089**

Editorial note

For 'It is not yet in force, but at the time that Civil Procedure 2004 went to press, it appeared likely that it would be implemented sometime during 2004. There will be separate commencement orders for England and Wales." substitute:

It was brought into force in England on June 30, 2004 by the Anti–social Behaviour Act 2003 (Commencement No.3 and Savings) Order 2004 S.I. 2004 No. 1502 (C.61). There will be a separate commencement order for Wales. **3A–1093**

Rules and directions

Delete existing text and substitute:

See CPR Part 65 and PD65. **3A–1095**

Editorial note

For 'It is not yet in force, but at the time that Civil Procedure 2004 went to press, it appeared likely that it would be implemented sometime during 2004. There will be separate commencement orders for England and Wales." substitute:

It was brought into force in England on June 30, 2004 by the Anti–social Behaviour Act 2003 (Commencement No.3 and Savings) Order 2004 S.I. 2004 No. 1502 (C.61). There will be a separate commencement order for Wales. **3A–1097**

Member of another's family

In "Ghaidan v. Godin–Mendoza", for "[2002] EWCA Civ 1533; [2003] Ch. 380; [2003] 2 W.L.R. 478" substitute:

Ghaidan v. Godin–Mendoza [2004] UKHL 30; [2004] 3 W.L.R. 113 **3A–1099**

Note

For 'The repeal is not yet in force, but at the time that Civil Procedure 2004 went to press, it appeared likely that it would be implemented sometime during 2004. There will be separate commencement orders for England and Wales." substitute:

In England the repeal and new sections 153A–E were implemented on June 30, 2004 by the Anti–social Behaviour Act 2003 (Commencement No.3 and Savings) Order 2004 S.I. 2004 No. 1502 (C.61). There will be a separate commencement order for Wales. **3A–1100.1**

Power to grant injunctions against anti-social behaviour

3A-1105 *Delete paragraphs 3A-1105 and 3A-1106.*

Note

For 'The repeal is not yet in force, but at the time that Civil Procedure 2004 went to press, it appeared likely that it would be implemented sometime during 2004. There will be separate commencement orders for England and Wales." substitute:

3A-1107.1 In England the repeal and new sections 153A-E were implemented on June 30, 2004 by the Anti-social Behaviour Act 2003 (Commencement No.3 and Savings) Order 2004 S.I. 2004 No. 1502 (C.61). There will be a separate commencement order for Wales.

Editorial note

In the first paragraph, for 'It is not yet in force, but at the time that Civil Procedure 2004 went to press, it appeared likely that it would be implemented sometime during 2004. There will be separate commencement orders for England and Wales." substitute:

3A-1117 It was brought into force in England on June 30, 2004 by the Anti-social Behaviour Act 2003 (Commencement No.3 and Savings) Order 2004 (S.I. 2004 No. 1502) (C.61). There will be a separate commencement order for Wales.

Minors

Add new paragraphs 3A-1122.1 to 3A-1122.3:

3A-1122 In *Enfield LBC v. B (A Minor)* [2000] 1 W.L.R. 2259, CA, the Court of Appeal doubted but left open the proposition that former s.152 could not apply to minors—but see *H v. H (A Child) (Occupation Order: Power of Arrest)* [2001] 1 F.L.R. 641; [2001] 1 F.C.R. 370; [2001] Fam. Law 261, CA. (The court has the power to attach a power of arrest to an occupation order made under Family Law Act 1996, s.47(2) against a minor. By suggesting that such a power of arrest could not be made against a 17 year old, wording was implied upon the provisions of s.47(2) of the Act that just was not there) and *Wookey v. Wookey* [1991] Fam. 121; [1991] 3 W.L.R. 135, CA. But see *G v Harrow LBC* [2004] EWHC 17 (QB). (Complaints against 14 year old. The council obtained an injunction against him under Housing Act 1996, s.152 with a power of arrest. Roderick Evans J. granted the appeal. G was too young to be sent to prison for contempt. In the absence of evidence to the contrary, common sense and experience dictated that G would have no source of income or goods that could be sequestered. The injunction could not be properly or effectively enforced and so should not have been granted. Roderick Evans J. stated that if a council did seek an injunction against a minor, it should be in a position to place evidence before the judge of the minor's circumstances which would make enforcement by a way of a fine or sequestration of assets an effective sanction for breach.)

Procedure

3A-1122.1 The County Court (Amendment) Rules 1997 set out the procedure to be followed on applications for injunctions to restrain anti-social behaviour under Housing Act 1996, ss.152 and 153 by creating a new CCR O.49, r.6B, as amended by the Civil Procedure (Amendment No.4) Rules 2001. They have been replaced by a new CPR, Part 65 (Anti-social Behaviour and Harassment) and PD 65. CPR, Pt 65 also contains provisions dealing with demoted tenancies, ASBOs and the Protection from Harassment Act 1997. The old procedure was also partly governed by a Practice Direction made by the Lord Chancellor on August 28, 1997. It has been revoked and not replaced.

(i) *Applications for anti-social behaviour injunctions.* Applications for injunctions under ss.153A, 153B or 153D must be made in Form N16A and follow the Part 8 procedure. They must be made in the court for the district in which the defendant resides or the conduct complained of occurred. (CPR, r.65.3; PD65, para.1; *cf.* CCR O.49, r.6B(1))

(ii) All applications must state the terms of the injunction applied for and be supported by written evidence. They must be made on two days notice unless the court otherwise directs. The defendant must be served personally. If the application is made without notice the affidavit should explain why notice has not been given. (CPR, r.65.3; *cf.* CCR O.49, r.6B(2) – (4))

(iii) Unless otherwise directed applications made on notice should be heard in public. (CPR, r.39.2; *cf.* PD to CCR O.49, r.6B(5))

(iv) Applications for injunctions must be made in Form N16A (PD65, para.1). Injunctions should be in Form N16. Wherever possible the claimant should file a draft of the order sought with the application and a disc with the draft order should be available to the court (PD25, para.2.4). Injunctions must be "framed in terms appropriate and proportionate to the facts of the case". If there is a risk of significant harm to a particular person or persons it is usually appropriate for the injunction to identify that person or those persons. However, in order to justify granting a wider injunction, restraining someone from causing a nuisance or annoyance to, "a person of a similar description," it is normally necessary for the judge to make a finding that there has been use or threats of violence to persons of a similar description, and that there is a risk of significant harm to persons of a similar description if an injunction is not granted in respect of them. (*Manchester City Council v. Lee* [2003] EWCA Civ 1256; [2004] 1 W.L.R. 349).

(v) If a power of arrest is sought, each provision which is to be subject to the power of arrest, must be set out in a separate clause of the injunction (CPR, r.65.4). Powers of arrest may be sought in claim forms, acknowledgements of service or Part 23 applications. They must be supported by written evidence. If made on notice, not less than two days notice must be given (CPR, r.65.9) It is important to spell out in the injunction the specific activities which are forbidden and confine the power of arrest to those specific activities alone. Under ECHR law, citizens must be able, if necessary with appropriate advice, to foresee to a reasonable degree the consequences that a given action may produce (*Silver v. United Kingdom* (1983) 5 E.H.H.R. 347, at paras 87–8). Summary arrest and detention are clearly an extremely serious interference with a person's private life, which can only be justified by an order which is "particularly precise" (*Kopp v. Switzerland* (1991) 27 E.H.R.R. 91, at para.72). See too *Manchester City Council v. Lee* [2003] EWCA Civ 1256; [2004] 1 W.L.R. 349 and, in a domestic violence context, *Hale v. Tanner* [2000] 1 W.L.R. 2377, CA, which suggests a power of arrest be attached only to paragraphs prohibiting violence or physical proximity. This is confirmed by s.153C.

(vi) A without notice court order with a power of arrest attached deserves and demands early re–consideration, ideally within 14 days. It is good practice to limit the time for the injunction and power of arrest to no longer than the time of the return hearing (*Horgan v. Horgan* [2002] EWCA Civ 1371).

(vii) The claimant must deliver a copy of an injunction with a Power of Arrest to any police station for the area where the conduct occurred—but if it was granted without notice, only after service on the defendant (CPR, r.65.4 and Form N110A; *cf.* CCR O.49, r.6B(6)). The claimant must immediately inform the police station if an injunction containing a power of arrest is varied or discharged.

(viii) The question of jurisdiction has been dealt with by an amendment to PD2B. The former position was that the jurisdiction of the court under ss.152 and 153 could be exercised by district judges as well as circuit judges. The amendment to PD2B makes it clear that district and deputy district judges have jurisdiction to grant anti–social behaviour injunctions and to commit for contempt. There is no longer any requirement that district judges and deputy district judges have to have had appropriate training before exercising the jurisdiction (*cf.* the Practice Direction made by the Lord Chancellor on August 28, 1997 which has been revoked and not replaced.) Notwithstanding the suggestion in some quarters that the former rule giving district judges jurisdiction was *ultra vires*, it is now accepted that this is not the case—see County Courts Act 1984, s.75(3)(d), repealed by Civil Procedure Act 1997 Sched.2, but Sched.1 of that Act provides that the Civil Procedure Rules may deal with the subjects contained in the former rules.

(ix) An application for a warrant of arrest under s.155(3) must be made in accordance with CPR Part 23 and may be made without notice. A claimant seeking a warrant must file an affidavit setting out grounds for the application or give oral evidence. A warrant shall not be issued unless the application is substantiated on oath and the judge has reasonable grounds for believing the defendant has failed to comply with the injunction (CPR, r.65.5).

(x) The judge before whom an arrested person is brought may deal with the matter or adjourn proceedings (CPR, r.65.6). In such circumstances the arrested person may be remanded or released. If the person is released, the matter shall be dealt with by the same or another judge within 28 days of the date the arrested person appears in court. At least two days notice of the adjourned hearing must be given. (CPR, r.65.6; *cf.* CCR O.49, r.6B(8B))

(xi) Applications for bail. An application for bail made by a person arrested under a power of arrest attached to an injunction or a warrant of arrest issued under s.155(3) may be made either orally or in an application notice. An application notice seeking bail must contain (1) the full name of the person making the application; (2) the address of the place where the person making the application is detained; (3) the address where s/he would reside if bail were granted; (4) the amount of any proposed recognizance; and (5) the grounds for the application and, where a previous application has been refused, full details of any change in circumstances which has occurred since that refusal. A copy of the application notice must be served on the person who obtained the injunction. (PD65, para.2; *cf.* PD to CCR O.49, r.6B)

(xii) If a person is bailed, subject to a recognizance, the recognizance may subsequently be taken by a judge, a justice of the peace, a justice's clerk, a senior police officer or the governor of a prison (CPR, r.65.7; *cf.* CCR O.49, r.6B(11)).

Sentences for breach of s.153A injunctions

3A–1122.2 In *Tower Hamlets LBC v. Long* (2000) 32 H.L.R. 219, CA, the Court of Appeal held that an immediate sentence of imprisonment was appropriate where a tenant had waged a personal vendetta against another tenant in breach of an injunction. However a prison sentence of three months was reduced to three weeks. In *Nottingham City Council v. Cutts* (2001) 33 H.L.R. 7, CA, the Court of Appeal dismissed an appeal against an immediate sentence of twelve months imprisonment where there had been previous breaches and where the actual breaches consisted of attempts to punch, racist and other foul language, threats to kill and kicking and banging of doors. The judge "was undoubtedly right in the case to impose a substantial term of imprisonment". Although the sentence was "a stiff one" it was not "manifestly excessive". See too *Leicester City Council v. Lewis* (2001) 33 H.L.R. 37, CA.

In *Barnet LBC v. Hurst* [2002] EWCA Civ 1009; [2003] 1 W.L.R. 722, the Court of Appeal held that a sentence of nine months imprisonment for a defendant who had breached an undertaking not to assault, threaten, harass or cause nuisance to anyone residing in or visiting a block of flats where his father lived by being loud and noisy and disturbing the neighbours' sleep was manifestly too long. The sentence was reduced to three months. The maximum sentence of two years imprisonment should be reserved for the worst cases (*Turnbull v. Middlesbrough BC* [2003] EWCA Civ 1327).

Time spent in custody on remand is not deducted from the sentence imposed on a committal for contempt of court (*Delaney v. Delaney* [1996] Q.B. 387, CA; *Sevketoglu v. Sevketoglu* [2003] EWCA Civ 1570).

Editorial note

For 'It is not yet in force, but at the time that Civil Procedure 2004 went to press, it appeared likely that it would be implemented sometime during 2004. There will be separate commencement orders for England and Wales." substitute:

3A–1124 It was brought into force in England on June 30, 2004 by the Anti–social Behaviour Act 2003 (Commencement No.3 and Savings) Order 2004 S.I. 2004 No. 1502 (C.61). There will be a separate commencement order for Wales.

Editorial note

In the first paragraph, for "It is not yet in force, but at the time that Civil Procedure 2004 went to press, it appeared likely that it would be implemented sometime during 2004. There will be separate commencement orders for England and Wales." substitute:

3A–1135 It was brought into force in England on June 30, 2004 by the Anti–social Behaviour Act 2003 (Commencement No.3 and Savings) Order 2004 S.I. 2004 No. 1502 (C.61). There will be a separate commencement order for Wales.

Editorial note

For "It is not yet in force, but at the time that Civil Procedure 2004 went to press, it appeared likely that it would be implemented sometime during 2004. There will be separate commencement orders for England and Wales." substitute:

3A–1140 It was brought into force in England on June 30, 2004 by the Anti–social Behaviour Act 2003 (Commencement No.3 and Savings) Order 2004 S.I. 2004 No. 1502 (C.61). There will be a separate commencement order for Wales.

Powers of arrest: ex–parte applications for injunctions

In subsection 154(1), for "section 152(6) or section 153" substitute:

3A–1142 **154.**—(1) section 153C(3) or 153D(4)

In subsection 154(1)(b), for "152(1)(a) or section 153(5)(a)" substitute:

(b) section 153A(4)

Powers of arrest: ex parte applications for injunctions

Delete existing text and substitute:

See commentary to ss.153A–E. **3A-1143**

Section 154 has been amended by Anti–social Behaviour Act, 2003 s.13(4).

The amendments were brought into force in England on June 30, 2004 by the Anti–social Behaviour Act 2003 (Commencement No.3 and Savings) Order 2004 S.I. 2004 No. 1502 (C.61). There will be a separate commencement order for Wales.

Arrest and remand

In subsection 155(1), for "section 152(6) or section 153" substitute:

155.—(1) section 153C(3) or 153D(4) **3A-1144**

In subsection 155(3), for "section 152(6) or section 153" substitute:

(3) section 153C(3) or 153D(4)

Note

Delete existing text and substitute:

Section 155 has been amended by Anti–social Behaviour Act, 2003 s.13(5). **3A-1145**

The amendments were brought into force in England on June 30, 2004 by the Anti–social Behaviour Act 2003 (Commencement No.3 and Savings) Order 2004 S.I. 2004 No. 1502 (C.61). There will be a separate commencement order for Wales.

Powers of arrest: supplementary provisions

In subsection 157(1), for "section 152(6) or section 153"

157.—(1) section 153C(3) or 153D(4) **3A-1151**

In subsection 157(3), for "section 152(6) or section 153"

(3) section 153C(3) or 153D(4)

Note

Delete existing text and substitute:

Section 157 has been amended by Anti–social Behaviour Act, 2003 s.13(6). **3A-1152**

They were brought into force in England on June 30, 2004 by the Anti–social Behaviour Act 2003 (Commencement No.3 and Savings) Order 2004 S.I. 2004 No. 1502 (C.61). There will be a separate commencement order for Wales.

Note

Delete the second paragraph and substitute:

It was brought into force in England on June 30, 2004 by the Anti–social Behaviour Act 2003 (Commencement No.3 and Savings) Order 2004 S.I. 2004 No. 1502 (C.61). There will be a separate commencement order for Wales. **3A-1155**

"available for his occupation"

In "R. (B) v. Southwark LBC", for " [2003] EWHC 1678 (Admin); The Times, July 30, 2003" substitute:

R. (B) v. Southwark LBC [2003] EWHC 1678 (Admin); [2004] H.L.R. 3 **3A-1160**

Guidance by the Secretary of State

For the last sentence beginning "If a local housing authority..." substitute:

The Code of Guidance is not a source of law. Although councils must take it into account and give reasons for departing from it, it is not binding on them (*R.(on the application of Khatun) v. Newham LBC* [2004] EWCA Civ 55; [2004] 3 W.L.R. 417). Where the Code of Guidance is in conflict with the Act, the words of the Act prevail (*Griffin v. Westminster City Council* [2004] EWCA Civ 108). **3A-1183**

Persons from abroad not eligible for housing assistance

For the fifth paragraph substitute:

3A–1205 Secondly, Homelessness (England) Regulations 2000 No. 701, para. 4, as amended by the Allocation of Housing & Homelessness (Amendment) (England) Regulations 2004 S.I. 2004 No. 1235, lists four classes of persons who, even though they are not habitually resident in the Common Travel Area, are eligible for housing assistance. They are—

(a) a person who is a worker for the purposes of Council Regulation (EEC) No.1612/68 or (EEC) No.1251/70;

(b) a person who is an accession state worker requiring registration who is treated as a worker for the purpose of the definition of "qualified person" in regulation 5(1) of the Immigration (European Economic Area) Regulations 2000 pursuant to regulation 5 of the Accession (Immigration and Worker Registration) Regulations 2004;

(c) a person with a right to reside pursuant to the Immigration (European Economic Area) Regulations 2000, which is derived from Council Directive No.68/360/EEC, No.73/148/EEC or No.75/34/EEC;

(d) a person who left the territory of Montserrat after November 1, 1995 because of the effect on that territory of a volcanic eruption.

Add at end:

When considering an application for interim accommodation under s.188, local authorities have a duty to make enquiries, but where the Secretary of State has refused a non–EEA national's application for a resident's permit, a local authority is entitled to take such a refusal at face value. It is reasonable not to make further enquiries (*R. (on the application of Burns) v. Southwark LBC* [2004] EWHC 1901 (Admin.)).

Vulnerable

Add at end:

3A–1235 Although the Code of Guidance (July 2002) para 8.13 states that the critical test in applying s.189(1)(c) is whether an applicant is less likely to be unable to fend for himself so that he is likely to suffer injury or detriment, the Court of Appeal has noted that the word 'likelihood' does not appear in the relevant provisions of the Act. Although local authorities must have regard to the Code of Guidance when exercising their functions under the Act, where the Code of Guidance is in conflict with the Act, the words of the Act prevail. The correct test under s.189(1)(c) is whether homeless persons are less able to fend for themselves so that they will suffer injury or detriment, not whether they are likely to suffer injury or detriment. It is not necessary to put the gloss of likeliness into the statutory test (*Griffin v. Westminster City Council* [2004] EWCA Civ 108; *The Times*, February 4, 2004). See too *Chowdhoury v. Islington LBC* [2004] EWCA Civ 08; January 13, 2004.

Settled accommodation

In the third paragraph, for "Knight v. Vale Royal BC [2003] EWCA Civ 1258; The Times, September 4, 2003 ; July 31, 2003" substitute:

3A–1256 *Knight v. Vale Royal BC* [2003] EWCA Civ 1258; [2004] H.L.R. 9

They are satisfied that the accommodation is suitable (s.193(7F))

Add new paragraph 3A–1281.1:

3A–1281.1 See s.210 below and commentary at para. 3A–1284, sub–paragraph (b).

Duty to persons with priority need who are not homeless intentionally

In sub–paragraph (b) after "Legal Action 22, November 27, 2001, QBD Admin Ct)." add:

3A–1284 (b) The requirement that accommodation be suitable means suitable for the persons to whom the duty is owed. It encompasses considerations of the range, nature and location of accommodation as well as its standard of condition, and likely duration of the applicant's occupancy (*Codona v. Mid–Bedfordshire DC* [2004] EWCA Civ 925).

In the penultimate paragraph, add at end:

After a determination has been made, if a council considers that it was wrong, it may conduct a further 'extra–statutory review'. Decisions under Housing Act 1996 as to whether applicants are in priority need or whether they are intentionally homeless are questions of public law. Accordingly once a decision has been taken the authority is permitted to revisit its conclusion (*Crawley BC v. B* (2000) 32 H.L.R. 636, CA). See too *Porteous v. West Dorset DC* [2004] EWCA Civ 244).

Reviews

Add at end:

3A–1285 After a determination has been made, if a council considers that it was wrong, it may conduct a further "extra–statutory review". Decisions under Housing Act 1996 as to whether applicants are in priority need or whether they are intentionally homeless are questions of public law. Accordingly once a decision has been taken the authority is permitted to revisit its conclusion (*Crawley BC v. B* (2000) 32 H.L.R. 636, CA. See too *Porteous v. West Dorset DC* [2004] EWCA Civ 244; [2004] HLR 30).

Section 194 – Power exercisable after minimum period of duty

Note

For the first sentence substitute:

3A–1286 Section 194 has been repealed by Homelessness Act 2002, s.6(4) which provides that Housing Act 1996, s.194 (power to continue to secure accommodation after minimum period of two years, formerly contained in s.193) shall cease to have effect.

At the end, delete "Note—Section 194 has been repealed."

Referral of case to another local housing authority

In the fifth paragraph, for "(Al–Ameri v. Kensington and Chelsea RLBC [2003] EWCA Civ 235; [2003] 1 W.L.R. 1289; [2003] 2 All E.R. 1; The Times, March 19, 2003)." substitute:

3A–1307 (*Al–Ameri v. Kensington and Chelsea RLBC* [2004] UKHL 4; [2004] 2 W.L.R. 354—although the effect of this decision will be reversed on implementation of Asylum & Immigration (Treatment of Claimants, etc) Act 2004, s.11 which will add new ss.(6) and (7) to s.199—see para. 3A–1310 below.)

Local connection

After subsection 199(5) add:

3A–1310 **199.**—(6) A person has a local connection with the district of a local housing authority if he was (at any time) provided with accommodation in that district under section 95 of the Immigration and Asylum Act 1999 (support for asylum seekers).

(7) But subsection (6) does not apply—

(a) to the provision of accommodation for a person in a district of a local housing authority if he was subsequently provided with accommodation in the district of another local housing authority under section 95 of that Act, or

(b) to the provision of accommodation in an accommodation centre by virtue of section 22 of the Nationality, Immigration and Asylum Act 2002 (c.41) (use of accommodation centres for section 95 support).

Note

Add new paragraph 3A–1310.1:

3A–1310.1 Subsections (6) and (7) were added by the Asylum & Immigration (Treatment of Claimants, etc) Act 2004, s.11. They are due to be brought into force by commencement order. The effect of the amendment is to reverse the effect of *Al–Ameri v. Kensington and Chelsea RLBC* [2004] UKHL 4; [2004] 2 W.L.R. 354; [2004] 1 W.L.R. 1104.

Reviews

In the penultimate paragraph, add at end:

3A–1329 Where issues have been put to an applicant in interview, there is no reason why a review panel should offer an oral hearing. (*Lomotey v. Enfield LBC* [2004] EWCA Civ 627. See too *Connors v. Northampton BC* [2004] EWCA Civ 427).

Failure to apply for review within 21 days

Delete closing bracket at end and add:

3A–1331 . See too *R.(Minhas) v. Wandsworth LBC* [2004] EWHC 805).

Reasons

In "Hijazi v. Kensington and Chelsea RLBC", for "[2003] EWCA Civ 692; May 7, 2003" substitute:

3A–1333 *Hijazi v. Kensington and Chelsea RLBC* [2003] EWCA Civ 692; [2003] H.L.R. 72

Editorial note

For "It is not yet in force, but at the time that Civil Procedure 2004 went to press, it appeared likely that it would be implemented sometime during 2004. There will be separate commencement orders for England and Wales." substitute:

3A–1388 It was brought into force in England on June 30, 2004 by the Anti–social Behaviour Act 2003 (Commencement No.3 and Savings) Order 2004 S.I. 2004 No. 1502 (C.61). There will be a separate commencement order for Wales.

Commencement of section 12

3A–1393 *Delete paragraph 3A–1393.*

CRIME AND DISORDER ACT 1998

Crime and Disorder Act 1998

(1998 c.37)

Add new paragraphs 3A–1401.1 to 3A–1401.22:

3A–1401.1

PART I

PREVENTION OF CRIME AND DISORDER

CHAPTER I

ENGLAND AND WALES

Crime and disorder: general

Anti–social behaviour orders.

1.—(1) An application for an order under this section may be made by a relevant authority if it appears to the authority that the following conditions are fulfilled with respect to any person aged 10 or over, namely—

(a) that the person has acted, since the commencement date, in an anti–social manner, that is to say, in a manner that caused or was likely to cause harassment, alarm or distress to one or more persons not of the same household as himself; and

(b) that such an order is necessary to protect relevant persons from further anti–social acts by him.

(1A) In this section and sections 1B and 1E 'relevant authority' means—

(a) the council for a local government area;

(aa) in relation to England, a county council;

(b) the chief officer of police of any police force maintained for a police area;
(c) the chief constable of the British Transport Police Force;
(d) any person registered under section 1 of the Housing Act 1996 (c. 52) as a social landlord who provides or manages any houses or hostel in a local government area; or
(e) a housing action trust established by order in pursuance of section 62 of the Housing Act 1988.

(1B) In this section 'relevant persons' means—
(a) in relation to a relevant authority falling within paragraph (a) of subsection (1A), persons within the local government area of that council;
(aa) in relation to a relevant authority falling within paragraph (aa) of subsection (1A), persons within the county of the county council;
(b) in relation to a relevant authority falling within paragraph (b) of that subsection, persons within the police area;
(c) in relation to a relevant authority falling within paragraph (c) of that subsection—
   (i) persons who are on or likely to be on policed premises in a local government area; or
   (ii) persons who are in the vicinity of or likely to be in the vicinity of such premises;
(d) in relation to a relevant authority falling within paragraph (d) or (e) of that subsection—
   (i) persons who are residing in or who are otherwise on or likely to be on premises provided or managed by that authority; or
   (ii) persons who are in the vicinity of or likely to be in the vicinity of such premises.

[...]

(3) Such an application shall be made by complaint to the magistrates' court whose commission area includes the local government area or police area concerned.

(4) If, on such an application, it is proved that the conditions mentioned in subsection (1) above are fulfilled, the magistrates' court may make an order under this section (an "anti–social behaviour order") which prohibits the defendant from doing anything described in the order.

(5) For the purpose of determining whether the condition mentioned in subsection (1)(a) above is fulfilled, the court shall disregard any act of the defendant which he shows was reasonable in the circumstances.

(6) The prohibitions that may be imposed by an anti–social behaviour order are those necessary for the purpose of protecting persons (whether relevant persons or persons elsewhere in England and Wales) from further anti–social acts by the defendant.

(7) An anti–social behaviour order shall have effect for a period (not less than two years) specified in the order or until further order.

(8) Subject to subsection (9) below, the applicant or the defendant may apply by complaint to the court which made an anti–social behaviour order for it to be varied or discharged by a further order.

(9) Except with the consent of both parties, no anti–social behaviour order shall be discharged before the end of the period of two years beginning with the date of service of the order.

(10) If without reasonable excuse a person does anything which he is prohibited from doing by an anti–social behaviour order, he is guilty of an offence and liable—

(a) on summary conviction, to imprisonment for a term not exceeding six months or to a fine not exceeding the statutory maximum, or to both; or

(b) on conviction on indictment, to imprisonment for a term not exceeding five years or to a fine, or to both.

(10A) The following may bring proceedings for an offence under subsection (10)—

(a) a council which is a relevant authority;

(b) the council for the local government area in which a person in respect of whom an anti–social behaviour order has been made resides or appears to reside.

(10B) If proceedings for an offence under subsection (10) are brought in a youth court section 47(2) of the Children and Young Persons Act 1933 (c. 12) has effect as if the persons entitled to be present at a sitting for the purposes of those proceedings include one person authorised to be present by a relevant authority.

(11) Where a person is convicted of an offence under subsection (10) above, it shall not be open to the court by or before which he is so convicted to make an order under subsection (1)(b) (conditional discharge) of section 1A of the Powers of Criminal Courts Act 1973 ("the 1973 Act") in respect of the offence.

(12) In this section—

'British Transport Police Force' means the force of constables appointed under section 53 of the British Transport Commission Act 1949 (c. xxix);

"the commencement date" means the date of the commencement of this section;

"local government area" means —

(a) in relation to England, a district or London borough, the City of London, the Isle of Wight and the Isles of Scilly;

(b) in relation to Wales, a county or county borough.

'policed premises' has the meaning given by section 53(3) of the British Transport Commission Act 1949.

Note

3A–1401.2 Section 1 has been amended by the Police Reform Act 2002, s.61 and by the Anti–social Behaviour Act 2003, s.85.

Anti–social behaviour order

3A–1401.3 Such an order (an ASBO) may be granted if a person has acted in an anti–social manner, that is to say, in a manner that caused or was likely to cause harassment, alarm or distress to one or more persons not of the same household as himself and such an order is necessary to protect relevant persons from further anti–social acts (s.1(1)). When considering whether a person's conduct has caused or is likely to cause harassment, alarm or distress to others within the meaning of Crime and Disorder Act 1998, s.1(1)(a) "likely" means "more probable than not". The likelihood has to be proved to the criminal standard (see *Chief Constable of Lancashire v. Potter* [2003] EWHC 2272 (Admin) and *R.(on the application of McCann) v. Manchester Crown Court* [2002] UKHL 39; [2003] 1 A.C. 787; [2002] 3 W.L.R. 1313). An ASBO may prohibit the defendant from doing anything described in the order. The prohibitions that may be imposed by an ASBO are "those necessary for the purpose of protecting persons (whether relevant persons or persons elsewhere in England and Wales) from further anti–social acts by the defendant." (s.1(4) and (6)). ASBOs have effect for the period (not less than two years) specified in the order or until further order (s.1(7)). Breach of an ASBO may be punished on summary conviction by imprisonment for a term not exceeding six months or a fine or both; or on conviction on indictment, by imprisonment for a term not exceeding five years or to a fine, or to both (s.1(10)).

A relevant authority

3A–1401.4 See s.1(1A), namely the council for a local government area, a county council, the chief officer of police of any police force maintained for a police area, the chief constable of the British Transport Police Force, a social landlord who provides or manages any houses or hostel which is registered under Housing Act 1996, s.1 or a housing action trust (see Housing Act 1988, s.62).

Relevant persons

3A–1401.5 See s.1(1B).

An application

3A–1401.6 Applications for ASBOs could originally only be made by complaint in the Magistrates Court, but see s.1B below (introduced by Police Reform Act 2002, s.63) which provides that ASBOs can be made in the county court if a relevant authority considers it is reasonable to make such an application. If the relevant authority or the person against whom the ASBO is sought is not already a party to the principal proceedings, an application can be made for him or her to be joined as a party. However a person may only be joined if his or her anti–social acts are material in relation to the principal proceedings (see s.1B(3C) below).

Power of Secretary of State to add to relevant authorities

3A–1401.7 **1A** The Secretary of State may by order provide that the chief officer of a body of constables maintained otherwise than by a police authority is, in such cases and circumstances as may be prescribed by the order, to be a relevant authority for the purposes of section 1 above.

By order

3A–1401.7.1 No such order has been made.

Orders in county court proceedings

3A–1401.8 **1B**—(1) This section applies to any proceedings in a county court ("the principal proceedings").

(2) If a relevant authority—

(a) is a party to the principal proceedings, and

(b) considers that a party to those proceedings is a person in relation to whom it would be reasonable for it to make an application under section 1,

it may make an application in those proceedings for an order under subsection (4).

(3) If a relevant authority—

(a) is not a party to the principal proceedings, and

(b) considers that a party to those proceedings is a person in relation to whom it would be reasonable for it to make an application under section 1,

it may make an application to be joined to those proceedings to enable it to apply for an order under subsection (4) and, if it is so joined, may apply for such an order.

(3A) Subsection (3B) applies if a relevant authority is a party to the principal proceedings and considers—

(a) that a person who is not a party to the proceedings has acted in an anti–social manner, and

(b) that the person's anti-social acts are material in relation to the principal proceedings.

(3B) The relevant authority may—

(a) make an application for the person mentioned in subsection (3A)(a) to be joined to the principal proceedings to enable an order under subsection (4) to be made in relation to that person;

(b) if that person is so joined, apply for an order under subsection (4).

(3C) But a person must not be joined to proceedings in pursuance of subsection (3B) unless his anti-social acts are material in relation to the principal proceedings.

(4) If, on an application for an order under this subsection, it is proved that the conditions mentioned in section 1(1) are fulfilled as respects that other party, the court may make an order which prohibits him from doing anything described in the order.

(5) Subject to subsection (6), the party to the principal proceedings against whom an order under this section has been made and the relevant authority on whose application that order was made may apply to the county court which made an order under this section for it to be varied or discharged by a further order.

(6) Except with the consent of the relevant authority and the person subject to the order, no order under this section shall be discharged before the end of the period of two years beginning with the date of service of the order.

(7) Subsections (5) to (7) and (10) to (12) of section 1 apply for the purposes of the making and effect of orders made under this section as they apply for the purposes of the making and effect of anti-social behaviour orders.

Note

3A-1401.9 Section 1B was inserted by the Police Reform Act 2002, s.63 and has been amended by the Anti-social Behaviour Act 2003, s.85.

A relevant authority

3A-1401.10 See s.1(1A), namely the council for a local government area, a county council, the chief officer of police of any police force maintained for a police area, the chief constable of the British Transport Police Force, a social landlord who provides or manages any houses or hostel which is registered under Housing Act 1996, s.1 or a housing action trust (see Housing Act 1988, s.62).

Anti-social acts

3A-1401.11 See s.1(1)(a) which refers to behaviour that has caused or was likely to cause harassment, alarm or distress.

Principal proceedings

3A-1401.12 See s.1B(1).

Procedure

3A-1401.13 Applications for relevant authorities or persons against whom ASBOs are sought to be joined to the principal proceedings are made in accordance with CPR Part 65. See CPR, r.65.23 and the commentary thereto. Note that a person may only be joined if his or her "anti-social acts are material in relation to the principal proceedings" (s.1B(3C)).

Orders on conviction in criminal proceedings

3A-1401.14 **1C**—(1) This section applies where a person (the 'offender') is convicted of a relevant offence.

(2) If the court considers—

(a) that the offender has acted, at any time since the commencement date, in an anti-social manner, that is to say in a manner that caused or was likely to cause harassment, alarm or distress to one or more persons not of the same household as himself, and

(b) that an order under this section is necessary to protect persons in any place in England and Wales from further anti-social acts by him,

it may make an order which prohibits the offender from doing anything described in the order.

(3) The court may make an order under this section—

(a) if the prosecutor asks it to do so, or

(b) if the court thinks it is appropriate to do so.

(3A) For the purpose of deciding whether to make an order under this section the court may consider evidence led by the prosecution and the defence.

(3B) It is immaterial whether evidence led in pursuance of subsection (3A) would have been admissible in the proceedings in which the offender was convicted.

(4) An order under this section shall not be made except—

(a) in addition to a sentence imposed in respect of the relevant offence; or

(b) in addition to an order discharging him conditionally.

(5) An order under this section takes effect on the day on which it is made, but the court may provide in any such order that such requirements of the order as it may specify shall, during any period when the offender is detained in legal custody, be suspended until his release from that custody.

(6) An offender subject to an order under this section may apply to the court which made it for it to be varied or discharged.

(7) In the case of an order under this section made by a magistrates' court, the reference in subsection (6) to the court by which the order was made includes a reference to any magistrates' court acting for the same petty sessions area as that court.

(8) No application may be made under subsection (6) for the discharge of an order before the end of the period of two years beginning with the day on which the order takes effect.

(9) Subsections (7), (10) and (11) of section 1 apply for the purposes of the making and effect of orders made by virtue of this section as they apply for the purposes of the making and effect of anti-social behaviour orders.

(9A) The council for the local government area in which a person in respect of whom an anti-social behaviour order has been made resides or appears to reside may bring proceedings under section 1(10) (as applied by subsection (9) above) for breach of an order under subsection (2) above.

(9B) Subsection (9C) applies in relation to proceedings in which an order under subsection (2) is made against a child or young person who is convicted of an offence.

(9C) In so far as the proceedings relate to the making of the order—

(a) section 49 of the Children and Young Persons Act 1933 (c.

12) (restrictions on reports of proceedings in which children and young persons are concerned) does not apply in respect of the child or young person against whom the order is made;

(b) section 39 of that Act (power to prohibit publication of certain matter) does so apply.

(10) In this section—

"child" and "young person"have the same meaning as in the Children and Young Persons Act 1933 (c. 12);

'the commencement date' has the same meaning as in section 1 above;

'the court' in relation to an offender means—

(a) the court by or before which he is convicted of the relevant offence; or

(b) if he is committed to the Crown Court to be dealt with for that offence, the Crown Court; and

'relevant offence' means an offence committed after the coming into force of section 64 of the Police Reform Act 2002 (c. 30).

Note

3A–1401.15 Section 1C was inserted by Police Reform Act 2002, s.64.

Interim orders

3A–1401.16 **1D**—(1) The applications to which this section applies are—

(a) an application for an anti–social behaviour order; and

(b) an application for an order under section 1B.

(2) If, before determining an application to which this section applies, the court considers that it is just to make an order under this section pending the determination of that application ("the main application"), it may make such an order.

(3) An order under this section is an order which prohibits the defendant from doing anything described in the order.

(4) An order under this section—

(a) shall be for a fixed period;

(b) may be varied, renewed or discharged;

(c) shall, if it has not previously ceased to have effect, cease to have effect on the determination of the main application.

(5) Subsection (6), (8) and (10) to (12) of section 1 apply for the purposes of the making and effect of orders under this section as they apply for the purposes of the making and effect of anti–social behaviour orders.

Note

3A–1401.17 Section 1D was inserted by Police Reform Act 2002, s.65.

Interim ASBOs

3A–1401.18 The court may make an interim ASBO if it considers that it is just to make such an order pending the determination of the main application. Interim ASBOs should be made for a fixed period, but may be varied, renewed or discharged. An interim ASBO obtained without notice to the defendant does not breach the right to a fair trial under ECHR Article 6 (*R.(on the application of M) v. Secretary of State for Constitutional Affairs* [2004] EWCA Civ 312; [2004] 1 W.L.R. 2298).

Consultation requirements

3A–1401.19 **1E**—(1) This section applies to—

(a) applications for an anti-social behaviour order; and
(b) applications for an order under section 1B.

(2) Before making an application to which this section applies, the council for a local government area shall consult the chief officer of police of the police force maintained for the police area within which that local government area lies.

(3) Before making an application to which this section applies, a chief officer of police shall consult the council for the local government area in which the person in relation to whom the application is to be made resides or appears to reside.

(4) Before making an application to which this section applies, a relevant authority other than a council for a local government area or a chief officer of police shall consult—

(a) the council for the local government area in which the person in relation to whom the application is to be made resides or appears to reside; and
(b) the chief officer of police of the police force maintained for the police area within which that local government area lies.

(5) Subsection (4)(a) does not apply if the relevant authority is a county council for a county in which there are no districts.

Note

3A-1401.20 Section 1E was inserted by Police Reform Act 2002, s.66 and amended by the Anti-social Behaviour Act 2003, s.85.

A relevant authority

3A-1401.21 See s.1(1A), namely the council for a local government area, a county council, the chief officer of police of any police force maintained for a police area, the chief constable of the British Transport Police Force, a social landlord who provides or manages any houses or hostel which is registered under Housing Act 1996, s.1 or a housing action trust (see Housing Act 1988, s.62).

Consultation

3A-1401.22 See McC v. Wigan MBC [2003] EWHC (Admin), October 30, 2003 where the lead role in seeking ASBOs was taken by a management company, which, although solely owned by the council, was a separate entity to the council. As such, in the absence of authorisation form the council, it was not authorised to consult. It was also apparent that there was a lack of knowledge on the part of the tenancy relations manager about the Home Office Guidance and an unstructured approach to the process. However these failings did not result in a substantial failure to comply with the consultation requirements. The requirement for consultation between the police and local authority in s.1E is fulfilled by substantial compliance, even though there may not have been full compliance. Information had been exchanged before making the application.

Implementation and Transitional Provisions

In the first paragraph, for "although parts are likely to come into force on October 13, 2004." substitute:

3A-1432 although 98(1) and para.5(4) and (5) of Schedule 6 and, to the extent that it relates thereto, s.97 were not brought into force until October 13, 2004.

Chapter 5 - Other Provisions About Leases

Implementation and Transitional Provisions

Delete existing text and substitute:

3A-1459 See the Commonhold and Leasehold Reform Act 2002 (Commencement No.1, Savings and Transitional Provisions) (England) Order 2002 S.I. 2002 No. 1912 (C.58), the Commonhold and Leasehold Reform Act 2002 (Commencement No.1, Savings and Transitional

Provisions) (Wales) Order 2002 S.I. 2002 No. 3012 (W.284) (C.96), the Commonhold and Leasehold Reform Act 2002 (Commencement No.2 and Savings) (England) Order 2003 S.I. 2003 No. 1986 (C.82) and the Commonhold and Leasehold Reform Act 2002 (Commencement No.2 and Savings) (Wales) Order 2004 S.I. 2004 No. 669 (W.62) (C.25).

Implementation

Add new paragraph 3A–1460.1:

3A–1460.1 Section 150 was brought into force on September 30, 2003 in England and on March 30, 2004 in Wales by the Commonhold and Leasehold Reform Act 2002 (Commencement No.2 and Savings) (England) Order 2003 S.I. No. 1986 (C.82) and the Commonhold and Leasehold Reform Act 2002 (Commencement No.2 and Savings) (Wales) Order 2004 S.I. 2004 No. 669 (W.62) (C.25).

Implementation

Add new paragraph 3A–1461.1:

3A–1461.1 Section 151 (introducing new Landlord and Tenant Act 1985, ss.20 and 20ZA) was brought into force on October 31, 2003 in England and on March 30, 2004 in Wales by the Commonhold and Leasehold Reform Act 2002 (Commencement No.2 and Savings) (England) Order 2003 S.I. No. 1986 (C.82) and the Commonhold and Leasehold Reform Act 2002 (Commencement No.2 and Savings) (Wales) Order 2004 S.I. 2004 No. 669 (W.62) (C.25) but has no effect in relation to qualifying works begun before the commencement date. Note also the Service Charges (Consultation Requirements) (England) Regulations 2003 S.I. 2003 No. 1987 and the Service Charges (Consultation Requirements) (Wales) Regulations 2004 S.I. 2004 No. 684 (W.72).

Implementation

Add new paragraph 3A–1465.1:

3A–1465.1 Section 152 (introducing new Landlord and Tenant Act 1985, ss.21 and 21A) was brought into force in so far as it confers power to make regulations on July 26, 2002 in England and on January 1, 2003 in Wales by the Commonhold and Leasehold Reform Act 2002 (Commencement No.1, Savings and Transitional Provisions) (England) Order 2002 S.I. 2002 No. 1912 (C.58) and the Commonhold and Leasehold Reform Act 2002 (Commencement No.1, Savings and Transitional Provisions) (Wales) Order 2002 S.I. 2002 No. 3012 (W.284) (C.96).

Implementation

Add new paragraph 3A–1469.1:

3A–1469.1 Section 153 (introducing new Landlord and Tenant Act 1985, s.21B) was brought into force in so far as it confers power to make regulations on July 26, 2002 in England and on January 1, 2003 in Wales by the Commonhold and Leasehold Reform Act 2002 (Commencement No.1, Savings and Transitional Provisions) (England) Order 2002 S.I. 2002 No. 1912 (C.58) and the Commonhold and Leasehold Reform Act 2002 (Commencement No.1, Savings and Transitional Provisions) (Wales) Order 2002 S.I. 2002 No. 3012 (W.284) (C.96).

Implementation

Add new paragraph 3A–1475.1:

3A–1475.1 Section 157 and Sched.10 were brought into force, subject to savings, on September 30, 2003 in England and on March 30, 2004 in Wales by the Commonhold and Leasehold Reform Act 2002 (Commencement No.2 and Savings) (England) Order 2003 S.I. 2003 No. 1986 (C.82) and the Commonhold and Leasehold Reform Act 2002 (Commencement No.2 and Savings) (Wales) Order 2004 S.I. 2004 No. 669 (W.62) (C.25).

Implementation

Add new paragraph 3A–1476.1:

3A–1476.1 Section 158 and Sched.11 were brought into force, subject to savings, on September 30, 2003 in England and on March 30, 2004 in Wales by the Commonhold and Leasehold Reform Act 2002 (Commencement No.2 and Savings) (England) Order 2003 S.I. 2003 No. 1986 (C.82) and the Commonhold and Leasehold Reform Act 2002 (Commencement No.2 and Savings) (Wales) Order 2004 S.I. No. 669 (W.62) (C.25).

Implementation

Add new paragraph 3A–1477.1:

3A–1477.1 Section 166 was brought into force in so far as it confers power to make regulations on July 26, 2002 in England and on January 1, 2003 in Wales by the Commonhold and Leasehold Reform Act 2002 (Commencement No.1, Savings and Transitional Provisions) (England) Order 2002 S.I. 2002 No. 1912 (C.58) and the Commonhold and Leasehold Reform Act 2002 (Commencement No.1, Savings and Transitional Provisions) (Wales) Order 2002 S.I. 2002 No. 3012 (W.284) (C.96).

Implementation

Add new paragraph 3A–1479.1:

3A–1479.1 Section 167 was brought into force in so far as it confers power to make regulations on July 26, 2002 in England and on January 1, 2003 in Wales by the Commonhold and Leasehold Reform Act 2002 (Commencement No.1, Savings and Transitional Provisions) (England) Order 2002 S.I. 2002 No. 1912 (C.58) and the Commonhold and Leasehold Reform Act 2002 (Commencement No.1, Savings and Transitional Provisions) (Wales) Order 2002 S.I. 2002 No. 3012 (W.284) (C.96).

Implementation

Add new paragraph 3A–1487.1:

3A–1487.1 Section 171 was brought into force in so far as it confers power to make regulations on July 26, 2002 in England and on January 1, 2003 in Wales by the Commonhold and Leasehold Reform Act 2002 (Commencement No.1, Savings and Transitional Provisions) (England) Order 2002 S.I. 2002 No. 1912 (C.58) and the Commonhold and Leasehold Reform Act 2002 (Commencement No.1, Savings and Transitional Provisions) (Wales) Order 2002 S.I. 2002 No. 3012 (W.284) (C.96).

Implementation

Add new paragraph 3A–1489.1:

3A–1489.1 Section 172 was partially brought into force, on 30 September 2003 in England and on March 30, 2004 in Wales by the Commonhold and Leasehold Reform Act 2002 (Commencement No.2 and Savings) (England) Order 2003 S.I. 2003 No. 1986 (C.82) and the Commonhold and Leasehold Reform Act 2002 (Commencement No.2 and Savings) (Wales) Order 2004 S.I. 2004 No. 669 (W.62) (C.25).

Asylum and Immigration (Treatment of Claimants, etc.) Act 2004

(2004c.19)

Add new paragraphs 3A–1508 to 3A–1510:

Accommodation for asylum seekers: local connection

3A–1508

11—(2) Subsection (3) applies where—

(a) a local housing authority would (but for subsection (3)) be obliged to secure that accommodation is available for occupation by a person under section 193 of the Housing Act 1996 (homeless persons),

(b) the person was (at any time) provided with accommodation in a place in Scotland under section 95 of the Immigration and Asylum Act 1999 (support for asylum seekers),

(c) the accommodation was not provided in an accommodation centre by virtue of section 22 of the Nationality, Immigration and Asylum Act 2002 (use of accommodation centres for section 95 support), and

(d) the person has neither—

(i) a local connection with the district of a local housing authority (in England or Wales) within the meaning of section 199 of the Housing Act 1996 as amended by subsection (1) above, nor

(ii) a local connection with a district (in Scotland) within the meaning of section 27 of the Housing (Scotland) Act 1987 (c. 26).

(3) Where this subsection applies—

(a) the duty of the local housing authority under section 193 of the Housing Act 1996 in relation to the person shall not apply, but

(b) the local housing authority—

(i) may secure that accommodation is available for occupation by the person for a period giving him a reasonable opportunity of securing accommodation for his occupation, and

(ii) may provide the person (or secure that he is provided with) advice and assistance in any attempts he may make to secure that accommodation becomes available for his occupation.

Implementation

3A–1509 This section is due to be brought into force by commencement order.

Note

3A–1510 The purpose of his section is to reverse the effect of *Al–Ameri v. Kensington and Chelsea RLBC* [2004] UKHL 4; [2004] 2 W.L.R. 354. Subsection (1) is an amendment to Housing Act 1996, s.199 and is printed at para. 3A–1310.

3B BUSINESS TENANCIES

notice of proposal

Add at end:

3B–24 Where a tenant serves a notice under s.3 stating an intention to carry out improvements, but then withdraws the notice after the landlord has served a counter notice, the landlord is not entitled to carry out the improvements (*Norfolk Capital Group Ltd v. Cadogan Estates Ltd* [2004] EWHC 385 (ChD); *The Times*, March 12, 2004).

Service of notices.

After subsection 23(1) add:

3B–79 **23.**—(1A) Occupation or the carrying on of a business—

(a) by a company in which the tenant has a controlling interest; or

(b) where the tenant is a company, by a person with a controlling interest in the company,

shall be treated for the purposes of this section as equivalent to occupation or, as the case may be, the carrying on of a business by the tenant.

(1B) Accordingly references (however expressed) in this Part of this Act to the business of, or to use, occupation or enjoyment by, the tenant shall be construed as including references to the business of, or to use, occupation or enjoyment by, a company falling within subsection (1A)(a) above or a person falling within subsection (1A)(b) above.

Note

Add at end:

and by the Regulatory Reform (Business Tenancies) (England and Wales) Order 2003 S.I. 2003 No. 3096. The latter amendment came into force June 1, 2004. **3B–80**

service of notices

After "Price v. West London Investment Building Society Ltd [1964] 1 W.L.R. 616; [1964] 2 All E.R. 318, CA" add:

; *cf. Arundel Corp. v Khokher* [2003] EWCA Civ 1784; [2004 148 S.J.L.B. 25 **3B–83**

In "Blunden v. Frogmore Investments Ltd", for " [2002] EWCA Civ 573; [2003] 29 E.G. 153" substitute:

Blunden v. Frogmore Investments Ltd [2002] EWCA Civ 573; [2003] 2 P. & C.R. 6; [2003] 29 E.G. 153

In "CA Webber (Transport) Ltd v. Network Rail Infrastructure Ltd (formerly Railtrack Plc)", for "[2003] EWCA Civ 1167; The Times, August 5, 2003" substitute:

CA Webber (Transport) Ltd v. Network Rail Infrastructure Ltd (formerly Railtrack Plc) [2003] EWCA Civ 1167; [2004] 1 W.L.R. 320; *The Times*, August 5, 2003

Editorial note

Add "Editorial note" paragraph:

Landlord and Tenant Act 1954, Part II contains provisions regulating security of tenure as between landlords and tenants of business premises. Significant amendments have been made by the Regulatory Reform (Business Tenancies) (England and Wales) Order 2003 S.I. 2003 No. 3096. These amendments apply to cases where the landlord gave a statutory notice of termination, or the tenant made a statutory request for a new tenancy on or after June 1, 2004—see the Regulatory Reform (Business Tenancies) (England and Wales) Order 2003 S.I. 2003 No. 3096 para. 29(1). The full text of para. 29 is as follows: **3B–89**

Transitional provisions

29.—(1) Where, before this Order came into force—

(a) the landlord gave the tenant notice under section 25 of the Act; or

(b) the tenant made a request for a new tenancy in accordance with section 26 of the Act,

nothing in this Order has effect in relation to the notice or request or anything done in consequence of it.

(2) Nothing in this Order has effect in relation—

(a) to an agreement—

(i) for the surrender of a tenancy which was made before this Order came into force and which fell within section 24(2)(b) of the Act; or

(ii) which was authorised by the court under section 38(4) of the Act before this Order came into force; or

(b) to a notice under section 27(2) of the Act which was given by the tenant to the immediate landlord before this Order came into force.

(3) Any provision in a tenancy which requires an order under section 38(4) of the Act to be obtained in respect of any subtenancy shall, so far as is necessary after the coming into force of this Order, be construed as if it required the procedure mentioned in section 38A of the Act to be followed, and any related requirement shall be construed accordingly.

(4) If a person has, before the coming into force of this Order, entered into an agreement to take a tenancy, any provision in that agreement which requires an order under section 38(4) of the Act to be obtained in respect of the tenancy shall continue to be effective, notwithstanding the repeal of that provision by Article 21(2) of this Order, and the court shall retain jurisdiction to make such an order.

(5) Article 20 above does not have effect where the tenant quit the holding before this Order came into force.

(6) Nothing in Articles 23 and 24 above applies to a notice under section 40 of the Act served before this Order came into force.

Note that the 1954 Act in its un–amended form applies where notices were served before that date.

The Order implements most of the recommendations of the Law Commission contained in their 1992 paper Business Tenancies: A Periodic Review of the Landlord and Tenant Act Part II (Law Com No.208).

In brief, the Order—

- changes the procedures to be followed to renew a tenancy or to terminate it without renewal. Both landlords and tenants are permitted to apply to the court for the terms of a new tenancy to be settled. Landlords are permitted to apply for an order that the tenancy be terminated without renewal if they can make out one of the statutory grounds for opposition. The requirement for a tenant to serve a counter–notice to a landlord's notice of termination is abolished.
- substitutes new time limits for applications to the court to renew tenancies and enable the parties to agree to extend these.
- widens the circumstances in which landlord and tenant can operate the statutory procedures of Part II. An individual and any company s/he controls should be treated as one and the same for the purposes of those procedures. Companies controlled by one individual should be treated as members of a group of companies.
- introduces several changes relating to interim rent. Tenants as well as landlords are allowed to apply to the court for interim rent. The date from which any interim rent determined by the court is payable becomes the earliest date for renewal of the tenancy which could have been specified in the statutory notice served by the landlord or tenant. A new method for the calculation of the amount of interim rent is introduced where the landlord does not oppose renewal. The interim rent is set at the same level as the rent for the new tenancy (*i.e.* usually, the open market rent), but subject to adjustment where market conditions or the occupational terms of the tenancy change significantly during the interim period. In other circumstances, the rules for calculation of interim rent formerly in section 24A(3), and now contained in section 24D(2), continue to apply.
- amends the rules relating to the compensation that tenants may claim where their tenancies are not renewed. It changes the method of calculation of compensation where the tenant has occupied different parts of premises for different periods of time, and where different landlords control different parts. It also enables a tenant to claim compensation if induced not to apply to court, or to withdraw an application for renewal, because of a misrepresentation.
- replaces the requirement for both parties to apply to court for approval to an agreement to exclude security of tenure or to surrender a tenancy. The new procedure requires a landlord to serve a prescribed notice on the tenant at least 14 days before the parties enter into such an agreement. Tenants must sign a simple declaration that they have received and accepted the consequences of the notice. If the parties wish to waive the 14 day period, tenants have to sign a statutory declaration, rather than a simple declaration, that they have received and accepted the consequences of the notice. In the case of an agreement to exclude security of tenure, the declaration must be made before the tenant enters into the tenancy or becomes contractually bound to do so. In the case of an agreement to surrender, the declaration must be made before entering into the agreement. The forms of the notice, the simple declaration and the statutory declaration are set out in Schedules 1 to 4 to the Order.
- increases the categories of information which a landlord and tenant can require the other to provide towards the end of a tenancy term, in order to enable effective use of the statutory renewal or termination process. They also impose an obligation to keep such information up to date for six months, make provision for parties which transfer their interests and clarify the powers of the court where a party fails to comply with obligations to provide or update information.
- clarifies what a tenant must do to terminate a tenancy to which Part II applies. If a tenant has ceased to occupy the business premises at the expiry of the contractual term, no continuation tenancy arises. Where a tenancy has continued beyond the

end of the fixed contractual term, the tenant must give three months notice, ending on any day. Where necessary, rent is apportioned.

- increases the length of the term of a new tenancy that the court may order from 14 to 15 years.

Continuation of tenancies to which Part II applies and grant of new tenancies.

In subsection 24(1), for "subject to the provisions of section 29 of this Act, the tenant under such a tenancy may apply to the court for a new tenancy" substitute:

3B–97

[**24.**—(1) subject to the following provisions of this Act either the tenant or the landlord under such a tenancy may apply to the court for an order for the grant of a new tenancy

After subsection 24(2) add:

(2A) Neither the tenant nor the landlord may make an application under subsection (1) above if the other has made such an application and the application has been served.

(2B) Neither the tenant nor the landlord may make such an application if the landlord has made an application under section 29(2) of this Act and the application has been served.

(2C) The landlord may not withdraw an application under subsection (1) above unless the tenant consents to its withdrawal.

Note

After "Law of Property Act 1969, s.15, Sched. 1." add:

3B–98

It was amended by the Regulatory Reform (Business Tenancies) (England and Wales) Order 2003 S.I. 2003 No. 3096. Those amendments came into force June 1, 2004.

Applications for determination of interim rent while tenancy continues

For section 24A substitute:

3B–105

24A.(1) Subject to subsection (2) below, if—

(a) the landlord of a tenancy to which this Part of this Act applies has given notice under section 25 of this Act to terminate the tenancy; or

(b) the tenant of such a tenancy has made a request for a new tenancy in accordance with section 26 of this Act,

either of them may make an application to the court to determine a rent (an "interim rent") which the tenant is to pay while the tenancy ("the relevant tenancy") continues by virtue of section 24 of this Act and the court may order payment of an interim rent in accordance with section 24C or 24D of this Act.

(2) Neither the tenant nor the landlord may make an application under subsection (1) above if the other has made such an application and has not withdrawn it.

(3) No application shall be entertained under subsection (1) above if it is made more than six months after the termination of the relevant tenancy.

Note

Delete text and substitute:

3B–106 New s.24A was inserted by the Regulatory Reform (Business Tenancies) (England and Wales) Order 2003 S.I. 2003 No. 3096. Those amendments came into force June 1, 2004.

Add new paragraphs 3B–110.1 to 3B–110.6:

3B–110.1

Date from which interim rent is payable

24B.—(1) The interim rent determined on an application under section 24A(1) of this Act shall be payable from the appropriate date.

(2) If an application under section 24A(1) of this Act is made in a case where the landlord has given a notice under section 25 of this Act, the appropriate date is the earliest date of termination that could have been specified in the landlord's notice.

(3) If an application under section 24A(1) of this Act is made in a case where the tenant has made a request for a new tenancy under section 26 of this Act, the appropriate date is the earliest date that could have been specified in the tenant's request as the date from which the new tenancy is to begin.

Note

3B–110.2 New s.24B was inserted by the Regulatory Reform (Business Tenancies) (England and Wales) Order 2003 S.I. 2003 No. 3096. This amendment came into force June 1, 2004.

Amount of interim rent where new tenancy of whole premises granted and landlord not opposed

3B–110.3

24C.—(1) This section applies where—

(a) the landlord gave a notice under section 25 of this Act at a time when the tenant was in occupation of the whole of the property comprised in the relevant tenancy for purposes such as are mentioned in section 23(1) of this Act and stated in the notice that he was not opposed to the grant of a new tenancy; or

(b) the tenant made a request for a new tenancy under section 26 of this Act at a time when he was in occupation of the whole of that property for such purposes and the landlord did not give notice under subsection (6) of that section, and the landlord grants a new tenancy of the whole of the property comprised in the relevant tenancy to the tenant (whether as a result of an order for the grant of a new tenancy or otherwise).

(2) Subject to the following provisions of this section, the rent payable under and at the commencement of the new tenancy shall also be the interim rent.

(3) Subsection (2) above does not apply where—

(a) the landlord or the tenant shows to the satisfaction of the court that the interim rent under that subsection differs substantially from the relevant rent; or

(b) the landlord or the tenant shows to the satisfaction of the court that the terms of the new tenancy differ from the terms of the relevant tenancy to such an extent that the interim rent under that subsection is substantially different from the rent which (in default of such agreement) the court would have determined under section 34 of this Act to be payable under a tenancy which commenced on the same day as the new tenancy and whose other terms were the same as the relevant tenancy.

(4) In this section "the relevant rent" means the rent which (in default of agreement between the landlord and the tenant) the court would have determined under section 34 of this Act to be payable under the new tenancy if the new tenancy had commenced on the appropriate date (within the meaning of section 24B of this Act).

(5) The interim rent in a case where subsection (2) above does not apply by virtue only of subsection (3)(a) above is the relevant rent.

(6) The interim rent in a case where subsection (2) above does not apply by virtue only of subsection (3)(b) above, or by virtue of subsection (3)(a) and (b) above, is the rent which it is reasonable for the tenant to pay while the relevant tenancy continues by virtue of section 24 of this Act.

(7) In determining the interim rent under subsection (6) above the court shall have regard—

(a) to the rent payable under the terms of the relevant tenancy; and

(b) to the rent payable under any sub–tenancy of part of the property comprised in the relevant tenancy,

but otherwise subsections (1) and (2) of section 34 of this Act shall apply to the determination as they would apply to the determination of a rent under that section if a new tenancy of the whole of the property comprised in the relevant tenancy were granted to the tenant by order of the court and the duration of that new tenancy were the same as the duration of the new tenancy which is actually granted to the tenant.

(8) In this section and section 24D of this Act "the relevant tenancy" has the same meaning as in section 24A of this Act.

Note

3B–110.4

New s.24C was inserted by the Regulatory Reform (Business Tenancies) (England and Wales) Order 2003 S.I. 2003 No. 3096. This amendment came into force June 1, 2004.

Amount of interim rent in any other case

3B–110.5

24D.—(1) The interim rent in a case where section 24C of this Act does not apply is the rent which it is reasonable for the tenant to pay while the relevant tenancy continues by virtue of section 24 of this Act.

(2) In determining the interim rent under subsection (1) above the court shall have regard—

(a) to the rent payable under the terms of the relevant tenancy; and

(b) to the rent payable under any sub–tenancy of part of the property comprised in the relevant tenancy,

but otherwise subsections (1) and (2) of section 34 of this Act shall apply to the determination as they would apply to the determination of a rent under that section if a new tenancy from year to year of the whole of the property comprised in the relevant tenancy were granted to the tenant by order of the court.

(3) If the court—

(a) has made an order for the grant of a new tenancy and has ordered payment of interim rent in accordance with section 24C of this Act, but

(b) either—

(i) it subsequently revokes under section 36(2) of this Act the order for the grant of a new tenancy; or

(ii) the landlord and tenant agree not to act on the order, the court on the application of the landlord or the tenant shall determine a new interim rent in accordance with subsections (1) and (2) above without a further application under section 24A(1) of this Act.

Note

3B–110.6 New s.24D was inserted by the Regulatory Reform (Business Tenancies) (England and Wales) Order 2003 S.I. 2003 No. 3096. This amendment came into force June 1, 2004.

Termination of tenancy by the landlord.

In subsection 25(1), after "Provided that this subsection has effect subject to" add:

3B–111 **25.**—(1) the provisions of section 29B(4) of this Act and

For subsections 25(5) and 25(6) substitute:

(5) ...

(6) A notice under this section shall not have effect unless it states whether the landlord is opposed to the grant of a new tenancy to the tenant.

(7) A notice under this section which states that the landlord is opposed to the grant of a new tenancy to the tenant shall not have effect unless it also specifies one or more of the grounds specified in section 30(1) of this Act as the ground or grounds for his opposition.

(8) A notice under this section which states that the landlord is not opposed to the grant of a new tenancy to the tenant shall not have effect unless it sets out the landlord's proposals as to—

(a) the property to be comprised in the new tenancy (being either the whole or part of the property comprised in the current tenancy);
(b) the rent to be payable under the new tenancy; and
(c) the other terms of the new tenancy.

Note

Add at beginning:

3B–112 Subsection (5) was repealed by the Regulatory Reform (Business Tenancies) (England and Wales) Order 2003 S.I. 2003 No. 3096 which also inserted new subsections (6) to (8). Those amendments came into force June 1, 2004. They only apply where a landlord has given a tenant notice under section 25 or a tenant has made a request for a new tenancy in accordance with section 26 on or after that date.

Requirements of a s.25 notice

In sub-paragraph (e) delete the first sentence and substitute:

3B–117 (e) See the Landlord and Tenant Act 1954, Part 2 (Notices) Regulations 2004 S.I. 2004 No. 1005

In the second sentence for "of the 1983 regulations" substitute:

of the 2004 regulations

service of notice

In "CA Webber (Transport) Ltd v. Network Rail Infrastructure Ltd (formerly Railtrack Plc)", for "[2003] EWCA Civ 1167; The Times, August 5, 2003" substitute:

3B–118 *CA Webber (Transport) Ltd v. Network Rail Infrastructure Ltd (formerly Railtrack Plc)* [2003] EWCA Civ 1167; [2004] 1 W.L.R. 320

more than one notice

For "Pennycook v. Shuns (EAL) Ltd [2003] EWHC 2769 (Ch); [2003] 45 E.G. 176." substitute:

Pennycook v. Shaws (EAL) Ltd [2004] EWCA Civ 100; [2004] 18 E.G. 102. (It is not open to a tenant to serve a negative counter–notice, in response to a landlord's notice terminating a tenancy, where a positive counter–notice has already been served.) **3B–121**

Tenant's request for a new tenancy.

In subsection 26(1), for "tenancy under which he holds for the time being (hereinafter referred to as "the current tenancy")" substitute:

26.—(1) current tenancy **3B–122**

In section 26(5), for "subsection (2) of section thirty–six" substitute:

(5) sections 29B(4) and 36(2)

Note

Add at end:

It was amended by the Regulatory Reform (Business Tenancies) (England and Wales) Order 2003 S.I. 2003 No. 3096. The amendment came into force June 1, 2004. It only applies where a landlord has given a tenant notice under section 25 or a tenant has made a request for a new tenancy in accordance with section 26 on or after that date. **3B–123**

prescribed form

Delete the first paragraph and substitute:

See the Landlord and Tenant Act 1954, Part 2 (Notices) Regulations 2004 S.I. 2004 No. 1005. **3B–128**

Termination by tenant of tenancy for fixed term.

After subsection 27(1) add:

[27.—(1A) Section 24 of this Act shall not have effect in relation to a tenancy for a term of years certain where the tenant is not in occupation of the property comprised in the tenancy at the time when, apart from this Act, the tenancy would come to an end by effluxion of time. **3B–131**

In subsection 27(2), for "section 24 of this Act may be brought to an end on any quarter day" substitute:

(2) shall not come to an end by reason only of the tenant ceasing to occupy the property comprised in the tenancy but may be brought to an end on any day

After subsection 27(2) add:

(3) Where a tenancy is terminated under subsection (2) above, any rent payable in respect of a period which begins before, and ends after, the tenancy is terminated shall be apportioned, and any rent paid by the tenant in excess of the amount apportioned to the period before termination shall be recoverable by him.

Note

Delete full stop at the end and add:

and amended by the Regulatory Reform (Business Tenancies) (England and Wales) Order 2003 S.I. 2003 No. 3096. The amendment came into force June 1, 2004. It does not have effect in relation to a notice served or request made or anything done in consequence of them prior to that date. **3B–132**

For existing section 29 substitute:

Order by court for grant of new tenancy or termination of current tenancy **3B–141**

29.—(1) Subject to the provisions of this Act, on an application under section 24(1) of this Act, the court shall make an order for the grant of a new tenancy and accordingly for the termination of the current tenancy immediately before the commencement of the new tenancy.

(2) Subject to the following provisions of this Act, a landlord may apply to the court for an order for the termination of a tenancy to which this Part of this Act applies without the grant of a new tenancy—

(a) if he has given notice under section 25 of this Act that he is opposed to the grant of a new tenancy to the tenant; or

(b) if the tenant has made a request for a new tenancy in accordance with section 26 of this Act and the landlord has given notice under subsection (6) of that section.

(3) The landlord may not make an application under subsection (2) above if either the tenant or the landlord has made an application under section 24(1) of this Act.

(4) Subject to the provisions of this Act, where the landlord makes an application under subsection (2) above—

(a) if he establishes, to the satisfaction of the court, any of the grounds on which he is entitled to make the application in accordance with section 30 of this Act, the court shall make an order for the termination of the current tenancy in accordance with section 64 of this Act without the grant of a new tenancy; and

(b) if not, it shall make an order for the grant of a new tenancy and accordingly for the termination of the current tenancy immediately before the commencement of the new tenancy.

(5) The court shall dismiss an application by the landlord under section 24(1) of this Act if the tenant informs the court that he does not want a new tenancy.

(6) The landlord may not withdraw an application under subsection (2) above unless the tenant consents to its withdrawal.

Note

For existing text substitute:

3B–142 A new s.29 was substituted by the Regulatory Reform (Business Tenancies) (England and Wales) Order 2003 S.I. 2003 No. 3096. The amendment came into force June 1, 2004.

Add new paragraphs 3B–150.1 to 3B–150.4:

3B–150.1 Time limits for applications to court

29A.—(1) Subject to section 29B of this Act, the court shall not entertain an application—

(a) by the tenant or the landlord under section 24(1) of this Act; or

(b) by the landlord under section 29(2) of this Act,

if it is made after the end of the statutory period.

(2) In this section and section 29B of this Act "the statutory period" means a period ending—

(a) where the landlord gave a notice under section 25 of this Act, on the date specified in his notice; and

(b) where the tenant made a request for a new tenancy under section 26 of this Act, immediately before the date specified in his request.

(3) Where the tenant has made a request for a new tenancy under sec-

tion 26 of this Act, the court shall not entertain an application under section 24(1) of this Act which is made before the end of the period of two months beginning with the date of the making of the request, unless the application is made after the landlord has given a notice under section 26(6) of this Act.

Note

3B–150.2 New s.29A was substituted by the Regulatory Reform (Business Tenancies) (England and Wales) Order 2003 S.I. 2003 No. 3096. The amendment came into force June 1, 2004.

Agreements extending time limits

3B–150.3 **29B.**—(1) After the landlord has given a notice under section 25 of this Act, or the tenant has made a request under section 26 of this Act, but before the end of the statutory period, the landlord and tenant may agree that an application such as is mentioned in section 29A(1) of this Act, may be made before the end of a period specified in the agreement which will expire after the end of the statutory period.

(2) The landlord and tenant may from time to time by agreement further extend the period for making such an application, but any such agreement must be made before the end of the period specified in the current agreement.

(3) Where an agreement is made under this section, the court may entertain an application such as is mentioned in section 29A(1) of this Act if it is made before the end of the period specified in the agreement.

(4) Where an agreement is made under this section, or two or more agreements are made under this section, the landlord's notice under section 25 of this Act or tenant's request under section 26 of this Act shall be treated as terminating the tenancy at the end of the period specified in the agreement or, as the case may be, at the end of the period specified in the last of those agreements.

Note

3B–150.4 New s.29B was substituted by the Regulatory Reform (Business Tenancies) (England and Wales) Order 2003 S.I. 2003 No. 3096. The amendment came into force June 1, 2004.

Opposition by landlord to application for new tenancy.

In subsection 30(1), for "subsection (1) of section 24 of this Act" substitute:

3B–151 [**30.**—(1) section 24(1) of this Act, or make an application under section 29(2) of this Act,

After subsection 30(1) add:

(1A) Where the landlord has a controlling interest in a company, the reference in subsection (1)(g) above to the landlord shall be construed as a reference to the landlord or that company.

(1B) Subject to subsection (2A) below, where the landlord is a company and a person has a controlling interest in the company, the reference in subsection (1)(g) above to the landlord shall be construed as a reference to the landlord or that person.

In subsection 30(2) after "entitled to oppose an application" add:

(2) under section 24(1) of this Act, or make an application under section 29(2) of this Act,

After subsection 30(2) add:

(2A) Subsection (1B) above shall not apply if the controlling interest was acquired after the beginning of the period of five years which ends with the termination of the current tenancy, and at all times since the acquisition of the controlling interest the holding has been comprised in a tenancy or successive tenancies of the description specified in section 23(1) of this Act.

Note

Delete full stop at end and add:

3B–152 and amended by the Regulatory Reform (Business Tenancies) (England and Wales) Order 2003 S.I. 2003 No. 3096. The amendments came into force June 1, 2004.

Dismissal of application for new tenancy where landlord successfully opposes.

In subsection 31(2), for "Where in a case not falling within the last foregoing subsection the landlord opposes an application under the said subsection (1) on one or more of the grounds specified in paragraphs (d), (e) and (f) of subsection (1) of the last foregoing section but establishes none of those grounds to the satisfaction of the court, then if the court would have been satisfied of any of those grounds" substitute:

3B–167 **31.**—(2) Where the landlord opposes an application under section 24(1) of this Act, or makes an application under section 29(2) of this Act, on one or more of the grounds specified in section 30(1)(d) to (f) of this Act but establishes none of those grounds, and none of the other grounds specified in section 30(1) of this Act, to the satisfaction of the court, then if the court would have been satisfied on any of the grounds specified in section 30(1)(d) to (f) of this Act,

Note

Add new paragraph 3B–167.1:

3B–167.1 Note s.31 was amended by the Regulatory Reform (Business Tenancies) (England and Wales) Order 2003 S.I. 2003 No. 3096. The amendments came into force June 1, 2004.

Grant of new tenancy in some cases where s. 30(1)(f) applies.

In subsection (1) after "paragraph (f) of section 30(1) of this Act" add:

3B–170 **[31A.**—(1) , or makes an application under section 29(2) of this Act on that ground,

Note

Delete full stop at end and add:

3B–171 and amended by the Regulatory Reform (Business Tenancies) (England and Wales) Order 2003 S.I. 2003 No. 3096. The amendment came into force June 1, 2004.

Duration of new tenancy.

In section 33, for "a term not exceeding fourteen years" substitute:

3B–180 **33.** a term not exceeding fifteen years

Note

Add new paragraph 3B–180.1:

3B–180.1 Section 33 was amended by the Regulatory Reform (Business Tenancies) (England and Wales) Order 2003 S.I. 2003 No. 3096. The amendment came into force June 1, 2004.

Rent under new tenancy.

In subsection 34(2)(a), for "application for the new tenancy" substitute:

[**34.**—(2) (a) application to the court **3B–184**

After subsection 34(2) add:

(2A) If this Part of this Act applies by virtue of section 23(1A) of this Act, the reference in subsection (1)(d) above to the tenant shall be construed as including—

(a) a company in which the tenant has a controlling interest, or
(b) where the tenant is a company, a person with a controlling interest in the company.

Note

Add at end:

Section 34(2)(a) was amended and s.34(2A) inserted by the Regulatory Reform (Business Tenancies) (England and Wales) Order 2003 S.I. 2003 No. 3096. The amendment came into force June 1, 2004. **3B–185**

Other terms of new tenancy.

In subsection 35(1) after "the rent payable thereunder)" add:

[**35.**—(1) , including, where different persons own interests which fulfil the conditions specified in section 44(1) of this Act in different parts of it, terms as to the apportionment of the rent, **3B–191**

Note

Delete full stop at end and add:

and amended by the Regulatory Reform (Business Tenancies) (England and Wales) Order 2003 S.I. 2003 No. 3096. The amendment came into force June 1, 2004. **3B–192**

Compensation where order for new tenancy precluded on certain grounds.

For subsection 37(1) substitute:

[**37.** (1) Subject to the provisions of this Act, in a case specified in subsection (1A), (1B) or (1C) below (a "compensation case") the tenant shall be entitled on quitting the holding to recover from the landlord by way of compensation an amount determined in accordance with this section. **3B–202**

(1A) The first compensation case is where on the making of an application by the tenant under section 24(1) of this Act the court is precluded (whether by subsection (1) or subsection (2) of section 31 of this Act) from making an order for the grant of a new tenancy by reason of any of the grounds specified in paragraphs (e), (f) and (g) of section 30(1) of this Act (the "compensation grounds") and not of any grounds specified in any other paragraph of section 30(1).

(1B) The second compensation case is where on the making of an application under section 29(2) of this Act the court is precluded (whether by section 29(4)(a) or section 31(2) of this Act) from making an order for the grant of a new tenancy by reason of any of the compensation grounds and not of any other grounds specified in section 30(1) of this Act.

(1C) The third compensation case is where—

(a) the landlord's notice under section 25 of this Act or, as the case may be, under section 26(6) of this Act, states his opposition to the grant of a new tenancy on any of the compensation grounds and not on any other grounds specified in section 30(1) of this Act; and

(b) either—

(i) no application is made by the tenant under section 24(1) of this Act or by the landlord under section 29(2) of this Act; or

(ii) such an application is made but is subsequently withdrawn.

In subsection 37(2), for "subsections (5A) to [(5E)] the said amount" substitute:

(2) the following provisions of this section, compensation under this section

In subsection 37(2)(a) after "the next following subsection are satisfied" add:

(a) in relation to the whole of the holding

After subsection 37(3) add:

(3A) If the conditions specified in subsection (3) above are satisfied in relation to part of the holding but not in relation to the other part, the amount of compensation shall be the aggregate of sums calculated separately as compensation in respect of each part, and accordingly, for the purpose of calculating compensation in respect of a part any reference in this section to the holding shall be construed as a reference to that part.

(3B) Where section 44(1A) of this Act applies, the compensation shall be determined separately for each part and compensation determined for any part shall be recoverable only from the person who is the owner of an interest in that part which fulfils the conditions specified in section 44(1) of this Act.

In subsection 37(4), for "the circumstances mentioned in subsection (1) of this section" substitute:

(4) a compensation case

Note

Delete full stop at end and add:

3B–203 and by the Regulatory Reform (Business Tenancies) (England and Wales) Order 2003 S.I. 2003 No. 3096. The latter amendment came into force June 1, 2004.

Add new paragraphs 3B–210.1 and 3B–210.2:

3B–210.1 Compensation for possession obtained by misrepresentation

37A.—(1) Where the court—

(a) makes an order for the termination of the current tenancy but does not make an order for the grant of a new tenancy, or

(b) refuses an order for the grant of a new tenancy,

and it subsequently made to appear to the court that the order was obtained, or the court was induced to refuse the grant, by misrepresentation or the concealment of material facts, the court may order the landlord to pay to the tenant such sum as appears sufficient as compensation for damage or loss sustained by the tenant as the result of the order or refusal.

(2) Where—

(a) the tenant has quit the holding—

(i) after making but withdrawing an application under section 24(1) of this Act; or

(ii) without making such an application; and

(b) it is made to appear to the court that he did so by reason of misrepresentation or the concealment of material facts,

the court may order the landlord to pay to the tenant such sum as appears sufficient as compensation for damage or loss sustained by the tenant as the result of quitting the holding.

Note

New section 37A was inserted by the Regulatory Reform (Business Tenancies) (England and Wales) Order 2003 S.I. 2003 No. 3096. The amendment came into force June 1, 2004. **3B–210.2**

Restriction on agreements excluding provisions of Part II.

In subsection 38(1), for "subsection (4) of this section" substitute:

[**38.**—(1) section 38A of this Act **3B–211**

In subsection 38(2), for "the last foregoing section" substitute:

(2) section 37 of this Act

In subsection 38(3), for "the last foregoing section" substitute:

(3) section 37 of this Act

Delete subsection 38(4).

Note

Delete full stop at end and add:

and was amended by the Regulatory Reform (Business Tenancies) (England and Wales) Order 2003 S.I. 2003 No. 3096. The amendment came into force June 1, 2004. It does not apply to an agreement for the surrender of a tenancy which was made or authorised by the court under section 38(4) before that date. **3B–212**

Agreements to exclude sections 24 to 28

Add new paragraphs 3B–219.1 and 3B–219.2:

Agreements to exclude provisions of Part 2 **3B–219.1**

38A.—(1) The persons who will be the landlord and the tenant in relation to a tenancy to be granted for a term of years certain which will be a tenancy to which this Part of this Act applies may agree that the provisions of sections 24 to 28 of this Act shall be excluded in relation to that tenancy.

(2) The persons who are the landlord and the tenant in relation to a tenancy to which this Part of this Act applies may agree that the tenancy shall be surrendered on such date or in such circumstances as may be specified in the agreement and on such terms (if any) as may be so specified.

(3) An agreement under subsection (1) above shall be void unless—

(a) the landlord has served on the tenant a notice in the form, or substantially in the form, set out in Schedule 1 to the Regulatory Reform (Business Tenancies) (England and Wales) Order 2003 ("the 2003 Order"); and

(b) the requirements specified in Schedule 2 to that Order are met.

(4) An agreement under subsection (2) above shall be void unless—

(a) the landlord has served on the tenant a notice in the form, or substantially in the form, set out in Schedule 3 to the 2003 Order; and

(b) the requirements specified in Schedule 4 to that Order are met.

Note

3B–219.2 New s.38A was inserted by the Regulatory Reform (Business Tenancies) (England and Wales) Order 2003 S.I. 2003 No. 3096. The amendment came into force June 1, 2004. It does not apply to an agreement for the surrender of a tenancy which was made or authorised by the court under section 38(4) before that date.

For existing section 40 substitute:

3B–223 Duty of tenants and landlords of business premises to give information to each other

40.—(1) Where a person who is an owner of an interest in reversion expectant (whether immediately or not) on a tenancy of any business premises has served on the tenant a notice in the prescribed form requiring him to do so, it shall be the duty of the tenant to give the appropriate person in writing the information specified in subsection (2) below.

(2) That information is—

(a) whether the tenant occupies the premises or any part of them wholly or partly for the purposes of a business carried on by him;

(b) whether his tenancy has effect subject to any sub–tenancy on which his tenancy is immediately expectant and, if so—

(i) what premises are comprised in the sub–tenancy;

(ii) for what term it has effect (or, if it is terminable by notice, by what notice it can be terminated);

(iii) what is the rent payable under it;

(iv) who is the sub–tenant;

(v) (to the best of his knowledge and belief) whether the sub–tenant is in occupation of the premises or of part of the premises comprised in the sub–tenancy and, if not, what is the sub–tenant's address;

(vi) whether an agreement is in force excluding in relation to the sub–tenancy the provisions of sections 24 to 28 of this Act; and

(vii) whether a notice has been given under section 25 or 26(6) of this Act, or a request has been made under section 26 of this Act, in relation to the sub–tenancy and, if so, details of the notice or request; and

(c) (to the best of his knowledge and belief) the name and address of any other person who owns an interest in reversion in any part of the premises.

(3) Where the tenant of any business premises who is a tenant under such a tenancy as is mentioned in section 26(1) of this Act has served on a reversioner or a reversioner's mortgagee in possession a notice in the prescribed form requiring him to do so, it shall be the duty of the person on whom the notice is served to give the appropriate person in writing the information specified in subsection (4) belo

(4) That information is—

(a) whether he is the owner of the fee simple in respect of the premises or any part of them or the mortgagee in possession of such an owner,

(b) if he is not, then (to the best of his knowledge and belief)—

(i) the name and address of the person who is his or, as the case may be, his mortgagor's immediate landlord in respect of those premises or of the part in respect of which he or his mortgagor is not the owner in fee simple;

(ii) for what term his or his mortgagor's tenancy has effect and what is the earliest date (if any) at which that tenancy is terminable by notice to quit given by the landlord; and

(iii) whether a notice has been given under section 25 or 26(6) of this Act, or a request has been made under section 26 of this Act, in relation to the tenancy and, if so, details of the notice or request;

(c) (to the best of his knowledge and belief) the name and address of any other person who owns an interest in reversion in any part of the premises; and

(d) if he is a reversioner, whether there is a mortgagee in possession of his interest in the premises and, if so, (to the best of his knowledge and belief) what is the name and address of the mortgagee.

(5) A duty imposed on a person by this section is a duty—

(a) to give the information concerned within the period of one month beginning with the date of service of the notice; and

(b) if within the period of six months beginning with the date of service of the notice that person becomes aware that any information which has been given in pursuance of the notice is not, or is no longer, correct, to give the appropriate person correct information within the period of one month beginning with the date on which he becomes aware.

(6) This section shall not apply to a notice served by or on the tenant more than two years before the date on which apart from this Act his tenancy would come to an end by effluxion of time or could be brought to an end by notice to quit given by the landlord.

(7) Except as provided by section 40A of this Act, the appropriate person for the purposes of this section and section 40A(1) of this Act is the person who served the notice under subsection (1) or (3) above.

(8) In this section—

"business premises" means premises used wholly or partly for the purposes of a business;

"mortgagee in possession" includes a receiver appointed by the mortgagee or by the court who is in receipt of the rents and profits, and "his mortgagor" shall be construed accordingly;

"reversioner" means any person having an interest in the premises, being an interest in reversion expectant (whether immediately or not) on the tenancy;

"reversioner's mortgagee in possession" means any person being a mortgagee in possession in respect of such an interest; and

"sub-tenant" includes a person retaining possession of any premises by virtue of the Rent (Agriculture) Act 1976 or the Rent Act 1977 after the coming to an end of a sub-tenancy, and "sub-tenancy" includes a right so to retain possession.

Note

For existing text substitute:

3B–224

New s.40 was inserted by the Regulatory Reform (Business Tenancies) (England and Wales) Order 2003 S.I. 2003 No. 3096. The amendment came into force June 1, 2004. It does not apply to a notice under s.40 served before that date.

prescribed form

Delete the first paragraph and substitute:

3B–227 See the Landlord and Tenant Act 1954, Part 2 (Notices) Regulations 2004 S.I. 2004 No. 1005.

Add new paragraphs 3B–229.1 to 3B–229.4:

3B–229.1 Duties in transfer cases

40A.—(1) If a person on whom a notice under section 40(1) or (3) of this Act has been served has transferred his interest in the premises or any part of them to some other person and gives the appropriate person notice in writing—

(a) of the transfer of his interest; and

(b) of the name and address of the person to whom he transferred it,

on giving the notice he ceases in relation to the premises or (as the case may be) to that part to be under any duty imposed by section 40 of this Act.

(2) If—

(a) the person who served the notice under section 40(1) or (3) of this Act ("the transferor") has transferred his interest in the premises to some other person ("the transferee"); and

(b) the transferor or the transferee has given the person required to give the information notice in writing—

(i) of the transfer; and

(ii) of the transferee's name and address,

the appropriate person for the purposes of section 40 of this Act and subsection (1) above is the transferee.

(3) If—

(a) a transfer such as is mentioned in paragraph (a) of subsection (2) above has taken place; but

(b) neither the transferor nor the transferee has given a notice such as is mentioned in paragraph (b) of that subsection,

any duty imposed by section 40 of this Act may be performed by giving the information either to the transferor or to the transferee.

Note

3B–229.2 New s.40A was inserted by the Regulatory Reform (Business Tenancies) (England and Wales) Order 2003 S.I. 2003 No. 3096. The amendment came into force June 1, 2004. It does not apply to a notice under s.40 served before that date.

Proceedings for breach of duties to give information

3B–229.3 **40B.** A claim that a person has broken any duty imposed by section 40 of this Act may be made the subject of civil proceedings for breach of statutory duty; and in any such proceedings a court may order that person to comply with that duty and may make an award of damages.

Note

3B–229.4 New s.40B was inserted by the Regulatory Reform (Business Tenancies) (England and Wales) Order 2003 S.I. 2003 No. 3096. The amendment came into force June 1, 2004. It does not apply to a notice under s.40 served before that date.

Partnerships.

In subsection 41A(6), for "section 29(1) of this Act for the grant of a new tenancy on an application made by the business tenants it may order the grant to be made to them or to them jointly" substitute:

[41A.—(6) section 29 of this Act for the grant of a new tenancy it may order the grant to be made to the business tenants or to them jointly **3B–235**

Note

Delete full stop at the end and add:

and amended by by the Regulatory Reform (Business Tenancies) (England and Wales) Order 2003 S.I. 2003 No. 3096.

Groups of companies.

In subsection 42(1) after "subsidiaries of a third body corporate" add:

[42.—(1) or the same person has a controlling interest in both **3B–239**

Note

Delete full stop at end and add:

and by the Regulatory Reform (Business Tenancies) (England and Wales) Order 2003 S.I. 2003 No. 3096. The latter amendment came into force June 1, 2004. **3B–240**

Meaning of "the landlord" in Part II, and provisions as to mesne landlords, etc.

In subsection 44(1), for "Subject to the next following subsection," substitute:

[44.—(1) Subject to subsections (1A) and (2) below, **3B–250**

After subsection 44(1) add:

(1A) The reference in subsection (1) above to a person who is the owner of an interest such as is mentioned in that subsection is to be construed, where different persons own such interests in different parts of the property, as a reference to all those persons collectively.

Note

Delete full stop at end and add:

and amended by the Regulatory Reform (Business Tenancies) (England and Wales) Order 2003 S.I. 2003 No. 3096. The latter amendment came into force June 1, 2004. **3B–251**

Interpretation of Part II.

At the beginning before "In this Part of this Act:—" add subsection number (1).

In new subsection 46(1), delete existing definition of "current tenancy" and substitute: **3B–255**

"current tenancy" means the tenancy under which the tenant holds for the time being;"

In new subsection 46(1), add after definition of "the holding":

"interim rent" has the meaning given by section 24A(1) of this Act;

Add at end:

(2) For the purposes of this Part of this Act, a person has a controlling interest in a company, if, had he been a company, the other company would have been its subsidiary; and in this Part—

"company" has the meaning given by section 735 of the Companies Act 1985; and

"subsidiary" has the meaning given by section 736 of that Act.

Note

Add new paragraph 3B–255.1:

3B–255.1 Section 46 was amended by the Regulatory Reform (Business Tenancies) (England and Wales) Order 2003 S.I. 2003 No. 3096. The amendment came into force June 1, 2004.

Interim continuation of tenancies pending determination by court.

In subsection 64(1)(b), for "the said Part II" substitute:

3B–258 **64.**—(1) (b) under section 24(1) or 29(2) of this Act

prescribed ... by statutory instrument

Delete the first paragraph and substitute:

3B–262 See the Landlord and Tenant Act 1954, Part 2 (Notices) Regulations 2004 S.I. 2004 No. 1005

For "of the 1983 regulations" substitute:

of the 2004 Regulations

not to be unreasonably withheld

Add new paragraph 3B–283.1:

3B–283.1 Unless it can be shown that a trial judge has misdirected himself by erring in principle or by reaching a conclusion that no reasonable judge could have reached, the Court of Appeal will be slow to differ from his measurements of reasonableness (*Arundel Corporation v. Khokher* [2003] EWCA Civ 1784; December 9, 2003).

damages

Add new paragraph 3B–285.1:

3B–285.1 Where a landlord has all relevant information to enable it to make a decision under s.1(3) as to whether or not to give licence to assign, but fails to respond and operates in a cynical way designed to frustrate the assignment of premises, the court may mark its disapproval by awarding a sum of exemplary damages that would cause the landlord to consider seriously its future conduct (*Design Progression Ltd v. Thurloe Properties Ltd* [2004] EWHC 324 (Ch); *The Times*, March 2, 2004—award of £25).

3D PROCEEDINGS UNDER THE HUMAN RIGHTS ACT 1998

Add at end:

3D–9.1 For a recent example see *R. (on the application of Middleton) v. HM Coroner for Western Somerset* [2004] UKHL 10; [2004] 2 W.L.R. 800, HL, where the House of Lords held that the scheme for the conduct of inquests which had been enacted by and under the authority of Parliament had to be respected, save to the extent that a change of interpretation was required to honour the international obligations of the United Kingdom under the Convention. The House of Lords confirmed that a court should propose no greater revision of the existing regime than is necessary to secure compliance with the Convention, particularly when legislative decisions, when made, will doubtless take account of policy, administrative and financial considerations which are not the concern of the courts (at paragraph 34).

At the end of the first paragraph add:

3D–10.1 It is not necessary to transfer proceedings to the High Court merely because a breach of a Convention right is alleged, nor is it necessary where an application for a declaration of incompatibility has no chance of success: *V (A Child) (Care Proceedings: Human Rights Claims), Re* [2004] EWCA Civ 54; [2004] 1 W.L.R. 1433.

Section 6(6)

In the first paragraph, for "Aston Cantlow and Wilmcote with Billesley Parochial Church Council v. Wallbank [2003] UKHL 37" substitute:

3D–12.1 *Aston Cantlow and Wilmcote with Billesley Parochial Church Council v. Wallbank* [2003] UKHL 37; [2004] 1 A.C. 546

In the first paragraph, delete last sentence and add:

See also *Hampshire CC v. Beer (t/a Hammer Trout Farm), sub nom. R. (on the application of*

Beer (t/a Hammer Trout Farm)) v. Hampshire Farmers Markets Ltd [2003] EWCA Civ 1056; [2004] 1 W.L.R. 233, CA and *R. (on the application of West) v. Lloyds of London* [2004] EWCA Civ 506.

In the second paragraph, for "Marcic v. Thames Water Utilities [2001] 3 All E.R. 698, TCC" substitute:

Marcic v. Thames Water Utilities [2003] UKHL 66; [2003] 3 W.L.R. 1603, TCC

In the third paragraph, for "B & C v. A [2002] EWCA Civ 337; [2002] H.R.L.R. 25, para. 4, CA." substitute:

A v. B Plc [2002] EWCA Civ 337; [2003] Q.B. 195; [2002] 3 W.L.R. 542.

Sections 7(1) and 7(7)

For "Human Rights, Law & Practice (Lester & Pannick, eds, Butterworths 1999)" substitute:

3D–13.1 Lester & Pannick, eds, *Human Rights, Law & Practice* (2nd Edition, Lexis Nexis, Butterworths, 2004)

Add at end:

A person may continue to claim to be a victim where there is a continuing violation of a positive procedural obligation, notwithstanding that he has received compensation for feelings of frustration, distress and anxiety from the European Court of Human Rights: *McKerr's Application for Judicial Review, Re* [2004] UKHL 12; [2004] 1 W.L.R. 807, HL.

Section 7(2)

After the penultimate paragraph add:

3D–13.2 It is not necessary to transfer proceedings to the High Court merely because a breach of a Convention right is alleged, nor is it necessary where an application for a declaration of incompatibility has no chance of success: *V (A Child) (Care Proceedings: Human Rights Claims), Re* [2004] EWCA Civ 54; [2004] 1 W.L.R. 1433, CA.

Section 12(3)

After the first sentence add:

3D–18.2 Thus, the subsection does not give either Article 8 or Article 12 pre–eminence over the other: *S (A Child) (Identification: Restrictions on Publication), Re* [2003] EWCA Civ 963; [2004] Fam. 43; [2003] 3 W.L.R. 1425, paragraph 52, Hale L.J.

For "B & C v. A [2002] EWCA Civ 337; [2002] H.R.L.R. 25, para. 11(iii)" substitute:

A v B Plc [2002] EWCA Civ 337; [2003] Q.B. 195; [2002] 3 W.L.R. 542, para. 11(iv)

Add at end:

The general approach of the Court of Appeal in these cases has been endorsed by the House of Lords in *Campbell v. Mirror Group Newspapers Ltd* [2004] UKHL 22; [2004] 2.W.L.R. 1232.

Delete the second paragraph and substitute:

3D–29 Section 6(1) applies to an unlawful killing which occurred after the Act came into force but not to one which took place before that date. The obligation to hold an investigation was triggered by the death and was consequential upon it: *McKerr, Re* [2004] UKHL 12; [2004] 1 W.L.R. 807, HL.

Add at the end:

A bankruptcy petition brought by a public authority is a proceeding brought by or at the instigation of a public authority. However, after the bankruptcy order was made the continuing proceedings were no longer within section 7(1)(b) unless the particular application in question was brought by the public authority: *Malcolm v. Mackenzie* [2004] EWHC 339 (Ch).

3E INSOLVENCY PROCEEDINGS

16A. Bankruptcy Restriction Orders

Add new section 16A:

3E–16.1

Making the application

16A.1 An application for a bankruptcy restrictions order is made as an ordinary application in the bankruptcy.

16A.2 The application must be made within one year beginning with the date of the bankruptcy order unless the court gives permission for the application to be made after that period. The one year period does not run while the bankrupt's discharge has been suspended under section 279(3) of the Insolvency Act 1986.

16A.3 An application for a bankruptcy restrictions order may be made by the Secretary of State or the Official Receiver ('the Applicant'). The application must be supported by a report which must include:

(a) a statement of the conduct by reference to which it is alleged that it is appropriate for a bankruptcy restrictions order to be made; and

(b) the evidence relied on in support of the application (r.6.241 Insolvency Rules 1986).

16A.4 The report is treated as if it were an affidavit (r.7.9(2) Insolvency Rules 1986) and is prima facie evidence of any matter contained in it (r.7.9(3)).

16A.5 The application may be supported by evidence from other witnesses which may be given by affidavit or (by reason of r.7.57(5) Insolvency Rules 1986) by witness statement verified by a statement of truth.

16A.6 The court will fix a first hearing which must be not less than 8 weeks from the date when the hearing is fixed (r.6.241(4) Insolvency Rules 1986).

16A.7 Notice of the application and the venue fixed by the court must be served by the Applicant on the bankrupt not more than 14 days after the application is made. Service of notice must be accompanied by a copy of the application together with the evidence in support and a form of acknowledgment of service.

16A.8 The bankrupt must file in court an acknowledgment of service not more than 14 days after service of the application on him, indicating whether or not he contests the application. If he fails to do so he may attend the hearing of the application but may not take part in the hearing unless the court gives permission.

Opposing the application

16A.9 If the bankrupt wishes to oppose the application, he must within 28 days of service on him of the application and the evidence in support (or such longer period as the court may allow) file in court and (within three days thereof) serve on the Applicant any evidence which he wishes the court to take into consideration. Such evidence should normally be in the form of an affidavit or a witness statement verified by a statement of truth.

16A.10 The Applicant must file any evidence in reply within 14 days of receiving the evidence of the bankrupt (or such longer period as the court may allow) and must serve it on the bankrupt as soon as reasonably practicable.

Hearings

16A.11 Any hearing of an application for a bankruptcy restrictions order must be in public (r.6.241(5) Insolvency Rules 1986). The hearing will generally be before the registrar or district judge in the first instance who may:

(1) adjourn the application and give directions;
(2) make a bankruptcy restrictions order; or
(3) adjourn the application to the judge.

Making a bankruptcy restrictions order

16A.12 When the court is considering whether to make a bankruptcy restrictions order, it must not take into account any conduct of the bankrupt prior to 1 April 2004 (art. 7 Enterprise Act (Commencement No 4 and Transitional Provisions and Savings) Order 2003).

16A.13 The court may make a bankruptcy restrictions order in the absence of the bankrupt and whether or not he has filed evidence (r.6.244 Insolvency Rules 1986).

16A.14 When a bankruptcy restrictions order is made the court must send two sealed copies of the order to the Applicant (r.6.244(2) Insolvency Rules 1986), and as soon as reasonably practicable after receipt, the Applicant must send one sealed copy to the bankrupt (r.6.244(3)).

16A.15 A bankruptcy restrictions order comes into force when it is made and must specify the date on which it will cease to have effect, which must be between two and 15 years from the date on which it is made.

Interim bankruptcy restriction orders

16A.16 An application for an interim bankruptcy restrictions order may be made any time between the institution of an application for a bankruptcy restrictions order and the determination of that application (Sch 4A para. 5 Insolvency Act 1986). The application is made as an ordinary application in the bankruptcy.

16A.17 The application must be supported by a report as evidence in support of the application (r.6.246(1) Insolvency Rules 1986) which must include evidence of the bankrupt's conduct which is alleged to constitute the grounds for making an interim bankruptcy restrictions order and evidence of matters relating to the public interest in making the order.

16A.18 Notice of the application must be given to the bankrupt at least two business days before the date fixed for the hearing unless the court directs otherwise (r.6.245).

16A.19 Any hearing of the application must be in public (r.6.245).

16A.20 The court may make an interim bankruptcy restrictions order in the absence of the bankrupt and whether or not he has filed evidence (r.6.247).

16A.21 The bankrupt may apply to the court to set aside an interim bankruptcy restrictions order. The application is made by ordinary application in the bankruptcy and must be supported by an affidavit or witness statement verified by a statement of truth stating the grounds on which the application is made (r.6.248(2)).

16A.22 The bankrupt must send the Secretary of State, not less than 7 days before the hearing, notice of his application, notice of the venue, a copy of his application and a copy of the supporting affidavit. The Secretary of State may attend the hearing and call the attention of the court to any matters which seem to him to be relevant, and may himself give evidence or call witnesses.

16A.23 Where the court sets aside an interim bankruptcy restrictions order, two sealed copies of the order must be sent by the court, as soon as reasonably practicable, to the Secretary of State.

16A.24 As soon as reasonably practicable after receipt of sealed copies of the order, the Secretary of State must send a sealed copy to the bankrupt.

Bankruptcy restrictions undertakings

16A.25 Where a bankrupt has given a bankruptcy restrictions undertaking, the Secretary of State must file a copy in court and send a copy to the bankrupt as soon as reasonably practicable (r.6.250).

16A.26 The bankrupt may apply to annul a bankruptcy restrictions undertaking. The application is made as an ordinary application in the bankruptcy and must be supported by an affidavit or witness statement verified by a statement of truth stating the grounds on which it is made.

16A.27 The bankrupt must give notice of his application and the venue together with a copy of his affidavit in support to the Secretary of State at least 28 days before the date fixed for the hearing.

16A.28 The Secretary of State may attend the hearing and call the attention of the court to any matters which seem to him to be relevant and may himself give evidence or call witnesses.

16A.29 The court must send a sealed copy of any order annulling or varying the bankruptcy restrictions undertaking to the Secretary of State and the bankrupt.

The EC Regulation on Insolvency Proceedings

In the second paragraph, for "Re a bankrupt (No. 136 of 2003) [2003] All E.R. (D) 36 (Dec).)." substitute:

3E–24 , *Re a bankrupt (No. 136 of 2003)* [2003] All E.R. (D) 36 (Dec) and *Re Salvage Association* [2003] B.C.C. 504.)

Company

Add at end:

3E–25 As to jurisdiction in relation to a company incorporated by royal charter, see *Re Salvage Association* [2003] B.C.C. 504.

Applications to fix an office holder's remuneration

Add at end:

3E–85 Detailed guidance on office holders' remuneration is contained in the Report (July 1998), Statement of Insolvency Practice 9 (Recovery Professionals) and the Practice Statement—The Fixing and Approval of the Remuneration of Appointees (2004) [the text of which is reproduced below].

PRACTICE STATEMENT—THE FIXING AND APPROVAL OF THE REMUNERATION OF APPOINTEES (2004)

Part One

General

Add new Practice Statement:

1. **Definitions and Interpretation** 3E–85.1

1.1 In this Practice Statement:

(1) "appointee" means:

(i) a provisional liquidator appointed under Section 135 of the Insolvency Act;

(ii) a special manager appointed under Section 177 or Section 370 of the Insolvency Act;

(iii) a liquidator appointed by the members of a company or partnership or by the creditors of a company or partnership or by the Secretary of State pursuant to Section 137 of the Insolvency Act, or by the court pursuant to Section 140 of the Insolvency Act;

(iv) an administrator of a company appointed to manage the property, business and affairs of that company under the Insolvency Act or other enactment and to which the provisions of the Insolvency Act are applicable;

(v) a trustee in bankruptcy (other than the Official Receiver) appointed under the Insolvency Act;

(vi) a nominee or supervisor of a voluntary arrangement under Part I or Part VIII of the Insolvency Act;

(vii) a licensed insolvency practitioner appointed by the court pursuant to Section 273 of the Insolvency Act;

(viii) an interim receiver appointed by the court pursuant to Section 286 of the Insolvency Act;

(2) "appointment" means the appointment as an appointee;

(3) "assessor" means a person appointed in accordance with Rule 35.15 of the CPR;

(4) "CPR" means the Civil Procedure Rules 1998 (as amended);

(5) "the court" means the court exercising jurisdiction in respect of the appointment in accordance with the Insolvency Act and the Insolvency Rules or other relevant enactment and/or applicable rules;

(6) "the guiding principles" means the statements of principle contained in paragraph 3.4;

(7) "Insolvency Act" means the Insolvency Act 1986 (as amended);

(8) "Insolvency Rules" means the Insolvency Rules 1986 (as amended);

(9) "the objective" means the objective stated in paragraph 3.2.

1.2 References to paragraphs are references to paragraphs of this Practice Statement.

2. **Applicability** 3E–85.2

2.1 This Practice Statement shall, save to the extent and as may otherwise be ordered by the court, apply to all appointees in respect of:

(1) any application to the court by an appointee for the fixing and approval of his remuneration where his remuneration has not otherwise already been fixed and approved;

(2) any application to the court by an appointee for the fixing and approval of his remuneration in circumstances where he considers that the amount of his remuneration as fixed and approved by resolution of the members of the partnership or company or the creditors' committee or the liquidation committee or by resolution of the general body of creditors (as appropriate) is insufficient;

(3) any application by a person who may be permitted to apply under the Insolvency Act, the Insolvency Rules, or otherwise including by reference to the jurisdiction of the court to supervise the conduct of one of its officers and the inherent jurisdiction of the Supreme Court and is dissatisfied with the remuneration of an appointee that has otherwise been fixed and approved on the basis that such remuneration is excessive.

2.2 This Practice Statement shall come into effect on 1 October 2004 and shall apply to all applications for the fixing and approval of the remuneration of an appointee issued after that date.

3E–85.3 3. **The Objective and the Guiding Principles**

3.1 This Practice Statement is supplemental to the Insolvency Act, the Insolvency Rules and such other enactments or rules as have been or may be introduced and which are relevant to the fixing and approval of the remuneration of an appointee.

3.2 The objective of this Practice Statement is to ensure that the remuneration of an appointee which is fixed and approved by the court is fair, reasonable and commensurate with the nature and extent of the work properly undertaken by the appointee in any given case and is fixed and approved by reference to a process which is consistent and predictable.

3.3 Set out below are the guiding principles by reference to which applications for the fixing and approval of the remuneration of appointees are to be considered both by applicants, in the preparation and presentation of their application, and by the court which is required to determine such applications.

3.4 The guiding principles are as follows:

(1) "Justification": It is for the appointee who seeks to be remunerated at a particular level and/or in a particular manner to justify his claim and in order to do so the appointee should be prepared to provide full particulars of the basis for and the nature of his claim for remuneration.

(2) "The benefit of the doubt": The corollary of guiding principle (1) is that on any application for the fixing and approval of the remuneration of an appointee, if after considering the evidence before it and after having regard to the guiding principles (in particular guiding principle (3)), the matters contained in paragraph 5.2 (in particular paragraph 5.2(10)) and the matters referred to in paragraph 5.3 (as appropriate) there remains any element of doubt as to the appropriateness, fairness or reasonableness of the amount sought to be fixed and approved (whether arising from a lack of particularity as to the basis for and the nature of the appointee's claim to re-

muneration or otherwise) such element of doubt should be resolved by the court against the appointee.

(3) "Professional integrity": The court should give weight to the fact that the appointee is a member of a regulated profession (where such is the case) and as such is subject to rules and guidance as to professional conduct and (where such is the case) the fact that the appointee is an officer of the court.

(4) "The value of the service rendered": the remuneration of an appointee should reflect and should be fixed and approved so as to reward the value of the service rendered by the appointee, not simply to reimburse the appointee in respect of time expended and cost incurred.

(5) "Fair and reasonable": the amount of the remuneration to be fixed and approved by the court should be fair and reasonable and represent fair and reasonable remuneration for the work properly undertaken or to be undertaken.

(6) "Proportionality":

  (i) "proportionality of information": in considering the nature and extent of the information which should be provided by an appointee in respect of an application for the fixing and approval of his remuneration the court, the appointee and any other parties to the application shall have regard to what is proportionate by reference to the amount of remuneration to be fixed and approved, the nature, complexity and extent of the work to be completed (where the application relates to future remuneration) or that has been completed by the appointee and the value and nature of the assets and liabilities with which the appointee will have to deal or has had to deal;

  (ii) "proportionality of remuneration": the amount of remuneration to be fixed and approved by the court should be proportional to the nature, complexity and extent of the work to be completed (where the application relates to future remuneration) or that has been completed by the appointee and the value and nature of the assets and/or potential assets and the liabilities and/or potential liabilities with which the appointee will have to deal or has had to deal, the nature and degree of the responsibility to which the appointee has been subject in any given case, the nature and extent of the risk (if any) assumed by the appointee and the efficiency (in respect of both time and cost) with which the appointee has completed the work undertaken;

(7) "Professional guidance": In respect of an application for the fixing and approval of the remuneration of an appointee, the appointee may have regard to the relevant and current statements of practice promulgated by any relevant regulatory and professional bodies in relation to the fixing and approval of the remuneration of an appointee. In considering an application for the fixing or approval of the remuneration of an appointee, the court may also have regard to such statements of practice and the extent of compliance with such statements of practice by the appointee.

(8) "Impracticability": where the appointee has not, either upon or shortly after the commencement of his appointment, sought to have the basis upon which his remuneration is to be fixed approved by the members of the partnership or the company, the creditors' committee, the liquidation committee or the general body of creditors (as appropriate) and in circumstances where the appointee considers that it will be impracticable to have his remuneration fixed and/or approved in such a manner, he may, as soon as reasonably practicable after his appointment, apply to the court to have the basis upon which he is to be remunerated fixed and for directions as to the manner in which his remuneration is to be approved (which may include provision for payments to be made on account). In circumstances where such an application may be made, to the extent that such an application is not made but the appointee subsequently makes an application to the court for the fixing and approval of the whole or any part of his remuneration, an explanation as to why no earlier application was made shall be provided to the court.

Part Two

The Fixing and Approval of Remuneration

3E–85.4 4. **Distribution of Business**

4.1 All applications for the fixing and approval of the remuneration of an appointee shall in the first instance (unless otherwise ordered by the court, having regard to the particular circumstances of an application) be made, where the court is the High Court to a Registrar or a District Judge in the appropriate District Registry of the High Court or, where the court is a County Court, a District Judge in the appropriate County Court.

4.2 On the hearing of the application the court shall consider the evidence then available to it and may either summarily determine the application or adjourn it giving such directions as it thinks appropriate. Such directions may include a direction that:

(1) an assessor or a Costs Judge prepare a report to the court in respect of the remuneration which is sought to be fixed and approved; and/or

(2) the application be heard by the Registrar or the District Judge sitting with or without an assessor or a Costs Judge or by a Judge sitting with or without an assessor or a Costs Judge.

4.3 In the usual course an application for the fixing and approval of the remuneration of an appointee should be determined by a Registrar or a District Judge sitting without an assessor or a Costs Judge and without the need for a report from an assessor or a Costs Judge.

4.4 The court may give the directions referred to in paragraphs 4.2(1) and (2) where it considers this to be appropriate having regard to the size and complexity of the case or in the event that the application gives rise to complicated issues of fact or of law. The court ought only to make an order for the involvement of a Costs Judge in circumstances where it considers the involvement of an assessor is (for whatever reason) not appropriate and that the application can only properly be determined by reference to the particular expertise and assistance that can be provided by a Costs Judge.

4.5 A list of suitably qualified persons appointed by the court to act as assessors in respect of applications for the fixing and approval of the remuneration of an appointee is available from the court.

4.6 The reasonable costs of an assessor appointed by the court shall be paid from the assets under the control of the appointee.

5. **Relevant Criteria and Procedure** **3E–85.5**

5.1 When considering an application for the fixing and approval of the remuneration of an appointee the court shall have regard to the objective, the guiding principles and all relevant circumstances including the matters referred to in paragraph 5.2 and where appropriate paragraph 5.3, each of which should be addressed in the evidence placed before the court.

5.2 On any application for the fixing and approval of the remuneration of an appointee, the appointee should:

(1) Provide a narrative description and explanation of:

(i) the background to, the relevant circumstances of and the reasons for the appointment;

(ii) the work undertaken or to be undertaken in respect of the appointment and in respect of which work the remuneration of the appointee is sought to be fixed and approved, which description should be divided, insofar as possible, into individual tasks or categories of task. General descriptions of work, tasks, or categories of task should (insofar as possible) be avoided;

(iii) the reasons why it is or was considered reasonable and/or necessary and/or beneficial for such work to be conducted, giving details of why particular tasks or categories of task were undertaken and why such tasks or categories of task are to be undertaken or have been undertaken by particular individuals and in a particular manner;

(iv) the amount of time to be spent or that has been spent in respect of work to be completed or that has been completed and in respect of which the fixing and approval of remuneration is sought and which it is considered is fair, reasonable and proportionate;

(v) what is likely to be and has been achieved, the benefits that are likely to and have accrued as a consequence of the work that is to be or has been completed, the manner in which the work required in respect of the appointment is progressing and what, in the opinion of the appointee, remains to be achieved.

(2) Provide details sufficient for the court to determine the application by reference to the criteria which is required to be taken into account by reference to the Insolvency Rules and any other applicable enactments or rules relevant to the fixing and approval of the remuneration of an appointee.

(3) Provide a statement of the total number of hours of work undertaken or to be undertaken in respect of which the fixing and approval of remuneration is sought, together with a breakdown of such hours by individual member of staff and individual tasks or categories of tasks to be performed or that have been performed. Details should also be given of:

(i) the tasks or categories of tasks to be undertaken as a proportion of the total amount of work to be undertaken in respect of which the fixing and approval of remuneration is sought and the tasks or categories of tasks that have been undertaken as a proportion of the total amount of work that has been undertaken in respect of which the fixing and approval of remuneration is sought; and

(ii) the tasks or categories of task to be completed by individual members of staff or grade of personnel including the appointee as a proportion of the total amount of work to be completed by all members of staff including the appointee in respect of which the fixing and approval of remuneration is sought, or the tasks or categories of task that have been completed by individual members of staff or grade of personnel as a proportion of the total amount of work that has been completed by all members of staff including the appointee in respect of which the fixing and approval of remuneration is sought.

(4) Provide a statement of the total amount to be charged for the work to be undertaken or that has been undertaken in respect of which the fixing and approval of remuneration is sought which should include:

(i) a breakdown of such amounts by individual member of staff and individual task or categories of task performed;

(ii) details of the time expended and the remuneration charged in respect of each individual task or category of task as a proportion (respectively) of the total time expended and the total remuneration charged.

In respect of an application pursuant to which the amount of the appointee's remuneration is to be fixed and approved on the basis of a percentage of the value of the assets realised and/or distributed, the appointee shall provide (for the purposes of comparison) the same details as are required by this paragraph (4), but on the basis of what would have been charged had he been seeking remuneration on the basis of the time properly spent by him and his staff.

(5) Provide details of each individual to be engaged or who has been engaged in work in respect of the appointment and in respect of which the fixing and approval of remuneration is sought, including details of their relevant experience, training, qualifications and the level of their seniority.

(6) Provide an explanation of:

(i) the steps, if any, to be taken or that have been taken by the appointee to avoid duplication of effort and cost in respect of the work to be completed or that has been completed in respect of which the fixing and approval of the remuneration is sought; and

(ii) the steps to be taken or that have been taken to ensure that the work to be completed or that has been completed is to be or was undertaken by individuals of appropriate experience and seniority relative to the nature of the work to be or that has been undertaken.

(7) Provide details of the individual rates charged by the appointee and members of his staff in respect of the work to be

completed or that has been completed and in respect of which the remuneration is sought to be fixed and approved. Such details should include:

(i) a general explanation of the policy adopted in relation to the fixing or calculation of such rates;

(ii) in relation to charges in respect of secretarial, administrative and cashiering services (and/or such other charges as might also otherwise be regarded as an overhead cost forming a component part of the rates charged by the appointee and members of his staff), an explanation as to why (where this is the case) such costs are to be or have been charged for separately together with confirmation that where such work is to be or has been charged for separately such work will not or has not also been charged for as part of the rates that are to be or have been charged by the appointee and/or members of his staff;

(8) Where the application for the fixing and approval of remuneration is in respect of a period of time during which the charge out rates of the appointee and/or members of his staff engaged in work in respect of the appointment have increased, provide an explanation of the nature, extent and reason for such increase and the date when such increase took effect. This paragraph (8) does not apply to applications to which paragraph 5.3 applies.

(9) Provide details of any remuneration previously fixed and approved in relation to the appointment (whether by the court or otherwise) including in particular the amounts that were previously sought to be fixed and approved and the amounts that were in fact fixed and approved and the basis upon which such amounts were fixed and approved.

(10) In order that the court may be able to consider the views of those persons which the appointee considers have an interest in the assets that are under his control, provide details of:

(i) what (if any) consultation has taken place between the appointee and those persons and if no such consultation has taken place an explanation should be given as to the reason why; and

(ii) the number and value of the interests of the persons consulted including details of the proportion (by number and by value) of the interests of such persons by reference to the entirety of those persons having an interest in the assets under the control of the appointee.

(11) Provide such other relevant information as the appointee considers, in the circumstances, ought to be provided to the court.

5.3 This paragraph applies to applications where the remuneration of the appointee is to be fixed and approved on the basis of a percentage of the value of the assets realised and/or distributed. On such applications in addition to the matters referred to in paragraph 5.2 (as applicable) the appointee shall:

(1) Provide a full description of the basis of and reasons for his remuneration being sought to be fixed and approved by reference to a percentage of the value of the assets realised and/or distributed.

(2) Provide a full explanation of the basis upon which the percentage rates to be applied to the values of the assets realised and/or distributed have been chosen.
(3) Provide a statement that to the best of the appointee's belief the percentage rates which are sought to be applied are similar to the percentage rates that are applied or have been applied in respect of other appointments of a similar nature.
(4) By reference to the matters contained in paragraph 5.2 (as applicable), provide a comparison of the amount to be charged by reference to a percentage of the value of the assets realised and/or distributed and an estimate of the amount that would otherwise have been charged if the remuneration was to be fixed by reference to the time properly given by him and his staff.
(5) Provide a comparison between the amounts to be charged by reference to a percentage of the value of the assets realised and/or distributed using the percentage rates sought to be fixed and approved by the court and the percentage rates provided for by the scale of fees referred to in Schedule 6 to the Insolvency Rules.

5.4 If and insofar as any of the matters referred to in paragraph 5.2 or 5.3 (as appropriate) are not addressed in the evidence placed before the court on the hearing of an application for the fixing and approval of the remuneration of an appointee an explanation for why this is the case should be included in such evidence.

5.5 Notwithstanding that the expenses and disbursements of the appointee and his staff are not required to be approved by the court on any application by the appointee for the fixing and approval of his remuneration, a summary of the amount and nature of such expenses and disbursements incurred during the relevant period should be provided as should an explanation of the steps taken by the appointee to subject such expenses and disbursements to critical scrutiny.

5.6 There should be included in the evidence placed before the court by the appointee in respect of any application for the fixing and approval of the remuneration of an appointee the following documents:
(1) A copy of the most recent receipts and payments account;
(2) Copies of any reports by the appointee to the persons having an interest in the assets under his control relevant to the period for which the remuneration sought to be fixed and approved relates;
(3) Schedules or such other representations of the information referred to in paragraphs 5.2 and 5.3 such as are likely to be of assistance to the court in fixing and approving the remuneration of the appointee.
(4) Evidence of consultation with those persons having an interest in the assets under the control of appointee in relation to the fixing and approval of the remuneration of the appointee.

5.7 On any application for the fixing and approval of remuneration of an appointee the court may make an order permitting payments of remuneration to be made on account subject to final approval whether by the court or otherwise.

5.8 Unless otherwise ordered by the court (or as may otherwise be provided for in any enactment or rules of procedure) the costs of and occasioned by an application for the fixing and/or approval of the remuneration of an appointee shall be paid from the assets under the control of the appointee.

Bankruptcy (Part IX Insolvency Act 1986)

3E–107

Existing paragraph 3E–108 has been renumbered "3E–107".

Discharge

Add new paragraph 3E–108:

3E–108

Section 279 of the Insolvency Act 1986 (as inserted by s.256, Enterprise Act 2000) provides for automatic discharge for the majority of bankrupts after one year (s.279(1)) or earlier if the official receiver files notice (see rule 6.214A) that the affairs of the bankrupt do not require investigation or that such investigation has been concluded (s.279(2)) in which case the bankrupt is discharged when the notice is filed. The trustee (where one has been appointed) or a creditor may, within 28 days of receiving notice from the official receiver of his intention to file a notice under s.279(2), inform the official receiver that he objects to the proposed course of action (rule 6.214A(5)). Reasons for objection must be given. The official receiver may reject the objection, he must also give reasons and the trustee or creditor may appeal (rule 6.214A(5)(b) and rule 7.50, Insolvency Rules 1986). Any appeal must be made within 14 days of the notification by the official receiver of his decision (rule 7.50(2)). The official receiver may still apply to suspend discharge if a bankrupt fails to comply with his obligations. Section 279(3) provides that the official receiver may apply to suspend discharge until the end of a specified period or until the fulfilment of a specified condition (see also rule 6.215).

The bankrupt's home

Add new paragraph 3E–109:

3E–109

Section 283A of the Insolvency Act 1986 (inserted by s.261, Enterprise Act 2000) introduces restrictions on the right of a trustee to realise the home of the bankrupt. Under this provision, where the bankrupt had an interest in a dwelling–house which was the sole or principal residence of the bankrupt, the bankrupt's spouse or former spouse at the date of the bankruptcy order, that interest ceases to be comprised in the bankrupt's estate at the end of three years beginning with the date of the bankruptcy and revests automatically in the bankrupt unless the trustee makes an application within the three year period or takes any of the other steps set out in the section. The three year period may be extended (s.283A(6)).

Section 313A, Insolvency Act 1986 (inserted by s.261, Enterprise Act 2000) provides that the court must dismiss an application made in respect of a low value home. What will constitute a low value home is not yet clear.

Bankruptcy Restrictions Order

Add new paragraph 3E–110:

3E–110

Section 257 of the Enterprise Act 2000 (headed Post–discharge restrictions) inserts a new s.281A and Schedule 4A into the Insolvency Act 1986 and thereby introduces the bankruptcy restrictions order and undertaking.

The Secretary of State for Trade and Industry or the official receiver may make the application for a bankruptcy restrictions order (para. 1, Schedule 4A, Insolvency Act 1986). It is made as an ordinary application in the bankruptcy and must be supported by a report setting out the conduct relied on (rule 6.241). The timing of the application is crucial and it must be made before the end of one year, beginning with the commencement of the bankruptcy (*i.e.* the making of the bankruptcy order) unless the discharge period has been suspended (para. 3, Schedule 4A). The application and supporting evidence must be served not more than 14 days after making the application (rule 6.242(1)) and the defendant must file an acknowledgment of service indicating whether or not he contests the application not more than 14 days after service upon him (rule 6.242(3)). Evidence in opposition must be filed within 28 days of service of the application and served on the Secretary of State within 3 days of filing it at the court (rule 6.243(1)). The Secretary of State must file any evidence in reply within 14 days of receipt of the evidence in opposition and serve this on the bankrupt as soon as is reasonably practicable (rule 6.243(2)).

A number of grounds of conduct likely to lead to the making of an order are set out in para. 2(2) of Schedule 4A but these are not exhaustive. The making of an order is obligatory if the court reaches the conclusion that it is appropriate to make one having regard to the bankrupt's conduct (para. 2(1), Schedule 4A). The order comes into force when it is made and may be for a period of between two and fifteen years (para. 3, Schedule 4A). The Act and the Rules also allow the court to make an interim bankruptcy restrictions order (see rules 6.245 to 6.248, Insolvency Rules 1986).

A bankrupt may enter into an undertaking, which has the same effect as an order (paras 7 to 9, Schedule 4A; see also rule 6.249, Insolvency Rules 1986).

3E–111 *Paragraph 3E–107 has been renumbered "3E–111".*

3F PERSONAL INJURY

Amendments

Delete "Sched. 15 para. 1" and substitute:

3F–13 Sched. 15 para. 11.

Add new sub–paragraphs (bb) and (bbb)

3F–15 "**69.**—(1)(bb) a Primary Care Trust established under section 16A of that Act,

(bbb) a Local Health Board established under section 16BA of that Act,

[(fa) an NHS foundation Trust,]

Add at end:

Note: the text in square brackets was added by the Health and Social Care (Community Health and Standards) Act (2003 c.43) Sched. 4 para. 107.

Fees

Delete the full stop at the end and add:

3F–19 , and as substituted by the Secretary of State for Constitutional Affairs Order (S.I. 2003 No. 1887) Sched. 2 para. 9 (1)(a).

Note

After i.e. add:

3F–31 in force from

Pending repeals and substitutions

For "substituted for the sections in italics above " substitute:

3F–32 replaced by the sections in italics

Note

Delete the first sentence and substitute:

3F–37 Section 10 of the Civil Evidence Act 1995 (see 9B–268) provides that the H.M. Government Actuary's Department's tables known as the Ogden Tables are admissible in evidence when that section comes into force. In practice such tables are regularly used in court in any event: see *Wells v. Wells and Ors.* [1999] 1 AC 345 referred to more fully below, and *Longden v. British Coal Corp* (1998) AC 653 at 671; [1997] 3 W.L.R. 1336 and in Scotland it has been held that the court can take judicial notice of the Ogden Tables at least for some purposes: *O'Brien's Curator Bonis v. British Steel Plc* 1991 S.C. 315.

Bereavement

Delete "£7,500" and substitute:

3F–68 **1A.**—(3) £10,000

Note

Delete existing text and substitute:

3F–69 Amended by the Damages for Bereavement (Variation of Sum) (England and Wales) Order S.I. 2002 No. 644.

Agreement to exclude liability towards passengers is of no effect

At the start of the quoted text delete "147" and substitute:

"**149** 3F–84

Amendments

delete subs. (3) and substitute:

subs.(2) 3F–91

Bankruptcy, death and sequestration of assets do not affect cover

After "sequestration of assets" add:

(or makes a composition or arrangement with his creditors, or grants a trust deed for his creditors) 3F–95

Measure of damages

Delete section 2 and substitute:

2.— [...] 3F–98

(4) In an action for damages for personal injuries (including any such action arising out of a contract), there shall be disregarded, in determining the reasonableness of any expenses, the possibility of avoiding those expenses or part of them by taking advantage of facilities under the National Health Service Act 1977 or the National Health Service (Scotland) Act 1978, or of any corresponding facilities in Northern Ireland.

[...]

Note

Delete the full stop at the end and add:

; subs. (1), (1A), (3), and (6) omitted by the Social Security (Recovery of Benefits) Act 1997 (1997 c.27), Sched. 3 para. 1. 3F–99

"Rights"—"value of rights"

Delete paragraphs 3F–100 to 3F–104 inclusive and substitute:

For the procedure in relation to Recoupment of Benefits from damages awards in personal injury cases see the Social Security (Recovery of Benefits) Act 1997 (1997 c.27) and regulations thereunder. 3F–100

3G DATA PROTECTION ACT 1998

DATA PROTECTION ACT 1998

Notes

In the first paragraph, delete the last sentence and add:

The point was not specifically considered in the House of Lords but appears to have been accepted, *per* Lord Nicholls of Birkenhead at para. 32: "It is not necessary for me to pursue the claim based on the Data Protection Act 1998. The parties were agreed that this claim stands or falls with the outcome of the main claim." If the House did not accept that publication in these circumstances fell under the Data Protection Act, the claim under that Act would have failed irrespective of the failure or success of the main claim. 3G–13

Notes

In the third paragraph, for "the Borough paid £50,000" substitute:

the Borough paid £5,000 3G–27

In the fourth paragraph, for "although the judgment was overturned on appeal." substitute:
although the judgment was overturned by Court of Appeal it was reinstated by the House of Lords which considered the case under the application of the law of confidence rather than as a Data Protection Act claim, see para. 3G–13.

3H CONSUMER CREDIT AND CONSUMER LAW

Meaning of credit

Subs. (1)

After the first paragraph add:

3H–16 Whether a contract provides credit is to be determined as at the time the contract is made. Where at that time it is uncertain whether the arrangements between the parties will give rise to a debt at all, there is no "credit" merely because the contract postpones any obligation to pay until the possible indebtedness has crystallised: *Nejad v. City Index Ltd* [2000] C.C.L.R. 7; *McMillan Williams v. Range* [2004] EWCA Civ 294; [2004] C.C.L.R. 3. A publishing contract, which provided for the author to be paid an advance on royalties coupled with a requirement for the author to repay after three years such amount of the advance as the sales in those three years had failed to earn, would not provide the author with credit. That conclusion might be different, however, if the amount of the advance was so great as to show that it was in reality a loan dressed up as an advance on royalties.

Exempt agreements

In the sixth bullet point paragraph, for "Threw v. Cole, King v. Daltry [2003] EWCA Civ 1828" substitute:

3H–36
- *Threw v. Cole, King v. Daltry* [2003] EWCA Civ 1828; [2004] C.C.L.R. 2

Multiple agreements

Add at end:

3H–41 The matter was fully argued for the first time in *Ocwen v. Coxall and Coxall* [2004] C.C.L.R. 7, where H.H. Judge Holt held that Bennion's views were to be preferred to those of Professor Goode. Francis Bennion's article and his addendum to it (written after the decision in *National Westminster Bank v. Story* [1999] Lloyd's Rep. Bank. 261; [1999] C.C.L.R. 70) can both be seen (as separate items) on Francis Bennion's website at www.francisbennion.com

Pre–contract information

Existing title is amended. Delete existing paragraph and substitute:

3H–54 The Consumer Credit (Disclosure of Information) Regulations 2004, which come into force on May 31, 2005, are the first regulations to be made under this section. They require certain stated information to be given to the debtor or hirer before a regulated agreement is made. The information must be provided in a document which is: (i) on paper or another durable medium; (ii) separate from the agreement itself; (iii) headed "Pre–contract Information", and; (iv) of such a nature that it can be removed by the debtor or hirer from the place where it is disclosed to him. The information must be legible, not generally interspersed with any other information and must all (apart from headings) be of equal prominence. Failure to comply with the regulations will result in the agreement being improperly executed (see ss.66(1) and 65). These sections—and the regulations—do not apply to agreements listed in ss.74(1) and 82(4). Also the regulations do not apply either to any agreement to which s.58 applies or to any regulated agreement which is a "distance contract" (as defined by the regulations). In the case of distance contracts, however, the Financial Services (Distance Marketing) Regulations 2004 set out, with effect from May 31, 2005, pre–contract disclosure requirements where the debtor is an individual acting outside any business he may carry on.

Form and content of agreements

After "Consumer Credit (Agreements) Regulations 1983 (S.I. 1983 No. 1553)" add:

3H–67 , as amended with effect from May 31, 2005 by the Consumer Credit (Agreements)(Amendment) Regulations 2004 (S.I. 2004 No. 1482),

Modifying agreements

Before ss.57–65 add:

s.55 and

3H–127

Rebate on early settlement

Delete "The Consumer Credit (Rebate on Early Settlement) Regulations 1983 (S.I. 1983 No. 1562)" and substitute:

3H–158

The first regulations under this section were the Consumer Credit (Rebate on Early Settlement) Regulations 1983 (S.I. 1983 No. 1562). Those regulations are replaced by the Consumer Credit (Early Settlement) Regulations 2004 (S.I. 2004 No. 1483) in respect of any agreement made on or after May 31, 2005. In respect of an agreement made before that date, the 1983 regulations continue to apply until either May 31, 2007 (if the agreement was for a term of 10 years or less) or May 31, 2010 (if the agreement was for a term exceeding 10 years). The calculation of the rebate is different under the two sets of regulations. Both the 1983 and the 2004 regulations, however,

At the beginning of the penultimate sentence delete "If" and substitute:

The rebate

Duty to give information

Delete paragraph and substitute:

3H–162

Until May 31, 2005, the prescribed period is 12 working days (the Consumer Credit (Settlement Information) Regulations 1983 (S.I. 1983 No. 1564)). The prescribed period is reduced to seven working days in the case of an agreement made on or after May 31, 2005 (the same regulations as amended by S.I. 2004 No. 1483). In respect of an agreement made before that date, the prescribed period will continue to be 12 working days until either May 31, 2007 (if the agreement was for a term of 10 years or less) or May 31, 2010 (if the agreement was for a term exceeding 10 years). The 1983 regulations also prescribe the "form"and "particulars". Where the agreement provides for a rebate in excess of the statutory rebate (under s.95), the settlement figure shown in the statement issued in response to a request for a settlement, must be calculated on the basis of the more favourable rebate provided in the contract (*Home Insulation Ltd v. Wadsley* [1988] C.C.L.R. 25, DC). A contractual provision giving a rebate less than the statutory rebate, is void (s.173(1)).

Remedies

Add at end:

3H–381

See also *Feldaroll Foundry Plc v. Hermes Leasing (London) Ltd* [2004] EWCA Civ 747; [2004] C.C.L.R. 8.

Implied terms as to title

For "(at 3B–415)" substitute:

(at 3H–440)

3H–384

In the course of a business

In the sentence which begins "This decision" for "is now" substitute:

seemed

3H–425

Before the sentence that begins "The amendments effected by the" add:

It was nevertheless followed and applied by the Court of Appeal in *Feldaroll Foundry Plc v. Hermes Leasing (London) Ltd* [2004] EWCA Civ 747; [2004] C.C.L.R. 8.

Consumer's additional rights for non–conformity

For "3B–412" substitute:

3H–423

3H–469

Consumer's additional rights for non–conformity

For "3B–453.3" substitute:

3H–469

3H–484

SECTION 4

HOUSE OF LORDS APPEALS

4A CIVIL APPEALS

Admissibility of petitions

Add new sub–paragraph (e) and its accompanying footnote:

4A–5 (e) an appeal from a decision of a judge of the High Court or Court of Session on an application for review of a decision of the Immigration Appeal Tribunal.[1]

16.

BOUND VOLUMES

After "amicus curiae" add:

4A–54 (e) (*i.e.* advocate to the court)

35.

FEES: WAIVER OF

Add new paragraph 35.2:

4A–79 35.2 In determining "financial hardship" for the purposes of Standing Order XIII, the Clerk of the Parliaments applies the provisions of the Supreme Court Fees Order 1999 (S.I. 1999 No. 687) as amended.

SECTION 6

ADMINISTRATION OF FUNDS, PROPERTY AND AFFAIRS

6A COURT FUNDS

Note

For "see C.F.O. Form 104 except for" substitute:

6A–53 see C.F.O. Form 100 for High Court and County Court lodgments, or C.F.O. Form 101 for Chancery lodgments except for

THE INVESTMENT OF FUNDS IN COURT

Common Investment Funds

For "(the Common Investment Funds Scheme 1991 (S.I. 1991 No. 1209)" substitute:

6A–161 (the Common Investment Funds Scheme 2004 (S.I. 2004 No. 266))

Dormant funds in court

In the first paragraph for "five" substitute:

6A–163 ten

Sources of information

Delete the line "Stewart House" from the address for Public Trustee Matters

[1] s. 101 Nationality, Asylum and Immigration Act 2002; see also s. 26 Asylum and Immigration (Treatment of Claimants, etc) Act 2004.

The High Court of Justice

Public Trustee Matters **6A–165**
Apply in the first instance to:
The Official Solicitor and Public
Trustee Office
81 Chancery Lane
London WC2A 1DD

6B COURT OF PROTECTION

GENERAL

The Court of Protection

Delete the existing Fax number and substitute:
0870 739 5780. **6B–2**

APPOINTMENT AND DISCHARGE OF RECEIVER

(a) First Application

General note

Delete the existing Commencement fee and substitute:
£230.00. **6B–12**

Mode of application

Delete the existing Commencement fee and substitute:
£230.00. **6B–13**

Documents and evidence

Delete sub–paragraph (ii) and substitute:
(ii) Statement of assets and income (Form C.P. 5). The statement includes provision for details of the applicant and the proposed receiver. **6B–17**

Add new sub–paragraph (iii)
(iii) Receiver's Declaration

Appointment Fee

Delete the existing appointment fee and substitute:
£300.00. **6B–23A**

After "2002" add:
and 2004.

Security

Delete existing text of subparagraph (b) and substitute:
(b) *By use of a simplified arrangement with HSBC Insurance Brokers Limited* in which case an endorsement supplied by the Public Guardianship Office should be signed, witnessed and sent to HSBC Insurance Brokers Limited together with the premium. **6B–24**

Delete existing subparagraphs (c) and (d) and the two subsequent paragraphs.

Existing subparagraph (e) is renumbered (c).
(c)

In the fourth paragraph of new subparagraph (c), delete "To increase security where it has been effected by lodgment in court of cash or securities, the necessary lodgment direction will issue for the additional cash or securities to be lodged."

In the fifth paragraph of new subparagraph (c), delete "Where security has been effected by lodgment in court, reduction will be effected by a direction under the Court Funds Rules 1987, r.7."

(b) Appointment of New Receiver

Documents and evidence

Add new sub–paragraph (v):

6B–29 (v) Receiver's Declaration

Delete the existing Transaction fee and substitute:

£190

Vacation of receiver's security

In the first paragraph, delete "Where, however, security has been effected by lodgment in court a direction to the Accountant General of the Supreme court to transfer the fund standing to the "Receiver's Security Account" to the former receiver, or his personal representatives, will be included in the order."

6B–33 *In the second paragraph, delete "Where the security has been effected by lodgment in court a separate direction to the Accountant General of the Supreme court will be prepared by the court. See r.65."*

(c) Application on Recovery of Patient

Transfer out of fund in Court

In the last paragraph, for "Common Investment Fund units" substitute:

6B–38 Equity Index Tracker Fund units

Vacation of security

In the first paragraph, delete "Where, however, security has been effected by lodgment in court a direction to the Accountant General of the Supreme Court to transfer the "Receiver's Security Account" to the receiver will be included in the order."

6B–39 *In the second paragraph, delete "Where security has been effected by lodgment in court a separate direction to the Accountant General of the Supreme Court will be prepared. See r.65."*

(d) Final Order or Direction on Death of Patient

Death of patient

Delete the existing winding up fee and substitute:

6B–41 £275

APPOINTMENT OF NEW TRUSTEES AND VESTING ORDERS

(b) Application to Exercise Patient's Power of Appointment under Mental Health Act 1983, s.96(1)(k)

Mode of application and applicants

Delete the existing Transaction fee and substitute:

6B–65 £125

Delete the existing Commencement fee and substitute:

£230

(c) Application to Exercise Patient's Power of Retirement under Mental Health Act 1983, s.96(1)(k)

Mode of application and applicants

Delete the existing Transaction fee and substitute:

6B–71 £125

(d) Application to Appoint New Trustee under Trustee Act 1925, s.54(2)

The order

Delete the existing Transaction fee and substitute:
£125 **6B–77**

(e) Application for Leave to Appoint New Trustee under Trustee Act 1925, s.36(9)

Certificate of leave

Delete the existing Transaction fee and substitute:
£125 **6B–81**

Delete the existing Transaction fee and substitute:
£230

MANAGEMENT AND ADMINISTRATION

Investments

In the fourth paragraph, for "the Common Investment Funds" substitute:
the Equity Index Tracker Fund **6B–85**

Equity Index Tracker Fund

Existing title is amended.

In the first paragraph, for "there are now two types of trust units, i.e. Capital and High Yield. The scheme now has a private sector manager." substitute: **6B–86**
there is now one type of trust unit, the Equity Index Tracker Funds units. The Fund is managed by Legal and General.

For the second paragraph substitute:
The Fund is substantially an equity fund. It tracks the FTSE All Share Index (80 per cent) and the FTSE World index Ex UK (20 per cent).

In the third paragraph, for "These funds have certain advantages" substitute:
The fund has certain advantages

In the third paragraph, delete "No brokerage or commission is payable."

In the fourth paragraph, for both instances of "the Capital Fund" substitute:
the Equity Index Tracker Fund

For the fifth paragraph substitute:
When income is of importance the court's investments strategies will determine the proportion invested.

For the sixth paragraph substitute:
The units can be held by the Accountant General, in a client's name or in nominees names but they are not transferable. They must therefore be realized on the death of a client but can be retained in the event of recovery.

Fees

Delete the existing Transaction fee and substitute:
£160 **6B–96**

Estate agent's charges

Exercise of power (including power to consent)

Delete the existing Transaction fee and substitute:
£125 **6B–106**

5. The terms of the trust

Statutory wills

Delete the existing transaction fee and substitute:

6B–136 £520

Accounts

Duty to account

Add at end:

6B–149 An account fee of 95 is payable on the tweny–eighth day after the last day of the period in respect of which an account is to be delivered under rule 61(1) or 65(2).

Costs

Short Form Bill of Costs

Add new paragraphs 6B–163A and 6B–163B:

6B–163A With effect from 1st June 2004 the Supreme Court Costs Office will accept a short form bill of costs where the amount of the bill does not exceed £3000, excluding VAT and disbursements. A model form for a short form bill is printed hereunder. When lodging the request for assessment, the following should be submitted:

1. Short Form Bill
2. Request for Assessment (Form N258B)
3. Fee of £100
4. The document giving the right to detailed assessment.
5. A statement giving the name and address for service of any person having a financial interest in the outcome of the assessment.
6. The relevant papers in support of the bill including the correspondence and attendance file for the period covered by the claim in the bill. No duplicates should be lodged.
7. Any fee notes of counsel and receipts or accounts for other disbursements relating to items claimed.

Model Short Form Bill **6B–163B**

IN THE COURT OF PROTECTION

Case No: - ....

SCCO reference ....
(to be completed by the court)

IN THE MATTER OF

.... (A patient)

Short form bill of costs of the Receiver of *(e.g.) General Management for the period* ....
to be assessed pursuant to the First General Order dated .... *and General Direction dated* ***19/11/82***

Summary of work carried out

Fee earner category .... Rate claimed ....

Work done:-			**Charge:-**
Time spent in personal attendances *e.g. 22/9/02* *45mins* *Upon patient*			....
Time spent in travel			....
Letters Sent			....
Telephone Calls	....		
Time spent on documents	....		
Other work *(give details)*			
....			
....			....
		Sub Total	....
		V.A.T.	....
Disbursements (list below)			
....			
....		Disbursements	....
		V.A.T.	....
		Grand Total	....

I certify that this bill is both accurate and complete.

.... (name and position)

Name, address and reference of person filing bill

Short form bill of costs for use in Court of Protection assessments where the total costs claimed do not exceed £3000 excluding VAT and disbursements

Final accounts

Rule 65(1) is revoked by the Court of Protection (Amendment) Rules 2004 (S.I. 2004 No. 1291)

65.—(1) [Revoked] **6B–291**

Delete paragraph (1) and substitute:

(6) paragraph (3)

Accounting by other persons

Delete "Rules 63 to 65" and substitute:

66. Rules 61 and 63 to 65 **6B–292**

PART XVII

FEES

Appendix of fees

Delete "rules 77A, 78, 79 and 82" and substitute:

6B–302 **76.**—(3) rules 77A, 78 and 78A

Administration fee

Delete 78(1) and substitute:

6B–304 **78.**—(1) An administration fee shall be payable—

(a) on the first and every subsequent anniversary of the date of the appointment of a receiver, until the termination of the proceedings; and

(b) at such other times either during the proceedings or at their termination as the court may direct, and

where the period for which the administration fee is payable is for less than one year, the fee payable shall be the proportion of the full fee as such period bears to one year.

Rule 78(5) is revoked by the Court of Protection (Amendment) Rules 2004 (S.I. 2004 No. 1291)

(5) [Revoked]

Account fee

Add new rule 78A:

6B–304A **78A.**—(1) An account fee shall be payable on the twenty–eighth day after the last day of the period in respect of which an account is to be delivered under rule 61(1) or 65(2).

(2) Where the court dispenses with the passing of an account under rule 61(4) or 65(3) the account fee—

(a) if paid, shall be refunded; or

(b) if not paid, shall cease to be payable.

Fees where officer of the court appointed receiver

Add new rule 80A:

6B–306A **80A.**—(1) Subject to paragraph (2), an appointment fee shall be payable, as set out in paragraph 4A of the Appendix, on the appointment of an officer of the court as receiver for a patient.

(2) Where proceedings are terminated within 4 weeks after the appointment, the fee referred to in paragraph (1) shall cease to be payable and any fee paid in accordance with that paragraph shall be refunded.

(3) Where an officer of the court has been appointed receiver for a patient—

(a) a fee shall be payable, as set out in paragraph 4B of the Appendix, in respect of completing an Inland Revenue tax return on behalf of the patient;

(b) a receivership administration fee shall be payable, as set out in paragraph 4C of the Appendix—

(i) on the first and every subsequent anniversary of the date of the officer's appointment as receiver until the termination of the proceedings; and

(ii) at such other times either during the proceedings or at their termination as the court may direct, and

where the period for which the receivership administration fee is payable is for less than one year, the fee payable shall be the proportion of the full fee as such period bears to one year; and

(c) the court shall annually, or at such other intervals as it may direct, issue a certificate in respect of each patient stating—

(i) the amount of the receivership administration fee payable in respect of the patient at the date of the certificate;

(ii) the period in respect of which that fee in payable; and

(iii) the name of the person who must make the payment.

(4) Upon the issue of a certificate under paragraph (3)(c) the amount of the fee shall be charged upon the patient's estate, and the payment shall be made within such time (not exceeding one month from the date of the certificate) as the court may allow.

(5) In any case in which it appears to the court that the amount of the fee certified under paragraph (3)(c) has been wrongly assessed, the court may direct that the fee is to be adjusted as it appears to it to be convenient.

PART XVIII

COSTS

Costs generally

After "or paid out of his estate" add:

84.—(1) or paid

6B–310

Delete exisitng table and substitute:

PART XXI

REVOCATION

Revocation of previous rules

APPENDIX COURT OF PROTECTION FEES

Column 1	Column 2
Commencement fee (rule 77)	
1. On the first application for the appointment of a receiver or other originating process.	£230.00
Receivership appointment fee (rule 77A)	
1A. Receivership appointment fee	£300.00

Column 1	Column 2
Administration fee (rule 78)	
2. Annually from the appointment of a receiver.	£230.00
Account fee (rule 78A)	
2A. On the twenty–eighth day after the last day of the period in respect of which an account is to be delivered under rule 61(1) or 65(2).	£95.00
Transaction fee (rule 79)	
3.—(1) On any order (or, as the case may be, on any approval given by the court under an order) or, as the case may be, on any application for such an order or approval, made by the court in the exercise of powers conferred by:—	
(i) the following paragraphs of section 96(1) of the Act:—	
(d) (settlement or gift of property) (h) (carrying out of contract) or (ii) section 1(3) of the Variation of Trusts Act 1958 (variation of trusts for the benefit of patient)	£100.00 or, in a "special case" 1/4% of the pecuniary consideration as referred to in rule 79 if greater than £100.00
provided that no fee under sub–paragraph (i) or (ii) shall be taken if the property is worth less than £100.00 and no such fee shall exceed £1000.00	
(iii) section 100 of the Act vesting of stock in curator appointed outside England and Wales)	£60.00
(iv) section 96(1)(k) of the Act (exercise of powers)	£120.00
(v) section 54 of the Trustee Act 1925 (concurrent jurisdiction with High Court over trusts)	£125.00
(vi) section 20 of the Trusts of Land and Appointment of Trustees Act 1996 (authorisation of person to Act as trustee).	£125.00
(2) On an application for an order or direction to be made by the court in exercise of the powers conferred by section 36(9) of Trustee Act 1925 (appointment of trustees).	£125.00
(3) On an application for an order or authority to be made by the court under section 96(1)(e) of the Act (execution of will).	£520.00
(4) On the application for the appointment of a new receiver.	£190.00

Column 1	Column 2
(5) On an application for an order or direction under section 96(1)(b) or (c) of the Act ordering or authorising the sale or purchase of any land.	£160.00
Detailed assessment of costs (rule 80)	
4.—(1) On the filing of a request for a detailed assessment of costs—	
(i) where the bill of costs does not exceed £3,000 excluding VAT and disbursements	£100.00
(ii) in all other cases	£200.00
(2) On an appeal against a decision made in a detailed assessment of costs or on an application to set aside a default costs certificate	£60.00
Fees where officer of the court appointed receiver (rule 80A)	
4A. On the appointment of an officer of the court as receiver	£1,000.00
4B. On the completion of an Inland Revenue tax return on behalf of the patient, where an officer of the court has been appointed receiver	£500.00
4C. Receivership administration fee, where an officer of the court has been appointed receiver	£3,500.00
Note – Paragraph 5 and 6 were omitted in their entirety in the Court of Protection (Amendment) Rules 2002	
Winding up fee (rule 82)	
7. On the death of a patient:	
(i) where an officer of the court has been appointed receiver	£850.00
(ii) otherwise	£275.00

TRANSITIONAL PROVISIONS

Transitional provisions

Add new paragraph 6B–318A:

6B–318A

(1) Where an appointment fee is payable under rule 77A upon the appointment of a receiver but the application for his appointment was received by the court before 1st June 2004, the Court of Protection Rules 2001 ("the 2001 Rules") shall have effect as if—

(a) rule 10(3) of these Rules had not been made; and

(b) in column 2 of paragraph 1A of the Appendix to the 2001 Rules for "£515.00", there were substituted "£460.00".

(2) Where—

(a) a transaction fee under rule 79(1) is payable which, by virtue of rule 79(4)(a), is to be taken upon the approval of the transaction; and

(b) the application for approval was received by the court before 1st June 2004, the 2001 Rules shall have effect as if rules 10(6) and 10(7) of these Rules had not been made.

(3) No transaction fee under rule 79(1) shall be payable where—

(a) an officer of the court is receiver for the patient;
(b) but for this paragraph that fee would, by virtue of rule 79(4)(a), be taken upon the approval of the transaction; and
(c) the application for such approval was received by the court before 1st June 2004.

(4) No appointment fee under rule 80A(1) shall be payable where the application for the appointment of a receiver was received by the court before 1st June 2004.

(5) Where a receivership administration fee is payable under rule 80A(3)(b) on an anniversary date falling before 31st May 2005, the fee payable shall be the proportion of the full fee as the period between 1st June 2004 and the anniversary bears to one year.

6D TRUSTEES

"Fees"

For "and the Public Trustee (Fees) (Amendment) Order 2003 (S.I. 2003 No. 690)." substitute:

6D–68 , the Public Trustee (Fees) (Amendment) Order 2003 (S.I. 2003 No. 690) and the Public Trustee (Fees) (Amendment) Order 2004 (S.I. 2004 No. 799)

SECTION 7

LEGAL REPRESENTATIVES – COSTS AND LITIGATION FUNDING

FUNDING ARRANGEMENTS

CONDITIONAL FEES

Add at end:

7A–32 For an explanation of the transitional provisions contained in the Access to Justice Act 1999 (Transitional Provisions) Order 1999 see *C v. M* [2003] EWHC 250 (Fam) Sumner J. Where a claimant has entered into a CFA prior to April 1, 2000 no success fee is recoverable from the paying party.

INSURANCE PREMIUMS

Recoverability of Insurance Premiums

Add at end:

7A–33 The Costs Judge had been correct to "deconstruct" the sum of money payable for legal costs insurance by claimant clients of The Accident Group to establish how much of that money was properly to be regarded as recoverable premium within the meaning of Section 29 of the 1999 Act. The fee paid to AIL (an associate company) was a referral fee. It had not been properly payable by the panel solicitors and had not therefore been chargeable to their clients and was certainly not recoverable from the paying party. The arrangement viewed objectively was that the fee had been compulsory for any solicitor wishing to be sent cases by TAG: *Sharratt* v. London Central Bus Co & Other Cases (No.2), The Accident Group Test Cases [2004] EWCA Civ 575; [2004] 3 All E.R. 325, CA.

Recoverability of Success Fees and Insurance Premiums

After the penultimate paragraph add:

7A–33.1 The Court of Appeal in *Callery v. Gray* (above) had been dealing with a case which involved success fees in simple claims. The court upheld the allowance of a success fee of 87% in a claim by the widow of the original claimant in a mesothelioma case, in which the damages awarded were £185,000. The Court of Appeal held that advising on quantum was not straightforward, particularly in the instant case where there had been several factors affecting the final award. Whilst liability issues and quantum issues could be considered separately, ultimately a single success fee was to be arrived at on an assessment of the prospect of winning: *Smiths Dock Ltd v. Edwards* [2004] EWHC 1116, (QBD) Crane J.

Particular allegations of breach

Add at end:

7A–33.4.4 Where a CFA made no mention of the fee deferral element in its schedule, although the body of the agreement stated that this was set out in the schedule, the solicitors argued that Section 58(1) of the Courts and Legal Services Act 1990 should be interpreted by inserting words such as "to the extent that it does not satisfy all requirements" so that the court could assess the effect of a particular breach. If the consequences were comparatively trivial this would penalise the solicitor far less than rendering the whole agreement unenforceable. The Court of Appeal rejected that argument pointing out that in *Hollins v. Russell* the court had found: "there is no graduated response to different types of breach: it is all or nothing." The words "shall be unenforceable" mean what they say. The court held that Parliament had decided that unless a CFA satisfied all the conditions applicable to it, by virtue of Section 58(1), it would not be exempt from the general rules as to the unenforceability of CFAs at common law: *Spencer v.Wood (t/a Gordon's Tyres)* [2004] EWCA Civ 352.

A CFA with a contingent uplift as a success fee was held to be enforceable as the fact that an agreement was a conditional fee agreement under the Courts and Legal Services Act 1990 was sufficient to render it enforceable regardless of how the success fee was calculated: *Benaim (UK) Ltd v. Davies Middleton & Davies Ltd* [2004] EWHC 737 (TCC) HHJ Rich Q.C.

REMUNERATION—GENERAL

Payment of the bill

Add at end:

7C–118 A firm of solicitors consisting of three partners rendered a bill to their client relating to the administration of an estate. A number of charities who were residuary beneficiaries of the estate sought detailed assessment because sums equal to the full amount of the bill had already been paid to them to one of the partners before he joined the firm. They sought repayment of any amounts found on assessment to have been overpaid. The partner to whom the money was originally paid had since disappeared. The Costs Judge found that the remaining partners were bound by representations made by the partner who had disappeared, even though the representations were made before the partnership was formed. The court rejected the suggestion that there was a novation which had the effect of rendering the firm liable for matters arising in the course of the prior retainer. The court also rejected the argument that the partners were estopped from denying that there had been a novation, nor was it persuaded that there was any statutory liability to pay under sections 70 and 71 of the Solicitors Act 1974. The continuing partners were therefore held to be not liable to repay any sum by which the bill was reduced, the only person being so liable being the partner who had disappeared: *Marsden v. Guide Dogs for the Blind Association* [2004] EWHC 593 (Ch); [2004] 3 All E.R. 222, also known as *Burton Marsden Douglas (A Firm), Re*, Lloyd J.

Note

In the third paragraph, for "Jemma Trust Co. Ltd v. Liptrott [2003] EWCA Civ 1476" substitute:
Jemma Trust Co. Ltd v. Liptrott [2003] EWCA Civ 1476; [2004] 1 W.L.R. 646, CA **7C–203**

NOTES ON THE GENERAL LAW RELATING TO SOLICITORS

2. RIGHTS, PRIVILEGES AND AGENCY OF SOLICITORS

Authority of solicitors

Conflict of interests

Add at end:

7C–225 It is beyond doubt that communications by a client to her solicitor are of a confidential nature. Therefore conclusions reached by the solicitor from that information are also confidential. It is not open to a solicitor without the client's consent to communicate information passed by that client to a solicitor involved under another retainer. The mere fact that two solicitors were employed on different matters by the same client is insufficient to justify the passing of confidential information from one solicitor to the other. Where the client had limited intellectual capacity leading to her being unable to manage her affairs this would mean that she would be unable to relax the duty of confidence between her and her solicitor. The mere fact of low intellect cannot justify a breach of confidence. The solicitor's duty of confidence is absolute unless there has been some relaxation by law or by the client: *Marsh v. Sofaer (Application to Strike Out)* [2003] EWHC 3264 (Ch) Sir Andrew Morritt V.C.

SECTION 8

LIMITATION

Scope and operation of the Act

In the first paragraph, delete from "It repeals and re–enacts these earlier statutes..." to the end of the paragraph.

8–3 *Delete the second paragraph and substitute:*

The Limitation Act 1963 was designed to mitigate the injustice caused to a plaintiff who did not know that he had suffered injury until after the expiry of the current period of limitation and thus had his claim barred without knowing that he had a claim (see *Cartledge v. Jopling (E.) and Sons Ltd* [1963] A.C. 758).

In the third paragraph for "See, for the recommendations on which the reform was based, the Law Reform Committee's 24th Report (Latent Damage: Cmnd. 9390) of November 1984. And, furthermore," substitute:

Furthermore

In the sixth paragraph delete "under the former Rules of the Supreme Court, O.18, r.8(1)); and now"

In the penultimate paragraph delete: "Third, in relation to the power to the Court, prior to the introduction of the CPR"...up to and including "The position as it now applies following the introduction of the CPR is an open one in the sense that whilst the Court has a very wide power to strike out proceedings" and substitute:

Third, following the introduction of the CPR, whilst the Court has a very wide power to strike out proceedings

Actions for damages for personal injuries or death

In the first paragraph delete the second sentence.

8–26 **Knowledge of plaintiff in negligence actions**

In the first paragraph delete from the second sentence "(as in the case of earlier reform in relation to actions involving personal injuries)"

8–34 *In the first paragraph delete from the fourth sentence "See in particular the 24th Report of the Law Reform Committee (Cmnd. 9390, November 1984) and" and substitute:*

See

Section 21—actions for breach of trust and actions for breach of fiduciary duty

Delete the first two sentences and substitute:

8–47 *Paragon Finance Plc v. DB* elucidates the true nature of the distinction between two different classes of persons described as constructive trustees, namely (1) those holding on trust by virtue of taking possession of property on trust for or on behalf of others before the occurrence of the transaction impeached, and (2) those to whom the description applies only by reason of that transaction.

Effect of this section

In the first paragraph delete the second sentence.

8–57 Note

In the second paragraph, delete the first two sentences.

In the second paragraph delete the last sentence. **8–66**

Delete the third paragraph.

Discretionary power to override time limits in actions for personal injuries or death

Delete the second paragraph.

Action begun within primary limitation period **8–69**

In the first paragraph delete the first sentence and substitute:

8–70 The new discretionary power under this section is limited and restricted in its operation, this was how the section was interpreted by the House of Lords.

Delete the fifth paragraph and substitute:

In *Firman v. Ellis* [1978] Q.B. 886 Lord Denning M.R. said that the grant by Parliament of the wide discretion to the Courts under s.2D (now s.33), *i.e.* to override time limits, is a revolutionary and valuable change which will enable justice to be done even at the expense of some certainty; the relevant words of the statute are so clear that they cannot be construed restrictively as applying only to exceptional cases (*ibid.*); see especially the judgment of Geoffrey Lane L.J.

SECTION 9

JURISDICTIONAL AND PROCEDURAL LEGISLATION

9A MAIN STATUTES

Head of Civil Justice

Add new paragraph 9A–10.1:

9A–10.1 The Lord Chancellor must appoint a Head of Civil Justice. No person may be so appointed unless he is (a) the Master of the Rolls, (b) the Vice–Chancellor, or (c) an ordinary judge of the Court of Appeal (Courts Act 2003, s.62).

Note

Add new paragraph 9A–26.1:

9A–26.1 From a date yet to be fixed, in this section para. (b) of sub–section (1) is amended, and sub–section (2) is substituted, by the Courts Act 2003, s.65(1), s.109(1) and Sched.8, para. 259.

Judicial bias – judge "incapable of acting"

At the end of the sixth paragraph add:

9A–44.1 *Garratt v. Saxby (Practice Note)* [2004] EWCA Civ 341; [2004] 1 W.L.R. 2152, CA (offer to settle inadvertently disclosed to judge). In the Scottish case of *Davidson v. Scottish Ministers (No. 2)* [2004] UKHL 34, *The Times* July 16, 2004, HL, it was held that a risk of apparent bias is liable to arise where a judge who had participated in the drafting or promotion of legislation during the parliamentary process is called up to rule judicially on the effect of the legislation.

Restrictions on appeals

At the end of the second paragraph add:

9A–55 In *R. (South West Yorkshire Mental Health NHS Trust) v. Crown Court at Bradford* [2003] EWCA Civ 1857; [2004] 1 W.L.R. 1664, CA, it was held that, although an order made by the Crown Court upon a verdict being entered was made under a statute empowering the court to make a custodial order in the absence of conviction (in this instance, the Criminal Procedure (Insanity) Act 1964, s.5(2)(a)), the order did not for that reason cease to be an order in a criminal cause or matter. In determining whether an appeal is in a criminal cause or matter it is appropriate for the court to take an overall view and not to enter into a detailed order by order analysis.

Appeals from Crown Court and inferior courts

9A–75 *In section 28(2)(b), delete "the Licensing Act 1964".*

Note

Add at end:

9A–76 Further amended by the Licensing Act 2003, s.99 and Sched.7.

Mandatory, prohibiting and quashing orders

Existing title is amended.

9A–80 *For section 29(1) substitute:*

29. (1) The orders of mandamus, prohibition and certiorari shall be known instead as mandatory, prohibiting and quashing orders respectively.

(1A) The High Court shall have jurisdiction to make mandatory, prohibiting and quashing orders in those classes of case in which, immediately before 1st May 2004, it had jurisdiction to make orders of mandamus, prohibition and certiorari.

In section 29(3), for "orders of mandamus, prohibition or certiorari" substitute:

(3) mandatory, prohibiting and quashing orders

In section 29(3A), for "orders of mandamus, prohibition or certiorari" substitute:

(3A) mandatory, prohibiting and quashing orders

In section 29(4), for "order of mandamus" substitute:

(4) mandatory order

For section 29(5) substitute:

(5) In any statutory provision —

(a) references to mandamus or to a writ or order of mandamus shall be read as reference to a mandatory order;

(b) references to prohibition or to a writ or order of prohibition shall be read as reference to a prohibiting order;

(c) references to certiorari or to a writ or order of certiorari shall be read as reference to a quashing order; and

(d) references to the issue or award of a writ of mandamus, prohibition and certiorari shall be read as references to the making of the corresponding mandatory, prohibiting or quashing order.

Note

Add at end:

9A–81 With effect from May 1, 2004, amended by the Civil Procedure (Modification of Supreme Court Act 1981) Order 2004 (S.I. 2004 No. 1033), so as to provide that orders of mandamus, prohibition and certiorari should be known instead as mandatory, prohibiting and quashing orders respectively.

Application for judicial review

For section 31(1)(a) substitute:

9A–84 **31.**—(1) (a) a mandatory, prohibiting or quashing order,

In section 31(2)(a), for "orders of mandamus, prohibition or certiorari" substitute:

(2) (a) mandatory, prohibiting and quashing orders

For section 31(4) substitute:

(4) On an application for judicial review the High Court may award to the applicant damages, restitution or the recovery of a sum due if—

(a) the application includes a claim for such an award arising from any matter to which the application relates; and

(b) the court is satisfied that such an award would have been made if the claim had been made in an action begun by the applicant at the time of making the application.

In subsection 31(5), for "an order of certiorari" substitute:

(5) a quashing order

Note

Add at end:

9A–85 With effect from May 1, 2004, subsections (1), (2) and (5) amended, and subsection (4) substituted, by the Civil Procedure (Modification of Supreme Court Act 1981) Order 2004 (S.I. 2004 No. 1033), as a consequence of amendments to s.31, see para. 9A–81 above. Subsection (4) provided that, on an application for judicial review, in certain circumstances the High Court should have power to award damages. As substituted, the subsection (4) provides that the Court has, in addition to the power to award damages, power to award restitution or the recovery of a sum due.

Applications for order

Add at end:

9A–134 For power of court to make civil restraint orders, see CPR r.3.11.

Power of High Court to vary sentence on application for quashing order

Existing title is amended.

9A–136 *In section 43(1), for "an order of certiorari" substitute:*

43.(1) a quashing order

Note

Add at end:

9A–137 With effect from May 1, 2004, amended by the Civil Procedure (Modification of Supreme Court Act 1981) Order 2004 (S.I. 2004 No. 1033), as a consequence of amendments to s.31, see para. 9A–81 above.

"costs ... shall be in the discretion of the court"

Delete the full stop at the end of the second paragraph and add:

9A–265 , *Gulf Azov Shipping Co. Ltd v. Idisi* [2004] EWCA Civ 292; March 15, 2004, CA, unrep.

After the second paragraph add:

The approach of the courts to the making of an award of costs against a non–party has had to accommodate the change in public policy which has recognised that access to justice can properly be procured by giving those who provide legal services an interest in the outcome of litigation through conditional fee agreements (*Gulf Azov Shipping Co. Ltd v. Idisi* [2004] EWCA Civ 292; March 15, 2004, CA, unrep., *per* Lord Phillips M.R. at para. 35).

Add at end:

In giving the judgment of the Court of Appeal in *Gulf Azov Shipping Co. Ltd v. Idisi* [2004] EWCA Civ 292; March 15, 2004, CA, unrep., Lord Phillips M.R. said (at para. 34) it was unfortunate that the application for costs against a non-party funder was heard, not by the judge who had dealt with the principal proceedings giving rise to the application, or by any other judge of the Commercial Court who had been involved with the litigation, but by a deputy High Court judge who had had no previous connection with the proceedings.

Circuit judges not to sit on certain appeals

9A–284 *With effect from January 26, 2004, s.56A was repealed by the Courts Act 2003, s.67 and Sched.10 (see Courts Act 2003 (Commencement No. 1) Order 2003 (S.I. 2003 No. 3345)).*

Committal for trial: alteration of place of trial

For subsection 76(4) substitute:

9A–342 **76.**—(4) [Repealed]

Note

Add at end:

9A–343 With the coming into effect on May 1, 2004, of s.86 of the Courts Act 2003, an application under s.76(3) is no longer required to be heard in open court by a judge of the High Court and accordingly subsection (4) was repealed by s.109(3) and Sched.10 of the 2003 Act.

Bail

In section 81(1)(e), for "an order of certiorari" substitute:

9A–349 **81.**—(1) (e) a quashing order

Note

Add at end:

9A–350 Para. (e) of subsection (1) amended by the Civil Procedure (Modification of Supreme Court Act 1981) Order 2004 (S.I. 2004 No. 1033), as a consequence of amendments to s.31, see para. 9A–81 above. The Criminal Justice Act 2003, s.17(3) (brought into effect on April 5, 2004) states that the inherent power of the High Court to entertain an application in relation to bail where the Crown Court has determined an application under paras (a), (b), (c) or (g) of s.81 is abolished. Further, the High Court is to have no power to entertain an application in relation to bail where the Crown Court has determined an appeal under s.16 of the 2003 Act (s.17(4)).

Effect of writs of execution against goods

With effect from March 15, 2004, s.138 was repealed by the Courts Act 2003, upon the coming into force of s.99 and Sched.7 (High Court writs of execution) of that Act.

9A–447 *Delete paragraphs 9A–448 and 9A–449.*

Sales under executions

With effect from March 15, 2004, s.138A was repealed by the Courts Act 2003, upon the coming into force of s.99 and Sched.7 (High Court writs of execution) of that Act.

9A–450 *Delete paragraph 9A–451.*

Protection of officer selling goods under execution

With effect from March 15, 2004, s.138 was repealed by the Courts Act 2003, upon the coming into force of s.99 and Sched.7 (High Court writs of execution) of that Act.

9A–452 *Delete paragraph 9A–453.*

Effects of warrants of execution

In section 99(2)(b), for "delivered to and remained unexecuted in the hands of the sheriff." substitute:

99.—(2) (b) delivered to an enforcement officer or other officer charged with the execution of the writ and remained unexecuted in the hands of that person. **9A–696**

In section 99(4), add before sub–paragraph (a):

(4) (za) "enforcement officer" means an individual who is authorised to act as an enforcement officer under the Courts Act 2003;

Delete section99(4)(b).

Effects of warrants of execution

Add at end:

With effect from March 15, 2004, subsections (2)(b) and (4) were amended by the Courts Act 2003, s.109(1) and Sched.8, para. 274. **9A–697**

Information as to writs and warrants of execution

For existing text substitute:

104.—(1) Where a writ against the goods of any person issued from the High Court is delivered to an enforcement officer who is under a duty to execute the writ or to a sheriff, then on demand from the district judge of a county court that person shall— **9A–708**

(a) in the case of an enforcement officer, by writing signed by that officer or a person acting under his authority, and

(b) in the case of a sheriff, by writing signed by any clerk in the officer of the under–sheriff,

inform the district judge of the precise time the writ was delivered to him.

(2) A bailiff of a county court shall on demand show his warrant to any enforcement officer, any person acting under the authority of an enforcement officer and any sheriff's officer.

(3) Any writing purporting to be signed as mentioned in subsection (1) and the endorsement on any warrant issued from a county court shall respectively be sufficient justification to any district judge, or enforcement officer or sheriff, acting on it.

(4) In this section "enforcement officer" means an individual who is authorised to act as an enforcement officer under the Courts Act 2003.

Information as to writs and warrants of execution

Add at end:

This section was substituted by the Courts Act 2003, s.109(1) and Sched.8, para. 275, with effect from March 15, 2004. **9A–709**

Power to make consequential and other amendments to enactments

In the first paragraph after "Civil Procedure (Modification of Enactments) Order 2002 (S.I. 2002 No. 439)" add:

9A–838 , Civil Procedure (Modification of Supreme Court Act 1981) Order 2004 (S.I. 2004 No. 1033)

Definition of "practice directions"

In the third paragraph, for "See further Vol. 1, para. 2.3.3.1" substitute:

9A–841.1 See further Vol. 1, para. 2.3.4

Add at end:

Practice directions are not made by statutory instrument. They are not laid before Parliament or subject to either the negative or positive resolution procedures in Parliament. They go through no democratic process at all, although if approved by the Lord Chancellor he will bear ministerial responsibility for them to Parliament. There is no ministerial responsibility for practice directions made for the Supreme Court by the Heads of Division (In *Re C (Legal Aid: Preparation of Bill of Costs)* [2001] 1 F.L.R. 602, CA, at para. 21 *per* Hale L.J.).

SECTION 10

COURT FEES

In the table, for section 3 substitute:

10–32

SCHEDULE 1

FEES TO BE TAKEN

Column 1 Number and description of fee	*Column 2* Amount of fee
3. Special applications 3.1 For a duplicate or second or subsequent grant (including one following a revoked grant) in respect of the same deceased person, other than a grant preceded only by a grant limited to settled land, to trust property, or to part of the estate	£15
3.2 On an application for a grant in respect of an estate exempt from inheritance tax by virtue of section 154 of the Inheritance Tax Act 1984 (exemption for members of the armed forces etc). Paragraph 3 of Non Contentious Probate Fees (Amendment) Order 2003 (coming into force 30 May 2003) *This order* [which introduces fee 3.2] applies in respect of deaths [of members of the armed forces of the Crown certified to have been killed on active service] occurring on or after 20th March 2003, and in respect of a death occurring before that date the Fees Order shall have effect as if this Order had not been made. (2) Paragraph (3) of this article applies where— (a) a fee or fees other than the fee prescribed by paragraph 3(2) of Scehdule 1 to the Fees Order ("the special fee") is paid on application for a grant; and (b) the grant applied for is in respect of an estate exempt from inheritance tax by virtue of section 154 of the Inheritance Tax Act 1984. (3) Where this paragraph applies the Lord Chancellor shall upon receiving a written application refund the difference between the fee or fees actually paid and the special fee.	£8

Column 1 Number and description of fee	*Column 2* Amount of fee
NOTE. The words in square brackets (above) are provided as an aid to understanding and are not part of the statute. The fees that would be payable but for the above order are £50 for a grant and £80 for a personal application.	

Add new paragraph 10–72

DIRECTORY OF HIGH COURT ENFORCEMENT OFFICERS – LISTED ALPHABETICALLY BY POSTAL DISTRICT

District	Code	Name
Bath	BA	ANDERSON, Michael ASKER, David BARNETT, Simon BASTIN, Simon BULLOCK, Richard CHANNER, Gervase COOMBE, Geoffrey DUNCAN, Andrew EGMORE, Angela EVANS, Philip FARRINGTON, Patrick GATER, Jonathan GRIFFITHS, Richard HARGROVE, John HATHAWAY, John HORNER, Nigel JAMES, John KIMBER, Michael LEYSHON, Martin PEPPER, Nigel SANDBROOK, Claire SMITH, Alan TRICKEY, David WENT, Richard WHELLER, Jonathan
Birmingham	B	ANDERSON, Michael ASKER, David BULLOCK, Richard BUTLER, Malcolm DEAN, Paul DUNCAN, Andrew EVANS, Philip FARRINGTON, Patrick GATER, Jonathan GRIFFITHS, Richard HARGROVE, John HATHAWAY, John HORNER, Nigel JAMES, John KIMBER, Michael LEYSHON, Martin MARSTON, John MORGAN, Ian PEPPER, Nigel SANDBROOK, Claire SMITH, Alan

District	Code	Name
Blackburn	BB	ASKER, David DEAN, Derek DEAN, Gordon DEAN, Paul HARGROVE, John HARRISON, Karl LAING, John SANDBROOK, Claire SMITH, Alan THOMPSON, Patricia WILSON, Andrew
Bolton	BL	ASKER, David DEAN, Derek DEAN, Gordon DEAN, Paul HARGROVE, John HARRISON, Karl SANDBROOK, Claire SMITH, Alan THOMPSON, Patricia VANN, Edward WILSON, Andrew
Bournemouth	BH	ASKER, David BARNETT, Simon BASTIN, Simon COOMBE, Geoffrey EGMORE, Angela HARGROVE, John SANDBROOK, Claire SMITH, Alan TRICKEY, David
Bradford	BD	ASKER, David HARGROVE, John HARRISON, Dion HARRISON, Karl LAING, John SANDBROOK, Claire SMITH, Alan THOMPSON, Patricia TOWERS, Jonathan WHITWORTH, Frank WILSON, Andrew
Brighton	BN	ASKER, David HARGROVE, John SANDBROOK, Claire SMITH, Alan

District	Code	Name
Bristol	BS	ALEXANDER, Nicholas ANDERSON, Michael ASKER, David BULLOCK, Richard CHANNER, Gervase DUNCAN, Andrew EVANS, Philip EWART–JAMES, Andrew FARRINGTON, Patrick GATER, Jonathan GRIFFITHS, Richard HARGROVE, John HATHAWAY, John HORNER, Nigel JAMES, John KIMBER, Michael LEYSHON, Martin PEPPER, Nigel SANDBROOK, Claire SMITH, Alan WENT, Richard WHELLER, Jonathan
Bromley	BR	ASKER, David BUTLER, Malcolm HARGROVE, John MARSTON, John MORGAN, Ian SANDBROOK, Claire SMITH, Alan
Cambridge	CB	ASKER, David CONSTANT, Bryan HALL, Brian HARGROVE, John SANDBROOK, Claire SILLS, Tim SMITH, Alan STEPHENS, Martin WATT, Peter
Canterbury	CT	ASKER, David HARGROVE, John SANDBROOK, Claire SMITH, Alan
Cardiff	CF	ANDERSON, Michael ASKER, David BOWEN, David BULLOCK, Richard DUNCAN, Andrew EVANS, Philip FARRINGTON, Patrick GATER, Jonathan GRIFFITHS, Richard HARGROVE, John HATHAWAY, John HORNER, Nigel JAMES, John KIMBER, Michael LEYSHON, Martin PEPPER, Nigel SANDBROOK, Claire SMITH, Alan

District	Code	Name
Carlisle	CA	ASKER, David DEAN, Derek DEAN, Gordon DEAN, Paul FITZGERALD, Hugh HARGROVE, John HARRISON, Karl SANDBROOK, Claire SMITH, Alan THOMPSON, Patricia WILSON, Andrew
Chelmsford	CM	ASKER, David BUTLER, Malcolm HARGROVE, John MARSTON, John MORGAN, Ian SANDBROOK, Claire SMITH, Alan TUNSTILL, Peter WILLIAMS, James
Chester	CH	ANDERSON, Michael ARNOLD, John ASKER, David BULLOCK, Richard DEAN, Derek DEAN, Gordon DEAN, Paul DUNCAN, Andrew EVANS, Philip FARRINGTON, Patrick GATER, Jonathan GREGORY, John GRIFFITHS, Richard GUEST, Robin HARGROVE, John HARRISON, Karl HATHAWAY, John HORNER, Nigel JAMES, John KIMBER, Michael LEYSHON, Martin MASON, David MORRIS–JONES, Gareth PARRY, Anthony PEPPER, Nigel SANDBROOK, Claire SMITH, Alan SOUTHERN, Norman THOMPSON, Patricia WILSON, Andrew
Cleveland (Teeside)	TS	ASKER, David DAVIES, Malcolm ELLIOTT, Chris FELLOWS, Kathleen HARGROVE, John HARRISON, Karl SANDBROOK, Claire SMITH, Alan STOREY, Roy THOMPSON, Patricia TOWERS, Jonathan WILSON, Andrew

District	Code	Name
Colchester	CO	ASKER, David GRAHAM, Brian HARGROVE, John SANDBROOK, Claire SMITH, Alan STEPHENS, Martin
Coventry	CV	ANDERSON, Michael ASKER, David BULLOCK, Richard BUTLER, Malcolm DUNCAN, Andrew EVANS, Philip FARRINGTON, Patrick GATER, Jonathan GRIFFITHS, Richard HARGROVE, John HATHAWAY, John HORNER, Nigel JAMES, John KIMBER, Michael LEYSHON, Martin MARSTON, John MORGAN, Ian PEPPER, Nigel SANDBROOK, Claire SMITH, Alan
Crewe	CW	ANDERSON, Michael ARNOLD, John ASKER, David BULLOCK, Richard DEAN, Gordon DEAN, Paul DUNCAN, Andrew EVANS, Philip FARRINGTON, Patrick GATER, Jonathan GRIFFITHS, Richard HARGROVE, John HARRISON, Karl HATHAWAY, John HORNER, Nigel JAMES, John KIMBER, Michael LEYSHON, Martin MASON, David PEPPER, Nigel SANDBROOK, Claire SMITH, Alan SOUTHERN, Norman THOMPSON, Patricia WILSON, Andrew
Croydon	CR	ASKER, David BUTLER, Malcolm HARGROVE, John MARSTON, John MORGAN, Ian SANDBROOK, Claire SMITH, Alan

District	Code	Name
Darlington	DL	ASKER, David
		DAVIES, Malcolm
		ELLIOTT, Chris
		FELLOWS, Kathleen
		HARGROVE, John
		HARRISON, Karl
		SANDBROOK, Claire
		SMITH, Alan
		STOREY, Roy
		THOMPSON, Patricia
		TOWERS, Jonathan
		WILSON, Andrew
Dartford	DA	ASKER, David
		BUTLER, Malcolm
		HARGROVE, John
		MARSTON, John
		MORGAN, Ian
		SANDBROOK, Claire
		SMITH, Alan
Derby	DE	ANDERSON, Michael
		ASKER, David
		BULLOCK, Richard
		BUTLER, Malcolm
		DEAN, Paul
		DUNCAN, Andrew
		EVANS, Philip
		FARRINGTON, Patrick
		GATER, Jonathan
		GRIFFITHS, Richard
		HARGROVE, John
		HARRISON, Karl
		HATHAWAY, John
		HORNER, Nigel
		JAMES, John
		KIMBER, Michael
		LEYSHON, Martin
		MARSTON, John
		MORGAN, Ian
		PEPPER, Nigel
		SANDBROOK, Claire
		SMITH, Alan
		THOMPSON, Patricia
		WILSON, Andrew
Doncaster	DN	ASKER, David
		BAITSON, Helen
		BAITSON, Michael
		BUTLER, Malcolm
		DEAN, Paul
		HARGROVE, John
		HARRISON, Dion
		HARRISON, Karl
		MARSTON, John
		McGARRAGH, Robert
		MORGAN, Ian
		SANDBROOK, Claire
		SMITH, Alan
		THOMPSON, Patricia
		TOWERS, Jonathan
		WILSON, Andrew

District	Code	Name
Dorchester	DT	ASKER, David BARNETT, Simon BASTIN, Simon COOMBE, Geoffrey EGMORE, Angela HARGROVE, John SANDBROOK, Claire SMITH, Alan TRICKEY, David
Dudley	DY	ANDERSON, Michael ASKER, David BULLOCK, Richard BUTLER, Malcolm DUNCAN, Andrew EVANS, Philip FARRINGTON, Patrick GATER, Jonathan GRIFFITHS, Richard HARGROVE, John HATHAWAY, John HORNER, Nigel JAMES, John KIMBER, Michael LEYSHON, Martin MARSTON, John MORGAN, Ian PEPPER, Nigel SANDBROOK, Claire SMITH, Alan
Durham	DH	ASKER, David DAVIES, Malcolm ELLIOTT, Chris HARGROVE, John HARRISON, Karl SANDBROOK, Claire SMITH, Alan THOMPSON, Patricia WILSON, Andrew
Enfield	EN	ASKER, David BUTLER, Malcolm HARGROVE, John MARSTON, John MORGAN, Ian SANDBROOK, Claire SMITH, Alan TUNSTILL, Peter WILLIAMS, James
Exeter	EX	ASKER, David BARNETT, Simon BASTIN, Simon CHANNER, Gervase COOMBE, Geoffrey EGMORE, Angela HARGROVE, John SANDBROOK, Claire SMITH, Alan TRICKEY, David WENT, Richard WHELLER, Jonathan

District	Code	Name
Fylde (Blackpool)	FY	ASKER, David
		DEAN, Derek
		DEAN, Gordon
		DEAN, Paul
		HARGROVE, John
		HARRISON, Karl
		SANDBROOK, Claire
		SMITH, Alan
		THOMPSON, Patricia
		WILSON, Andrew
Gloucester	GL	ALEXANDER, Nicholas
		ANDERSON, Michael
		ASKER, David
		BOWEN, David
		BULLOCK, Richard
		DUNCAN, Andrew
		EVANS, Philip
		EWART–JAMES, Andrew
		FARRINGTON, Patrick
		GATER, Jonathan
		GRIFFITHS, Richard
		HARGROVE, John
		HATHAWAY, John
		HORNER, Nigel
		JAMES, John
		KIMBER, Michael
		LEYSHON, Martin
		PEPPER, Nigel
		SANDBROOK, Claire
		SMITH, Alan
Guildford	GU	ANDERSON, Michael
		ASKER, David
		BUTLER, Malcolm
		DUNCAN, Andrew
		EVANS, Philip
		FARRINGTON, Patrick
		GATER, Jonathan
		GRIFFITHS, Richard
		HARGROVE, John
		HATHAWAY, John
		HORNER, Nigel
		JAMES, John
		KIMBER, Michael
		LEYSHON, Martin
		MARSTON, John
		MORGAN, Ian
		PEPPER, Nigel
		SANDBROOK, Claire
		SMITH, Alan
Halifax	HX	ASKER, David
		HARGROVE, John
		HARRISON, Dion
		HARRISON, Karl
		LAING, John
		SANDBROOK, Claire
		SMITH, Alan
		THOMPSON, Patricia
		TOWERS, Jonathan
		WHITWORTH, Frank
		WILSON, Andrew

District	Code	Name
Harrogate	HG	ASKER, David
		HARGROVE, John
		HARRISON, Dion
		HARRISON, Karl
		LAING, John
		SANDBROOK, Claire
		SMITH, Alan
		THOMPSON, Patricia
		TOWERS, Jonathan
		WHITWORTH, Frank
		WILSON, Andrew
Harrow	HA	ASKER, David
		BUTLER, Malcolm
		GATER, Jonathan
		GRIFFITHS, Richard
		HARGROVE, John
		KIMBER, Michael
		MARSTON, John
		MORGAN, Ian
		SANDBROOK, Claire
		SMITH, Alan
Hemel Hempstead	HP	ANDERSON, Michael
		ASKER, David
		BULLOCK, Richard
		BUTLER, Malcolm
		COUZENS, James
		DUNCAN, Andrew
		EVANS, Philip
		FARRINGTON, Patrick
		GATER, Jonathan
		GRIFFITHS, Richard
		HARGROVE, John
		HATHAWAY, John
		HORNER, Nigel
		JAMES, John
		KIMBER, Michael
		LEGGETT, John
		LEYSHON, Martin
		MARSTON, John
		MORGAN, Ian
		O'NEILL, Mick
		PEPPER, Nigel
		SANDBROOK, Claire
		SMITH, Alan
		TUNSTILL, Peter
		WILLIAMS, James

District	Code	Name
Hereford	HR	ALEXANDER, Nicholas ANDERSON, Michael ASKER, David BOWEN, David BULLOCK, Richard BUTLER, Malcolm DUNCAN, Andrew EVANS, Philip EWART–JAMES, Andrew FARRINGTON, Patrick GATER, Jonathan GRIFFITHS, Richard HARGROVE, John HATHAWAY, John HORNER, Nigel JAMES, John KIMBER, Michael LEYSHON, Martin MARSTON, John MORGAN, Ian PEPPER, Nigel SANDBROOK, Claire SMITH, Alan
Huddersfield	HD	ASKER, David DEAN, Paul HARGROVE, John HARRISON, Dion HARRISON, Karl LAING, John SANDBROOK, Claire SMITH, Alan THOMPSON, Patricia TOWERS, Jonathan WHITWORTH, Frank WILSON, Andrew
Hull	HU	ASKER, David BAITSON, Helen BAITSON, Michael HARGROVE, John HARRISON, Dion HARRISON, Karl McGARRAGH, Robert SANDBROOK, Claire SMITH, Alan THOMPSON, Patricia TOWERS, Jonathan WILSON, Andrew
Ilford	IG	ASKER, David BUTLER, Malcolm HARGROVE, John MARSTON, John MORGAN, Ian SANDBROOK, Claire SMITH, Alan

District	Code	Name
Ipswich	IP	ASKER, David CONSTANT, Bryan GRAHAM, Brian HALL, Brian HARGROVE, John SANDBROOK, Claire SILLS, Tim SMITH, Alan STEPHENS, Martin WATT, Peter
Kingston upon Thames	KT	ASKER, David BUTLER, Malcolm GATER, Jonathan GRIFFITHS, Richard HARGROVE, John KIMBER, Michael MARSTON, John MORGAN, Ian SANDBROOK, Claire SMITH, Alan
Lancaster	LA	ASKER, David DEAN, Derek DEAN, Gordon DEAN, Paul FITZGERALD, Hugh HARGROVE, John HARRISON, Karl SANDBROOK, Claire SMITH, Alan THOMPSON, Patricia WILSON, Andrew
Leeds	LS	ASKER, David HARGROVE, John HARRISON, Dion LAING, John SANDBROOK, Claire SMITH, Alan THOMPSON, Patricia TOWERS, Jonathan WHITWORTH, Frank WILSON, Andrew

District	Code	Name
Leicester	LE	ANDERSON, Michael
		ASKER, David
		BULLOCK, Richard
		BUTLER, Malcolm
		DUNCAN, Andrew
		EVANS, Philip
		FARRINGTON, Patrick
		GATER, Jonathan
		GRIFFITHS, Richard
		HARGROVE, John
		HARRISON, Karl
		HATHAWAY, John
		HORNER, Nigel
		JAMES, John
		KIMBER, Michael
		LEYSHON, Martin
		MARSTON, John
		MORGAN, Ian
		PEPPER, Nigel
		SANDBROOK, Claire
		SMITH, Alan
		STEPHENS, Martin
		WATT, Peter
Lincoln	LN	ASKER, David
		BAITSON, Helen
		BAITSON, Michael
		BULLOCK, Richard
		BUTLER, Malcolm
		HARGROVE, John
		HARRISON, Karl
		MARSTON, John
		McGARRAGH, Robert
		MORGAN, Ian
		SANDBROOK, Claire
		SMITH, Alan
		THOMPSON, Patricia
		WILSON, Andrew
Liverpool	L	ARNOLD, John
		ASKER, David
		DEAN, Derek
		DEAN, Gordon
		DEAN, Paul
		HARGROVE, John
		HARRISON, Karl
		MASON, David
		SANDBROOK, Claire
		SMITH, Alan
		THOMPSON, Patricia
		WILSON, Andrew

District	Code	Name
Llandridnod Wells	LD	ANDERSON, Michael
		ASKER, David
		BOWEN, David
		BULLOCK, Richard
		DUNCAN, Andrew
		EVANS, Philip
		FARRINGTON, Patrick
		GATER, Jonathan
		GRIFFITHS, Richard
		HARGROVE, John
		HATHAWAY, John
		HORNER, Nigel
		JAMES, John
		KIMBER, Michael
		LEYSHON, Martin
		PEPPER, Nigel
		SANDBROOK, Claire
		SMITH, Alan
Llandudno	LL	ANDERSON, Michael
		ASKER, David
		BULLOCK, Richard
		DEAN, Derek
		DEAN, Gordon
		DEAN, Paul
		DUNCAN, Andrew
		EVANS, Philip
		FARRINGTON, Patrick
		GATER, Jonathan
		GREGORY, John
		GRIFFITHS, Richard
		GUEST, Robin
		HARGROVE, John
		HARRISON, Karl
		HATHAWAY, John
		HORNER, Nigel
		JAMES, John
		KIMBER, Michael
		LEYSHON, Martin
		MORRIS–JONES, Gareth
		OWEN, William
		PARRY, Anthony
		PEPPER, Nigel
		SANDBROOK, Claire
		SMITH, Alan
		THOMPSON, Patricia
		WILSON, Andrew
London East	E	ASKER, David
		BUTLER, Malcolm
		HARGROVE, John
		MARSTON, John
		MORGAN, Ian
		SANDBROOK, Claire
		SMITH, Alan
London East Central	EC	ASKER, David
		BUTLER, Malcolm
		CAUCHI, Col. George
		HARGROVE, John
		MARSTON, John
		MORGAN, Ian
		SANDBROOK, Claire
		SMITH, Alan

District	Code	Name
London North	N	ASKER, David BUTLER, Malcolm HARGROVE, John MARSTON, John MORGAN, Ian SANDBROOK, Claire SMITH, Alan
London North West	NW	ASKER, David BUTLER, Malcolm GATER, Jonathan GRIFFITHS, Richard HARGROVE, John KIMBER, Michael MARSTON, John MORGAN, Ian SANDBROOK, Claire SMITH, Alan
London South East	SE	ASKER, David BUTLER, Malcolm HARGROVE, John MARSTON, John MORGAN, Ian SANDBROOK, Claire SMITH, Alan
London South West	SW	ASKER, David BUTLER, Malcolm HARGROVE, John MARSTON, John MORGAN, Ian SANDBROOK, Claire SMITH, Alan
London West	W	ASKER, David BUTLER, Malcolm GATER, Jonathan GRIFFITHS, Richard HARGROVE, John KIMBER, Michael MARSTON, John MORGAN, Ian SANDBROOK, Claire SMITH, Alan
London West Central	WC	ASKER, David BUTLER, Malcolm GATER, Jonathan GRIFFITHS, Richard HARGROVE, John KIMBER, Michael MARSTON, John MORGAN, Ian SANDBROOK, Claire SMITH, Alan

District	Code	Name
Luton	LU	ASKER, David CONSTANT, Bryan COUZENS, James HALL, Brian HARGROVE, John HATHAWAY, John LEGGETT, John O'NEILL, Mick SANDBROOK, Claire SILLS, Tim SMITH, Alan STEPHENS, Martin WATT, Peter
Manchester	M	ARNOLD, John ASKER, David DEAN, Derek DEAN, Gordon DEAN, Paul HARGROVE, John HARRISON, Karl MASON, David SANDBROOK, Claire SMITH, Alan THOMPSON, Patricia VANN, Edward WILSON, Andrew
Medway	ME	ASKER, David BUTLER, Malcolm HARGROVE, John MARSTON, John MORGAN, Ian SANDBROOK, Claire SMITH, Alan
Milton Keynes	MK	ASKER, David HALL, Brian HARGROVE, John LEGGETT, John O'NEILL, Mick SANDBROOK, Claire SILLS, Tim SMITH, Alan STEPHENS, Martin WATT, Peter CONSTANT, Bryan COUZENS, James
Newcastle	NE	ASKER, David DAVIES, Malcolm ELLIOTT, Chris HARGROVE, John HARRISON, Karl SANDBROOK, Claire SMITH, Alan THOMPSON, Patricia WILSON, Andrew

District	Code	Name
Newport	NP	ALEXANDER, Nicholas ANDERSON, Michael ASKER, David BOWEN, David BULLOCK, Richard DUNCAN, Andrew EVANS, Philip EWART–JAMES, Andrew FARRINGTON, Patrick GATER, Jonathan GRIFFITHS, Richard HARGROVE, John HATHAWAY, John HORNER, Nigel JAMES, John KIMBER, Michael LEYSHON, Martin PEPPER, Nigel SANDBROOK, Claire
Northampton	NN	ASKER, David CONSTANT, Bryan HALL, Brian HARGROVE, John SANDBROOK, Claire SILLS, Tim SMITH, Alan STEPHENS, Martin WATT, Peter
Norwich	NR	ASKER, David CONSTANT, Bryan HALL, Brian HARGROVE, John SANDBROOK, Claire SILLS, Tim SMITH, Alan STEPHENS, Martin WATT, Peter
Nottingham	NG	ANDERSON, Michael ASKER, David BULLOCK, Richard BUTLER, Malcolm DEAN, Paul DUNCAN, Andrew EVANS, Philip FARRINGTON, Patrick GATER, Jonathan GRIFFITHS, Richard HARGROVE, John HARRISON, Karl HATHAWAY, John HORNER, Nigel JAMES, John KIMBER, Michael LEYSHON, Martin MARSTON, John MORGAN, Ian PEPPER, Nigel SANDBROOK, Claire SMITH, Alan THOMPSON, Patricia WILSON, Andrew

District	Code	Name
Oldham	OL	ASKER, David DEAN, Gordon DEAN, Paul HARGROVE, John HARRISON, Karl LAING, John SANDBROOK, Claire SMITH, Alan THOMPSON, Patricia VANN, Edward WHITWORTH, Frank WILSON, Andrew
Oxford	OX	ALEXANDER, Nicholas ANDERSON, Michael ASKER, David BULLOCK, Richard COUZENS, James DUNCAN, Andrew EVANS, Philip EWART–JAMES, Andrew FARRINGTON, Patrick GATER, Jonathan GRIFFITHS, Richard HARGROVE, John HATHAWAY, John HORNER, Nigel JAMES, John KIMBER, Michael LEGGETT, John LEYSHON, Martin O'NEILL, Mick PEPPER, Nigel SANDBROOK, Claire SMITH, Alan
Peterborough	PE	ASKER, David CONSTANT, Bryan HALL, Brian HARGROVE, John SANDBROOK, Claire SILLS, Tim SMITH, Alan STEPHENS, Martin WATT, Peter
Plymouth	PL	ASKER, David BARNETT, Simon BASTIN, Simon CLAPCOTT, Gerald COOMBE, Geoffrey EGMORE, Angela HARGROVE, John HUGHES, David POTE, David REED, Philip SANDBROOK, Claire SMITH, Alan TRICKEY, David

District	Code	Name
Portsmouth	PO	ANDERSON, Michael
		ASKER, David
		DUNCAN, Andrew
		EVANS, Philip
		FARRINGTON, Patrick
		GATER, Jonathan
		GRIFFITHS, Richard
		HARGROVE, John
		HORNER, Nigel
		JAMES, John
		KIMBER, Michael
		LEYSHON, Martin
		PEPPER, Nigel
		SANDBROOK, Claire
		SMITH, Alan
Preston	PR	ASKER, David
		DEAN, Derek
		DEAN, Gordon
		DEAN, Paul
		HARGROVE, John
		HARRISON, Karl
		LAING, John
		SANDBROOK, Claire
		SMITH, Alan
		THOMPSON, Patricia
		WILSON, Andrew
Reading	RG	ANDERSON, Michael
		ASKER, David
		BULLOCK, Richard
		COUZENS, James
		DUNCAN, Andrew
		EVANS, Philip
		FARRINGTON, Patrick
		GATER, Jonathan
		GRIFFITHS, Richard
		HARGROVE, John
		HATHAWAY, John
		HORNER, Nigel
		JAMES, John
		KIMBER, Michael
		LEGGETT, John
		LEYSHON, Martin
		O'NEILL, Mick
		PEPPER, Nigel
		SANDBROOK, Claire
		SMITH, Alan
Redhill	RH	ASKER, David
		BUTLER, Malcolm
		HARGROVE, John
		MARSTON, John
		MORGAN, Ian
		SANDBROOK, Claire
		SMITH, Alan
Romford	RM	ASKER, David
		BUTLER, Malcolm
		HARGROVE, John
		MARSTON, John
		MORGAN, Ian
		SANDBROOK, Claire
		SMITH, Alan

District	Code	Name
Salisbury	SP	ASKER, David
		BARNETT, Simon
		BASTIN, Simon
		COOMBE, Geoffrey
		EGMORE, Angela
		HARGROVE, John
		HATHAWAY, John
		SANDBROOK, Claire
		SMITH, Alan
		TRICKEY, David
Sheffield	S	ASKER, David
		BULLOCK, Richard
		BUTLER, Malcolm
		DEAN, Paul
		HARGROVE, John
		HARRISON, Dion
		HARRISON, Karl
		LAING, John
		MARSTON, John
		MORGAN, Ian
		SANDBROOK, Claire
		SMITH, Alan
		THOMPSON, Patricia
		TODD, Nicholas
		TOWERS, Jonathan
		WILSON, Andrew
Shrewsbury	SY	ANDERSON, Michael
		ARNOLD, John
		ASKER, David
		BULLOCK, Richard
		DUNCAN, Andrew
		EVANS, Philip
		FARRINGTON, Patrick
		GATER, Jonathan
		GRIFFITHS, Richard
		HARGROVE, John
		HATHAWAY, John
		HORNER, Nigel
		JAMES, John
		KIMBER, Michael
		LEYSHON, Martin
		MASON, David
		PEPPER, Nigel
		SANDBROOK, Claire
		SMITH, Alan

District	Code	Name
Slough	SL	ANDERSON, Michael ASKER, David BULLOCK, Richard COUZENS, James DUNCAN, Andrew EVANS, Philip FARRINGTON, Patrick GATER, Jonathan GRIFFITHS, Richard HARGROVE, John HATHAWAY, John HORNER, Nigel JAMES, John KIMBER, Michael LEGGETT, John LEYSHON, Martin O'NEILL, Mick PEPPER, Nigel SANDBROOK, Claire SMITH, Alan
Southall (Uxbridge)	UB	ASKER, David BUTLER, Malcolm GATER, Jonathan GRIFFITHS, Richard HARGROVE, John KIMBER, Michael MARSTON, John MORGAN, Ian SANDBROOK, Claire SMITH, Alan
Southampton	SO	ANDERSON, Michael ASKER, David DUNCAN, Andrew EVANS, Philip FARRINGTON, Patrick GATER, Jonathan GRIFFITHS, Richard HARGROVE, John HATHAWAY, John HORNER, Nigel JAMES, John KIMBER, Michael LEYSHON, Martin PEPPER, Nigel SANDBROOK, Claire SMITH, Alan
Southend on Sea	SS	ASKER, David BUTLER, Malcolm HARGROVE, John MARSTON, John MORGAN, Ian SANDBROOK, Claire SMITH, Alan
St. Albans	AL	ASKER, David BUTLER, Malcolm HARGROVE, John MARSTON, John MORGAN, Ian SANDBROOK, Claire SMITH, Alan TUNSTILL, Peter WILLIAMS, James

District	Code	Name
Stevenage	SG	ASKER, David
		BUTLER, Malcolm
		CONSTANT, Bryan
		HALL, Brian
		HARGROVE, John
		MARSTON, John
		MORGAN, Ian
		SANDBROOK, Claire
		SILLS, Tim
		SMITH, Alan
		STEPHENS, Martin
		TUNSTILL, Peter
		WATT, Peter
		WILLIAMS, James
Stockport	SK	ARNOLD, John
		ASKER, David
		BUTLER, Malcolm
		DEAN, Derek
		DEAN, Gordon
		DEAN, Paul
		HARGROVE, John
		HARRISON, Dion
		HARRISON, Karl
		MARSTON, John
		MASON, David
		MORGAN, Ian
		SANDBROOK, Claire
		SMITH, Alan
		THOMPSON, Patricia
		VANN, Edward
		WILSON, Andrew
Stoke on Trent	ST	ANDERSON, Michael
		ASKER, David
		BULLOCK, Richard
		BUTLER, Malcolm
		DEAN, Paul
		DUNCAN, Andrew
		EVANS, Philip
		FARRINGTON, Patrick
		GATER, Jonathan
		GRIFFITHS, Richard
		HARGROVE, John
		HARRISON, Karl
		HATHAWAY, John
		HORNER, Nigel
		JAMES, John
		KIMBER, Michael
		LEYSHON, Martin
		MARSTON, John
		MORGAN, Ian
		PEPPER, Nigel
		SANDBROOK, Claire
		SMITH, Alan
		THOMPSON, Patricia
		WILSON, Andrew

District	Code	Name
Sunderland	SR	ASKER, David
		DAVIES, Malcolm
		ELLIOTT, Chris
		HARGROVE, John
		HARRISON, Karl
		SANDBROOK, Claire
		SMITH, Alan
		THOMPSON, Patricia
		WILSON, Andrew
Sutton	SM	ASKER, David
		BUTLER, Malcolm
		HARGROVE, John
		MARSTON, John
		MORGAN, Ian
		SANDBROOK, Claire
		SMITH, Alan
Swansea	SA	ANDERSON, Michael
		ASKER, David
		BULLOCK, Richard
		DUNCAN, Andrew
		EVANS, Philip
		FARRINGTON, Patrick
		GATER, Jonathan
		GRIFFITHS, Richard
		HARGROVE, John
		HATHAWAY, John
		HORNER, Nigel
		JAMES, John
		JENKINS, Anthony
		KIMBER, Michael
		LEYSHON, Martin
		PEPPER, Nigel
		REES, Pamela
		SANDBROOK, Claire
		SMITH, Alan
Swindon	SN	ALEXANDER, Nicholas
		ANDERSON, Michael
		ASKER, David
		BULLOCK, Richard
		DUNCAN, Andrew
		EVANS, Philip
		EWART–JAMES, Andrew
		FARRINGTON, Patrick
		GATER, Jonathan
		GRIFFITHS, Richard
		HARGROVE, John
		HATHAWAY, John
		HORNER, Nigel
		JAMES, John
		KIMBER, Michael
		LEYSHON, Martin
		PEPPER, Nigel
		SANDBROOK, Claire
		SMITH, Alan

District	Code	Name
Taunton	TA	ASKER, David BARNETT, Simon BASTIN, Simon CHANNER, Gervase COOMBE, Geoffrey EGMORE, Angela HARGROVE, John HATHAWAY, John SANDBROOK, Claire SMITH, Alan TRICKEY, David WENT, Richard WHELLER, Jonathan
Telford	TF	ANDERSON, Michael ASKER, David BULLOCK, Richard DUNCAN, Andrew EVANS, Philip FARRINGTON, Patrick GATER, Jonathan GRIFFITHS, Richard HARGROVE, John HARRISON, Karl HATHAWAY, John HORNER, Nigel JAMES, John KIMBER, Michael LEYSHON, Martin PEPPER, Nigel SANDBROOK, Claire SMITH, Alan THOMPSON, Patricia WILSON, Andrew
Tonbridge	TN	ASKER, David BUTLER, Malcolm HARGROVE, John MARSTON, John MORGAN, Ian SANDBROOK, Claire SMITH, Alan
Torquay	TQ	ASKER, David BARNETT, Simon BASTIN, Simon CHANNER, Gervase COOMBE, Geoffrey EGMORE, Angela HARGROVE, John SANDBROOK, Claire SMITH, Alan TRICKEY, David WENT, Richard WHELLER, Jonathan

District	Code	Name
Truro	TR	ASKER, David BARNETT, Simon BASTIN, Simon CLAPCOTT, Gerald COOMBE, Geoffrey EGMORE, Angela HARGROVE, John HUGHES, David POTE, David REED, Philip SANDBROOK, Claire SMITH, Alan TRICKEY, David
Tweeddale (Berwick upon Tweed)	TD	ASKER, David DAVIES, Malcolm ELLIOTT, Chris HARGROVE, John HARRISON, Karl SANDBROOK, Claire SMITH, Alan THOMPSON, Patricia WILSON, Andrew
Twickenham	TW	ASKER, David BUTLER, Malcolm GATER, Jonathan GRIFFITHS, Richard HARGROVE, John KIMBER, Michael MARSTON, John MORGAN, Ian SANDBROOK, Claire SMITH, Alan
Wakefield	WF	ASKER, David DEAN, Paul HARGROVE, John HARRISON, Dion HARRISON, Karl LAING, John SANDBROOK, Claire SMITH, Alan THOMPSON, Patricia TOWERS, Jonathan WHITWORTH, Frank WILSON, Andrew

District	Code	Name
Walsall	WS	ANDERSON, Michael ASKER, David BULLOCK, Richard BUTLER, Malcolm DUNCAN, Andrew EVANS, Philip FARRINGTON, Patrick GATER, Jonathan GRIFFITHS, Richard HARGROVE, John HATHAWAY, John HORNER, Nigel JAMES, John KIMBER, Michael LEYSHON, Martin MARSTON, John MORGAN, Ian PEPPER, Nigel SANDBROOK, Claire SMITH, Alan
Warrington	WA	ARNOLD, John ASKER, David DEAN, Derek DEAN, Gordon DEAN, Paul HARGROVE, John HARRISON, Karl MASON, David SANDBROOK, Claire SMITH, Alan SOUTHERN, Norman THOMPSON, Patricia WILSON, Andrew
Watford	WD	ASKER, David BUTLER, Malcolm HARGROVE, John MARSTON, John MORGAN, Ian SANDBROOK, Claire SMITH, Alan TUNSTILL, Peter WILLIAMS, James
Wigan	WN	ARNOLD, John ASKER, David DEAN, Derek DEAN, Gordon DEAN, Paul HARGROVE, John HARRISON, Karl MASON, David SANDBROOK, Claire SMITH, Alan THOMPSON, Patricia WILSON, Andrew

District	Code	Name
Wolverhampton	WV	ANDERSON, Michael
		ASKER, David
		BULLOCK, Richard
		BUTLER, Malcolm
		DUNCAN, Andrew
		EVANS, Philip
		FARRINGTON, Patrick
		GATER, Jonathan
		GRIFFITHS, Richard
		HARGROVE, John
		HATHAWAY, John
		HORNER, Nigel
		JAMES, John
		KIMBER, Michael
		LEYSHON, Martin
		MARSTON, John
		MORGAN, Ian
		PEPPER, Nigel
		SANDBROOK, Claire
		SMITH, Alan
Worcester	WR	ALEXANDER, Nicholas
		ANDERSON, Michael
		ASKER, David
		BULLOCK, Richard
		BUTLER, Malcolm
		DUNCAN, Andrew
		EVANS, Philip
		EWART–JAMES, Andrew
		FARRINGTON, Patrick
		GATER, Jonathan
		GRIFFITHS, Richard
		HARGROVE, John
		HATHAWAY, John
		HORNER, Nigel
		JAMES, John
		KIMBER, Michael
		LEYSHON, Martin
		MARSTON, John
		MORGAN, Ian
		PEPPER, Nigel
		SANDBROOK, Claire
		SMITH, Alan
York	YO	ASKER, David
		BAITSON, Helen
		BAITSON, Michael
		FELLOWS, Kathleen
		HARGROVE, John
		HARRISON, Dion
		HARRISON, Karl
		LAING, John
		SANDBROOK, Claire
		SMITH, Alan
		STOREY, Roy
		THOMPSON, Patricia
		TOWERS, Jonathan
		WILSON, Andrew

Add new paragraph 10–73

DIRECTORY OF HIGH COURT ENFORCEMENT OFFICERS – ADDRESSES AND CONTACT DETAILS FOR APPOINTED ENFORCEMENT OFFICERS

Name	Postal Address *(DX Address in italics)*	Phone Number(s) *(Mobile or out of hours numbers in italics)*	Fax Number	Email address *(Web address in italics)*
ALEXANDER, Nicholas	2nd Floor 65 London Road Gloucester Gloucestershire GL1 3HF *Dx 7514 Gloucester*	01452 429883 *01531 636108*	01452 300922	nalexander@whitemans.com
ANDERSON, Michael	141 Walter Road Swansea SA1 5RW *DX 52966 Swansea*	01792 466771	01792 455755	mike@mleyshon.co.uk *www.mleyshon.co.uk*
ARNOLD, John	Birch Cullimore, Solicitors Friars White Friars Chester CH1 1XS *DX 19985 Chester*	01244 321066	01244 312582	john.arnold@bclaw.co.uk
ASKER, David	20–21 Tooks Court London EC4A 1LB *DX 70 LONDON/ CHANCERY LANE WC2*	020 7025 2550 *07775 590469*	020 7025 2556	sysman@sheriffs.co.uk *www.sherforce.co.uk*
BAITSON, Helen	The Edwardian Auction Galleries Wiltshire Road Hull HU4 6PG	01482 500500 *07860 649230*	01482 500501	Info@gilbert–baitson.co.uk *www.gilbert–baitson.co.uk*
BAITSON, Michael	The Edwardian Auction Galleries Wiltshire Road Hull HU4 6PG	01482 500500 *07860 674714*	01482 500501	info@gilbert–baitson.co.uk *www.gilbert–baitson.co.uk*

Name	Postal Address *(DX Address in italics)*	Phone Number(s) *(Mobile or out of hours numbers in italics)*	Fax Number	Email address *(Web address in italics)*
BARNETT, Simon	Cherry's Limited 2nd Floor Lloyds Bank Chambers 30 High Street Crediton Devon EX17 3AH *DX 54207 Crediton*	01363 775118	01363 773009	shb@hceo.fsbusiness.co.uk
BASTIN, Simon	Cherry's Limited 2nd Floor Lloyds Bank Chambers 30 High Street Crediton Devon EX17 3AH *DX 54207 Crediton*	01363 775118	01363 773009	scb@hceo.fsbusiness.co.uk
BOWEN, David	Victoria Chambers 11 Clythia Park Road Newport South Wales NP20 4PB *DX 33204 Newport (South Wales)*	01633 264194 01633 266595	01633 841146 01633 220827	bowen@colbornes.demon.co.uk
BULLOCK, Richard	Freethhcartwright LLP Cumberland Court 80 Mount Street Nottingham NG1 6HH *DX 10039 Nottingham*	0115 9369396	0115 8599617	richard.bullock@freethcartwright.co.uk

Name	Postal Address *(DX Address in italics)*	Phone Number(s) *(Mobile or out of hours numbers in italics)*	Fax Number	Email address *(Web address in italics)*
BUTLER, Malcolm	John Marston & Co 24/26 Broadway North Walsall West Midlands WS1 2AJ *DX 12143 Walsall*	01922 720 777	01922 647 222	post@johnmarston.co.uk *www.hceo.co.uk*
CAUCHI, Col. George	Central Criminal Court Old Bailey London EC4M 7EH *DX 5426 Stratford (London)*	020 7248 3277 ext 2326/ 2323/ 2338	020 7489 8451	colonel.cauchi@corpoflondon.gov.uk
CHANNER, Gervase	41 St James Street Taunton Somerset TA1 1JR *DX 32115 Taunton*	01823 284444	01823 270869	
CLAPCOTT, Gerald	Cornwall High Court Recovery Graham & Graham Solicitors High Cross House St Austell PL25 4AE *DX 81253 St Austell*	01726 75565	01726 61484	sheriff@graham–graham.co.uk
COOMBE, Geoffrey	Cherry's Limited 2nd Floor Lloyds Bank Chambers 30 High Street Crediton Devon EX17 3AH *DX 54207 Crediton*	01363 775118	01363 773009	gpc@hceo.fsbusiness.co.uk

Name	Postal Address *(DX Address in italics)*	Phone Number(s) *(Mobile or out of hours numbers in italics)*	Fax Number	Email address *(Web address in italics)*
CONSTANT, Bryan	Invicta House 71 High Street Riseley Bedford MK44 1DD *DX 5641 Bedford*	01234 708044 01234 708688	01234 708177	sheriffsofficer@kbnet.net
COUZENS, James	14 Bourbon Street Aylesbury Bucks HP20 2RS	01296 318505	01296 318531	james.couzens@parrott–coales.co.uk
DAVIES, Malcolm	32 Front Street Whickenham Tyne & Wear NE16 4DT *DX 60414 Whickham*	0191 4888800	0191 4888811	info@elliottdavies.com
DEAN, Derek	A & D Dean Trident House 31/33 Dale Street Liverpool L2 2DA *DX 14104 Liverpool*	0151 236 4751 0151 236 6406	0151 236 8071	sheriff@a–d–dean.co.uk
DEAN, Gordon	A & D Dean Trident House 31/33 Dale Street Liverpool L2 2DA *DX 14104 Liverpool*	0151 236 4751 0151 236 6406	0151 236 8071	sheriff@a–d–dean.co.uk
DEAN, Paul	A & D Dean Trident House 31/33 Dale Street Liverpool L2 2DA *DX 14104 Liverpool*	0151 236 4751 0151 236 6406	0151 236 8071	sheriff@a–d–dean.co.uk

Name	Postal Address *(DX Address in italics)*	Phone Number(s) *(Mobile or out of hours numbers in italics)*	Fax Number	Email address *(Web address in italics)*
DUNCAN, Andrew	16 The Tything Worcester WR1 1HD *DX 716264 Worcester*	01905 732881	01905 22347	a.duncan@wwf.co.uk
EGMORE, Angela	Cherry's Limited 2nd Floor Lloyds Bank Chambers 30 High Street Crediton Devon EX17 3AH *DX 54207 Crediton*	01363 775118	01363 773009	are@hceo.fsbusiness.co.uk
ELLIOTT, Chris	32 Front Street Whickenham Tyne & Wear NE16 4DT *DX 60414 Whickham*	0191 4888800	0191 4888811	info@elliottdavies.com
EVANS, Philip	22 St Andrews Crescent Cardiff CF10 3DD *DX 50752 Cardiff 2*	029 20229716	029 20377761	pevans@ardiff–law.co.uk
EWART–JAMES, Andrew	2nd Floor 65 London Road Gloucester Gloucestershire GL1 3HF *DX 7514 Gloucester*	01452 429883 *01453 872470*	01452 300922	aewartjames@whitemans.com
FARRINGTON, Patrick	17 Martin Street Stafford ST16 2LF *DX 14554 Stafford 1*	01785 211411	01785 248573	pfarrington@hmo.co.uk

Name	Postal Address *(DX Address in italics)*	Phone Number(s) *(Mobile or out of hours numbers in italics)*	Fax Number	Email address *(Web address in italics)*
FELLOWS, Kathleen	Storey & Fellows Albert Chambers 50 Albert Road Middlesbrough TS1 1QD *DX 60534 Middlesbrough*	01642 218819	01642 246456	k.fellows@virgin.net
FITZGERALD, Hugh	39 High Street Wigton Cumbria CA7 9PE *DX 714666 Wigton*	016973 43241	016973 44820	hugh__f@atkinsonoritson.co.uk
GATER, Jonathan	Blandy & Blandy 1 Friar Street Reading Berkshire RG1 1DA *DX 4008 Reading*	0118 951 6947	0118 958 3032	hceo@blandy.co.uk
GRAHAM, Brian	24–26 Museum Street Ipswich Suffolk IP1 1HZ *DX 3206 Ipswich 1*	01473 406265 *07880 741707*	01473 406391	brian–graham@birketts.co.uk
GREGORY, John	95 High Street Mold CH7 1BJ *DX 26556 Mold*	01352 753882	01352 758927	office@keeneandkelly.fsnet.co.uk
GRIFFITHS, Richard	Blandy & Blandy 1 Friar Street Reading Berkshire RG1 1DA *DX 4008 Reading*	0118 951 6947	0118 958 3032	hceo@blandy.co.uk

Name	Postal Address *(DX Address in italics)*	Phone Number(s) *(Mobile or out of hours numbers in italics)*	Fax Number	Email address *(Web address in italics)*
GUEST, Robin	95 High Street Mold CH7 1BJ *DX 26556 Mold*	01352 753882	01352 758927	office@keeneandkelly.fsnet.co.uk
HALL, Brian	6 Bedford Road Sandy Bedfordshire SG19 1EN *DX 47801 Sandy*	01767 680251	01767 691775	brian.hall@leedssmith.co.uk *www.leedssmith.co.uk*
HARGROVE, John	20–21 Tooks Court London EC4A 1LB *DX 70 LONDON/ CHANCERY LANE WC2*	020 7025 2551 *07775 590475*	020 7025 2556	j–hargrove@sheriffs.co.uk *www.sherforce.co.uk*
HARRISON, Dion	Ashfield House Illingworth Street Ossett West Yorkshire WF5 8AL *DX 707162, Ossett 2*	01924 279005	01924 280114	sheriffs@cwharrison.net
HARRISON, Karl	The Sheriffs Office 26 Missouri Avenue Salford Manchester M50 2NP *DX 710252 Manchester 3*	0161 925 1800	0161 925 1801	karl.harrison@northernsheriffs.com *www.northernsheriffs.com*
HATHAWAY, John	42 Brook Street Warwick Warwickshire CV34 4BL *DX 18109 Warwick*	01926 492407	01926 401424	heath.blenkinson@btopenworld.com

Name	**Postal Address** *(DX Address in italics)*	**Phone Number(s)** *(Mobile or out of hours numbers in italics)*	**Fax Number**	**Email address** *(Web address in italics)*
HORNER, Nigel	16 The Tything Worcester WR1 1HD *DX 716264 Worcester*	01905 732881	01905 22347	n.horner@wwf.co.uk
HUGHES, David	Cornwall High Court Recovery Graham & Graham Solicitors High Cross House St Austell PL25 4AE *DX 81253 St Austell*	01726 75565	01726 61484	sheriff@graham–graham.co.uk
JAMES, John	17 Martin Street Stafford ST16 2LF *DX 14554 Stafford 1*	01785 211411	01785 248573	info@hmo.co.uk *www.hmo.co.uk*
JENKINS, Anthony	Messrs Ungoes Thomas and King Gwynne House Quay Street Carmarthen SA33 3JX	01267 237441 (Switchboard) 01267 239192 (Direct Line) *07974 071739*	01267 238317	ajenkins@utk.co.uk
KIMBER, Michael	6 Bellman Court Great Knollys Street Reading RG1 7HU *DX 54731 Reading 2*	0118 939 1816 *07831 436112*	0118 958 8258	sheriff@erksandoxon.co.uk michael.kimber@thimbleby–shorland.co.uk
LAING, John	C N Gaunt & Son 12 New John Street Bradford West Yorkshire BD1 2QZ *DX 11701 Bradford*	01274 391929/ 01274 721711	01274 734773	post@cngaunt.co.uk

Name	**Postal Address** *(DX Address in italics)*	**Phone Number(s)** *(Mobile or out of hours numbers in italics)*	**Fax Number**	**Email address** *(Web address in italics)*
LEGGETT, John	14 Bourbon Street Aylesbury Bucks HP20 2RS	01296 318501	01296 318531	john.legett@parrott–coales.co.uk
LEYSHON, Martin	141 Walter Road Swansea SA1 5RW *DX 52966 Swansea*	01792 466771	01792 455755	martin@mleyshon.co.uk *www.mleyshon.co.uk*
McGARRAGH, Robert	PO Box 654 Lincoln LN2 2XP	01673 862899 *07785 902352*	01673 862899	r.mcgarrach@tiscali.coluk
MARSTON, John	John Marston & Co 24/26 Broadway North Walsall West Midlands WS1 2AJ *DX 12143 Walsall*	01922 720 777	01922 647 222	post@hceo.co.uk *www.hceo.co.uk*
MASON, David	Birch Cullimore, Solicitors Friars White Friars Chester CH1 1XS *DX 19985 Chester*	01244 321066	01244 312582	david.mason@claw.co.uk
MORGAN, Ian	John Marston & Co 24/26 Broadway North Walsall West Midlands WS1 2AJ *DX 12143 Walsall*	01922 720 777	01922 647 222	post@johnmarston.co.uk *www.hceo.co.uk*
MORRIS–JONES, Gareth	95 High Street Mold CH7 1BJ *DX 26556 Mold*	01352 753882	01352 758927	office@keeneandkelly.fsnet.co.uk

Name	Postal Address *(DX Address in italics)*	Phone Number(s) *(Mobile or out of hours numbers in italics)*	Fax Number	Email address *(Web address in italics)*
O'NEILL, Mick	14 Bourbon Street Aylesbury Bucks HP20 2QD *DX 4100 Aylesbury*	01296 318525 *07860 238941*	01296 318526	hceo@parrott–coales.co.uk
OWEN, William	314 High Street Bangor Gwynedd LL57 1YA	01248 353357	01248 372272	wowenestate@yahoo.co.uk
PARRY, Anthony	9 Chester Street Mold CH7 1EG *DX 26556 Mold*	01352 752552	01352 752542	auctions.dodds@tesco.net dodds@door_key.com
PEPPER, Nigel	17 Martin Street Stafford ST16 2LF *DX 14554 Stafford 1*	01785 211411	01785 248573	npepper@hmo.co.uk
POTE, David	Cornwall High Court Recovery Graham & Graham Solicitors High Cross House St Austell PL25 4AE *DX 81253 St Austell*	01726 75565	01726 61484	sheriff@graham–graham.co.uk
REED, Philip	Cornwall High Court Recovery Graham & Graham Solicitors High Cross House St Austell PL25 4AE *DX 81253 St Austell*	01726 75565	01726 61484	sheriff@graham–graham.co.uk

Name	Postal Address *(DX Address in italics)*	Phone Number(s) *(Mobile or out of hours numbers in italics)*	Fax Number	Email address *(Web address in italics)*
REES, Pamela	18 Kings Road Llandybie Carms SA18 2TN	01269 850280	01269 850280	silver.star@lineone.net
SANDBROOK, Claire	Shergroup Westwood Park London Road Little Horkesley Colchester Essex CO6 4BS *DX 3654 COLCHESTER*	01206 274255 *07775 590454*	01206 274176	c–sandbrook@sheriffs.co.uk *www.sherforce.co.uk*
SILLS, Tim	6 Bedford Road Sandy Bedfordshire SG19 1EN *DX 47801 Sandy*	01767 680251	01767 691775	tim.sills@leedssmith.co.uk *www.leedssmith.co.uk*
SMITH, Alan	12 Greek Street Leeds LS1 5RU *DX 26416 LEEDS PARK SQUARE*	0113 2855979 *07717 508105*	0113 2855977	asmith@sheriffs.co.uk *www.sherforce.co.uk*
SOUTHERN, Norman	A & D Dean Trident House 31/33 Dale Street Liverpool L2 2DA *DX 14104 Liverpool*	0151 236 4751 0151 236 6406	0151 236 8071	sheriff@a–d–dean.co.uk
STEPHENS, Martin	Beattie Son & Leslie 35 Palmerston Road Northampton NN1 5EU	01604 605400 *07860 762736*	01604 605069	sheriffs@supanet.com

Name	Postal Address *(DX Address in italics)*	Phone Number(s) *(Mobile or out of hours numbers in italics)*	Fax Number	Email address *(Web address in italics)*
STOREY, Roy	Storey & Fellows Albert Chambers 50 Albert Road Middlesbrough TS1 1QD *DX 60534 Middlesbrough*	01642 218819	01642 246456	k.fellows@virgin.net
THOMPSON, Patricia	The Sheriffs Office 26 Missouri Avenue Salford Manchester M50 2NP *DX 710252 Manchester 3*	0161 925 1800	0161 925 1801	tricia.thomson@northernsheriffs.com *www.northernsheriffs.com*
TODD, Nicholas	The Old Bull's Head Dun Street Sheffield S3 8SL *DX 10531 Sheffield*	0114 2729667 *07764 559748*	0114 276160	info@ewbauctions.co.uk
TOWERS, Jonathan	17 Lendel York YO1 8AQ *DX 61502 York*	01904 466000	01904 672212	jhnt@undersheriff.fsbsiness.co.uk
TRICKEY, David	Cherry's Limited 2nd Floor Lloyds Bank Chambers 30 High Street Crediton Devon EX17 3AH *DX 54207 Crediton*	01363 775118	01363 773009	dt@hceo.fsbusiness.co.uk

Name	Postal Address *(DX Address in italics)*	Phone Number(s) *(Mobile or out of hours numbers in italics)*	Fax Number	Email address *(Web address in italics)*
TUNSTILL, Peter	Breeze & Wyles 114 Fore Street Hertford Hertfordshire SG14 1AG *DX 57901 Hertford*	01992 558411	01992 503889	peter.tunstill@breezeandwyles.co.uk
VANN, Edward	2–12 Crescent Salford Manchester M5 4PF *DX 14331 Manchester 1*	0161 737 9889 *07979 774422*	0161 737 9449	esvann@prima.net
WATT, Peter	Beattie Son & Leslie 35 Palmerston Road Northampton NN1 5EU	01604 605400	01604 605069	sheriffs@supanet.com
WENT, Richard	12 Paul Street Taunton Somersert TA1 3PF *DX 32130 Taunton*	01823 335623	01823 334563	wwsomerset@hotmail.com
WHELLER, Jonathan	12 Paul Street Taunton Somersert TA1 3PF *DX 32130 Taunton*	01823 335623	01823 334563	wwsomerset@hotmail.com
WHITWORTH, Frank	17 Cloth Hall Street Huddersfield HD1 2DX *DX 713001 Huddersfield*	01484 427467 *07767 385223*	01484 484313	frank@whitworthsestateagents.co.uk
WILLIAMS, James	Breeze & Wyles 114 Fore Street Hertford Hertfordshire SG14 1AG *DX 57901 Hertford*	01992 558411	01992 503889	james.williams@breezeandwyles.co.uk

Name	Postal Address *(DX Address in italics)*	Phone Number(s) *(Mobile or out of hours numbers in italics)*	Fax Number	Email address *(Web address in italics)*
WILSON, Andrew	The Sheriffs Office 26 Missouri Avenue Salford Manchester M50 2NP *DX 710252 Manchester 3*	0161 925 1800	0161 925 1801	andrew.wilson@northernsheriffs.com *www.northernsheriffs.com*

SECTION 11

COURTS DIRECTORY

The Daily Cause List

Add at end:

11–1 1. The Daily Cause List is also available from the Court Service website: www.courtservice.gov.uk/cms/8039.htm

Amendments to Circuit Arrangements

For "Tel: 0161 833 1004/5" substitute:

11–4

	Central Manchester and Outer Manchester	Tel: 0161 833 1005

County Court Directory

In the table, details for the following courts are amended:

11–7

Court (Courts with Bankruptcy jurisdiction in bold)	*Address*	*Contact Nos*
ABERDARE AA	The Court House Cwmbach Road Aberdare Wales CF44 OJE	Tel: 01685 888575 Fax: 01685 883413 DX: 99600 Aberdare–2
ALTRINCHAM AL	Trafford Courthouse Ashton Lane Sale Cheshire M33 7NR	Tel: 0161 975 4760 Fax: 0161 975 4761 DX: 708292 Sale–6

Court (Courts with Bankruptcy jurisdiction in bold)	*Address*	*Contact Nos*
BARNET BT		DX: 122570 Finchley
BASILDON BQ		Email: e–filing@asildon.countycourt.gsi.gov.uk Email: bailiffs@asildon.countycourt.gsi.gov.uk Email: hearings@asildon.countycourt.gsi.gov.uk Email: enquiries@asildon.countycourt.gsi.gov.uk Email: family@asildon.countycourt.gsi.gov.uk
BEDFORD BE	May House 29 Goldington Road Bedford MK40 3NN	Tel: 01234 760400 Fax: 01234 327431 DX: 97590 Bedford–3
BIRKENHEAD BI	76 Hamilton Street Birkenhead Merseyside CH41 5EN	Tel: 0151 666 5800 Fax: 0151 666 5873 DX: 725000 Birkenhead–10
BIRMINGHAM BM, ZB	The Priory Courts 33 Bull Street Birmingham B4 6DS	Tel: 0121 681 4441 Fax: 0121 681 3001/2 DX: 701987 Birmingham–7 Email: e–filing@birmingham.countycourt.gsi.gov.uk Email: bailiffs@birmingham.countycourt.gsi.gov.uk Email: hearings@birmingham.countycourt.gsi.gov.uk Email: enquiries@birmingham.countycourt.gsi.gov.uk Email: family@birmingham.countycourt.gsi.gov.uk
BLACKPOOL BC	The Law Courts Chapel Street Blackpool Lancs FY1 5RJ	Tel: 01253 754020 Fax: 01253 295255 DX: 724900 Blackpool–10
BOURNEMOUTH BH	The Bournemouth Crown and County Courts The Courts of Justice Deansleigh Road Bournemouth BH7 7DS	Email: e–filing@bournemouth.countycourt.gsi.gov.uk Email: bailiffs@bournemouth.countycourt.gsi.gov.uk Email: hearings@bournemouth.countycourt.gsi.gov.uk Email: enquiries@bournemouth.countycourt.gsi.gov.uk Email: family@bournemouth.countycourt.gsi.gov.uk

Court (Courts with Bankruptcy jurisdiction in bold)	*Address*	*Contact Nos*
BRADFORD BD	Bradford Law Courts Exchange Square Drake Street Bradford West Yorkshire BD1 1JA	Tel: 01685 358222 Fax: 01685 359727 DX: 702083 Bradford–2
BRECKNOCK ZM	Cambrian Way Brecon Powys LD3 7HR	Tel: 01685 358222 Fax: 01685 359727 DX: 99582 Merthyr Tydfil 2
Brighton County Court–Family Centre	1 Edward Street Brighton BN2 0JD	Tel: 01273 811333 Fax: 01273 607638 DX: 142600 Brighton–12
BURNLEY	The Law Courts Hammerton Street Burnley Lancs BB11 1XD	Tel: 01282 416899 Fax: 01282 414911 DX: 724940 Burnley–4
CAERNARFON CJ	Llanberis Road Caernarfon Gwynedd LL55 2DF	Tel: 01286 684600 Fax: 01286 678965 DX: 702483 Caernarfon–2
CARDIFF CF	Cardiff Civil Justice Centre 2 Park Street Cardiff Wales CF10 1ET	Tel: (029) 20 376400 Fax: (029) 20 376475 DX: 99500 Cardiff–6
CARLISLE CA	Courts of Justice Earl Street Carlisle Cumbria CA1 1DJ	Tel: 01228 520619 Fax: 01228 590588 DX: 65335 Carlisle
CENTRAL LONDON CL Patents County Court	13–14 Park Crescent London W1B 1HT	Tel: (020) 7917 5000 Fax: (020) 7917 5014
CHESTER CH	Chester Civil Justice Centre Trident House Little St John Street Chester CH1 1SN	Tel: 01244 404200 Fax: 01244 404300 DX: 702460 Chester–4
COVENTRY CV	Coventry Combined Court Centre 140 Much Park Street Coventry West Midlands CV1 2SN	Tel: (024) 76 536166 Fax: (024) 76 520443 DX: 701580 Coventry–5
DARTFORD DA	Court House Home Gardens Dartford Kent DA1 1DX	Tel: 01322 629820 Fax: 01322 270902 DX: 98090 Dartford–2

Court (Courts with Bankruptcy jurisdiction in bold)	*Address*	*Contact Nos*
DERBY DE	Derby Combined Court Centre The Morledge Derby DE1 2XE	Tel: 01332 622600 Fax: 01332 622543 DX: 724060 Derby–21
EVESHAM EV	1st Floor 87 High Street Evesham Worcs WR11 4EE	Tel: 01386 442287 Fax: 01386 49203 DX: 701910 Evesham–3
GLOUCESTER GL	Combined Court Building Kimbrose Way Gloucester GL1 2DE	Tel: 01452 834900 Fax: 01452 834923 DX: 98660 Gloucester–5
GRANTHAM GR	Harlaxton Road Grantham Lincs NG31 7SB	Tel: 01476 539030 Fax: 01476 539040
HUNTINGDON HN	Ground Floor Godwin House George Street Huntingdon Cambs PE29 3BD	Tel: 01480 450932 Fax: 01480 435397 DX: 96650 Huntingdon–2
LAMBETH LB	Court House Cleaver Street Kennington Road London SE11 4DZ	Tel: (020) 7091 4410/4420 Fax: (020) 7735 8147 DX: 145020 Kennington–2
MACCLESFIELD MC	2nd Floor Silk House Park Green Macclesfield Cheshire SK11 7NA	Tel: 01625 412800 Fax: 01625 501262 DX: 702498 Macclesfield–3
MAYOR'S AND CITY OF LONDON MY	Guildhall Buildings Basinghall Street London EC2V 5AR	Tel: (020) 77965400 Fax: (020) 77965424 DX: 97520 Moorgate–2
MELTON MOWBRAY MM	The Court House Norman Way Melton Mowbray Leics LE13 1NH	Tel: 01664 458100 Fax: 01664 501869 DX: 701937 Melton Mowbray–2
MERTHYR TYDFIL MT	The Law Courts Glebeland Place Merthyr Tydfil Wales CF47 8BH	Fax: 01685 359727 DX: 99582 Merthyr Tydfil–2
MILTON KEYNES MK	351 Silbury Boulevard (Rear) Witan Gate East Central Milton Keynes MK9 2DT	Tel: 01908 302800 Fax: 01908 230063 DX: 136266 Milton Keynes 6

Court (Courts with Bankruptcy jurisdiction in bold)	*Address*	*Contact Nos*
NEWPORT (GWENT) NP	Olympia House 3rd Floor Upper Dock Street Newport Gwent NP20 1PQ	Tel: 01633 227150 Fax: 01633 263820 DX: 99480 Newport (South Wales)–4
NORTHAMPTON NN	85–87 Lady's Lane Northampton NN1 3HQ N.B. See Bulk Centre for bulk issue	Tel: 01604 470400 Fax: 01604 470445 (Family) Fax: 01604 4232398 (General) DX: 725380 Northampton–21
PENRITH PN	The Court House Lowther Terrace Penrith CA11 7QL	Tel: 01768 862535 Fax: 01768 899700 DX: 65207 Penrith
PLYMOUTH PL	The Law Courts 10 Armada Way Plymouth Devon PL1 2ER	Tel: 01752 677400 Fax: 01752 208286 DX: 98470 Plymouth–7
PONTYPRIDD PD	Courthouse Street Pontypridd Wales CF37 1JR	Tel: 01443 490800 Fax: 01443 480305 DX: 99620 Pontypridd–2
PRESTON PR	The Law Courts Openshaw Place Ring Way Preston Lancs PR1 2LL	Tel: 01772 844700 Fax: 01772 844710 DX: 702640 Preston–4
RAWTENSTALL RA	1 Grange Street Rawtenstall Lancs BB4 7RT	Tel: 01706 214614 Fax: 01706 219814 DX: 702565 Rawtenstall
St HELENS HW	1st Floor Rexmore House Cotham Street St Helens Merseyside WA10 1SE	Tel: 01744 27544 Fax: 01744 20484 DX: 725020 St Helens–4
SKEGNESS AND SPILSBY ZV Hearings and counter service available at: The Court House Park Avenue Skegness Lincs PE25 1BH	55 Norfolk Street Boston Lincs PE21 6PE	Tel: 01754 762429 Fax: 01754 761165 DX: 701922 Boston–2
SOUTHEND SS	Tylers House Tylers Avenue Southend–on–Sea Essex SS1 2AW	Tel: 01702 601991 Fax: 01702 603090 DX: 97780 Southend–on–sea–2

Court (Courts with Bankruptcy jurisdiction in bold)	*Address*	*Contact Nos*
SOUTH SHIELDS SH	Millbank Secretan Way South Shields Tyne & Wear NE33 1RG	Tel: 0191 456 3343 Fax: 0191 427 9503 DX: 65143 South Shields–3
SWINDON SN	The Law Courts Islington Street Swindon Wilts SN1 2HG	Tel: 01793 690500 Fax: 01793 690555 DX: 98430 Swindon–5
THANET TT	2nd Floor Cecil Square Margate Kent CT9 1RL	Tel: 01843 221722 01843 228771 Fax: 01843 222730 DX: 98210 Cliftonville–2
WALSALL WJ	Bridge House Bridge Street Walsall West Mids WS1 1JQ	Tel: 01922 728855 Fax: 01922 728891 DX: 701943 Walsall–2
WARWICK WW	Northgate South Side Warwick CV34 4RB	Tel: 01926 492276 Fax: 01926 474227 DX: 701964 Warwick–2
WATFORD WD	Cassiobury House 11/19 Station Road Watford Herts WD17 1EZ	Tel: 01923 699400/699401 Fax: 01923 251317 DX: 122740 Watford–5
WELLINGBOROUGH WE	Lothersdale House West Villa Road Wellingborough Northants NN8 4NF	Tel: 01933 226168/222393 Fax: 01933 272977 DX: 701883 Wellingborough–2
WEYMOUTH AND DORCHESTER WY	Westwey House Westwey Road Weymouth Dorset DT4 8TE	Tel: 01305 752510 Fax: 01305 788293 DX: 98820 Weymouth–3
WORCESTER WR	The Shirehall Foregate Street Worcester WR1 1EQ	Tel: 01905 730800 Fax: 01905 730801 DX: 721120 Worcester–11
WORTHING WG	The Law Courts Christchurch Road Worthing Sussex BN11 1JD	Tel: 01903 221920 Fax: 01903 235559 DX: 98230 Worthing–4

INDEX

References to paragraph numbers in square brackets are to Volume 2